Sounding Latin Music, Hearing the Americas

BIG ISSUES IN MUSIC
A PROJECT OF THE CHICAGO STUDIES IN ETHNOMUSICOLOGY SERIES
Edited by Philip V. Bohlman

Sounding Latin Music, Hearing the Americas

JAIRO MORENO

The University of Chicago Press   Chicago and London

The University of Chicago Press, Chicago 60637
The University of Chicago Press, Ltd., London
© 2023 by The University of Chicago
Published 2023
Printed in the United States of America

32 31 30 29 28 27 26 25 24 23   1 2 3 4 5

ISBN-13: 978-0-226-82566-3 (cloth)
ISBN-13: 978-0-226-82568-7 (paper)
ISBN-13: 978-0-226-82567-0 (e-book)
DOI: https://doi.org/10.7208/chicago/9780226825670.001.0001

This book has been supported by the Iberian and Latin American
Music Fund and the General Fund of the American Musicological
Society, supported in part by the National Endowment for the
Humanities and the Andrew W. Mellon Foundation.

Library of Congress Cataloging-in-Publication Data

Names: Moreno, Jairo, 1963– author.
Title: Sounding Latin music, hearing the Americas / Jairo
    Moreno.
Other titles: Big issues in music.
Description: Chicago : The University of Chicago Press, 2023. |
    Series: Big issues in music | Includes bibliographical references
    and index.
Identifiers: LCCN 2022038203 | ISBN 9780226825663 (cloth) |
    ISBN 9780226825687 (paperback) | ISBN 9780226825670
    (ebook)
Subjects: LCSH: Popular music—Latin America—History and
    criticism. | Latin Americans—United States—Music—History
    and criticism.
Classification: LCC ML3549 .M68 2023 | DDC 781.64098—dc23/
    eng/20220811
LC record available at https://lccn.loc.gov/2022038203

To Coco Moreno (2006–2019), in memoriam,
and to Lola and Gil

CONTENTS

PREFACE

This book lies at the affective and political intersection of alienation and familiarity. It is a book about musical migrancy, about leaving things behind, arriving elsewhere, and realizing that things are never really left behind and that elsewhere is everywhere: home and abroad exist in constant and mutual reconfiguration. Musicking, which I take in a rather broad sense to include not only music making but the entire set of conditions of possibility that inevitably accompany it, offers particular insights on this reconfiguration, taking place at multiple scales and in relations of mutual investment—one plays or sings or arranges well, others write songs or one does, things come together, the music feels good, it swings, someone listens, someone dances, someone pays, places are visited, recordings are made, there are hits and flops, relationships emerge and come apart, and much more. And yet, there remain little gaps, nodes in these relationships that reveal that with every note played, every beat articulated, every word sung, come histories of place, of time, of circulation, claims and hopes to the past, the present, and the future, and there appear complex senses of ownership of and belonging *with* music that belonging *in* music cannot overcome. The book speaks to these entanglements.

These entanglements too have been my own as musician, intellectual, and academic. I had the great fortune of making music, as an immigrant to the US, with musicians whom I knew back home, growing up, in Colombia, but only as stars in distant galaxies, often in New York City, whom I diligently studied in recordings. And it is perhaps my misfortune to also have been as, if not more, driven to the world of ideas. I write and think and listen and play from that double position of simultaneous alienation and familiarity, the intimacy of a shared tone or thought that at the same time resonates with the uncanny sense of being-with and being-without that feels familiar to immigrants, even today when all seems connected and known. This doubleness renders my writing here denser than I wish it were, and it compels a certain searching character in the book. Rendering the familiar strange and the strange familiar means that the work constantly crosses disciplines, that its writing modes can feel essayistic, impossibly abstract, and unbearably concrete, all in rhythms that insist on varying repetition and reiteration, as a reviewer noted. The ongoing present has the allure of open-endedness, and the significance and meanings of what I explore remain in process. Please, if you can, do not hold me to the standards of concision and pragmatic directness expected from American academia. Indulge me, if you would, in detours, in moments where the music recedes from earshot, only to reappear, louder, noisier with politics, at any point. I always hope that the rich densities I explore might yet take you back to those sounds and sung words, those rhythms and textures.

Introduction

Sounding Latin Music, Hearing the Americas addresses music making by musicians from or with declared roots in Latin America and the Spanish Caribbean who have migrated to and/or work in the US: Panamanian singer-songwriter Rubén Blades; Colombian pop superstar Shakira; Mexican-born American pianist and bandleader Arturo O'Farrill and his Afro Latin Jazz Orchestra; and Puerto Rican saxophonist, bandleader, and composer Miguel Zenón. The book asks: How is the sounding of their music heard, by whom, where, when, and why? In the US, as a direct effect of the sociocultural slot they occupy by virtue of their migrant or immigrant status, these musicians are heard to make "Latin music." Such hearing embodies fundamental contradictions at the foundations of the host nation's aesthetic, cultural, economic, historical, and political self-definitions. The sounding of "Latin Music" brings a degree of impropriety to these self-definitions. The book analyzes responses by recognized minorities in the US and by the so-called mainstream to this impropriety. This impropriety extends to the musicians' countries of origin and to the continent as a whole. In their countries, tensions emerge in connection to national belonging and to broader notions of Latin American history and sociopolitical orders. At home, their music generates either immense national pride or suspicion for national betrayal. Regionally, their music provides a sonic index of Latin American resonance in the world at large; it addresses the continent, and in turn the continent addresses the world. The book registers transformations in all these interrelationships. How then are sounding, hearing, Latin America, and the Americas conceived and experienced such that music making helps bring them into being?

Three conceptual spheres organize my analyses of the interrelations between sounding and hearing: migrant creativity, aural equality, and modernity's syncopations. The musicians I discuss have been celebrated for their creative contributions, even when critiqued. This creativity does not emanate solely from individual achievement, hard work, powers of invention, or talent, important as these are in relation to the collective labor of producers, critics, commentators, fans, and musicians. More importantly, *migrant creativity* signals the production of worlds and senses of the world in—not "out of"—the particular conjunction of Latin America and the US that constitutes the place and time of migrants' dwelling. Within this analytic, music making is not heard to reflect, express, transpose, or otherwise represent Latin America in the US. Latin America is not reduced to being a cause for the effect "Latin American music," and neither is migration or arrival to the US the music's final determination. Migrant creativity names the operations (aesthetic, affective, corporeal, cultural, ideological, material, political, symbolic) involved in music making and whose performative is to understand and articulate being in and becoming with the relation between Latin America and the US.[1]

Migrant creativity alludes to the fugitive nature of acting creatively, to its capacity to disrupt boundaries and usher in the new by taking a temporary place in an improper space and time. The analyses I present correspond to one period of Latin music's efflorescence. Blades's salsa songs, O'Farrill's amplification of his father's 1950s signal contributions to big-band music, Shakira's unprecedented bilingual conquest of a global market, and Zenón's inventive transformations of Puerto Rican music in an unheard-of jazz idiom all mark significant turning points. These turning points reconfigure the limits of what music making can, should, or must do at a given place and time; they challenge existing hegemonies that normatively distribute the sensible.[2] Such redistributions of the sensible entail "a multiplication of connections and disconnections that reframe the relation between bodies, the world they live in and the way in which they are equipped to 'adapt' to it"—an aesthetic experience.[3] *Sounding Latin Music* argues that migrant creativity constitutes an exercise in *aural equality* grounded in music making's capacity to redistribute the sensible. Simply put, musical enunciations inscribe what, having been heard, understood, and taken in, now become transformed. Such enunciations in turn compel listeners into coming to terms with these transformations. Through these aural encounters, I contend, "connections and disconnections" emerge that "reframe relations" between people, their worlds, and the ways in which "they are equipped to 'adapt' to it." The aural becomes an exercise to equally reframe relations. These reframings occur across the relational vectors that comprise music making: North and South distinctions, class and race difference, modes of production, circuits of circulation, forms of mediation, language use, and so on. For the people and institutions involved, these relational vectors help produce a sense of spatio-temporal location in the Americas that blurs but does not erase the traditional North–South poles that make of Latin America "Latin America." Because redistributions of the sensible alter these relational vectors, the redistributions are considered "political." How then to understand the political such that music making can perform these redistributions? My position follows from an axiomatic assignation of political function to aesthetic form. Music making, sounding, and hearing emerge as privileged mediations in migratory dynamics of displacement, both to create a sense of place in the place of arrival and to forge new links with the place of origin.[4] I supplement this understanding of migratory dynamics with an analytic of aesthetic form and politics, which Rancière defines as "the configuration of a specific space, the framing of a particular sphere of experience, of objects posited as common and as pertaining to a common decision, of subjects recognized as capable of designating these objects and putting forward arguments about them."[5] Such aesthetic-political configurations are functions of creative work executed in and through a simultaneously sensorial and intellectual operation.[6]

Sounding Latin Music explores how migrant creativity confronts certain expectations in breaching US modernity's aesthetic, historical, and sociopolitical coordinates. The senses of what music making does in the world change as musicians negotiate the US's sociopolitical terrains. But those senses equally bear traces of a Latin American modernity enmeshed with that of the US. I name that relationship between enmeshed but particular modernities *modernity's syncopations*. Syncopation (further elaborated later) grounds my analyses of how music making reveals the gaps and unthoughts in the encounters that migrant creativity necessarily entails. Syncopation organizes the temporal and spatial displacements of migration, and resounds the fraught politics of belonging to the host society, both of which question definitions of the US and Latin America.[7]

Politically complex and sonically pleasurable, Latin American music's soundings and hearings constitute feedback loops. These feedback loops exist in relation with the aurality through which music is heard to express and produce heterogeneous entanglements of the Americas. To take the cases that bookend *Sounding Latin Music*, Blades's highly literate salsa songs, recorded in New York City by a company with an interest in Latin American markets, speak to the heart of experience of working-class Puerto Rican migrants, address quintessential Latin American concerns with political strife, and more. By his own admission, he wanted to argue the case for Latin America and bring the migrant experience in touch with a history largely ignored in the North. In the South, these songs are heard to break through the hegemony of the lettered word at the same time that they are celebrated by the Latin American intelligentsia. In the US, Miguel Zenón, a Puerto Rican, receives the prestigious MacArthur Award in recognition of his rethinking of Puerto Rican traditions that sound out jazz in the twenty-first century. Zenón is heard to sound jazz ahead of itself. My analyses listen to and study these entanglements. Sounding—in the literal acoustic sense of emitting a sound—plays an important role in the book as resonance and fathoming.[8] Resonance refers to how music making mobilizes and is mobilized by affect, concepts, feelings, ideas, notions, histories, memories, places, spaces, and temporalities. Music making cannot be rendered solely as sonic form. Yes, it comprises carefully created songs, tracks, performances, and works that provide audible interfaces between musicians and audiences—but not only these. It also establishes cultural competences and expectations, excites pleasures and desires, and activates historical imaginations and sociopolitical realities. Resonance thus requires a qualification beyond the actually audible— namely, that music making be understood as *musicking,* an assemblage of heterogeneous elements including musical creativity, performance, listening, dancing, modes of production, infrastructure, marketing, circulation, songs, recordings, and critical commentary and discourse.[9] To sound (and to analyze sounding) is, in part, to fathom how musicking assemblages engage and produce affective, conceptual, feelingful, ideational, notional, historical, memorial, spatial, and temporal relations that are experienced variously as cultural kinship and/or alienation, and hierarchical and non-hierarchical sociopolitical organization. This book sounds out resonance and fathoming as methods for a critical perspective on entanglements both material and abstract that make musicking a matter of concern for understanding the Americas.

Sounding, hearing, aurality, and resonance have phenomenological and non-phenomenological aspects that require clarification. The phenomenological tradition distinguishes between indexical and communicative modes of listening.[10] In the former, sound indicates or conveys things or events, and listening works to identify those. In the latter, sound bears meanings within some semiotic system such as language or, in music, tonal syntax. Closer to aural comprehension, this latter mode of listening entails greater intentionality than the former. Another mode, non-indexical listening, entails selecting whatever sonic attributes may interest a listener who qualifies what she listens to without concern for indexes or meanings. Finally, hearing is the physio-acoustic fact of sound perception, of being struck by sound.

This book engages differently with these modes of listening. "Hearing" is more than the fact of sound perception; it refers to the fact that throughout the book subjects address their listening as indexical and communicative. For example, Blades says that his audiences, whether educated or not, will find meaning in his literate songs; Shakira's Miami-based producers dot a hit song with sonic indexes of Colombia or of a generalized "Middle East" that audiences will recognize. In those cases, indexical and communicative modes entail some kind of subject-object relation. But when I argue that "sounding Latin music" compels "hearing the Americas," the object of this hearing (which itself may be expressed as indexical or communicative listening) is not strictly discrete or acoustic. Under resonance and fathoming, I understand what happens when forms other than acoustic objects—for example, entangled histories, circulation feedback loops—emerge in relation to musical sound but are themselves sounded abstractly and heard non-phenomenologically.

Two interrelated issues follow: first, resonance and fathoming exist in relation to phenomenological listening modes; and second, although music is medium specific, its constitutive entanglement with other elements in an assemblage means that it is an event of mediation and not merely an object that mediates something for a subject. In Veit Erlmann's memorable quip, music becomes "a medium that mediates, as it were, mediation"; music "functions as an interactive social context, a conduit for other forms of interaction, other socially mediated forms of appropriation of the world."[11] Such linearity may be reversed, with mediation mediating the medium. Rather than insisting on a subject-object pair or on directional or bidirectional relations between the members of this pair, I propose understanding the configuration as an event.[12] In an event, objects are object-mediators that necessarily entail actions initiated elsewhere and that transform what happens (e.g., resonance, fathoming) such that they become transformed by this happening.[13] For Antoine Hennion, "this is what takes us out of a dual world (on the one hand, autonomous but inert things and on the other, pure social signs) to let us into a world of mediations and effects in which they are produced together, one by the other." Resonance and fathoming "are determinants and determined at the same time: they determine the impositions and renew the course of the things."[14] In the end, mediation—which encompasses "resonance" and "fathoming" as events—relates to aural equality and migrant creativity to the degree that "sounding" and "hearing" breach norms of musicking and renew the course of things. The course of things is the syncopated entanglement of the Americas.

In each case *Sounding Latin Music* presents, actors differently shape the conceptual spheres I consider. The book is thus comparative at its core. In exploring differences through time, the book, without being a "history of," is historical at heart. It pursues the significance of Latin American music in the US, identifies its dynamics, and clarifies its history. Next I will introduce the book's scaffold: Latin America, Latin Americanism, modernity, and syncopation.

Latin America

In this book, the Americas are heard in productive and contradictory entanglement. A simple maxim captures this entanglement: Latin America is born out of a thinking in twos. Here's a declaration of *L'Amerique latine* by Michel Chevalier, a Saint-Simonian historian who traveled the US and Mexico in the 1830s: "The two branches, Latin and Germanic, have reproduced in the New World. South America is, like meridional Europe, Catholic and Latin. The America to the North belongs to a Protestant and Anglo-Saxon population."[15] However imprecise, the idea of "Latin America" proved irresistible and subject to insisting discursive enunciation. Paris-based Colombian intellectual José María Torres Caicedo's 1856 poem "Las dos Américas": "the race of Latin America finds itself confronted by the Saxon race, mortal enemy who now threatens to destroy its liberty and its banner."[16] In 1856, the Chilean Francisco Bilbao gave a conference in Paris entitled "Initiative of America," reportedly using the expression "*lo latinoamericano*" (that which is Latin American) to describe that which properly belonged to the continent, excluding Paraguay and Brazil.[17] Torres Caicedo would propose in 1861 the foundation of the "Unión Latino-Americana," a bloc of nations to protect regional interests from US intervention.[18]

These enunciations harbor a set of Latin Americanist fundaments: first, its constitution in relation to an elsewhere geographically external to it that would suffuse its cultures and social orders; second, a corollary assertion setting it in antagonistic relation to another part of the Americas; third, a need to name, map, conceptualize, and historicize this relation. The ideal of continental unity constitutes a fourth and quintessential fundament for the idea of Latin America. A fifth fundament of Latin Americanism lies in its internal exclusions, both of nations and of vast sectors of society, mainly Indigenous and Afro-descendent peoples.[19] Despite such exclusions (and because of them), these fundaments will endure.

Not unlike the actors this book studies, Latin Americanist ideas were also enunciated by intellectuals and diplomats writing from the US.[20] Some embraced the US as a model for national projects.[21] Others, suspicious of the US, marked sharp distinctions between South and North.[22] The case of the Cuban José Martí is of particular interest. Martí (1853–1895) saw the US through astute anthropological eyes, articulating in chronicles, essays, and personal letters from New York City and, in the case of the chronicles, read throughout the continent, his diagnoses of the discontents of modernity and modernization at the very heart of the US's triumphant industrial capitalism: racial relations under Jim Crow, the politics of indentured labor and the economy of labor movements, the character of US popular culture and the urban everyday existence in the metropolis.[23] He sensed the troubling effects of modernization and its technological apparatuses on sociability, cultural production, and the distribution of classes under monopoly capitalism. He perceived one of the central themes of this book: the sociopolitical dynamics attending to the massive presence of what will later be called "Hispanics" and "Latinos" in the US, how these peoples will have negotiated home as "a portable cultural tradition to be cited, sung, or constructed," as Laura Lomas writes, and how the constant arrival of people contributes to ongoing struggles for the apportioning of political allocations in US democracy.[24] He witnessed the annexation of former Mexican nationals transformed into second-class citizens in their former land, at once denaturalized and re-naturalized. He imagined a unique challenge of the future to be the politics of classifying people and allotting for them a place in a society in perennial flux. Arriving by way of Guatemala and Mexico and having experienced the Euro-African society of Cuba, Martí was equipped "to negotiate comparatively the tension between the national and transnational forces in the Americas"; his travels "exposed [him] to the differing ethno-cultural complexities that imperialism had bequeathed to America."[25]

Martí helps us to understand the importance of mass media circulation and consumption for Latin Americanism and the enduring role the intellectual played in this, of how the historicity of Latin Americanisms and their refusals and critiques remain inseparable from the forces of coloniality, imperialism, capitalism, and republicanism that are of modernity as much as modernity is of them. He understood Latin America as a regional correlate for modernity. In Martí, unequal modernization, an incipient economy of dependency, different social entanglements between the masses and commodification, and their corollary impingements on culture and politics emerge as definitional characteristics of a modernity that needs to be understood at the intersection of inter-American relations, as "modernities."[26] This reflects a classic Latin Americanist trope: the self-consciousness that something called political and economic-industrial modernity was unfolding in which "America" was fully implicated and yet remained peripheral to.[27] Such optic on modernity is co-constitutive of Latin Americanism, being the occasion for the birth of an alternative modernity aware of the ills of an impending modernization that would destroy the very essence of Latin America. That essence needed description.

Forging this essence would beget and sustain an affective fidelity that constituted Latin America as reality and aspirational project, rendered in eloquent prose in Martí's essay "Our America."[28] "Our America" introduced the ideologeme defining the continent as the site for a natural predisposition toward the spirit and the communal, in contradistinction to the materialistic and individualistic Northern neighbor. Self-attributions of identity and value around the questions of race abound. "There is no racial hatred, because there are no races," exclaimed Martí.[29] "Our America's" nature frees it of artifice and the alienation of imported knowledge, owing nothing to "Madrid or Paris," to say nothing of the US. Throughout the continent and within each country, the "autochthonous mestizo" will defeat the "exotic Creole," affirming a constitutive mixture (i.e., mestizo) as the fundamental demographic category of "our America." For Martí, "the problem of independence did not lie in the change of forms but in change of Spirit."[30] A sixth fundament emerges: the ethical and moral predisposition of Latin America, its spirit.

Coupled with the draw of geography and cartography, these six fundaments produce an "excess of confidence . . . regarding the ontology of continental divides."[31] Mauricio Tenorio-Trillo argues that "'Latin America' has never designated a geographically or historically tangible reality. . . . the expression has worked as the title, as the generic name of a well-known plot that is both the autobiography of the term ('Latin America') and the story of a belief that has escaped extinction since its origins as an idea and a project in the 1850s."[32] The dual character of "idea" and "project" owes much to the political milieu in which, responding to the pressures of French imperialism, US expansionism, and the reaffirmation of Hispanic colonial foundations, Creole intellectuals carved for the continent a generalized identity.[33] This identity would be grounded in a disparate array of ideologemes held to be constitutive of the continent. "Latin America" messily affirms and/or negates a series of values inscribed in modernity: "progress and tradition," "empire and/or nation; *Gemeinschaft* [community] and *Gesellschaft* [society]; race and culture; alienation and authenticity; modern freedom through, or despite, history; identity as personal achievement, as ecstasy, or as a reluctant inevitability."[34] More recently, these ideologemes transform into "post–World War II theories of modernization, which took for granted the existence of a Latin part of the Americas . . . where a new social engineering could be applied."[35] There follows the period that corresponds to *Sounding Latin Music*, beginning in the 1960s and 1970s with the stirrings of revolutionary utopia associated with Latin America, the specters of modernization hovering over politically conflicted nations haunted by the modern promises of democracy and the realities of dictatorship and economic dependence, the maelstrom of globalization and neoliberalism, mass migration to the US, the emergence of postcolonial "coloniality," and alternative epistemic models that critique Latin America while preserving, somehow, the blueprint for the idea of Latin America.[36] Globalization would both threaten and strengthen this "blueprint." Throughout these various moments, "there has never been a meaning for Latin America that did not involve conterminously Europe and the Americas."[37] This conterminous relation expresses what I identify as the dialectic without synthesis of the Americas, South and North.

LATIN AMERICANISM

Latin America and Latin Americanism are co-constitutive. Latin Americanism is the discursive counterpart of the affective, material, and symbolic appeals Latin America makes. Alberto Moreiras defines Latin Americanism as "the set or the sum total of engaged representations providing a viable knowledge of the Latin American object of enunciation."[38] For Julio Ramos, Latin Americanism is "an ensemble of mediations between the local and the universal, the proper and the foreign, between the particularity of cultural expression and the necessity to translate and render legible the local register in function of the universality of global discussions."[39] Moreiras's "representation" and Ramos's "mediation" might seem conceptually different, the former more passive and dualist and the latter more dynamic and immanentist (i.e., the means of mediation are inherent to the object of mediation). Moreiras's sense definition of representation, after Stephen Greenblatt ("not detached scientific assessments but . . . representations that are relational, local, and historically contingent," fueled not by "reason but imagination"), is congruent with Ramos's appeal to the dynamic relational impetus of mediation, much as deconstruction guides the former and transculturation the latter. Notions such as a constitutive outside, relationality, contingency, enunciation, and imagination provide an updated lexicon to account, in Latin Americanism, for the enduring legacies of the old idea of Latin America.

Latin Americanism demands caution due to its relational character. Relations are ontologically porous and epistemically leaky. Relations are situated, forge power vectors, and have preponderant sites. Thus, Tenorio-Trillo critiques what he calls, in English, "*Latin America*," namely, the form the idea takes in the US academy but that includes music-specific articulations under the aegis of "the global reach of the English language and US mass culture."[40] This "reach" is responsible for making "'Latin America,' 'Latino,' and 'Latina' commonplace terms in contemporary languages" to the point that "Latin America" today exists almost exclusively in the US in a grotesque "text-book version" that obscures the historical specificities of the multiple societies inhabiting the continent.[41] This cautionary note cannot be heeded enough.

That said, the relational nature of Latin Americanism vis-à-vis the US complicates a simple dualism of interiority and exteriority. Latin Americanism is both an exotopic and an endotopic discourse.[42] It is a set of interested representational practices enunciated abroad and in Latin America and by Latin Americans and others. Intense debates in the US academy arise concerning, first, who gets to say and write what, and where, and second, what object of representation Latin America may be.[43] Román de la Campa speaks of a "coming of age" of Latin Americanism by its "scholarly legitimation" in academia's lingua franca, English, but also as part of a "transnational discursive community with a significant market for research and sales in the industrial capitals of the world."[44] De la Campa remarks on the gap between this phenomenon and Latin American cultural, political, and literary practices, a point forcefully made by Chilean theorist and critic Nelly Richard, for whom, as a "device of academic knowledge," Latin Americanism requires that Latin America be an "object of study," a "field of experience," and a "position of enunciation."[45] According to Neil Larsen, the object of study "Latin America" "is no doubt a holdover from the colonial past" compounded by the creation of a "theoretically 'regional' object with almost no connection with any real place."[46] Tenorio-Trillo reserves the expression "US-Centered Latin America" to describe this general field, insisting on the problematic construction of "difference" by "certain current US-Centered Latin Americanism" for which "only the indigenous people are real."[47] In the end, Latin America and Latin Americanism remain both impossible and necessary.

Uses of the expression "Latin Americanisms" cannot be relegated to "theoretical fictions," "institutional entelechies," or the symptom of a historiography too lazy to establish all the facts and dates before saying anything at all that transcends the local, national, or regional.[48] One is left with the non-choice of having to use the term "Latin America" as an empty signifier, a "placeholder for a founding universality, to be occupied by any element in a chain of equivalences that, through always contingent historical circumstances, develops a hegemonic function."[49] In this book, along with Latin Americanism, Latin America and Latin American index the performatives they embody in the assemblages I discuss. These performatives cannot be dismissed and taken to do the ideological labor of false consciousness. Neither do they rely on affirming the lowest common denominator among people and all manner of endeavors from the region as that which is culturally, socially, and politically valuable. Instead, these performatives help forge and maintain temporal-spatial relations. Rather than taking the nodal place that US-based articulations of Latin America give as a sign of its "ontological" and/or "conceptual" impurity (or purity), the term signifies its constitutive impurity and relational capaciousness. However critical of the ways in which "Latin America" and "Latin Americanism" underlie each other, this book focuses on the recent history of various articulations, their whys, wheres, and hows, all taking place at the intersection between what, for better or worse, one calls Latin America and the US.

MUSICAL LATIN AMERICANISM

The brief examples of Blades and Zenón above suggest that if migrant musicking animates diverse forms of Latin Americanism, the "power and allure" of an idea (i.e., Latin America) sustains that musicking as well. A musical Latin Americanism sounded out North, then, in and through which entanglements of the Americas are heard. Given my proposal for musicking, musical Latin Americanism materializes as emergent forms and processes that mobilize representational discourses in the public sphere while compelling powerful embodied affective and aesthetic experiences that push discourse to its limits. This capaciousness is already intimated by my choice of cases around song *and* instrumental music. And it too suggests that despite the difference between Blades's more traditional Latin Americanism and that articulated by the MacArthur Foundation, the exotopic/endotopic dualism is attenuated in musical Latin Americanism.

Two issues help locate the cases this book presents. First, when does Latin Americanism take musical form? Second, what forms does it take? Historian Pablo Palomino dates the consolidation of the category "Latin American music" to the 1930s.[50] In the preceding decades, national and incipiently regional genres existed without a sense of a wider continental frame. This earlier "continental patchwork" of genres conjoins with "transnational networks" of markets, scholarship, media, and geopolitics involving musicologists, diplomats, intellectuals, policymakers, artists, radio operators, and diplomats who shape the new category. For Palomino, the category harnessed and helped disseminate the idea of Latin America as a cultural conglomeration out of a heterogeneous field, music being "particularly effective to express the power of culture better than other aesthetic practices, because of its ubiquity, its cross-class nature, and its ability to link, through aesthetic, policy, and economic means, the local, the regional, the national, and the global."[51] By the 1950s, the category "Latin music" becomes firmly ensconced in the US, "the other of Latin America . . . although partially being Latin American itself."[52] Palomino's excellent chronicle ends in the 1960s, when the musicking I discuss comes into earshot.

Tenorio-Trillo adopts a nominalist perspective on musical Latin Americanism, noting that the term "Latin America" does not appear in any songs prior to repertoires inspired by the Cuban Revolution. The term derives from "the recent US-centered Latinization of everything tropical,

Spanish, Portuguese, indigenous, brown and exotic," somewhere around
the 1960s and 1970s.[53] What is worse, "the idea of Latin America was
never fully embraced by the masses, commoners, plebs of Mexico City,
Cochabamba, or São Luís de Maranhão. Not in 1900. Not even in 1970."[54]
This sweeping claim skips over the impact of the Latinization of Afro-
Cuban music in New York City throughout the 1950s. And it overlooks
the impact, throughout the 1960s, of the idea coalesced on large sectors
of working classes in Caracas, Callao, and Cali through salsa. From the
North, New York City–based musicians self-consciously were appealing to
their sense of connection with Latin America during that decade. Mediated by migratory movement to the US and the phonographic industry,
these developments produced three key spheres for the emergence of a
musical Latin Americanism: aural attunement, contemporaneousness,
and spatial connectedness.

   Sounding Latin Music outlines two broad categories of musical Latin
Americanism. The first one, in chapters one, two, and three, maps entanglements linking South and North. Within this category, there are three
types of musical Latin Americanism. The first one corresponds to Blades's
early work produced within the context of salsa, understood by its actors to be "Latin" music, or as I put it, Latino Latin Americanism.[55] The
second, Latin American Latin Americanism, describes Blades's work upon
return to Central America. The third, Cosmopolitan Latin Americanism,
refers to the emergence of Shakira as a global figure and leans on the singer's own claims to cosmopolitanism, as well as those of her hometown,
Barranquilla, Colombia, and of Colombian commentators. The second
broad category, in chapters four and five, focuses on US-Cuba and US-
Puerto Rico entanglements and highlights a US perspective on music. This
latter category is sensitive to the fraught relationship the Spanish Caribbean has with Latin America in light of imperial tensions in these islands.

Modernity

A sense that Latin America moves ahead or behind its others is as old
as the idea of Latin America itself. Politically, Latin America felt itself
as having overcome Europe's arcane ideas of nobility in favor of an
"American republican modernity."[56] Ethically, Martí's "our Americanism" asserts Latin America's spiritual superiority over the US. Martí's
and José Vasconcelos's ideas of racial organization hold Latin America
to be an alternative to US racial binaries. Political institutions, the life
of the spirit, and racial attitudes function as spheres where the continent
represents the future, the site for realizing modern sociopolitical ideals.
Soon enough, the North's industrial modernity (commercial, economic,

industrial, scientific) would lead to the future.[57] Latin America would be consigned to the past.

Another maxim: Latin American participation in modernity is its abiding concern. The question of marking the Latin American entrance or arrival to modernity could, one might say, only have been asked there, where convergences and divergences around the modern, modernization, and modernity are decisive for mapping the continent in world geography and establishing its place in history.[58] This concern is symptomatic of a classically modern notion of a temporality that, following Reinhart Koselleck, renders historical time as the premises and promises of freedom, unimpeded betterment, and progress.[59] These premises and promises provide coordinates for modernity. In these coordinates' grid, the future becomes the horizon of expectation for the present, and the present constantly becomes an experience of expecting what was an imagined future. The past becomes a byproduct of the nexus of present and future, a time left behind in which those relegated to the outside of modernity remain caught, forever lagging behind.[60] If Latin America is born out of a thinking of twos, modernity amplifies how these are out of joint. Modernity is itself this dislocation.

Dislocations produce rhythms. This section introduces my own mapping of the relation of temporal and spatial alignments and dis-alignments that I identify in modernity and that I conceive through the metaphor of syncopation. In Zenón's case, for instance, how might we account for the anticipation that "a new jazz language for the 21st century" raises in the US? At what scale may that anticipation operate? What entanglements bring together institutions, musical traditions, individuals, musical forms, and Puerto Rico's complex place in modernity vis-à-vis US imperialism? At first sight, the MacArthur Foundation's claims may seem implausible simply because existing historical accounts of jazz could hardly have anticipated the emergence of a figure like Zenón. Significantly, whatever Zenón achieved was done on the terrain of the US and in direct entanglement with African American cultural traditions that claim a direct stake on jazz. His is a story of encounter and collision. So are all of this book's stories. In the nexus of displacement and collision, I identify modernity's syncopation.

Modernity is all-encompassing. For Talal Asad, modernity "aims at institutionalizing . . . constitutionalism, moral autonomy, democracy, human rights, civil equality, industry, consumerism, freedom of the market—and secularism. It employs proliferating technologies (of production, warfare, travel, entertainment, medicine) that generate new experiences of space and time."[61] Jonathan Sterne summarizes widely circulated accounts of modernity: (1) capitalism, colonialism, and rise of industry; (2) growth and development of the sciences, changing cosmologies, massive population shifts, new forms of collective and corporate power, social movements, class struggle, and the rise of new middle classes, mass communication, nation states, and bureaucracy; (3) confidence in progress, a universal abstract humanist subject, and the world market; and (4) reflexive contemplation of constancy of change.[62]

Defining "modernity" might seem a fool's errand. One is left to opt for the kinds of general accounts just seen that place it partly as a broad epoch, partly as a set of social, political, economic, and scientific initiatives that constitute a worldview and a project for those who seek to attain it and for those who enforce its values. Struggles over these values are central to *Sounding Latin Music*, for in each case questions emerge around belonging in shared histories, affordances of literacy and language, diverging notions of racial organization in relation to tradition and historiography, citizenship, imperiality, and cultural sovereignty. Topically, the book resonates with efforts to reevaluate modernity and generating alternative historical narratives.[63]

One must examine modernity in its spatial economy of borders, boundaries, and limits, as well as its dynamics of inclusions and exclusions, similarities and differences, inequalities and equalities, and its temporal dimension as genealogy and futurology. Various densities are afforded to musically sonorous/discursive practices such that they can carry out the kind of work so often assigned to them, so they can move and circulate wherever and however they do or seem to. There is a strong possibility that there is no friction at all or resistance to its circulation—the "barricades and incentives" for it to move about. Diverse, if not divergent, populations, communities, places, regional links, and hemispheric alliances may be "constituted and stabilized by such circulations." In the end, who claims or is assigned the task of carrying these circulations and being responsible for their effects?[64]

Concerns with circulation and mobility resonate with the book's use of modernity in the plural, the result of encounters in displacement: migration, the mobility of creativity, the uneasy coexistence of competing histories and the need to negotiate them as part of music making, the dispersion of musical commodities, the linkages between diasporic expansion and racialization, and the politics of language. These queries dialogue with a critical position vis-à-vis modernity in contemporary analyses of Latin American modernity.

Mary Louise Pratt calls out hegemonic accounts of modernity for their "dramatic failure to recognize the diffusionist character of modernity."[65] Such accounts are enunciated from a self-ascribed center, with features that are made to appear noncontradictory: "democracy, nation-state, class formation, industrialization and industrial division of labor, high/low distinction in the cultural sphere, urbanization, mass culture, mass society, mass education, expansion of markets and capitalist growth, hegemonization of instrumental rationality, bureaucratization of society . . . privilege of reason as path to true knowledge, rise of individual and his [the individual is gendered as masculine] idea of his freedom, idea of progress, progressive time, change as inherently positive value."[66] The so-called periphery must endlessly negotiate its position in global orders and temporal developments.

For Beatriz Sarlo, "peripheral modernity" offers the distinct advantage of having a perspective on its own position and on the center's that the center itself remains blind to.[67] Immanuel Wallerstein reminds us that core-periphery relations are not static, even if hegemonic arrangements remain in place, because these relations are "relations of production." Thus, certain production processes may become more profitable in peripheral locations, giving these locations core-like processes.[68] Under processes of migration, peripheries internally populate the core itself.

Modernity cannot be but heterogeneous; heterogeneity demands regional reckoning. As Hermann Herlinghaus and Mabel Moraña noted in 2003, "today, discussions around modernity in Latin America offer a singularly heterogeneous landscape."[69] Since the 1980s, Latin American countries were pushed into "the abysses of an advanced globalization," giving to this landscape more than a modicum of "epistemic independence."[70] As a "matrix for historization, the present is 'modern' with regards to a constitutive disequilibrium," because "in the case of Latin America, modernity has always been a modernity in crisis and has provided the discursive grounds pro domo from which to formulate equally desires for identity and legitimacy as well as strategies for cultural difference."[71] The singularity of which they speak concerns how the values of modernity take form in the subcontinent. In the book, this results in the identification of particular issues drawn from this broad understanding of "modernity" that gain social relevance in their circulation in immigrant musicking.

Modernity is relatively uncommon as an analytic frame in Music Studies.[72] In Latin American Studies, however, the situation is quite different. Abril Trigo did not exaggerate when describing the concerns of "generations of artists and intellectuals, thinkers and activists [with] neocolonialism, the popular, the national, modernity, and modernization, as well as national and continental identities and their internal and external others," as an "obsessive questioning."[73] This questioning yields a proliferation of qualifiers expressing the particularity of nineteenth- and twentieth-century Latin American modernity, in some cases expanding the temporal register to include the beginning of modernity as the correlate of the "discovery" of America. Among these we find "peripheral modernity" (Beatriz Sarlo), "hybrid modernity" (Néstor García Canclini, Jorge Larraín), "divergent modernities" (Ramos), "heterogeneous modernity" (Hermann Herlinghaus and Mabel Moraña), "modernity out of phase" (*a destiempo*) (Carlos Monsiváis), "modernity as discontent" and "to the south of modernity" (Jesús Martín-Barbero), "Modernity/Coloniality" (Anibal Quijano, Walter Mignolo), "elusive" (Fernando Calderón, Martin Hopenhayn, and Ernesto Ottone), "uneasy" (Pablo Oyarzún), and, in a rare instance focused on music, "primitive" (Florencia Garramuño).[74] What would this book add to modernity's extensive bestiary? And why now, when debates about modernity and modernities appear to have tapered off?

First, arguing for its signal importance for understanding musicking, I return to the idea of modernity as an inter-American phenomenon animated by migration, by networks of musical circulation, and by the feedback loops that constitute differing senses of listening in relation to one another and, on each pole, to themselves: sounding, hearing, resonating, and fathoming are constituted by and help constitute modernity.

Second, aurality (the sonorous, hearing, and modes of listening) becomes "foundational to modern modes of knowledge, culture, and social organization."[75] Aurality becomes, in Ana María Ochoa Gautier's groundbreaking work, a central dispositive organizing social hierarchizations in Latin America.[76] David Novak aptly describes an entanglement of aurality and modernity applicable to the Americas when he writes that for the "mass technological mediation of sound, the emphasis on recordings was not something that merely happened to Japan, something that made its listening 'modern.' Rather, the reception of recordings was itself a crucial ground for the staging of Japanese musical modernity."[77] This could be said of listening to Blades in Colombia in 2009, or of Blades's listening to Willie Colón in Panama years before he would join the Nuyorican and change the course of salsa. Something similar could be said of the MacArthur Foundation's listening to Zenón, and of Zenón being spellbound by Ornette Coleman's music when he was in high school. Both express a relation that cannot be but modern: the consolidation of sung letters as the medium and form for Latin Americanism, in one case, and the unpredictable outcome of creativity sponsored in great part by American intervention in Puerto Rico, in the other. A guiding question, then: How does engaging with forms (musical genres, styles, recording, performances, commodities, etc.) help render listening into a modern project and active participant in the production of an aural modernity?[78]

Third, for the many insights that the work on Latin American modernity bequeaths us, there is little about the place of music, let alone musicking. To put it bluntly, in much of this work, literature and the visual arts have absorbed nearly all attention, and the same goes for the focus in the social sciences on questions of modernization and geopolitics. Modernity may be exhausting and perhaps even be exhausted, but for an idea of Music Studies that seeks to cross various scales of analysis, it still demands engagement.

Sounding Latin Music complements the work of scholars who have considered music and Latin American modernity,[79] transposing their concerns to a continent-wide sphere where some are intensified or attenuated and new ones emerge. In the example above, Blades's music engages with what are seen as new forms of enunciating politics via mass popular forms. These forms—a renewed sense of Latin American unity, for one—emerge as effects of his Latin American immigrant status in relation to the recognized minority status of Puerto Rican communities in New York City. Aesthetic modernism in relation to the nation, or the role of race in the making of popular music, do not figure as such in this case, but Blades's commitment to the idea of nation-state and his preoccupation with recognizing and overcoming class distinctions do play a part. This commitment and this preoccupation both express discontents with the premises and promises of Latin American modernity as it encounters the US's own. This dual concern has disciplinary implications for this book. The book works at the intersections of Latin American Cultural Studies, Latino Studies, American Studies, and Music Studies, probing the possibilities and constraints of a musicking that cannot but operate at these intersections and their corollary conjunctures and disjunctures.

Finally, I identify the mutual entanglement of temporal and spatial relationships that emerge from migratory musicking and circulation networks. I consider how competing senses of the present, past, and future emerge and new mappings of place and location appear—this mapping of temporality to place signals modernity's lingering effects.

SYNCOPATION

Modernity: the set of entanglements fostering and sustaining dislocated temporalities and their corollary historical and geopolitical hierarchies. Latin America: a thinking in twos in which, at any point and in endless oscillation, one of these twos stands in excess of the other as a condition of possibility for this thinking. "Latin" musicking in the US marks encounters *in* displacement—and not just for the obvious migratory condition of musicians—at the juncture of Latin America and the US but also within each of these. Modernity sets—but does not determine—the terrain and the temporality in which that juncture occurs. Zenón ushers in the future in great part because US modern governance in Puerto Rico afforded him a sense of a musical elsewhere, while he moves ahead of the time of jazz history by rethinking Puerto Rican musical traditions. Blades's lettered experimentation with popular song upheld and upturned values long encrusted in the Latin American lettered tradition. At the same time, by seeking to bring the Nuyorican communities in the US in line with the historical imperatives of Latin America, his efforts would be rejected by some for the excessively lettered character of his work. These encounters *in* displacement assemble varying social scales. Modern institutional forms and modes of governance may inflect the character of these encounters, they may arise in the context of venerable traditions, or in relation to the senses of history and political needs that made of aesthetics (e.g., literature) the index for Latin American creativity. *Sounding Latin Music* makes the case for, first, understanding musicking as a dynamic force for collaboration in disagreement, inclusion in exclusion, disruption in continuity, and difference in similarity that expresses an elision in the relation between the parts involved, an unthought and excess that emerges in the collision of parts, the coming together-apart that I call *syncopation*. The book also argues that migrant creativity embodies an unrelenting constitutive outside in the Americas.

The syncope marks a momentary, brief but consequential halt and suppression in the flow of things: in medicine, a missed heartbeat and its associated momentary loss of consciousness; in grammar and poetry, a skipped sound, syllable, or letter; in psychoanalysis, a well-placed interruption that might bring "shock and illumination"; in phenomenology, "the dialectic's tug of negation."[80] Out of this baroque patchwork of meanings, two main conceptions of the syncope guide my own: musical and philosophical.

In the Western tradition, a musical syncope indicates an off-beat rhythmic articulation in relation to the main beat. The beat is disturbed, elided but necessarily implied, raising the possibility of anticipation (the syncope) and expectation (the return of the main beat or the continuation of the disturbance). The French musical lexicographer Sébastien de Brossard wrote of the syncope: "[it] hits and collides with . . . the natural time of the measure."[81] Melodically, "the counter-time [contretemps] that the syncope causes nonetheless produces a leaping movement [un mouvement sautillant] that enlivens [égaye] and rejoices [réjouit]; harmonically, it creates an agreeable contrast of consonances and dissonances, producing all the beauty of modern music."[82] In syncopation, rhythmic, metrical, tonal, and expressive forces emerge that juxtapose preexisting norms (e.g., the "natural" order of alternating strong and weak pulses of a meter) and the disruption of these norms such that the two both blur into one another and remain discernible. Syncope: a generative disruption, pleasurable collision.

For Jean-Luc Nancy, "the syncope *simultaneously* attaches and detaches . . . . Of course, these two operations do not add up to anything, but neither do they cancel each other out."[83] Like touch, the syncope is as "an interruption in the continuity of being that becomes into what it is only after it has been interrupted," redolent of how a physiological syncope reveals the flux of consciousness by interrupting it.[84] Like in music, the syncope creates elisions *in* the contact between parts. These elisions express a constitutive tension not apparent to either part outside of the syncope: it is a withdrawal that affirms, without reaching synthesis, the relations from which it withdraws.

"Syncopation" in the expression "syncopated modernities" is not an adjective. In this book, syncopation is a heuristic to conceptualize a modernity in which the Americas are constitutive outsides of each other but also in which each one harbors elisions internal to their own societies.[85] Koselleck, recall, characterizes modernity by the emergence of the future as a horizon against which a society's present is organized. Modern societies live partly ahead of themselves. Off-beats in the grand historical rhythm of modernity are where other societies dwell which "lag" behind, until they appear to move ahead, as in the example of Zenón and the Puerto Rico he is heard to embody. The elision here reveals an unthought in US society, used to imposing its rhythms on others and now hearing what happens when the periphery makes claims on the temporal and spatial designs of US jazz history. For the Latin American lettered tradition, Blades's songs open up the gap in a tradition used to incorporating popular forms while radically excluding them under the quintessentially modern distinction between high and low forms. Like modernity, Latin America (South) and North America (North) remain entangled in the relational instability that I conceptualize under syncopation. Musicking not only stages the productive tensions of that entanglement, for it too sounds and makes audible that entanglement.

Sounding Latin Music departs from work that hears the musical syncope as an index of social disruption and resistance by way of Afro-diasporic musical forms that fractures modernity's linear historicism and totalization.[86] Paul Gilroy: for the African diaspora, "anteriority," as a form of anti-modernity, remains "inescapably both inside and outside of the dubious protection modernity offers."[87] Further, "[the Afro-diasporic] artistic and political formation has come to relish its measure of autonomy from the modern—an independent vitality that comes from the syncopated pulse of non-European philosophical and aesthetic outlooks."[88] The diaspora's temporality, artistic forms, and aesthetic principles guarantee their critical syncopation vis-à-vis modernity.

Racial particularity, anti-modernity, and antagonism against the West inform a fundamental thinker of salsa music, Puerto Rican sociologist Ángel Quintero Rivera. His hearing of Blades's song "Adán García":

> By means of an interesting combination of internal rhymes in the discursive affirmations and the musical phrases, an irregular meter is established that resembles the syncopated rhythms of Afro-Caribbean music. The combination of these elements (the sonorous syncope and the irregular poetic meter) gives the impression of an interplay of times that breaks through the circular regularity and/or a linear projection. This is a spontaneous resource of the singer-improviser [sonero] . . . thus, it is not a matter of a personal effort to present a particular cosmovision of temporality, rather it is a matter of archetypes of the collective unconscious that attest to cultural patterns in the manner that it is experienced.[89]

For Quintero Rivera, the syncope derives from an Afro-diasporic mode of experiencing time. Following the anthropological tradition of African retentions, Quintero Rivera asserts rhythm as the great legacy of African cultures, with polyrhythm and "what European musicology calls syncopated rhythms."[90] The importance of these retentions cannot be overstated. They represent a particular manner of experiencing corporal movement in relation to percussive sonority that disrupts or breaks the modes of synchronization of "Western" isorhythms and harmony, enabling a form of cultural resistance that drumming helps camouflage.[91] The dichotomy is generalized, since "the multiplicity of temporal intercrossings" of syncopation "musically express the subjective reality of the heterogeneity of human temporal experience (the time of emotions)," which "counter the lineal conception of time of the idea of progress in Western modernity."[92]

This critical framework sets up binaries—mind/body, motion/reason, linearity/syncopation—that enable moving across temporal and spatial scales without specifying the relationship between formal properties of the syncope and its metaphoric deployment. A racialized, immanent dissensual power in the rhythmic disruptions of syncopation is summoned to address questions of power inequalities of racism.[93] Throughout, the syncope emerges as a figure condensing various senses of time and temporality: as a transcendental category, as a phenomenon, as a focus and operation in historical discourse, as the historicity of events, as condition for and expression of subjective experience, and as a mode of musical organization. Without establishing the terms by which these produce and are produced by relations, its analytical purchase may lose traction. With Anna Tsing, we may wonder if the syncope might risk losing all friction once it is given free analytical rein to index and symbolize resistance to and subversion of hegemonic forces across all scales and registers.[94]

An important theorization of the syncope happens in Brazil. Beginning in the 1920s, the great Brazilian intellectual and writer (and trained musician) Mário de Andrade identified in the syncope a culturally and politically charged expression of the encounter between his society and others. Mário understood the syncope as a displacement of normative strong beats in the notated European tradition, which displacement he heard as a freeing of rhythm, in Brazilian popular and folkloric music, of this tradition's mensural order as well as a push toward prosody.[95] At this level, the syncope expressed how Brazilians "reconcile with foreign elements and accommodate their own proclivities."[96] In the end, Brazilian forms overcome the temporal subdivisions, even of the syncope, and free musico-poetic time.

Brazil's overcoming of the syncope is constitutive of its society. For Fernando Pérez Villalón, "[Mário's] notion of syncope articulates complex relations between rhythm, nation, the popular, and high culture."[97] Here, syncope indexes the key place that musicking held for Mário's notion of the national-popular. With the expression "syncopated modernity," Pérez Villalón deploys Mário's notion of the syncope "as a key to enter the relations between the national, modernity, the popular and aesthetics, a key that also may help us to think of the temporality of Brazilian modernism, of the regional and the cosmopolitan, of the machinic and the ritual, the popular and the erudite."[98] Pérez Villalón follows the Brazilian's intuition that a musical form informs a broader understanding of Brazil. Brazilian society emerges concurrently with the forces that give rise to those musical forms.

Fred Moten hears the syncope's disruptive character as indexing an asymmetric and asymptotic force in US Black radical aesthetics. His preferred figure is "the break," "a location at once internal and interstitial." Alongside "performance" and "the anarchic organization of phonic substance," "syncopation" delineates "an ontological field wherein black radicalism is set to work."[99] Moten considers "transfers" between "musical performances and strains in the history of that reproduction . . . the drives by which it's animated and punctuated"; he pursues "generative forces . . . in the asymptotic, syncopated nonconvergence of event, text, and tradition."[100] Irreducible to the event (of musical performance), text (the open weavings of improvisation and the kind of totality that it might yet be), or the tradition (the temporal operations that afford Black radical aesthetics a sense of temporal belonging negated by racism), the syncope compels "transfers" that cannot be mere ascriptions in a sociopolitical iconicity between the phenomenal experience of syncopation and phenomena that escape that experience. I take Moten's point to heart.

My own sense of syncopation shares in conceiving of syncopation in dialectical terms and, in this way, of conceptualizing simultaneous but heterogeneous spatio-temporal relations. Different from Pérez Villalón, Mário, and Quintero Rivera, I am not interested in tracing the putative origins of this dialectic (for the Puerto Rican, in the African diaspora, for the Brazilian, and for the Chilean critic, in the particular racial and cultural mixings of the nation) or in upholding musicking as the prototype for syncopation.[101] Syncopation as a figure of productive tension and irresolution, a model for the entanglements of the Americas. Musicking entails actions, events, and ideas in and through which the turbulence of time and space settles into a gentler sway of a harmonious temporality and emplacement. Blades overcomes the attenuation of the heyday of salsa beginning in the 1980s and sustains the once before achieved power of song to carry the weight of Latin American lettered practices. Zenón innovates jazz, a paradigmatic US contribution to modern music *tout court*. But there remains a tense undercurrent, a contradiction, a constitutive disorder that cannot be suppressed: the decline of the power of the written letter to harness Latin Americanist affect, for Blades, or the precarious place in the US polity of Puerto Rican citizens, in the case of Zenón.

Sounding Latin Music moves constantly, perhaps restlessly, back and forth across these tensions and the halting (syncopated) gaps. Syncopation affords this book a thinking that tries to capture the historicity of Latin American musicking as well as the structuring dynamics that help it establish senses of space and place. Syncopation: a manner and mode to produce time and space relations, simultaneous and nonsimultaneous temporalities, rhythms of change, the experience of displacement and dislocation, of anticipation, expectation and tension, of a possible resolution, and the eventual emergence of new tensions. Syncopation: a halt and a little gap at the heart of the encounter between things in their relentless march through time and space.

Chapter Overview

Chapter 1 brings into relief the tensions at the heart of a literate musical Latin Americanism, the divisions installed in the continent by the power of the lettered city being partly affirmed and partly challenged in the context of popular song and in New York City and various locales in the circum-Caribbean. While Blades asserts an equality of intelligence across classes, he also bemoans a lack of understanding of the sociopolitical woes of Latin America among his peers and audiences in New York City. Thus, unity (fourth fundament) collides with the constitutive internal exclusions of any Latin Americanism (sixth fundament).

In chapter 1, the Latin American lettered tradition—itself one of the great legacies of its colonial entanglements—becomes the terrain for friction between Blades and his Nuyorican colleagues and audiences circa 1979, at least in his account. At the same time, his immigrant position enables him the kind of perspective on Latin America that makes of New York City the site of core-like processes for an *idea* of Latin America, displacing Latin America's own core position in the production of Latin Americanism. Needless to say, this displacement works in tandem with core processes of the US's "Latin" phonographic industry, whose hegemony it reinforces.

In chapter 2, much as Blades's lettered ambitions remain in place in his turn-of-the-century projects, the Latin Americanism at stake relies on a new strategy: using musical forms to express a broader expanse of what he calls "Latin American feeling." That chapter finds the Panamanian recording in Costa Rica—as if "returning" to—the site of enunciation in Latin America, however, unable to suture the gap created by an ever more global definition of "Latin America." The Latin American "spirit" (sixth fundament) might have found its musical form in those recordings, but Latin America no longer seems to need a spokesperson to name its "condition" (third fundament)—to name, map, and historicize Latin America's constitutive relations to an outside.

Chapter 2 finds Blades working from Costa Rica at the turn of the century, seeking to expand his purview on "Latin American feeling" (his expression) by means of a heterogeneity of musical genres not readily available in his musical circles in the US. For the Costa Rican musicians in these projects, such heterogeneity was part and parcel of their voracious listening practices, including their expertise with the salsa styles they had heard coming from the US (and Puerto Rico and Cuba). They may well have represented the kind of perspectival modernity of Sarlo's. But Blades's Latin Americanism, anchored as it was on his own US perspective, found itself adrift with audiences no longer in need of Latin Americanist proclamations. The old Latin Americanism, which produced a sense of simultaneity between North and South, now rendered Blades's renewed Latin Americanism as nonsimultaneous with Latin America; the place of enunciation (a globalized Costa Rica) appeared as a space where emerging temporalities foretold a future without Latin Americanism. In this case, globalization had smoothed out the friction required for the idea of Latin America to gain traction.

This same globalization, in chapter 3, gives rise to the figure of Shakira as a superstar. In a significant reconfiguration of relations of production that centralized Colombia's place in the music industry relative to other Latin American countries, the Colombian singer and songwriter would challenge long-standing positions on US monolingualism. Meanwhile at home, debates would rage around the choice between a deracinated citizen and a citizen whose global visibility could in fact affirm the nation on the world stage. In Shakira, emerging forms of citizenship-as-consumption and of the individual as brand, persona, and subject reveal the coexistence of principles of modernity in what would well correspond to a postmodern dynamic in which core and periphery distinctions appear to melt away in a corporate cosmopolitanism, the nineteenth-century futures for a cosmopolitan capitalism foretold by Marx and Mill apparently fully realized in pop music.

The appearance of Colombian singer and songwriter Shakira on the global stage as a bona fide superstar appears to achieve the worldwide projection of the continent precisely as sonic traces of autochthony become unnecessary. The old constitutive outside (first fundament) might have become obsolete. And yet, her being from Latin America, or Colombia, continues to matter for emerging forms of Latinity in the US and elsewhere. Latin Americanism might well be a compulsion. The equally old antagonisms of the second fundament do not relent. Raging debates in Colombia about the character of both Colombian-ness and Latin American-ness, as well as anxieties expressed by US media and communication managers concerning the dissolution of a one-language policy for pop music, restore old concerns about what is "Latin" and what is not, of how "Latinity" may open up to unexpected transformations.

The modern links between race, exile, diaspora, and cultural ownership and its corollary historiography unravel in the encounter between institutionalized modes of jazz (Jazz at Lincoln Center) and those institutions' efforts to include associated migrant musical contributions (Afro-Cuban and Afro-Latin Jazz). Chapter 4 examines the temporal dynamics at play in one of modernities' signal terrains: the inclusions and exclusions of history. Exile, history, tradition, cultural inheritance, and familial kinship figure in chapter 4's discussion of the Afro Latin Jazz Orchestra at Lincoln Center led by Arturo O'Farrill. Initially sponsored by Jazz at Lincoln Center and Wynton Marsalis as a project for the recuperation of the deservedly admired repertoire of big-band "Latin" music from the 1940s and 1950s, O'Farrill's ensemble leaves this institutional fold and advocates both reclaiming for that music a place in an ecumenical conception of jazz and creating new music that he regards as more Pan American and worldly. O'Farrill will conjure up his father's spirit and that of the multiple ancestries that haunt and nourish Afro-Latin Jazz musicking. Marsalis would uphold a categorical distinction between African American Blackness and that of O'Farrill's music. This development is important for the way it inscribes US perspectives on race into the usually deracialized notions of Latin Americanism. How can two histories of exclusion dialogue?

In chapter 5, the progressive musical work of Miguel Zenón, placed in the future of jazz by the MacArthur Foundation, addresses the complexities of musical knowledge growing from the back-and-forth movement between Puerto Rico and the US. The MacArthur Foundation insists on naming the North–South relation in temporal terms: a Puerto Rican catches up with the relentless pace of musical modernism and even pushes ahead. Latin Americanism recedes from view at the same time that the old concerns with continental representation fade under the ever-pressing question of modernity in Puerto Rico, the musician engaging in a micropolitics of the event that find him bringing the jazz canon to peripheral locations across the Island while taking traditions from those locations to the "jazz for the 21st century." The continuing existence as an imperial outpost of Zenón's Puerto Rico in the new century would confirm Martí's greatest fears about the "Other" America's hemispheric designs. And still, Zenón would play America in advance of itself.

1 * Reckoning with Letters

"PEDRO NAVAJA" AND AURAL EQUALITY

Tú eres un pendejo, tú eres un pendejo.
(You are a jerk, you are a jerk.)

Edgardo Rodríguez Juliá (1983)

On the November 2009 bicentennial of Latin American independence, *El País* (Madrid) asked experts in economics, politics, science, arts, entertainment, and gastronomy in Hispanic America to list, in their view, Latin America's ten most prominent figures. On his list, Cuban critic and essayist Iván de la Nuez placed Pedro Navaja—from Panamanian singer-songwriter Rubén Blades's hit salsa song "Pedro Navaja"—eighth:

> Pedro Navajas [*sic*], by Rubén Blades: The lumpen immigrant. Brecht poached in Latin America and served in New York; a hero even to those who are illiterate in two languages.

> *Pedro Navajas* [sic], *de Rubén Blades. El emigrante lumpen. Brecht pasado por América Latina y servido en Nueva York. Un héroe, incluso, hasta para los que son analfabetos en dos lenguas.*[1]

With these two sentences, de la Nuez assembles a socioeconomic genealogy of immigration and its undergirding neocolonialism, a transnational intertextual trajectory, a public and an audience (these are distinct things), and "a people."[2] Much ado about salsa.

Writing in 1981, Édouard Glissant had identified salsa as a late stage in the process he termed "Plantation America." In fact, for Glissant, salsa was the sole phenomenon directly connecting the space and time of the continental US *back* to the Caribbean.[3] In the diagram reproduced in figure 1.1, Glissant retraced salsa's diasporic routes and conditions of possibility: from the eastern shores of the Americas; to the US "Deep South"; to the interlocked processes of urbanization, proletarization, and the marginalization of Black populations; to the creation of jazz, another musical complex. Glissant shows salsa, as it circles back to the Spanish Caribbean,

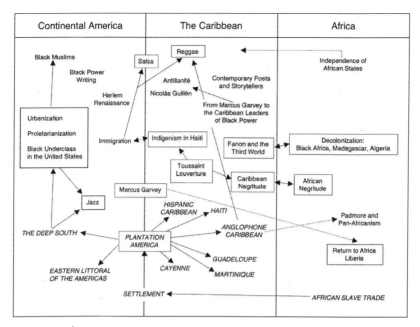

Figure 1.1. Édouard Glissant, *Caribbean Discourse*

in relation to migration (top of diagram). Tellingly, salsa remains in both "Continental America" and "The Caribbean."[4]

Glissant's rich historical materialist map elides the commodification and mass mediation of music that made "salsa" possible and that rendered it a paradigmatic capitalist product in the US. Nonetheless, it complements de la Nuez's pithy traversal of a related space and time.[5] For both, salsa traces an important historical trajectory that resonates with "nomadic evocations" of Caribbean migration to the US.[6]

These two mappings have a significant distinction. De la Nuez's commentary on "Navaja" broadens salsa's space of circulation to include points south of the Caribbean—what I will call "South," and in which I include the Spanish-speaking Caribbean. Such broadening produces an *immigrant* Latin American sphere different but inseparable from the *migrant* Latino minority who claim salsa as their cultural proper. In these spheres' political dynamics, languages cross over each other. Salsa becomes a phenomenon that, "although sung in Spanish, underlies the many characters of a culture generalized from New York City as being 'Latin.'"[7]

There emerges not just a larger mapping of salsa but several vectors connecting and separating Latin America, the Spanish Caribbean, the US, and Latino communities in the US (especially in New York City). Each vector inflects the politics of salsa (and salsa as politics) in unique though interrelated ways. These vectors constitute what I identify as Blades's *La-tino Americanist* Latin Americanism (hereafter Latino Latin Americanism): the composition of an idea and a practice of Latin America for which the perspective from the Latino sector of society in "America," entangled with that of Latin American immigrants, constitutes a primary condition of possibility.[8] In this chapter, this perspective establishes a set of dynamic relations between Latin America and specific Latino communities in the US. Blades's musical experiments condense listening modalities, corollary audiences, and publics in Latin America and the US. His projects of aesthetic renovation compel a political analysis of positionality and enunciation. In these projects, the work of musical-literary representation produces the "lumpen immigrant" as a signifier of a cultural ethos and a social type. These signifiers are symptoms of specific labor-related issues in US modernity. For instance, Leopoldo Tablante writes that in 1960, 60 percent of New York City's textile workers were Puerto Rican migrants who lost over 400,000 jobs between 1960 and 1980. Such massive changes in labor structures were compounded with New York City's mid-1970s fiscal crisis. By 1973, the Commission of Human Rights of New York declared that "the proportion of workers of Puerto Rican origin in the public sector was smaller than that of any ethnic group," a decline that "parallel[s] with the elimination of social assistance programs." Tablante writes that "the Nuyorican community has been forged out of three concrete obstacles: its cultural and ethnic difference, a level of education that only guaranteed low-level employment of high turnover, and an industry amidst transformation."[9]

Blades's experiments transform received aesthetic forms and adapt them to a renovated didacticism. This didacticism seeks to speak to and for a people (*demos*) and expresses Blades's immigratory trajectory. The translation of aesthetic forms across popular and cultural spheres and literary practices informed by the Latin American lettered tradition, with literature as its focal point, is both productive and contradictory. "Lettered tradition" refers broadly to the idea of the "lettered city," to urban intellectuals' (*letrados*) power to establish, regulate, and maintain social order since colonial times. Writing, proper orthography, grammar, and diction all comprised the medium and mediation for apportioning power, and regulated, sanctioned, or suppressed cultural alternatives.[10] The dialectic between productive and contradictory translation demands rethinking transculturation in order to account for how the song-chronicle "Pedro Navaja" performs the political work critics, audiences (listeners and dancers alike), and the author hold it to do.[11] This rethinking calls for the reconstitution of a new past for Latin American and Latino culture.

All this in a song called "Pedro Navaja." How is it that a song—a

New York City chronicle of a crime gone wrong for the titular assailant—should engage and mobilize the dynamic relations outlined above? Why does it take the form that it does? How is the song constituted by letters, which includes voice, speech, song, literature, and language as well as reading, speaking, writing, listening, and dancing? How does it constitute a logic of Latino Latin Americanism? How does it implicate an understanding of musical politics under such a logic? These are the questions with which I contend in this chapter.

If "Navaja" belongs in a musical category (i.e., "salsa") with stylistic features, aesthetic values, and a variety of subgenres, it too is an assemblage of heterogeneous affective, cognitive, commercial, corporeal, cultural, literary, musical, political, and technical components that operate at various and simultaneous temporal and spatial scales.[12] This song embodies the contingent sum of these components. It also produces specific sets of dynamic interrelations that both resonate and interfere in the syncopated encounter between an immigrant, the host migrant minority community in the US, and the continent. Listening is plural, which renders it a crucible for struggles over salsa's significance. At stake are the principles by which people—audiences, publics, critics, the singer-songwriter, arrangers—wager on their powers of intelligibility, to understand and be understood when words and musical sounds are at stake. These powers ground what I call aural equality. This, then, is a story about the travails of this equality.

Whence "Illiteracy"?

"Illiteracy in two languages." With this phrase, de la Nuez risks denigrating a sector of Latin American and mostly Puerto Rican immigrant laborers in New York City who, one presumes, although able to communicate bilingually, were not necessarily able to read and write. They also may not have partaken of the Latin American literary tradition, which for de la Nuez—a Cuban intellectual living in Barcelona—is perhaps the defining signal of Latin America's resonance in a globally conceived modernity.[13] The phrase conjures the politics of bilingualism in Puerto Rico. From the beginning of US control of Puerto Rico, bilingual education on the Island was meant to deliver cheap English-speaking labor to US corporations. This linguistic policy was carried out unevenly and remained intensely controversial.

The Island's two languages have existed in tense correlation. Early in the US occupation of Puerto Rico, "Spanish was intermittently, but consistently, forbidden" in schools.[14] From the prevalence of English-language education until about 1947 to the passage of the Spanish Only Law in

1991, official stances toward one language or the other have vacillated. According to the 2000 US Census, 71.9 percent of Puerto Ricans described their ability to speak English as "less than very well."[15] Intellectuals such as Arcadio Díaz-Quiñones and José Luis González consider Puerto Rican emigrants' bilingualism "a distorting element of the hispano-philic image of Puerto Rican culture,"[16] meaning that the Island's Spanish-only advocates would exclude the millions living in the US and disavow what Díaz-Quiñones considers "the mixtures and hybridity of our [Puerto Rican] tongue, and our many degrees of bilingualism."[17]

In the 1950s, "a significant part of the country's displaced agricultural proletariat"[18] migrated from Puerto Rico to New York City. This second great wave of laborers was linked to the 1952 establishment of the Island as Estado Libre Asociado (ELA) of the US (literally "Associated Free State," formally "Commonwealth of Puerto Rico"). This migratory movement was also linked to "Operation Bootstrap," the Island's post–World War II industrialization, which peaked in 1953 but continued for decades. Jorge Duany reports that "between 1948 and 1990 . . . 421,238 Puerto Ricans were recruited to work on the US mainland," with a high point of almost 25,000 in 1968 alone.[19] A majority of these workers, who settled in the Northeast (New York, New Jersey, Connecticut, Delaware, and Pennsylvania), "were men with little schooling and proficiency in the English language."[20] According to the 2010 Census, 64 percent of Puerto Ricans in New York City reported speaking English very well, compared to only 28 percent on the Island. In contrast, in Puerto Rico 85 percent reported speaking Spanish exclusively at home, while only 25 percent of them reported speaking Spanish at home when they were on the mainland, and 19.4 percent overall reported speaking English less than "very well."[21] As of 2008, more Puerto Ricans lived in the US than on the Island.[22] This migratory movement "drastically changed the character of the Puerto Rican immigrant community,"[23] generating what came to be known as the "Puerto Rican problem" (think *West Side Story* stereotypes). By the 1970s this migration helped consolidate an underclass beneath the working class, a social remainder of capitalism—in the midst of modernity's hyper-capitalism—unique in its bi- and inter-lingualism.

"*Analfabetos en dos lenguas.*" How could US modernity have engendered this social formation? And what might have been the relation of this formation to Latin American lettered understandings of and hierarchies between written/read and spoken language? After all, in relation to the Latin American literate tradition these "illiterate in two languages" would embody a diglossia rooted in the division between orality and writing/reading. This distinction is based more on class differences than on ethnic and cultural differences, as it is in the US. It has been used to understand 1960s and 1970s Puerto Rican communities in New York ("Nuyorican") as either "an immigrant group" or "an ethnic or racial minority."[24] These distinctions will inform Blades's work, but the emergence of a rich Nuyorican literature will not figure in that work, concerned as he was with the canonic, Spanish-language Latin American literary tradition.[25]

The co-constitutive relationships between the following are key: the social formation "illiterate in two languages," the category of the lumpen immigrant, and Blades's position as spokesperson for a renovated and renovating musical politics.[26] These all entail the traditional notions that, first, there exists a social reality that serves as the referent for some form of musical-literary representation, and second, that music that achieves a certain goal in its fidelity of representation itself becomes part of Latin American and Latino American "representativeness." Ángel Rama proposes "independence, originality, [and] representation" as three primary impulses behind Latin American literature. Representation of the "entire Latin American region," of nations, a "class," "a sociological reality," among others, appears as an ever-transforming constant in literature.[27] Thus, these relationships fall under the rubric of representation and its corollary functions of "portraying," "speaking about," "speaking for," "giving voice to," and "expressing the identity and values of the community." Before further unpacking the politics of representation at play in Blades's music, let's first consider the song and its musical form, understanding form as the relation between sonic materials and their handling.

THE FORM OF SONG

"Pedro Navaja" begins with a brass introduction accompanied by full rhythm section (see fig. 1.2). The stunning opening two measures of Luis "Perico" Ortiz's brilliant arrangement are voiced in parallel fourths and played by three trombones in a high, urgent register (labeled *a*). This opening sets up harmonic ambiguity abetted by the counterpoint between an ascending bass line and descending upper parts, all in a strictly homorhythmic pattern.[28] Each chord lacks the third scale degree, contributing to the distinct sonority of the harmonies and blurring both a major or minor mode tonality. The tonal approach might hint at a modal organization more typical of some jazz idioms than of salsa styles. Shifting to a melodic-strand-plus-accompaniment (homophony), the descending chromatic line against a static bass (i.e., a bass pedal) that follows (labeled *b*) retains and intensifies the previous two bars' unsettled character. The whole is grouped in a six-measure unit, varying most salsa songs' norma-

Figure 1.2. "Pedro Navaja," Introduction, arranged by Luis "Perico" Ortiz

tive four- or eight-bar phrases. The two-bar *clave* pattern, sacrosanct in New York City salsa dance culture, remains intact, for now (labeled 3–2 below the score).

In the background, the din of New York City—the commotion of distant sirens, the indistinct noise of cars, the anonymous hum of buildings—adds to the introduction's novel sonic texture. The introduction is mimetic of the soundscape of New York City, which turns out to be one of the song's key protagonists.[29] This buildup of tension releases unexpectedly by means of a variation of a standard closing formula borrowed from traditional Cuban *son* (labeled *c*). This release unambiguously affirms a tonal center (C major), in strong contrast with the preceding six-measure phrase's tonal ambiguity. In a way, within one measure we appear to traverse the imaginary space separating the epicenter of urban modernity's harmonic innovations from a rural periphery's traditions.

At this point something unusual happens: there is a break in the music—an actual silent seizure, a literal sonic syncope. For eight measures, the whole ensemble is suddenly pared down to the conga playing a standard *marcha* pattern (or march) at a noticeably slower tempo. Along with this breach in the musical texture, the tempo change disrupts the flow of dancing, even as it helps set a new tempo for dancers. In addition, the closing formula had occurred on the first measure of the two-bar clave pattern (i.e., the clave's "3-side") but the conga restarts the music on that same figure ("the 3-side"), effectively "crossing" the clave.[30] In all, the change in the musical setting helps direct our attention toward what happens next. Over the conga pattern, casual and colloquial street shouts and whistling sound in the background, one last "realist" touch before the narrative begins. "*Oye, Avelino, ven pa'ca!*" a voice shouts (the Spanish equivalent of "Hey, Avelino, c'mere!"). As these voices recede, the scene is set for Blades to begin. In a slightly nasal tenor and with a clear, almost clipped Spanish diction—articulated enunciation, long rolled *r*'s—Blades chronicles the events leading to the death of Pedro Navaja.

"Navaja" would not be all that it is without its musical arrangement.[31] As Blades put it, "arrangements are a key topic, which few people consider because in the majority of cases we who write songs do not have knowledge of orchestration[,] and the arranger becomes in part a composer. . . . The arranger can make or break a song. . . . the arranger takes a song that may have a certain level of importance and either transforms it into a special thing or destroys it."[32] As the song's arranger, Luis "Perico" Ortiz and his music contribute to the narrative process. Ortiz thus participates in the production of a kind of listener and a mode of listening, of a kind of dancer and a mode of dancing, and of audiences.

Ortiz's arrangement features a degree of experimentation that condenses his earlier innovations in orchestration, tonal resources, and formal expansion. His 1977 arrangement for Blades's "Pablo Pueblo" featured irregular uses of the clave considered sacrilegious by New York City salsa dancing's orthodoxy. The introduction of "Pablo" contains one measure in an odd meter, which would literally trip dancers up. Speaking of his arrangement for "Pablo," Ortiz recalled Fania executives' apprehension toward his proposal for the song's unusual sound. He unforgettably introduced the tuba to create a broad orchestral sound with cinematic effects.[33] Beginning with "Pablo," Ortiz felt an uncanny affinity with Blades, with whom he shared a sense of mission: "that we were there to educate the people—and I never stopped after that." Ortiz recalled becoming more daring in disrupting established norms: "An arrangement is like a road, a highway that one takes but from which one sometimes takes a shortcut in order to get back on the road." He relished taking such shortcuts ("*atajo*"), creating stark musical juxtapositions that to his ear were nonetheless interconnected. This technique, he remarked, he learned from legendary Puerto Rican bandleader Rafael Cortijo as filtered through his own background as a classical trumpeter seriously interested in jazz. Ortiz spearheaded what he called a "musical revolution" in 1970s New York City and contributed to the emergence of "urban *son*" ("*son urbano*") in a nod to salsa's roots in Afro-Cuban *son*.[34]

The startling opening of "Navaja" embodies this aesthetic of renovation. Take, for instance, the song's uncanny traversal of modern chromatic harmony, which arrives at a traditional diatonic break. Ortiz achieves this renovation by juxtaposing modernity's spaces and places, indexing temporalities at play with differential relations to the past and the present, and condensing in a few measures questions of memory in a challenging present in need of his "musical revolution." Through his music, Ortiz appears to address traditional and progressive audiences. But at the same time, his music asserts the possibility that this dualistic distinction, though audible, is no longer to be rendered as opposite poles but as positions within a single spectrum of musical intelligibility. Ortiz thus asserts the equality of audiences and the aural equality they all possess.

For all Ortiz's renovations, "Navaja" still obeys many of salsa's formal conventions. In its overall design, it follows a more or less standard succession of sections of 1970s salsa arrangements:

1. An instrumental introduction
2. A set of stanzas (here, ten stanzas)
3. A call-and-response section in which the singer improvises lines (*soneos*) against a repeated choir refrain
4. An instrumental interlude (*mambo*)
5. A second call-and-response section
6. A repetition of the instrumental interlude (*moña*, sometimes different from the mambo)
7. A brief final call-and-response section
8. An ending (here, a return to the introductory music, including the closing formula)[35]

In the main set of stanzas, "Navaja" narrates the fatal encounter in the streets of New York City between Pedro Navaja, a two-bit thief in his neighborhood, and a nameless woman, a prostitute. As Quintero-Herencia puts it, "Pedro Navaja" is the "musicalization of eviction, of the constitutive fracture of these modern subjects in the Big City."[36] In stunning detail and adhering to a strict chronological order of events, the singer relates how Navaja prowls the streets looking for someone to rob only to meet, by an act of radical chance, an untimely death at the hands of the woman. The woman, alas, suffers the same fate. Instead of a double murder, this is a doubled murder and a tragicomic, if not absurdist, shared death of two marginal subjects.[37]

The opening lines are as memorable as they are arresting:

Por la esquina del viejo barrio lo vi pasar,
Con el tumbao que tienen los guapos al caminar.

(I saw him pass by the corner of the old neighborhood,
With the swinging swagger that tough fellas have in their gait.)[38]

They are the words of an observant witness with a fine ear for setting, circumstance, and character, exemplifying how "storytellers tend to begin the story with a presentation of the circumstances in which they themselves learned what is to follow."[39] Or, as Blades put it, "all the themes are the product of lived experiences, or of something that happened where one was a witness."[40]

The second stanza adds bongos and timbales to the conga pattern, assembling salsa's classic percussion section. The narration stays with Navaja, whose clothing items, we are told, each carry a function: dark glasses hide what he sees; a wide-brimmed hat tipped to one side hides him; his sneakers would allow him to scram should he run into trouble; a golden tooth, which shines when he smiles, marks him as a tough guy.[41]

Next, we encounter the other main character, a prostitute who, like Navaja, is out in the street, "walking up and down the avenue," and, like him, eking out a precarious living in the city. At this point, the rest of the rhythm section (electric bass and acoustic piano) joins in the percussion as the instruments' mix comes to the center, no extraneous city sounds to be heard. The music is on.

Both characters labor in an environment pregnant with risk and void of possibilities: the streets of an impoverished neighborhood. Cops idle away in their patrol car, indifferent to what happens (fourth stanza). As fate would have it, when Navaja and the woman come into direct contact (eighth stanza), he meets an unexpected end: having chosen his victim for her presumed vulnerability, he did not anticipate that she too might have been armed. That day, she was carrying a gun that "would protect her from all evil," the narrator reports in a paraphrase of the Lord's Prayer. When Navaja attacks her, blade in hand, she happens to be fumbling inside her purse trying to grab a flask with liquor that might "ward off the cold," her revolver close at hand. As he stabs her, she shoots him. He falls mortally wounded; she does too. A drunkard stumbles upon their bodies, grabs a couple of dollars, steals the knife, and wanders off. Interrupting the omniscient narrator's voice, the drunkard (whom Blades imitates) slurs a maxim that may be one of the most memorable lines in all of salsa (tenth stanza): "*La vida te da sorpresas, sorpresas te da la vida, ¡Ay Dios!*" ("Life gives you surprises, surprises are given to you by life; ah, God!").

No commotion follows, no one cries, no one wonders why, how, or who, the narrator reports. Among the eight million stories unfolding in New York, as the singer will later remark, those involving this peculiar doubled murder and its exquisite paradox do not warrant even a byline in the newspapers' crime beat.

The narrative, now finished, gives way to an extended call-and-response in which, against the drunkard's refrain, Blades improvises his *soneos*. Deploying popular proverbs, statistics about New York City, parodies of radio news broadcasts, and references to Kafka, Blades dramatizes the chronicle's moral, the quotidian life in the contemporary metropolis, and the potentially deadly uncertainties of working in its informal economies.

Following salsa conventions, the improvisation is punctuated by an instrumental mambo. Here, Ortiz's unfettered creativity shines. First, he

Figure 1.3. "Pedro Navaja," mambo section

sets out the section with a five-bar phrase, which effectively undercuts the clave pattern by creating a crossed clave.

As figure 1.3 shows, the rhythmic feel of the first five-bar phrase occurs on a 2–3 clave (shown beneath the example). Were the clave to continue regularly, its repetition would turn around this feel by setting the same phrase on a 3–2 clave pattern. Dancers attuned to the subtle relationships between instrumental rhythms and clave would be bothered by this shift. But the clave is not actually played, making it possible to alternatively perceive that the first bar of the clave is repeated between the fifth bar of the mambo and its repetition. Heard this way, it produces two successive bars on the same "side" of the clave (the "two side"), which is to say, it forces dancers to take two steps with the same foot, anathema to New York–style dancing. Usually, the mambo is a place of greater energy release on the dance floor, allowing dancers—particularly, but not only, in New York City—to engage in elaborate turns, all while keeping to the strict steps dictated by a regular clave. But Ortiz seems determined to renovate this norm.

Second, Ortiz's arrangement moves suddenly from the key of E major to a harmonic sequence beginning with a C-dominant chord (altered in the style of modern jazz harmony) that leads to the key of E-flat major in the fourth bar. At this point, a harmonically ambiguous progression arrives at a polychord with E in the bass—this E is not the E that anchors the improvisations. Even if this formal harmonic interpretation is not apparent, the jagged and atonal melody in bars 4–5 of the mambo reveals Ortiz searching for new modes to create musical tension.

Third, particularly in the first two measures, the second part of this extended mambo (fig. 1.4) features a melodic line in the style of Brazilian samba. This line uncannily renders the simultaneously joyous and melancholy ethos of so many samba chorus lines. Like the mambo's previous five-bar phrase, this melodic strand combines a tonally settled part (the first four bars) and a more tonally agitated section (the second four bars). Ortiz again revels in sudden harmonic shifts. The section first suggests A minor (first two bars) via the succession of half-diminished seventh to altered-dominant chords, a classic jazz progression known as ii–V. It then swerves chromatically toward A-flat major. Bars 7–8 of this section shift again, this time suggesting a modulation to F major, a key distant from A-flat major.[42]

To end, Ortiz engages in a bit of (postmodern) pastiche (fig. 1.5). Fulfilling the tonal possibility of F major, he sets a famous phrase from Leonard Bernstein's and Stephen Sondheim's *West Side Story*, "America." This tune is known for its line "I like to live in America," which Bernstein set to a Mexican cross-rhythm in the style of huapango. The irony in the original is amplified in "Navaja." However, Ortiz juxtaposes this with an instrumental version of the refrain *"la vida te da sorpresas,"* from "Navaja," except that, as if to represent either a drunken voice or the yawning gap between the American Dream ("I like to live in America") and the realities of the characters in the song, Ortiz sets the refrain in another, wholly unrelated key: A major. The trombones play this line with a slightly overblown sound, coming across as if mocking the claim of "I like to live in America," the reality of immigrant life being closer to the gap and relation between these two strands, cleverly rendered in two distant keys. This harmonic technique is known as bitonality. Although it is a resource in some strands of European musical modernism, and only

Figure 1.4. "Pedro Navaja," second part of mambo section

Figure 1.5. "Pedro Navaja," mambo section lead-in to refrain

rarely in jazz, it is unheard of in salsa. Finally, out of this bitonal pastiche emerges a classic jazz sonority (an altered B-dominant chord) that, while it has little to do with either key (F major or A major), brings this unprecedented mambo back to the home key of E major, where Blades initiates his second set of improvisations. This music is nothing short of stunning.

As if to comply with a rigorous formalism, Blades's stanzas are set in an Alexandrine pattern.[43] This fourteen-syllable line format stands out from the more typical decasyllabic Caribbean *décima* or alternatives such as octosyllabic lines. It is a display of virtuosic poetics in canny counterpoint with the melody's relative simplicity. Dominating the major-key melody is a peculiarly repetitious, taunting, childlike motive oscillating between two notes that nonetheless lends the character of a recitation tone, as in sung prayers and sermons. As figure 1.6 indicates, the two tones are scale degrees 6 and 5 of the major scale. This is a variation of the song's model: Bertolt Brecht and Kurt Weill's "Die Moritat von Mackie Messer," widely known in its English version as "Mack the Knife" (which also includes scale degree 3).

Like Weill's song, "Navaja" follows an exacting course of stepwise ascending modulations from the initial key of C major to its final destination in E major. This tonal scheme gradually increases musical tension, paralleling the chronicle's narrative tautness. Once the bare circumstances of the story's scene have been presented, and once the characters in the opening three stanzas have been sketched, faster tonal modulations propel the action forward and away from the initial C major. Formal repetition and narrative continuity give the song a tightly knit texture, balanced by Ortiz's arrangement, which carefully avoids any repetitions in the trombone punctuations that dot the sung strophes.

Figure 1.6. Comparison between "Pedro Navaja" and "Mack the Knife"

At ten minutes, "Navaja" is long by salsa standards. A typical, contemporaneous salsa song lasted at most four minutes. Nonetheless, the song's ten stanzas and instrumental setting give it a sense of minimalist compression, all in the service of narrating the fatal events. Narration and temporality maintain the symbiotic relationship between this story's form, word(s), and world(s). In reality, "Navaja" is a sung chronicle, a form with a long tradition of narrating events in Latin American letters.

Chronicle-Song

In his foundational book about the music, Puerto Rican sociologist Ángel Quintero Rivera places "Navaja" within a salsa tradition of chronicle-song (*crónica-canción*). These chronicle-songs convey quotidian and historical matters by means of a temporally ordered account of events. Quintero Rivera cites chronicles by Ana Lydia Vega (b. 1948), such as "Letra para salsa y tres soneos por encargo," from her collection *Vírgenes y mártires* (1981), whose epigraph is the refrain "*La vida te da sorpresas, sorpresas te da la vida.*" The chronicle-"Navaja" connections continue. In Vega's short story, a woman turns the tables around on an aggressive male pursuer by becoming the pursuer herself. It deconstructs gender power relations in general and, in Frances Aparicio's words, critiques "the rigid sexual roles articulated through salsa music itself." Aparicio spares Blades this critique, in part because his refrain "signals a commitment on the part of musicians and writers alike to deconstruct social conventions reified by class, race, and gender boundaries."[44] The events the chronicles narrate may be actual or fictional, a distinction that does not annul their truthful expression of fundamental values already inscribed in the community, from which perspective they propose alternatives to institutional histories, silences, and exclusions. Blades is categorical on the matter: "I am reporter of the barrio and of the urbanized city," adding in 1983 that "we're doing musical urban chronicle in the same way that there is one [urban chronicle] in the literary world."[45]

The chronicle constitutes a literary production of temporality, as Spanish critic Aníbal González-Perez argues: "[The chronicle] moves in time and with time and at the same time reflects on that [double] movement."[46] Combined with its insistent reportage of events, this temporal operation of the chronicle performs what Susana Rotker calls an "archeology of the present."[47] In this sense, "Navaja" would excavate the social strata inscribed in and relations enacted by quotidian events in a modern urban environment, registering in "real time" transformations that other forms of reportage may not capture with the ease of the song's immediacy. "For those with no access to radio, cinema, television, the written press, music recovers its original reason, which was to inform," Blades affirmed in 1984, remarking that "the work I do is a reflexive labor of my situation as inhabitant of the Latin American city; as such, nothing can escape such reflection."[48]

As chronicle-song, "Navaja" amplifies the literary and journalistic character of the chronicle. It does so not by rendering the chronicle as song but by exploring and exploiting the character of storytelling as it pushes the relation between the fictional and the real. "I prefer to write about a reality of which I take elements to create a fictional figure, but one that may be identifiable, by virtue of its essence, with someone or with some people," Blades explained in 1980.[49] These attitudes are more associated with the lettered tradition than with popular song. Consider Mexican novelist and chronicler Juan Villoro's relevant comparison to the novel: "If the novelist searches for the creation of a unique and unrepeatable world, the chronicler, on the contrary, assimilates all kind of common places. Imaginary chronicles are a combination of both procedures."[50]

The song produces a singular antinomy by joining socioeconomic concerns with an unprecedented attention to form. On the one hand, the "fictional reality" of the marginalized irrupts in the "reality" of a broad community of listeners, making it possible that *audiences* become *publics*. On the other hand, song and form together constitute a means both to open ears to this marginalized "reality" and to break through the "walls against which the community comes up against." Specifically, these are walls of indifference and invisibility surrounding the immigrant neighborhood. Through this antinomy, the song records a community's "confrontation with reality," to use Glissant's remarks about Black jazz communities in the US.[51] Two discernible poles in the antinomy (a social field and a song, the documentary and the fictive) become mutually embedded, without either one being wholly subsumed in the other. This mutuality owes to the juxtaposition of rationalities that the song assembles—namely, social, economic, political, and poetic rationalities. Such tensions—between reality and fiction, form and politics—are easier understood within the framework of the chronicle-song.

Because of its double character as reportage and literature, the chronicle-song highlights the co-constitution of event and form. It straddles the overlap between history and literature, or what Hayden White called "fictions of factual representation."[52] Distinctions between these pairs entail preconceived notions of truth: the "truth of correspondence" between word and event and the "truth of coherence" between events and their narration.[53] At stake are the kinds of truth that matter most when making any distinctions, truths that emerge from specific social and political needs and demands. This compels further distinctions between politics variously understood as (1) the contestation and exercise of power often cast in terms of "resistance" (in this case, the chronicle-song as a counter-discourse);[54] (2) the conformation of social blocs seizing political meaning in antagonistic relation with an outside "other";[55] and (3) the redistribution of "space and time, place and identity, speech and noise, the visible and the invisible" and "the introduction of new objects and subjects onto the common stage."[56]

THE LATIN AMERICAN CHRONICLE AND
ITS SOCIOPOLITICAL FORMS

These political forms connect with an influential nineteenth-century Latin Americanist literary form: the chronicle. The chronicle emerged in the context of unprecedented growth of printed media, rising transnational mass communication, an emerging consumer class,[57] and the "internationalism of the modernizing period (1870–1910)," when "writers worked to transcend the restrictions of nineteenth-century nationalities and to reestablish the mythical common fatherland, which they called 'Latin America.'"[58] The chronicler, in turn, was the first professional in the world of Latin American letters, fusing into one the roles of journalist, writer, lettered emissary, and foreign correspondent. A new consumer, the reader, experienced the rush of a nascent public sphere locally while forming part of a novel regional configuration: a chronicle could be read simultaneously in several countries.[59] For the first time, writers adapted "to his permanent readers."[60] The form embodied a synergy between the written word and changing societal orders.[61]

The chronicle observed and registered customs and values of some sector of society, somewhere. Partly ethnographic and partly sociological, the chronicle skillfully relayed firsthand experiences, allowing readers to vicariously encounter worlds undergoing rapid transformation.[62] The chronicle, though, offered a critical perspective on these customs and values, being able to attend to the particularity (and peculiarity) of its object while drawing broad social diagnoses.[63] This duality made it an "archaeology of the present, dedicated to 'small facts,'" that "amused" and "informed" readers.[64] Complementing "an alignment with the real," the chronicle introduced a new truth: the truth of critique.[65] Still, it would dwell at the margins of true literature (i.e., poetry, novel, short story).

Three distinct social formations emerge. First, the readership; second, the *demos*, a national formation divided into the people as object of journalistic-literary representation and the people who seize control of that representation; third, the *public*. A public comes into being "by virtue of being addressed," not because that address may constitute it as such but rather because any address gains public character—a *res publica* or public matter—by the kind of response it earns: no reading or no listening means no response, and no response means no public.[66] From the perspective of the public, if readership constitutes the mediating force shaping it, a public appears as a condition of possibility for complex notions of the *demos*: "you are standing before a portrait of your country. Whether or not you are a catalogued archetype, you are a reader who moves among archetypes and, therefore, you exist doubly: verify (reflective) the moral achievement of the conduct of others and amuse yourself (frivolous) with the excesses of picturesqueness, vulgarity, or pretension."[67] The Latin American chronicle, then, harbored questions of self-definition, "a way to diagnosing's one's present," in a word, diagnosing "modernity."[68]

These formations entail a politics, and their relation pivots on the duty the chronicle had to the Latin Americanist principle of representativeness, *sensu* Rama. The *demos*, for example, was split; the continent remained largely illiterate for a long time. Such are the politics of the chronicle that neither its potential contestatory nature (the first sense of the political above), nor its capacity to conform social blocs in possible agonistic relation with others (the second sense of the political), nor its performance of staging new subjects and objects as part of the common (the third sense of the political) can autonomously operate as dispositives for social transformation. Any analytic of the chronicle—and of the chronicle-song, as we will soon see—must confront the inherent contradictions of these earlier political dynamics, which remain, *mutatis mutandis*, in place at the time Monsiváis writes (and Blades sings). And if the written word already suggested the potentials and shortcomings of reading, the sung word and its corollary aurality will give these a further and no less complicated turn.

THE DISCONTENTS OF REPRESENTATIVENESS

As Quintero Rivera observes, the chronicle-song narrates events that are either not recorded by institutional history or simply wouldn't come to public attention.[69] This duality of history and story in the chronicle-song of "Navaja" demands further questioning in two ways: first, the question of representation, itself consisting in the logic of correspondence (White) and the principle of representativeness (Rama); second, the question of temporality and history. Let's now return to the song.

As a salsa song, what is "Navaja" about? Critics and commentators offer three kinds of answers. The first and most widely held interpretation invokes what Quintero-Herencia calls the story's "concrete sociological referent," which makes it "the song with which the urban proletariat identifies."[70] Here belong, among others, Venezuelan writer César Miguel Rondón's notion of salsa as the music of the urban (largely poor) Hispanic circum-Caribbean (besides the hispanophone Caribbean islands, Venezuela, Panama, and Colombia); Puerto Rican essayist, novelist, and poet Mayra Santos-Febres's notion that "salsa is pueblo"; and US-based Puerto Rican literary critic Arcadio Díaz-Quiñones's claim that salsa lyrics give "the clearest and most continuous signal of national identity." Such signals were emitted out of the interaction of Puerto Ricans in New York City with other communities, as Juan Otero Garabís remarks.[71] The old nationalistic *demos* now index a new sociopolitical proper, the poor or "pueblo."

But there is a twist: salsa's work of representation circulates between the Caribbean, New York City, *and* Latin America. In this circum-Caribbean process, Rondón singles out Blades as the leading figure, particularly through his late 1970s songs. In a widely accepted and endlessly repeated gesture, Blades is credited not only for directly addressing the social and the political through salsa lyrics but also for introducing these matters to salsa. This is commonly cast as a matter of gaining "consciousness," as *salsa con consciencia* (salsa with consciousness). Salsa hereby becomes aware of itself, knowingly addressing matters of concern for the communities it most directly speaks to and from which it draws inspiration. Whatever their differences, critics within this tradition favor an imperative of mimetic fidelity to the community and its people, along with a suspicion of abstractions—notwithstanding the paradoxical appeal to "consciousness."[72] In the end, music and song faithfully transcribe a social reality and transduce social energies into sound. At the same time, singers, composers, and arrangers have the duty to speak to that reality from a point of enunciation authorized by their belonging to it.

A second critical perspective is exemplified by literary and cultural critic José David Saldívar. He remarks on Blades's "predilection for radically experimenting with the traditional salsa form and content."[73] Saldívar writes of the "eerie juxtaposition of the concrete and the abstract" in what he calls Blades's "new salsa 'undersongs'": songs recorded in 1987 based on short stories of Gabriel García Márquez, a repertoire that takes the work of "Navaja" to its ultimate literary consequences. Saldívar proclaims that "if mass cultural forms create conditions of possibility by expanding the present by informing it with memories of the past, Blades's cultural creations can present post-contemporary [that is, future] social contradictions while retaining the potential to play a role in the struggle for hegemony."[74] This heady program is tied to the idea that Blades's "'Nueva Canción' becomes transnational" and that the singer-songwriter is "open to two worlds and is formed within his local and global Borderlands." In the end, "[through the lived-in simultaneity of the Americas] the hybrid . . . becomes the ground for political analysis and social change."[75] Thanks to his immigrant cosmopolitanism and lettered erudition, Blades is able to speak to the encounter between the two Americas, and across the social class divides he traverses.

A third position refutes the mimetic populist interpretation. For example, Quintero-Herencia disavows what he considers the mimetic position's populist fundamentalism, noting its moralizing and prescriptive tendencies. He rejects identitarian claims of either class or ethnicity as the final horizon for signification as limited. He also refuses the privilege granted to "consciousness raising" advocated by intellectuals and the Latin American middle class whenever salsa addresses "social themes," critiquing any attempt at "affirmative intellectual civility."[76] Instead, he proposes that the song stages the radical dislocation, dispossession, and fragmentation of the modern metropolitan subject. Second, he understands the song as an "ethical emblem" of "an irreparable situation" in which fate governs all and can never be "administered or known."[77] Quintero-Herencia casts any "incitation to action" or "condemnations" heard in the song as "reading effects" ("*efectos de lectura*"), not as "final determinations of the possible senses in a song filled with citations, parodies, and allusions."[78] No celebration of Rondón's "urban proletariat" here. No possible contestation of hegemony under the auspices of transnational hybridization either. Only an ironic, melancholy expression of "what the 'American dream' means to many Hispanic American immigrants" whose "tragic invisibility is what is sung not what the song celebrates."[79] In "Navaja," the drunkard's famous words embody "the ironic laughter of an ending without transcendence."[80] This is a universalizing irony marked by an implacable fatalism and represents, for Quintero-Herencia, a possible "point of departure for political or discursive reflection of the song."[81]

With Quintero-Herencia's call to "discursive reflection" in mind, we may interrogate the song's representativeness and its politics of time. The story of "Navaja" lies at the intersection of its proximity to events of journalistic reportage and the literate will to weave words into form. By the same token, it appears as an interpretation of reality—*a* reality—and *as* invented reality. Audible traces of a reality understood as that which happens in the world compel critics' mimetic hearings of "Navaja." As Rama cast it, the chronicle is compelling because it is cut from the same cloth as "our dreams, desires, and guilt," and because no matter its form, its story still engages the "reality of the imagination of people."[82] In short, one need not rely on mimetic interpretations in order to hear in the song the social traces Rama describes. I adopt this position because of how it shifts matters from representation to a more dialogic and communicative exchange between singer-songwriter and listeners. This, in turn, has to do with a quintessential concern of modernity: experience. In storytelling, experience finds its expression.

STORYTELLING AND EXPERIENCE

Irreducible to but part of the chronicle's content and form in song, storytelling is a modality of shared experience in modernity. In this section, I consider storytelling in "Navaja" alongside three aspects of Walter Benjamin's storytelling analytic: sympathizing with crooks, psychological austerity, and sociability. For Benjamin, a loss of experience derived from a mechanized and mercantilized modernity in which "bodily experience" had been exchanged for "moral experience by those in power."[83] Direct communication in storytelling, even as "secondary orality,"[84] retains some of the worth of experience. At the same time, as a genre now remediated by a recording (i.e., not necessarily face-to-face), storytelling transforms relations of intimacy, expanding and contracting temporal and spatial senses in various ways.[85]

Much in the chronicle-song of "Navaja" engages storytelling dynamics, as Benjamin glossed them. For one, the song aligns itself with a tradition of sympathizing with crooks and tricksters.[86] In Cuban and Puerto Rican vernacular forms there is a long tradition of addressing delinquency, which speaks to the storyteller's acquaintance with local characters.[87] In this case, "Navaja" the song produced Navaja the character. More precisely, the relation between song and audience rendered the song and its main character "part of Puerto Rican folklore."[88]

Psychological austerity establishes another connection between storytelling in "Navaja" and Benjamin's storytelling analytic. In "Navaja," the two main characters' interior psychological worlds are left for listeners to only infer. This limited narrative purview gives the story "an amplitude that information lacks."[89] Although one could argue that in "Navaja" the rendering of events as if they were newsworthy requires that the story be both a mode *and* a form of communication and also that it share information. In the song's final section, underneath the urgent music of the instrumental introduction, a radio news parody reports the double homicide. It hints at the woman's identity with a barely audible "Josefina" in the fadeout: "*en la ciudad de Nueva York dos personas fueron encontradas muertas. Esta madrugada los cuerpos sin vida de Pedro Navaja y Josefina. . . .*" In 1984, Blades stated that "the way I see popular music today, as an alternative to express sentiments of the majority of people who inhabit the city and [who] have no access to radio, cinema, TV, and print press, music recovers its original antecedents: to inform."[90]

Psychological austerity constitutes also a mnemonic dispositive: "There is nothing that commends a story to memory more effectively than that chaste compactness which precludes psychological analysis," writes Benjamin. He adds that "the more natural the process by which the storyteller forgoes psychological shading, the greater becomes the story's claim to a place in the memory of the listener, the more completely is it integrated into his own experience."[91] As many recorded live performances of the song attest, the lyrics are firmly committed to memory and sung by audiences of thousands.[92]

And there is sociability. Just as "a man listening to a story is in the company of the storyteller," so too are listeners in the company of other listeners.[93] Singer (storyteller) and listener (audience) coexist in a dialectic and dialogic relation. If "the listener's naïve relationship to the storyteller is controlled by his interest in retaining what he is told,"[94] the listener helps constitute the storyteller as storyteller through a social relationship. One speaks, the other listens; one shapes events into form, the other remembers, interprets, and fills in the gaps. This aural/oral aesthetic distribution forges a common. At stake is a sharing of experience that links places and times. Such linkage takes place through the performance of communication as the evocation of an experience that relates something happening elsewhere. Knowledge of distant events is the result of the storyteller's travels. A Homeric imperative obliges the traveler—the immigrant musician, in Blades's case—to tell stories of what has been heard, learned, and seen. As a result, sociability is connected with movement.

As in Rama's characterization of the literary chronicle, a story needs to appeal to an audience by being both grounded in a reality, place, and time intelligible to them *and* malleable enough in their imagination (which extends to other places and times). Similarly, if "a great storyteller will always be rooted in the people," Benjamin proclaims, she too will be constituted in relation to an audience and to a public.[95] But if their relation is strictly dialectical, their common is proper to neither, being the product of their relation. Stories thus depend on a storyteller who adequately calibrates the *scale* of events reported to the scale of her audience. They also depend on storytellers who *intervene* in "reality." According to a 1981 statement, the music produced in New York City at the time Blades had arrived, though popular, "didn't represent the sentiment of the metropolis" and was limited to "speaking of small segments of the barrio and not of far more generalized and universal realities such as the reality of living in the city . . . [with] political repercussions and more collective situations."[96] Recognizing a heterogeneous Latin American social field—not a particular community, whether central, peripheral, or anywhere in between, or proposals for hybrid communities—we may begin to think of what Martín-Barbero identifies as schematism in expressive genres (e.g., salsa) that helps tether experience to social archetypes and of whatever in "Navaja" appears as an abstraction as the mutual interchange, indeed a literary-musical as well as aural-oral assembly, of experience and archetypes.[97] The fictional intervention in reality, then, transcends the exclusively local, while its rootedness in experience sanctions the validity of the literary intervention to audiences that occupy local positions wherever the story is heard. Storytelling sketches the general contours of the social life of audibility as potential grounds for aesthetic equality.

The storyteller accrues social authority from what they convey to listeners and from the endurance of that conveyance. Storytelling carries the duty to be useful, to convey some moral or practical advice from which the listener gains "counsel." And counsel, Benjamin remarks, "is less an answer to a question than a proposal concerning the continuation which is just unfolding."[98] The open-ended character of "counsel" coincides with another aspect of story: unlike information, which is punctual and self-explanatory, a story "doesn't expend itself" and remans potent "even after a long time."[99] Stories are malleable and resonate in listeners' imagination. Song and voice further accentuate this character.

The refrain of "Navaja" certainly resonated with Quintero-Herencia. For him, the drunkard's words mark both the end of the story and the beginning of "the wisdom of the chorus [refrain]."[100] "The out of tune, ruined voice of the drunkard authorizes the coming into wisdom of the chorus and sums up the message of the song," he writes. Some critics fail to hear the chorus's insistence that "*la vida te da sorpresas, sorpresas te da la vida ¡ay Dios!*" This phrase conveys "the lack of a definite sense to life" and the impossibility of controlling fate.[101] Critics who try to determine a meaning based on prior knowledge of "'communities' and their 'rebellious traditions'" end up disallowing surprise itself, exhausting the story's "counsel." If the stanzas' dispassionate reportage takes no particular moral position, it is not because there are no morals but because the moral of the story is discursively elaborated in the improvisations through proverbs, parodies, and literary allusions. It is because, in these stanzas, the chance encounters that rule the fate of human lives absolve anyone of guilt and dissolve moral conscience altogether.

A dissociative motive, more than the logic of causality, impels the story. Its events are realized within informal labor economies indifferent to the flux of chance encounters. The psychological dissociation of the character from the play of life and death sustains a fateful story that allows no morality. Instead, it stages a dichotomy between the irrepressible vitality of individuals striving to survive and the morbidity of a modernity indifferent to the barbarity it produces. There is a moral here, but no morality.

Quintero-Herencia makes room for the mimetic and dialectical interpretations I earlier outlined. He writes, "'Pedro Navaja' exceeded the public circuits and traditional listeners of salsa precisely because what it says and how it says it was not determined exclusively by the story of class or ethnic belonging of its characters or interpreters."[102] On its own, this observation in support of Quintero-Herencia's "ironic interpretation" wouldn't necessarily exclude traditional mimetic or progressive dialectical interpretations. Understood within the framework of storytelling, such interpretations constitute modalities of listening and effects of the social authority drawn from a people (mimetic interpretation) and of Blades's "presentation of contradictions" and experimentation with hybrid forms (the dialectical interpretation).

We might ask what relation exists between "fate" and the songwriter's authorial powers. To echo Rama's stunning reading of García Márquez's *Chronicle of a Death Foretold*, "fatality *is* the Narrator. He originates it, he consummates it."[103] Benjamin offers a further clue, proposing that storytelling extracts its authority from death itself. His proposal metonymically displaces death (the "natural" finitude of all storytellers and listeners) to the terrain of stories in which characters live and die. Storytelling, in this account, is rich in metalepsis, the "paradoxical contamination between the world of the telling and the world of the told."[104] As a narrative process, metalepsis undermines "the separation between narration and story,"[105] while also blurring distinctions between the rhetorical level of the "fictional world and the ontological level occupied by the author."[106] To tell a story is not only to fuse the time of the telling with the time of what is told, but also to broach questions about broader temporalities that address the story's past and its possible futures. It is to bring the invented reality of the chronicler into the reality of the listener, and vice versa. Story and history (and historicity besides) emerge as obverse sides of an experience shared among audiences and the chronicler, actual and possible, present, past, or yet to come.

The conjunction of chronicle-song and storytelling as shared experience in "Navaja" expresses the narrator's power to weave together events with a precision in which little is left to chance. Such precision is evident in the stanza's tight construction and in the self-conscious allusions, parodies, paraphrases, and quotations that make up the subsequent commentary on "fate" and "surprise." This poetics, however, entails more than a narrative will-to-form, for it has as a condition of possibility what Sheldon Pollock calls *literarization*: "the process by which oral, traditional forms of vernacular expression are accommodated to 'literature,' worthy of being cultivated, read and preserved."[107] This accommodation, in turn, works both ways: from the vernacular to the literary, and from the literary to the vernacular and their corollary figures (i.e., chronicler, singer, storyteller, listeners). These figures partake in processes of redistribution of Latin Americanist perspectives afforded by the South and the North, perspectives that, though shared, are proper to neither pole. Consider de la Nuez—a present-day lettered individual—alongside those he calls "illiterate in two languages." In Blades's literarized musicking, these positions constitute both new subjects of listening and objects of the sung word. Their listening and that of others would be marked by distinct positions given in and through their respective locations in the North and South as much as by how senses of the present and past appear from the role of popular song in the South.

Toward "a New Past of Latin American Culture"

In a lucid analysis of the century-long struggle in Latin America between "high" and "low" culture, Carlos Monsiváis zeroes in on "Pedro Navaja" as an index of the "immeasurable triumph" of salsa.[108] He understands the song as a fundamental part of "the need [throughout the 1970s] to establish a past, a new past of Latin American culture equidistant from high culture and original popular culture, one that might be at once textual evocation and fantasy, capitalist realism and communitarian utopia."[109]

Aided by cultural industrialization and mass mediation, the tide of mass popular forms and their associated technologies (film, radio, phonograph) will inevitably alter the perception of the popular and render it impossible to keep behind the curtain of letters, Monsiváis writes, in a Benjaminian key. Literature—Carlos Fuentes and Guillermo Cabrera Infante are paradigmatic—would begin staging within a single scenario the heterogeneity of the city in which millionaires, prostitutes, and poets coexist in a cultural continuum that cannot but be popular, Cabrera Infante sagaciously blurring the distinction between soap opera and "the feelings of security inside and outside the family," between "the idols . . . in the records and laic sainthood."[110] And then romantic song, "the unavoidable chapter in the sentimental education of Latin America," moves into the space of the written word, but only under the condition that figures—at once real and fictional—be the locus of attachment, as he writes of Cabrera Infante's character "La Freddy" (née Fredesvinda García Valdes [1935–1961]):

> The force of conviction of the bolero, its mode of making us aware of what we think, and of giving us the precise words to express ourselves at the moment what we feel, accesses another level. And the singer . . . is the symbol not only of Freddy, the real character on which the literary Freddy

is based, but also of all the women who filter emotions, sanction wildness, and lead to passion through the institutional byways of the record, the rockola, and radio.[111]

While the expansion of the middle class, access to education, and impulse toward autonomy help foster a reading market in which 1960s literature booms (including an unprecedented one million copies of García Márquez's 1981 *Chronicle of a Death Foretold*), music continues changing perceptions. Thus, parallel to literature's boom, rock rapidly overcomes stubborn mental schemes and shows the unity and diversity of Latin American culture in relation to its metropolis, the US. These mental schemes succeeded largely thanks to both transnational corporations' interests in the region and in dictatorships, and to tides of cultural stimulation without which hardly any nation would experience some form of "internationalism."[112]

Citing the second line from the first strophe of "Navaja" ("*Con el tumbao que tienen los guapos al caminar*"), Monsiváis introduces the conclusion of his argument—namely, that it makes no sense to insist on an "equally fantastic and oppressive" separation of cultures.[113] Perhaps this line from the chronicle-song embodies that impossible separation, rendering in colloquial language, exquisite form, and musico-poetic sound (tum*bao*/gua-pos, tie*nen*/cami*nar*) the union in diversity that the Mexican critic sees as the defining characteristic of 1980s Latin American culture:

> Following bloody failures, timid but hopeful recompositions, and with some countries in the midst of an absolutely unanimous economic crisis, Latin America, in the 1980s, constitutes a surprisingly unified ambit thanks to the experiences of the last twenty years: Thanks to historical disasters, to the mass media offensive, growing intercommunication, and shared cultural experiences, and thanks to the interrelation of the culture industry and literary creation—of the life of idols as a cultural theme.[114]

Sound plays an important role in the project of cultural unification that Monsiváis perceives. And nothing better captures the sonic, despite its much-vaunted ephemerality, than "the idols of song." With this term, the critic appeals to the poetic, constitutive power of the idols' voice: "The quality of voice transfigures and transforms" the singer into "transmitter and creator of modes of life and erotic presentiments, which become an absolute and definitive experience." This quality has everything to do with salsa's success, "which 'Pedro Navaja' takes to boundless triumph," and with how this music, both erudite and streetwise, addressed the need to establish a "new past of Latin American culture."[115]

This "past" entails the recognition that figures such as Mexicans Agustín Lara and José Alfredo Jiménez, or the Argentine Carlos Gardel, gave form earlier in the century to the "theme and the problematic of popular expressivity," singing poetry for "those who do not read poetry" but who love images held in the "collective unconscious." The present has already subterraneously reconciled literary form, both experimental and not, with the idols of popular life, giving the lie at last to any efforts to insist on the purity of letters.[116] Why? Because this phenomenon partakes of what Monsiváis calls a "social contract." While one side agrees and gains access to interpret and provide classical models of desires and obsessions, the other side makes a compromise to reproduce and creatively detract, in the minimal sphere it governs, the models it is offered. Both manipulative and alienating, this also constitutes an unfalsifiable recuperative experience for millions of Latin Americans. Popular myth and legend, in the end, have eluded the inquisitorial surveillance of (high) cultural prejudices. "*La vida te da sorpresas, sorpresas te da la vida,*" he concludes, as if the whole of twentieth-century cultural struggles around the waning powers of letters in Latin America were a massive act of fate and unpredictability and all parties involved (high, low, and in between) drunkards reaping the benefits of sociocultural chance.

It would take a perspective from outside and within literature—that is, Monsiváis's—to glean how forms could redistribute the aesthetic field as a whole. After all, the lettered city worked by folding the real city's speech into its forms. In some cases, this meant adopting orality, as in magical realism or *testimonio*. In others, it meant the emergence of subsidiary forms such as theater and popular music with literate aspirations like the bolero and the tango (which Rama tellingly labeled middlebrow music or "*mezzomusic*"): Argentine musicologist Carlos Vega coined the expression "*mesomúsica*" to describe "the set of [musical] creations functionally dedicated to leisure . . . salon dance, spectacles, ceremonies, acts, games, classroom, etc., accepted or adopted by listeners in culturally modern nations."[117] According to Vega, this music coexists with "high" music in urban settings and with "folklore." It is a music "for everyone." Vega aims to clarify the criteria by which "high" and "folkloric" music is classified, sometimes by social standards, sometimes by cultural standards. Mesomúsica obeys both social and cultural patterns.[118]

In place of this dialectical struggle and its formidable will to appropriation, Monsiváis suggests the emergence of a third space characterized by its "equidistance" from either pole (lettered and real, high and low) and irreducible to the "middlebrow" of Rama's "mezzomusic." Namely, he suggests that popular forms such as Blades's salsa songs partake of *both* "textual evocation *and* fantasy, capitalist realism *and* communitarian utopia." This third space indexes how after the 1960s high and low culture had each accommodated capitalism and communitarianism, evocation and fantasy.

Based on forms like Blades's salsa, Monsiváis's proposal offers an alternative to hybridization and transculturation, the classic operations by which cultural binaries have been mediated in Latin American theory and practice. In turn, Monsiváis's additive logic ("and . . . and") bypasses—without "sublating" or negating—critics' perennial anxiety that there is no breaking free from the lettered city's (or capitalism's, communitarianism's, or a politics of identity's) hegemonic oppression.[119] It is as an expression of the relation between each of these terms (i.e., the "and" in Monsiváis's pairs) that "Navaja" performs its Latin Americanism—the Mexican, however, does not foreground the immigrant character of this Latin Americanism. In fact, the gap that this copula bridges constitutes the syncopation that makes this music possible at the same time that this music exposes syncopation as a condition of possibility for its coming into being.

Monsiváis's intriguing idea of a "search for a new cultural past" warrants further elaboration. In his argument, the collapse (or uselessness) of a radical distinction between high and low culture in mass popular forms and in some literature from the 1970s and 1980s—the period that also marks the "fall of the lettered city," in Jean Franco's argument—can recuperate already existing poetics for what they were: poetics of immaculate creative power and invention in which the word as much as anything else—the sonic, for instance, and the voice—stands on the same ground, neither high nor low, not their hybridization, but otherwise than these.

The Mexican critic proposes a complex temporal operation. This "new cultural past" corresponds to a nonlineal vision of history. In it, the present redeems that which, although it had already "happened" in the past, remains to be realized (or redeemed, in Benjamin's expression). In this account, the present destabilizes the official version of the past (this is what "new cultural past" might entail) as much as the past arrives (because it never left) to destabilize the official version of the present. The present thus constitutes both a place of contradiction between whatever foundations the past might have offered and a future horizon in which the redeemed past will have constituted a new and broader sense of the present. This present is made out of the collision of times to which different social classes and ideologies contribute. It is one in which the folding of capitalism and utopia, of evocation and fantasy, inflects expressive forms and modes of perception, as Monsiváis hears and understands the matter. A refusal of any kind of reductivism—be it economic, communicational, communitarian, aesthetic, ideological, technological—becomes the signal of this present. The "new cultural past" constitutes a critique of transculturation, hybridity, fusion, and similar versions of cultural mixture. It is neither revisionist nor recuperative history. It is a traversal literate history of obverse processes—in particular, music.

Jean Franco offers a formidable analysis of the fall of the lettered city that shares with Monsiváis's own. In fact, Monsiváis emerges as a figure capable of relocating the claims of the lettered city to mass media, particularly radio and newspaper chronicles, but embracing the creative energies of the "real city," the name that Rama had given to all that the lettered city repressed in the name of authority. Franco is attentive to music's particularities and role, within the context of mass culture, in the lettered city's decline. In her argument, "mass culture has produced a certain egalitarianism at least in attitudes if not in wealth, and this means that hierarchies—political or religious—are no longer respected."[120]

Enter Blades: "Even Rubén Blades . . . is not immune from the general disrespect and is mocked as a 'pendejo' (a jerk)," as this chapter's epigraph reads.[121] Franco's reference here is to Edgardo Rodríguez Juliá's brilliant chronicle *El entierro de Cortijo* (1983), a stunning account of the wake and funeral of the genial Puerto Rican musician Rafael Cortijo (1928–1982), in the San Juan neighborhood where the musician lived. In the chronicle, Blades—who spoke during the actual funeral—is among the last people lingering in the cemetery. Bothered by the laughter of a group of young women offering Cortijo one last send-off at his tombstone, Blades hushes them. They retort, "*Tú eres un pendejo, tú eres un pendejo* . . ." ("you are a jerk, you are a jerk"), perhaps for being an outsider, perhaps because, like Rodríguez Juliá, he was white and middle class, or perhaps because although he was a proven *salsero*, and thus "one of them," he carried bourgeois airs and didn't understand that in Cortijo's world the dead require companionship (as Rodríguez Juliá actually writes).

The episode matters for how an incisive critic (Franco) frames music's powers, but also for how she perceives distributions between literature and other forms. While there is no longer a possibility for permanence in the social order, music "evokes the possibility of a kind of *permanencia* [*sic*] in the form of the musical phrase, which will be played, reinterpreted, transformed."[122] No longer being channeled to "patriotism, socialism, official religion, or even literature," affect lives on and survives in "music—the same notes played by different people at different moments—that corresponds to something like Lyotard's 'petit histoire,' a form of temporality that he described as 'simultaneously evanescent and immemorial.'"[123] Franco appeals to an aesthetic historicism that relies on an a priori division of labor between letters and reading, on the one hand, and the sonorous and listening, on the other.[124] This division allows the claim that letters (and literature) operate on a singular and non-evanescent temporality satiated with memory (and history) and with an inherent capacity for permanence. The sonorous (and music), in contrast, moves enigmatically in the throes of evanescence without permanence and without memory—phonography notwithstanding. If nothing else, as Rama insistently repeated, the lettered city had arrogated to itself the condition of transcendence, the real city having been contingent. From Franco's analysis emerge the rendering-contingent of letters and the correlate historicity of literature. Music, on this account, belongs to its future, but only on the basis of its quality as (or capacity to be) reiterated, having had no real history or only barely legible traces of one.

The story Franco tells is important on many accounts. She identifies mass-mediated forms such as Monsiváis's as part of the process and in terms that resonate with the Mexican chronicler's analysis of a "new cultural past." Music, however, is shorn of history. And where Franco, speaking from literary studies, looks for remnants of letters and sees mass culture's creation of fame at this time as literature's antagonist, particularly the pop idol's disruptive figure, Monsiváis hears this figure in redemptory terms and with an ear toward reconfigurations of perception.[125] If Franco thinks in terms of a substitution, Monsiváis thinks in terms of a displacement—the logic of the metaphor against that of metonymy.

SYNCOPATION, OR OTHER THAN TRANSCULTURATION

My analysis finds a correlation between: (1) the collisions of high *versus* low, communitarianism *versus* capitalism that Monsiváis exposes as characterizing Latin American cultural production throughout the twentieth century; (2) a present in which he detects a misunderstanding in the nature of those collisions as collisions and not as neutral encounters; and (3) the notion of a redemptive present in which those collisions are conditions of possibility for forms of expression to occur and that he sees as being able to resignify the past such that the "versus" becomes "and" (e.g., high *and* low, communitarianism *and* capitalism). This correlation constitutes a classic instance of what I call *syncopation*. The operations that Monsiváis proposes—in which the present hears the past anew as it (the present) readies to produce a new future on the basis of that reheard past—embody the push and pull that marks the experience of Blades's music, which audiences and publics sustain through incessant replays, re-hearings, and performances, and which is shot through with the many tensions that make up its very existence in the long haul, be it market forces of capitalist phonography, musical traditions and innovations, or the multiple manifestations of care for sung words and linguistic expression.[126]

Now, Monsiváis's juxtaposition of opposites, a third space, might seem like an optimal explanation for the perennial question of cultural mixtures in Latin America. But there is another issue—namely, that Blades and several figures from the world of letters in Latin America stake a claim on the musical transformation of the power of the sung word. Such a claim teeters on the brink of becoming literature and depends upon who listens, from where, and how. This corresponds to what Pollock describes as a "refiguration of the domestic Other" through the process of *literarization*.[127] Under literarization, something that could be called "literature can be produced in ignorance of writing, or at least without its use," such that "nonliterature can become literature if we choose to take it as such; or indeed, since the latently imaginative can always be detected in the overtly informational and vice versa, that the very binaries just mentioned above are inadequate and literature as such must remain indefinable."[128]

This valorization, part of the work of vernacularization—and which I believe figures in Monsiváis's analysis—has as a condition of possibility the fact that language had broken through into writing much before twentieth-century popular forms appeared (which Pollock calls *literization*). Nonetheless, literarization carries a set of important corollaries: the symbolic and political elevation of the written; the transformations that the text could undergo by virtue of its being written down; the emergence of levels of authority concerning who writes, who reads, who merely listens and speaks, along with "social, political, and even epistemological privileges"; and a metadiscursive sphere where writing is written about, deciphered, and decoded within a larger "aestheticized awareness" of language.[129]

We might consider the possibility that Monsiváis's analysis of popular song operates within the dynamics of vernacularization (with literarization and literization as two main operations) against *transculturation*. Vernacularization would be understood here as the equidistance from the high and the low, and from the capitalist and the communitarian where he locates popular forms. Transculturation would be a traversal across these categories and sociocultural and economic domains.

Transculturation's importance to Latin Americanism cannot be overstated. In Alberto Moreiras's words, "transculturation is the original sin of cultural production in the same sense in which Karl Marx said that primitive accumulation is the original sin of political economy: no capitalism without primitive accumulation, no Latin-American culture without transculturation."[130] Monsiváis regards transculturation ambiguously as being both "more and less."[131] It is "more" to the degree that it brings together the general and particular, and thus proposes to fulfill Latin America's need for global representation of its cultural forms. It is "less" because it cannot overcome the gap between the general and the particular and because mass popular forms (like rock or salsa music), which participate in transculturation, are not included within Rama's Latin Americanist scheme for representativeness, originality, and independence. In a deconstructive key, if transculturation accounts for everything in Latin American culture, "what would explain transculturation itself?"[132]

Transculturation arranges the global and the local and enforces specific creative hierarchies. Ana María Ochoa Gautier notes that, "while creative transculturation is a practice that can be embodied by certain figures (*avant garde* composers, folklorists, musicians of the popular identified as valid, and writers), it depends on others whose proper place is to represent the local, without deviating from it," creating a "sonic division of labor."[133] Here transculturation functions all too well to the degree that it mobilizes distinctions like the one Blades himself draws between the local and the universal. As Idelber Avelar has argued, transculturation involves a double movement: the "high" and the "low" must be transculturated, except that the "low" must retain the vigor of its sources.[134]

When transculturation fulfills its goal, it leaves a remainder that is itself transcultural. Perhaps this remainder (that the masses cannot attain the general status of representing Latin America) constitutes what Monsiváis considers to be "less" in transculturation. The transcultural inclusion of the marginalized itself constitutes a transcultural dispositive, and this is not simply legitimized as a social "truth" by the presumed authenticity of its origin. Inextricable from representation, debates about this "truth" are amplified, quite literally, by cultural industry's apparatuses that confer it the status of a new universal. Or, as Avelar puts it, "representativeness" (here, the inclusion of the "low" as emblematic of Latin American culture) is already a function of transculturation to which it (the inclusion) gives value, not something that transculturation attains.[135] There is no prior moment to transculturation, one might say, but neither is there a full transculturation that leaves nothing more to transculturate, no pre-transcultural past or post-transcultural future.

Monsiváis, then, appears to offer an analytic alternative to transculturation. He senses how literature—the classical Latin Americanist transcultural scene—finds in its mediation of modernity's exclusions a key strategy for legitimizing literature's existence and extending its hegemonic privileges. Against the background of this politics, it is not enough to point to transculturation's "cultural transitivity" and its linear chronotope.[136] By affording a "search of a new cultural past" and with their spiral-like temporality, popular mass media forms provide one counter-narrative to transculturation.

While Monsiváis's triadic framework helps us think of the complexities of cultural production under capitalism more productively than Rama's dyads, the perennial concern with the locus of enunciation reveals that this alternative is not without limitations. Monsiváis, speaking from the privileged place of public intellectual via radio broadcasts and newspaper chronicles (besides books), can reinvigorate the lettered city's power to signify and thus encompass a new mass and their aesthetic and expressive preferences. In other words, the possibility that there is no outside to the lettered city, only endless variations, even during its observable attenuation, remains in place.

Monsiváis's additive logic of both/and, however analytically productive, finds social traction and friction and cultural-historical push and pull—that is, syncopation—in the interrelations between: (1) the status of representativeness and the production of social realities in and as song during transformations in the lettered and real cities that were resignifying audiences and publics; (2) salsa's capacity to generalize and to obey, as in "Navaja," a complex calculus of "lived abstraction" that empowers the sung word to participate in emerging listening practices; (3) the consolidation of the megalopolis and the city as key articulators of the Latino local and specific to the Latin American regional and general; and (4) the apparent transcultural wager of "Brecht blanched in Latin America and served in New York."

Monsiváis's insights work quite well within a Latin American sphere. Blades, however, is doubly positioned there and in the Latino circuits of the US. His relation to the communities where salsa emerged creates asymmetries unexplainable within the dualisms of high and low culture and the equidistance gained by some popular forms. If Blades brings an openly "social" and "political" thematic to salsa via lettered practices and a popular musical language, how do we define the "social" and the "political" such that music constitutes the grounds for reckoning with a Latin American and Latino participation in late modernity? This is a modernity in which representations of Latinity as illiterate coexist with the lettered exercise of "Navaja." A modernity for which the labor of thought and reflection becomes consubstantial with the work, practices, and modalities of listening. Considering Blades's literate storytelling, how may we understand the degree to which "Navaja" assumes the lettered tradition's capacity to adapt, susceptibility to be transformed, and power to function in the face of social reconfigurations? The singer-songwriter's literary beginnings shed some light on the issues.

Becoming Literate, Becoming a Pedagogue

Born to a Colombian father with St. Lucian roots (hence the English last name), Blades had started singing semiprofessionally in Panama City at seventeen. He recalls his teenage occupation with a variety of music: British and US pop and rock, bossa nova, and Afro-Cuban and Puerto Rican standards. The Puerto Rican singer Cheo Feliciano was Blades's idol and most influential stylistic model, as was the great Cuban *sonero* Benny Moré. Blades recorded and performed with the well-known local groups Bush y los Magníficos and Ritmo Salvaje. His Cuban-born mother was a professional singer and radio soap-opera vocalist with a modest career but impeccable musical skills. His father was an accomplished amateur percussionist. Blades has said of his paternal grandmother, Emma Bosques Aizpuru, that she "gave me all the initial momentum towards comprehending social justice, education, politics, and respect of others. These principles come from her tutelage, which begins by teaching me how to read at age four. She delivered to me the power of reading, which defined me as a person forever." It was she who gave him a book by Georg Trakl as his first ever present.[137] A not inauspicious beginning for "the poet of salsa," "the singer of the nation and the neighborhood," and "universal Panamanian."

In 1974, law degree in hand, Blades returned to Miami, where his family had sought political exile. Soon afterward he moved to New York City. There, he found work in the mail room of Fania Records, the salsa world's dominant label.[138] No music had so insistently sought to address countries in the Caribbean basin (Panama, Colombia, Venezuela) as salsa, and no commercial project had ever directed its efforts more aggressively than Fania Records. By the mid-1970s, the company would hit gold in South America, with Blades as their bestselling artist.[139] Blades got there by using every possible occasion to introduce his songs to stars recording with Fania. He eventually caught a break when legendary percussionist Ray Barretto hired him as a lead vocalist. They would go on to record several hits together. Meanwhile, Blades lent his songs to established salsa stars like Héctor Lavoe, who in 1978 recorded a major hit with Blades's "El Cantante" ("The Singer"), a bittersweet, confessional account of life in the limelight.[140] Willie Colón, Lavoe's musical partner, arranged the song with rich strings and brass in a ten-minute-and-twenty-four-second track—an unprecedented length and a declaration of Fania's (and Colón's) artistic ambitions.

Colón, a Bronx-born trombonist, producer, arranger, and self-declared "bad boy" of salsa, paired off with Blades in 1977. They released the hit

"Pablo Pueblo" on their first record, *Metiendo Mano!* The song, a third-person portrait of a defeated worker, further cemented Blades's reputation as a singer-songwriter with a singular commitment to complex chronicles of the quotidian set in a condensed and highly literate language and form. It established his pattern of creating characters with which audiences might identify and sociopolitical and economic archetypes of the modern city.

Blades's writerly sensibilities were not new. "Pablo Pueblo" had been among the compositions Blades took on his first New York City trip, a sign of his precociousness. At the tender age of seven, the budding singer-songwriter had won a school prize for story writing. Blades would later list an eclectic constellation of writers as his literary genealogy:

> From the age of six to fourteen, I read everything that fell into my hands: Sir Walter Scott; Alexandre Dumas (father); Francisco de Quevedo; Homer; Virgil; Juan Ramón Jiménez; Johanna Spyri; Mark Twain; anything from *Reader's Digest*, whatever. From sixteen onward, the author with greatest impact was Albert Camus—his essays in *The Rebel* devastated me and deeply impacted me [*me calaron hondo*]; Balzac, for his capacity for thorough description; Michel de Zevaco, for his amusing and entertaining manner of creating historical fiction; Edgar Allan Poe, for his tortured vision and creation of horror as literary form; George [*sic*] Trakl, with his dark and dense symbolic poetry; Horacio Quiroga and [José] Eustasio Rivera, for their descriptions of the jungle and existential difficulty; Guy de Maupassant, for his excellent arguments and short stories; Ernest Hemingway, for his direct and sober prose; William Faulkner and his archetypes; Borges—*The South* is among the best ever written in short stories; Vinicius de Moraes; Vargas Llosa; Cortázar; Neruda and Benedetti. I read, and read a lot today, but I leave many authors out of this list.[141]

Blades's second album with Colón, *Siembra*, garnered ecstatic responses. From these, it would appear as if this impressive literary constellation itself deeply impacted the music and how it was translated in Latin America as an index of thinking itself. A 2009 byline in Colombia's leading newspaper, *El Tiempo*, announced the album's thirtieth-anniversary reissue with characteristic fanfare: "Before its release in 1979, salsa was identified with dance and with rhythm," but *Siembra* "took measure of the intelligence of its followers, who had to stop and listen to what they [Colón and Blades] were saying."[142] As the byline had it, the album divided salsa's trajectory in two. Fania would never again see the sales *Siembra* brought: 500,000 copies were officially sold, although unofficially it is said to have sold well over a million, making it the bestselling salsa record just as salsa began its inevitable decline. "Navaja" would become the greatest hit salsa ever produced.[143]

With *Siembra*, Blades developed his earlier concern with political reportage (e.g., his 1965 song "9 de Enero" addressing the 1964 Panama Canal riots against the US presence). The album addressed sociopolitical themes as a whole. Including "Pedro Navaja," it features the following songs and themes: "Plástico," which promotes Latino identity and pride in labor instead of "plastic" materialism; "Buscando Güayaba" describes the difficult search for guava, but possibly suggests a more metaphorical search; "Maria Lionza" praises the titular Venezuelan syncretic religious figure; "Ojos" uses descriptions of *ojos* (eyes) to gesture toward the range of human experience, and concludes by considering the "*ojos de mis pueblos*" and the future "*nuestra raza*" and Latin America; "Dime," a lovelorn request to "tell him" how to get rid of the pain of lost love; and "Siembra," in which Blades enjoins listeners to forget the superficial, sow Latino consciousness, and cultivate an example for "the seeds," or youth.[144]

Alongside Colón, Blades was said to present "music full of social, even political content, a move that began a new style called 'salsa with a conscience.'" Rondón affirmed that, "without doubt, by 1979, Rubén Blades had become the most important figure in salsa, and he sealed this achievement with *Siembra*." "Unlike other composers," he added, "Blades did not see the social theme as something tangential. . . . on the contrary, the themes that concerned the daily lives of the collective were the focal point of his work and were treated with a specific political criteria. . . . some considered him a protest singer, and others . . . did not waver in their judgment of him as a demagogue, a trickster, and a showoff." He concluded: "But Blades rose above the criticism . . . and the extreme labels they tried to pin him down with; he became an icon, an unusual personality who not only sold an impressive number of albums but who also *said* things and, more importantly, said them in the best ways salsa has ever known."[145]

Despite bordering on the hagiographic and betraying his own social position as a journalist and public intellectual in his native Venezuela—and a close friend of Blades—Rondón's assessment is typical of the critical reception of *Siembra*. The thematic constellation grouped under the "social" and the "political" comprises the nucleus of Blades's concern. More significant is Rondón's intuition that the singularity of the singer-songwriter "*said* things" and did so in "the best ways salsa has ever known." Although the manner and content of the singer's songs may have resonated with Rondón's particular preferences as a journalist, the latter also echoed ingrained regional concerns with and care for the craft of storytelling in vernacular song, which in Puerto Rico and Cuba draws extensively from poetic practices from the Iberian Peninsula. This all betrayed also an abiding need to demonstrate popular forms' capacity to convey and embody this care for storytelling and language.

Siembra expanded an already existing market in Latin America, an intervention inseparable from phonographic capitalism. But it too addressed a paradox: just as salsa music made in New York City established and formalized Latin America as a locus of interlocution during the 1960s and 1970s, its makers did not appear to have any insights into existing social, let alone historical relations there. This set of circumstances forms part of the inseparability of phonographic production from political intent. Blades could well have had in mind memories of a 1971 performance on Panamanian TV by Héctor Lavoe and Willie Colón that had made an impact on the young aspiring singer. In the video, from a Latin American tour, the musicians cut an impressive figure.[146] Blades had contacted Colón while he was on tour in Panama in 1969 or 1968, by his reckoning, offering him some of his songs. Of the occasion, he said that "they [Lavoe and Colón] were the first salsa group that I saw, again, that was composed of young people. They had an energy that was incredible. . . . We were all impressed by Héctor Lavoe and by Willie Colón. I mean, they were like really . . . that group had an energy that was unbelievable."[147] Nothing could be more impressive than these hip New York City musicians' singing of "Colombia" to the rhythm of Cuban *Son Montuno* and naming and praising specific cities in that country.

If salsa had addressed Latin America, Blades would recalibrate the music's message with an openly didactic intent. Catalino "Tite" Curet Alonso (1926–2003), arguably the most prolific and revered Puerto Rican salsa songwriter, affirmed how Blades's "salsa with a social message has produced a string of hits, and also smoothed out the genre a little, making young people think about the issues of the moment, of the everyday path."[148] Blades himself declared that "my music is not politics, or protest salsa. . . . my music is urban song, period . . . and song, besides entertaining, educates and informs. It is a work that requires dedication."[149] Entertainment, education, information, work, dedication, and effort: Blades's lexicon fits all too well within Brechtian didacticism, *mutatis mutandis*.

Blades stated in 1996 how his music constituted an intervention:

Something happened in the '70s . . . Every band had their own distinctive sound, but it was pretty much dancing music and rhythmic music with a tremendous emphasis on copying the Cuban models. There was a tremendous interest in everything African. So, everything sort of went towards Cuba, towards Africa. When I walked in, I was coming from Panamá. I was the first person to come into New York with a Latin American point of view which was also very much influenced by political happenings in Latin America, so that I saw music as a way of documenting realities from the urban cities of Latin America. That is very important because it explains why, in the midst of this golden era, we managed to outsell everybody, by singing songs that no one in New York quite understood. The [prevalent] emphasis, again, was dancing and rhythm. I came in with an emphasis on lyrics. What happened is that people bought records when people went dancing on the weekends or liked to hear the dancing music in the house. But when I came in with songs like "Plástico" and "Siembra" and "Pedro Navaja," all of a sudden, these songs were telling stories that were familiar to people in Latin America and what happened was that the albums were bought across the board: The grandmother, the mother, the worker, the student, the intellectual, the professional, the unemployed, everybody identified with the songs because they were descriptions of life in the city. So that where you sold 20,000, all of a sudden, we were selling 350,000 records. So, it was a big, huge impact that was caused by the fact of the lyrics, and that is why *Siembra* became the first million seller.[150]

A paradox haunted Blades's Latino Latin Americanism. On the one hand, as he put it, "my work never made any concessions; I never said to myself, 'I will sing this to this Latin people and this other thing to the other Latin people,' because to me they are people [*gente*], period." On the other hand, "the US Latino, by virtue of being of Hispanic background, has a different perspective on life. That is, in relation to the situation in Latin America, s/he doesn't understand well what is going on—not because of a lack of interest but rather because s/he is too busy trying to survive." His identitarian preoccupations emerged from a classic immigrant realization—namely, that he was not only a Panamanian, but became "Latin American" upon migrating to the US. "The work that we are trying to do is to make them [US Latin people] understand that there exists a commonality of interests among those who share the same heritage," he explained. Nonetheless, "we had many problems in New York with certain images: you try to explain to a US Latin what is a [State-mandated] curfew and s/he cannot understand. . . . In the US people practice a very basic Spanish, super elementary."[151] These tensions culminated in Blades's momentous decision to "argue the case for Latin America":

When I first came to New York, I found that the musicians here did not fully understand the impact they were having on Latin American life—that this music was not just producing fans, it was filling a *social need.* The radio and the songs were becoming companions of so many people. And sporadically, when a song would come on and *speak*, and talk about something more than *mira-mira*-let's-dance-baby-let's-dance, it struck a chord, a very sensitive spot in the audience. I found a total lack of understanding here— even among Latin musicians—of what Latin America was all about. So, when I got here, I had to argue the case for Latin America.[152]

Three songs from *Siembra* made this "argument" forcefully. "Plástico" offered a searing critique of middle-class consumerism by appealing to Bolivarian notions of Latin American unity. It ended with a well-known roll call of Latin American nations, including the famous line "Nicaragua without Somoza," years before the infamous dictator was deposed.[153] "Siembra" addressed the need to plant seeds of a greater Latin American consciousness, which included foregoing regional and ethnic differences and avoiding the seductions of US consumerism. "Navaja," like the earlier "Pablo Pueblo," was concerned with the marginal, the lumpen proletariat, and the precarity of the metropolitan informal working class. Released as a two-part follow-up album to *Siembra*, *Maestra Vida* (1980) narrated life and death across three generations of a single family, and is considered Blades's most ambitious project. In the songs, he said, "there are a lot of little jokes, ironies to listen for and make you think; little scenes, slices of life which can happen in any barrio in the world."[154] Calling the project "perhaps the most anti-commercial endeavor ever in salsa," he proposed his music to be Latin American City Folklore (FOCILA, or "Folclor de Ciudad Latinoamericana"). *Canciones del solar de los aburridos* (1981) introduced new archetypes (e.g., "Ligia Elena" as a middle-class young woman who falls in love with a poor musician, much to the consternation of her prejudiced parents) and "Tiburón" (Shark), a thinly veiled metaphor for US interventionist politics in Latin America. The song led to radio bans and threats, particularly in Miami's Cuban community. At this point, the singer-songwriter revealed that his characters—including "Navaja," "Pablo Pueblo," and others from earlier works—formed part of a "fictitious Republic of Hispania."[155]

Blades's songs were particularly tethered to the formidable tradition canonized in the 1960s literary boom. The late Gabriel García Márquez reportedly said that "Pedro Navaja" "represented what he really would have liked to have written."[156] In 2011, Blades appeared in a public interview on the eve of his participation as headline speaker at the Hay Festival in Cartagena, Colombia's largest literary festival.[157] In mentioning *Siembra*, the interviewer again cast Blades's contribution as salsa's irruption of storytelling in the Latin American lettered tradition. From this emerged the singer-songwriter as consummate narrator and storyteller, stories of urban life and streetscapes that could just as likely occur in Mexico City, New York City, or Caracas: they enlivened "the entire auditory scenario that they told, a new reality yet uncovered . . . of cities which songwriters were barely beginning to approach. . . . His was at once the vision of a narrator and an educated musician . . . not an easy task in the politicized milieu of Latin America during the 1970s. . . . His was another way of uttering the political."[158] During the interview, Blades paraphrased Mexican novelist Carlos Fuentes, who heard his songs as short stories, tightly organized and concentrated efforts that would take two-hundred-plus pages of a novel to unfold, instead of the few minutes of a song. Combined, this fraternity of men of letters, the critics, and the highly literate singer-songwriter himself agreed on one thing: if Blades's music was unique, it was because it took measure of the intelligence he thought audiences already possessed. Ortiz, the arranger, also held and enacted this position in his musical setting. Blades's chronicle-songs were an exercise in radical equality, not one of identitarian difference (Latin Americanist claims on the music notwithstanding).

Blades's lettered proclivities—exemplified by songs like "Ojos de Perro Azul" from *Agua de Luna* (1987), inspired by García Márquez's short stories—came at a cost. Rondón, who voiced the "narrator" in *Maestra Vida,* put it this way: "for [the usual listeners to and dancers of salsa], the figure of Blades became more and more difficult to decipher."[159] Rondón further remarked that "many critics [from the press and radio in the late 1970s]" began to speak about the "ruined salsa," the salsa "turned into protest," and of a "loss of virtue" in Blades's music.[160] Blades's "argument" together with his work's lettered ethos yielded mixed results for the constitution of audiences and publics at the same time that he oriented his efforts in constituting these audien:es and publics. Like the literate in relation to popular song, his didactics ran either ahead of or behind the political possibilities of his approach to salsa. This quarrel (which is not a simple antagonism between the high and low or between letters and popular song) undergirds the politics of aesthetics at play in Blades's music.

Equality and "equidistance" emerge as ways to "utter the political," but not perhaps as the Colombian interviewer might have thought. After all, "Navaja" was a remaking of a song with an illustrious political heritage. For besides the cost of Blades's lettered proclivities, his adaptation of Brecht raises questions of place and time,[161] but also about modernist didactics as a remaking of "modern souls" (Rancière's expression). Who, in other words, has the capacity to teach? How can the artist teach? And, crucially, how are his or her charges constituted such that an audience might learn? How could there be a transmission of class consciousness as such—if such a thing exists? Is it enough to wish to educate, teach, or argue on behalf of someone, as Blades claimed? And is this not redolent of

literary transculturation as the "vehicle for the cultural syncretism necessary to the formation of an inclusive nation-state," but now deployed on
behalf of a more inclusive Latin Americanism?[162] The creative vanguard
of Blades's song mobilizes the lumpen's proclivity for proverbs, rumors,
stories, forms of history, modes of political economy, and theories of
value. Such Brechtian didacticism is entangled with the relations of production of salsa itself, and Blades's perception of what the music did in
and for Latin America and what it could do for Latino America in relation
to the continent. De la Nuez's pithy remark about Brecht requires expansion, for the German's political art weighed on the political convulsions
of Latin America of which "Navaja" is an expression.

STAGING "NAVAJA"

It is unclear how directly Blades knew Brecht's work when "Navaja" was
written. "Navaja" has roots in the 1960 version of "Mack the Knife" by
Bobby Darin (in the English adaptation by Marc Blitzstein) that he learned
to mimic and perform at family gatherings as a youngster in Panama.
Shortly afterward, he claims, he familiarized himself with Brecht's work
by 1963.[163]

The release of "Pedro Navaja" in 1979 coincided with the 1978 pre-
miere, in São Paulo, Brazil, of Chico Buarque's *Ópera do Malandro*. The
work was a full theatrical adaptation of Brecht's work with music by
Buarque, one of Blades's favorite musicians.[164] Blades's own North-by-
South version compelled other versions. Inspired by Blades's song, the
Puerto Rican theater company Teatro del Sesenta (1960s Theater) premiered *La verdadera historia de Pedro Navaja* (The True Story of Pedro
Navaja) in San Juan, Puerto Rico, in 1980. Directed by Pablo Cabrera,
and with music by Pedro Rivera Toledo, the play featured "Navaja" as its
main musical theme. Cabrera is said to have insisted that Blades's song be
included in the final version of the play.[165] This intertextual web resonates
with broad definitions of political art in Latin America.

Political subjects (the "people," the "popular," "the masses," the
demos) were central to Latin American engagement with Brecht with the
proviso that, as Roberto Schwarz put it, "our Joe Nobody still needed to
be transformed into a respectable citizen, with a proper name; while for
Brecht overcoming the capitalist world, like the discipline of class warfare, depended on collective logic and on the critique of the bourgeois
mythology of the detached individual."[166] Political subjects were not a
priori social formations but rather were *produced* within an exclusionary
system grounded in history, tradition, and class and gender differences.[167]
In Marina Pianca's words,

In Latin America theater is not dramatized. It is not because Brecht appears that there is a search for the forms of an epic theater but rather because there exists an urgent need for a popular epic, an epic of popular events [*acontecimientos*]—in a word, an urgent need to narrate true history, to give testimony, to historicize the present . . . thus emerges collective creation, the search for a new popular public, for a new distribution, for a product resulting from a new relation of production. . . . What truly created a commotion in the theater was history itself, a history that demanded and demands a concrete position before history.[168]

Some perceived in theater political affordances distinct from literature's own. According to Diana Taylor, "Latin American theatre artists, as opposed to the famous Latin American novelists, had few possibilities for working if they separated themselves from the intense struggles affecting their societies."[169] In Latin America, Brecht's ideas played a foundational role in the creation of "Nuevo Teatro" ("New Theater"),[170] itself part of a revolutionary will strengthened by the Cuban Revolution, renewed interest in alternative forms of Marxism, and anti-fascistic and anti-capitalist critique through artistic means.[171]

Theater would both represent and enact a dynamic of inclusion and exclusion. Playwrights would unmask the social relations *producing* exclusion and explore how the oppressed might play a part in their oppression. It was crucial that theater expose the production of social relations rather than prescribe an emancipatory ideology.[172] For theater disavowed the notion of the committed artist (e.g., the Sartrean *écrivain engagé*), refused operations linking committed art to obvious political content, and rejected the aesthetics of realism (Lukács), mimetic identification and catharsis (Aristotle), and traditional theatrical *costumbrismo*. Engaged, mimetic, realist, and traditionalist art separated "political" content from "cultural" form, but in Brecht these were in dialectical relation. Brechtian art could produce relations by intervening on the conditions, forms, and instruments of production determining those relations.[173] The artist first had to respond to the demand that Benjamin, using Brecht as prototype, put curtly: "*to think*, to reflect on his position in the process of production."[174] Corresponding to a Brechtian vision of realism against the mimetic tendencies of social realism, these relations were given neither in the immediate appearance of a class nor in the sum of individual experiences of people in a social sector.[175] Instead, "all the conditions of life" needed to be "literarized" such that barriers between artistic forms "imposed by specialization" (e.g., writing, photography, and music) were breached and governing antitheses structuring artistic encounters (e.g., between performers and audiences) eliminated.[176]

Art acquired the character of a task. Instead of simply implementing changes in content to traditional forms, forms became transformed; or, as Benjamin argued in relation to Brecht, the instruments of production became enactments of a reflection on how they operated as modes of producing social relationships.[177] To achieve this, technique served to shift audience attention from content toward the arousal of its capacity for action. Dramaturges deployed a well-known set of technical dispositives: the alienating effect (*V-effekt*) that would distance actor from character and discourage spectators' emotional empathy with the events and actors; the appeal to the gestural language associated with the people in the scene (recall the opening lines in "Navaja"); the refusal of naturalistic mimesis and of humanist notions of realistic representation; the principle of objectivity, which would refuse psychological portraiture of characters. Along with the notion of "refunctioning" [*Umfunktionierung*], according to which art could be detached from its traditional function and transposed to other contexts,[178] these techniques had as a condition of possibility a classical modernist tenet: the capacity of aesthetic form to provoke social reflection and to produce new social relationships.

These ideas swirling around Brecht played out in the theatrical renderings of "Navaja." Writing in the Puerto Rican press, theater critic Donald Thompson reported in 1981 that *La verdadera historia de Pedro Navaja* "was one of the greatest successes of musical theatre ever produced in the Island."[179] The production was successfully staged in New York City in 1985, and has since been staged across the Americas numerous times.[180] In 1985, it was presented in New York City as part of the Festival Latino. Adam Versényi observed that the piece "owed much of its spirit to the salsa hit," adding how "music and dance form great part of the attractiveness of the piece," before concluding, surprisingly, that "the point is to entertain; teaching is secondary."[181] According to Versényi, Cabrera's use of soap opera as structure indexed the artificiality Brecht required of theater to properly entertain.[182] In his essay "A Short Organum for the Theatre," Brecht questioned whether theater shouldn't entertain but evaluate the form that entertainment ought to take. The most intense pleasures, he said, are complex and contradictory, in line with a modernist aesthetic that stakes in audience effort a measure of its worth and an index of how much they are willing to engage in reflection around one's social condition. In Brechtian poetics, "the spectator delegates to the character the power to act on her behalf but reserves the right to think by herself, even in contradiction to the character."[183]

Brecht had spoken of how theater "constructs its workable representations of society, which are then in a position to influence society, wholly and entirely as a game: for those who are constructing society [the theater] sets out society's experiences, past and present alike, in such a manner that the audience may 'appreciate' the feelings, insights and impulses which are distilled from daily events or from those of the century by the wisest, most active and most passionate among us from the events of the day or the century."[184] Cautiously, Brecht steers clear of the future, expressing perhaps a sense of the radical historicity of dramaturgical entertainment and of the fact that even dialectics, like pedagogies, do age—and not always graciously. Rancière suggests that, much as Brecht embraced the illusion of a Marxist truth in which the whole apparatus of production constitutes the fundamental condition for social relations in his time, the dramaturge used this truth not like the ironist (who uses a split truth) but like a dialectician ("using the truth as a splitting in two"): "the power of the truth would simply demystify the illusions of the petit-bourgeois spectator by showing him, in the form of an apologue, the way the ruling class manipulates the thoughts of their ilk."[185] But truth, Rancière remarks, "loses its obviousness in being represented."[186] Thus, the "*Three-penny* [*sic*] *Opera* delighted those it hoped to trash."[187]

And so, representation, refunctioning, adaptation, and historicity do not commute easily into truth, which suggests how easy it was for Versényi, the American theater critic, to take from *La verdadera historia de Pedro Navaja* everything that the Puerto Rican troupe would not have "meant." Ironically, music was what most strongly compelled his reading, in conjunction with the fact that things can get lost in the passage from the Island to New York City. Diana Taylor affirms that "selective use of Brechtian principles to think about localized sociopolitical conditions" corresponds to a process "whereby one cultural system receives and ultimately transforms material from another," in the fashion of transculturation. A series of transculturations attended the staging of "Navaja": Brechtian theater, salsa song made in New York, Puerto Rican musical-play, Puerto Rican musical-play staged in New York. Such transculturation cannot be seen as a set of unidirectional transformations. At each moment, different figures gain form and the process of refunctionalization cannot guarantee the kind of anti-hegemonic critique one might reasonably expect.

The alienated character of what appears on the stage—the social relations that produces the subjects and as part of which their actions need to be grasped—may not be recognized, in this case, partly because the artistic interpretation of social relations cannot compel refunctioning on its own and partly because *production*—the fundamental fact that "Navaja" traveled through the circuits of international phonographic capitalism—and *pedagogy*—pupils emerge as either audiences or publics through the circulation of music—too are of a piece. Hovering above these collapsed distinctions (between interpretation and transformation, between production and pedagogy) stands the figure of the educator in charge of demystifying the consciousness of its charges, here the vast and heterogeneous audiences and publics that greeted "Navaja" with unprecedented enthusiasm. We need to examine whether Blades's refusal of any predetermination between modes of expression and aesthetic form and specific audiences could have had the democratizing effect that he perhaps wished for.

The Principle of Equality

How to assess Curet Alonso's positive reception of Blades's music in relation to that of the critics that Rondón mentions? Where is there room for the claim that Blades grounds his work in the premise of the aural equality of all his audiences? What constitutes this equality? Is it a matter of positing a common that cuts across economic classes and their avatars in high and low culture in Latin America? One that bridges the particular histories of official minorities in the US and those of recent immigrants from the South? Is it, in the end, a struggle to bring people into some kind of consensus, staging in aesthetic form the proof that for all their differences audiences might share in their ability to make sense of music that is both pleasurable and challenging? To answer those questions, I take Blades's idea that people know a lot, Ortiz's sense that people needed and could be musically challenged by his arrangements, and Curet Alonso's view that Blades's music made "young people think." I measure these against Rancière's proposal that what is at stake in such claims to equality and intelligibility is the "distribution [*partage*] of the sensible": "the system of self-evident facts of sense perception that simultaneously discloses the existence of something in common and the delimitations that define the respective parts and positions within it."[188]

First, let me consider some alternative interpretations of the polemics surrounding Blades's music. One could dismiss the resistance to Blades's lettered experimentation by noting with Pierre Bourdieu that "disorientation and cultural blindness of the less-educated beholders are an objective reminder of the objective truth that art perception is a mediate deciphering operation."[189] The debates that Rondón refers to (i.e., that Blades became increasingly undecipherable) concern modes of intelligibility that, although often linked to questions of class, cannot be reduced to matters of economic status and its traditional correlates of education and literacy. To approach questions of intelligibility, we ought to consider the implications of what these critics considered a "loss of virtue" in the music, for instance. More broadly, we might consider what audiences (e.g.,

Rondón's "the usual listeners to and dancers of salsa") might have considered salsa's performative to be, what they perceived salsa to do for them, and the qualities of virtue that they sense were being lost or dissipated.

In combining art and awareness beyond passive and lethargic entertainment, Blades believes that even salsa music may become a genre conducive to physical engagement through dancing and listening, participating in the same "transparent" context alluded to by Brecht and thus uniting author or performer, and spectator. Whereas Brecht's goal was to incite awareness of the thematic and ideological discordance as to provoke action, for Blades, the action ideally and metonymically shifts from a physical movement of masses dancing communally to individual consciousness and intellectual stimulation, creating awareness for that which is behind the beats and dance steps. Blades's goal, therefore, is to popularize "narrative salsa," in which a whole story can be told in a song, since, according to the artist, "you can respect your conscience and the clave rhythm in the same song."[190]

We may begin from a general assumption that salsa, before Blades, functioned as a common for its audiences. For the audiences that Rondón invokes, this common would have been given in part by shared thematic concerns, for example, as was the case in "mimetic" interpretations of "Navaja." It also would have been given in the way the music contributed to the distribution of bodies and activities, for example, as dancers, and the designation of proper spaces for dancing. The common would then be a whole constituted in the coming together of people around thematic concerns and bodily distributions and actions. Music performs this particularly well, even and particularly in those instances in which the coming together does not require people to share an actual space. Although such coming together may obey a logic of association linking disparate parts (and which capitalist circulation of cultural commodities compel with singular force), it is quite possible to understand it under a logic of integration in which these parts fold into a larger whole.[191] A disruption to the common carries a disintegrative force that must be resisted.

These forms of the common correspond to Rancière's "distribution of the sensible." Sense (or "the sensible"), meaning both what appears before the senses and what produces a sense of things in the world, is taken to be axiomatically as "what is commonly distributed."[192] This is one reason why this common constitutes community but does so in a way that another, negative form of the common appears because distribution necessarily follows a logic of exclusion, which Rancière calls "delimitations." These delimitations mark out what can be visible, audible, and sayable within its domain and social formation (e.g., within the domain of "salsa" and the social formation of, say, traditional listeners and dancers), and they regulate how people and functions are allocated within a field.[193]

This arrangement constitutes a politics of aesthetics in which "politics is not the exercise, or struggle for power," but "the configuration of a specific space, the framing of a particular sphere of experience, of objects posited as common and as pertaining to a common decision, of subjects recognized as capable of designating these objects and putting forward arguments about them."[194] In this light, we perceive the same things and give them meaning in partaking of institutions of consensus (tradition, schools, media, etc.) that might enable agreement between what we see, say, hear, and think. Consensus along these lines produces and sustains sense experience such that it becomes self-evident. But because consensus about this or that distribution formally contains that which it excludes and because sense experience is not circumscribed to any particular formation, these politics of aesthetics may be challenged in moments of dissensus that disrupt prevalent or dominant categories of sense evidence and alter the stability of the common. Dissensus happens not because some radical alterity appears that upturns the status quo. Rather, because the radical equality of sense experience posits axiomatically that everyone senses and makes sense of things, whenever those who have been excluded in a particular partition stake a claim on inclusion, dissensus takes place. The politics of aesthetics rests on the possibility of acting on the axiomatic principle of equality (equality preexists any distribution of the sensible as its condition of possibility), not on the struggle for attaining it.

The importance of art here cannot be overestimated. A key implication of this political arrangement is that any social configuration is divided from itself in advance: those excluded are included as a part with no part. This arrangement counts, notably, artistic practices. Art reveals a form of partaking, a sharing in common, in the sensorial—aurally, visually, corporeally—and at the same time engages in a triple distribution: (1) of this sharing in common as that which is fundamentally or primarily sensorial (the arts) and other forms of doing and making; (2) of apportioning what belongs to specific arts; and (3) within the sensorial domain, of separating what is proper and improper (i.e., in music, a distribution between the audible and the inaudible).

This triple distribution is at work in the relation between music, social agreement over its constitution, and the possibility of disagreement. In order to be considered "music," the set of practices that constitute it and that could open its democratic potential actually regulates that potential. Thus, musical genres and styles represent an intensification of this regulation, seizing hold of social agreements over what is within a style and what oversteps its boundaries. At the same time, genres and styles remain constitutively susceptible to change. In some cases, change effects a new distribution, producing a dissensual moment. Such a moment disrupts categories of intelligibility, expressive assumptions, and social functions of music, so-called, compelling a reconsideration of things in accordance with a "polemical" common sense that, it turns out, might have been there all along. Isn't Blades's work a self-conscious effort to bring about change?

Within this framework, we can outline the domains and levels at which Blades might be said to engage in dissensual operations. Consider the claim that Blades incorporates into salsa a "social consciousness" it somehow lacked. From the perspective pursued here, this is nonsense, quite literally. To begin with, it would be impossible for salsa—mired in capitalist modernity and its sharp class, ethnic, gender, national, race, and regional distinctions—to be other than conscious of its own condition. Even the most casual review of the salsa repertoire would reveal an incisive awareness of the social.[195] Blades himself names Rafael Hernández, the great Puerto Rican songwriter, and Carlos Gardel, the tango giant, as paradigms of "social song."[196] As I argue, Blades acts on the presupposition of an equal intelligence already there. He redistributes—in relation to the values of the lettered city and its avatar, literature—audiences' critical powers to engage words, and to engage them in ways that have been barred from the consensual orderings of literature or relegated to literature's minor forms. We could say, then, that Blades operates at the level of the distribution that regulates the relation of specific art forms to their proper.

"Pedro Navaja" functions as a dissensual act that discloses the existence of something in common (i.e., an object such as precarity in the lives of the lumpen, the socially marginalized), repositions bodies as they partake of this common (i.e., new audiences come to salsa who may now listen and dance), and redistributes the field of subjects capable of designating this object and "putting forward arguments about" it (i.e., the public sphere discussion by de la Nuez or by audiences in general). Blades is explicit about such arguments, proposing quite openly the centrality of aurality to his politics of aesthetics and to what I argue is a sense of equality. "I start from the belief that a person who is listening to the song is critiquing it, understanding it; I am not a teacher who has to explain the same thing six times, I have no time. I assume that the person sees the irony of what I say," Blades said in 1982, speaking of "Navaja."[197] I thus want to return to Curet Alonso's idea that Blades's "salsa with a social message . . . smoothed out the genre a little, making young people to [sic] think about the issues of the moment, of the everyday path."[198] This raises two questions. First, what could the notion of "smoothing out" a genre mean? Second, what kind of dynamic within the redistribution of the sensible could "making young people think" imply?

The most obvious response to the first query affirms that by engaging forms associated with the lettered city, Blades uproots salsa from its proper popular origins in the "real city": "I prefer to write about a reality from which I take elements to create a fictional figure. . . . I like to go a little beyond reality in itself."[199] For Panamanian musicologist Don Michael Randel, this type of fictionalization "elevates" the genre to the ranks of middle- and upper-middle-class Latin American, Caribbean, and US Latino societies.[200] Randel's reading contains remnants of an unreflective populism that would overlook, for example, the sophisticated use of form, language, and narrative of Blades's peer in salsa songwriting, Curet Alonso—a working mailman, besides being a songwriter—whose over-two-thousand-song repertoire explores a wide thematic range of contemporary, historical, rural, urban, local, and Caribbean issues, often with a critical take on social injustice. Moreover, if one wishes to focus on "content" as reason for critique, Curet Alonso shares with Blades an interest in the plight of the poor, the marginalized, and the oppressed. Of Curet Alonso, Blades affirmed that "he made music that reached everyone for his handling of language [*idioma*]; he expressed people's situations and interpreted them with enormous lyrical richness."[201]

The expanding reach of Blades's and Curet Alonso's songwriting hinges on a principle of equality. For Blades, in addition to his sense that people know a lot (and for Curet Alonso, the idea that music can make young people think), the expanding reach of equality entailed showing "certain pseudo-intellectuals" that "there is no antinomy whatsoever in being a maraca player and an intellectual."[202] Rather than becoming undecipherable, Blades's intensification of what some took as excessive "protest" and others as distractive "literary experimentation" at the expense of danceability reveals audiences' capacity to understand what was at stake for them and to become a public by arguing about it. That is, only if the music was intelligible to the public could they protest its appearance and potential consolidation as a new musical hegemon. Now, by rejecting the new hegemony implied by Blades's popularity, the public exercised choice in a practical expression of redistribution. They too engaged in a dissensual act. This act demonstrated the music's intelligibility to them, not, as one might assume, that the music became unintelligible ("undecipherable," as Rondón reports). Dissensus expresses the equality that Blades assumed and which he identified as "listening." This aural equality indexes the shared capacity to apprehend the music and its stakes. In sum, if Blades engaged in a dissensual act by redistributing the sensible, the same happens when the public agree or disagree with that act and engage in a dissensual act themselves, expressing their equality in relation to the singer-songwriter. Dissensual politics means that any distribution remains divided from itself by inclusions that necessarily introduce new forms of exclusion. Equality furnishes dissensual politics with its dynamic forces, but it cannot regulate its outcome.

Dissensus cannot be settled on account of choice alone for at least two reasons. First, choice is itself an effect of certain political configurations, not a neutral expression of "freedom." Second, diverse audiences from across the class, gender, and race spectrums took part in the reception of Blades's music. Recall how lettered figures felt compelled to speak to their perceived inclusion in the poetics of Blades's popular song. Audiences other than those of the urban circum-Caribbean also heard in those songs a way to both dance *and* engage with his words, and many there too parted ways with Blades when the music became too focused on the literary. Consider again how Blades's music affirmed the lumpen while critiquing oppressive structures. For each of these audiences, music may have carried a different and, in some cases, incommensurable function. These different functions have everything to do with folds within the distribution of the sensible. Thus, for instance, the imperatives of dancing might have been intransitive to lettered men's appreciation of the same Blades song. For these lettered men, it would have sufficed that a song could incarnate the written word without needing that incarnation to take the form of dancing.[203] For the listeners and dancers that Rondón invokes, the classificatory regime implied by musical genres offered an affirmation of certain modes of being in and with music that could not be altered without a loss of sense; for them, there could be no radical disruptions to the genre regime even when such disruptions implied a democratization of salsa's subject matter. By democratization I mean that all subject matter comes to occupy the same place: there is nothing that lies outside the realm of possible thematic concern for salsa. In "Navaja," for example, both the marginal life of the lumpen as well as that life's ordinary happenings—a worn sneaker, a gold-capped tooth, a revolver, a drunk, the avenue, idling cops—coexist. They coexist as content with a form that itself coexists within an expressive practice (music) with other expressive practices (literature, the story, the chronicle) such that form and content matter for the ways in which their collaboration presents novel ways of relating the singable and the visible, words and worlds.[204]

This interpretation is not to uphold a romantic notion of autonomy of form-content relations but rather to insist on the autonomy of the sensory as an axiomatic political principle that links equality to democratization via language. Democratization takes place when the use of language draws new relationships "between the distinctive and the indistinctive, the proper and the improper, the poetic and the prosaic," between "description and narration." From this perspective, the distinctiveness of Blades's experimentations has to do less with "a specific use of language . . . [than with] a new way language can act by causing something to be seen and heard." "Navaja," to return to our key work, provides "a new identification of the art of writing . . . a system of relationships between practices, the forms of visibility of such practices, and modes of intelligibility." By "sharing of the perceptible," this song acts by creating a common that "defines the world we live in," not by mimetically representing an existing social reality. By "defining" I mean, with Rancière, rendering the world visible and audible, shaping the visible and audible into sound and word. But observing the dynamics of dissensual politics, I also mean that defining the world entails a kind of revelation of "capacities and incapacities" in how society meets the sharing of the perceptible.[205] What we find in the agonistic reception of Blades as well as in his sense of how he intervenes in the world are expressions of the challenges of sharing the perceptible, defining the world, and dealing with the attending disagreements that inevitably follow.

SALSA AND THE CONFIGURATIONS OF THE POLITICAL

The musical didactics of Blades's Latino Latin Americanism brings into relation two parties, the Latin American immigrant and the minority group in the US. Directed at both, Blades addresses what he perceives as a lack of history in the North, experiments with the possibilities of words and forms from the lettered tradition in the South, chronicles the woes of modernity in the metropolis for all, and stages the shared ground between intellectual reflection and pleasure. These relations create points of collision, such as we find in our analytic of syncopation, and are manifest as a refusal of Blades's political aesthetics.

Blades's Latino Latin Americanism pursued the old Latin Americanist project of bridging divides in the Americas. He did so in an exercise of redistribution that displaced dancers' corporeal energies, mobilized the economic dynamics of mass mediation, and harnessed the egalitarian principle of equal intelligence. The conflicts, impasses, and accomplishments we have found express the unpredictable outcome of a wager on the sensible. Listening becomes the crucible for a political struggle; a struggle over what "salsa" means, what it is, what it does to people who engage with it. This perspective on the political may be formulated as follows: "a party says (or does) salsa and another party says (or listens to) salsa but they disagree over what salsa is," or, likewise, "a party says

X and another says X but they cannot conceive that they may mean the same thing."²⁰⁶ At the core of such disagreement lies the reconfiguration of salsa's function in societies where it had been a dispositive for voicing social realities, for example, and gathering people to do certain things (to dance, to listen together). With these functions, salsa linked music to a people, not only to an audience or public. What salsa could say and not say and what could be said or not said through salsa defined its politics.

The critics that Rondón invokes and those who did not feel connected with Blades's literate experimentation both share in the belief that musical practices *must be* necessarily tethered to specific themes and not others, or that specific themes (and not others) ought to be expressed and represented by specific musical styles and genres (and not others). The reason for this is that such practices both express and sustain a common ethos, be it an actual social group or an idea. If Blades's critics disavowed his embrace of "protest" at the expense of the ludic, others might have found *Maestra Vida*'s extended form too removed from their milieu. And some dancers may have found Ortiz's use of odd-bar musical phrases, unorthodox clave, or tempo shifts in "Navaja" to assert formal priorities over choreographic ones. These disagreements correspond to the political commitments of the various parties: "archipolitical" for those upholding the idea of expressive forms corresponding to their understanding of what is proper to them, and "parapolitical" for those upholding the idea that specific expressive forms must address only specific matters and satisfy specific functions, not any others.²⁰⁷ But for both of these, dissensual politics entails an active understanding of what Blades's music means such that it does not satisfy their expectations. The principle of equality, it follows, enables Blades's and Ortiz's musical and literary interventions to redraw boundaries between what was acceptable in salsa and what was not. Under this analytic, any artistic practice constitutes what it is according to the ways in which it affirms or challenges the relations linking what is sayable (writable, singable). This presumption, however, cuts two ways. On the one hand, it must have been there in order for Blades to present his novel reconfigurations of musical genre, form, and thematic content and expect that it would be comprehended by all. On the other hand, that comprehension had as a central motivation the idea that, once taken on board, audiences could "learn" something, something which he, as master pedagogue, knew and was in a position to convey within the constraints and possibilities of musical form and of its then-established channels of circulation (radio, live performances, discotheques, at-home listening). The contradiction here makes for a complex politics.

To return to de la Nuez's "illiterate in two languages," we see now the principle of equality as an axiom for the production of music that bets on a marginalized sector to fully understand the rich aesthetics of "Navaja." But the transition from the axiomatic presentation of equality to a politics of inclusion within a broadly conceived Latin Americanism does not happen without introducing forms of exclusion, Blades's included. To begin with, in the New York City milieu that he considers paradigmatic of the Latin American–US Latino encounter, Blades appears to have occupied a place both inside the political space of equality and of solidarity with Latino minority audiences and, because of his immigrant status and lettered formation, outside of it. We have learned of his frustration with the sociocultural impasse that rendered immigrants unable to grasp the situation in the South, his perplexity with the nearly insurmountable obstacles of linguistic and political translation, and his befuddlement that his musician colleagues, despite their impact on the South, remained unconcerned with its "realities" and the fictions through which those realities were mediated. On the other hand, consider how, despite their successful collaboration, Colón saw Blades as a social other. "On a personal level, we didn't connect at all. Because Rubén was a guy that was raised by his mom and dad, and he went to the university, and he decided to come to New York to dabble, you know, in the ghettos, and to the music. So, he understood everything intellectually but he didn't know what it really is, you know, and I am a guy that was raised, you know, with holes in his shoes in El Barrio. It was very hard for us to work together."[208] Speaking of his early years at Fania, Blades said that because he was a lawyer his musical peers thought he had no "popular knowledge," ascribing this perception to a kind of social conditioning by which lower-class people saw education as a marker of irreconcilable difference. These socioeconomic perspectives split equality in advance of its axiomatic proclamation.

Voice was a key index of differentiation. One of salsa's most creative improvisers (*sonero*) alongside the Puerto Rican Héctor Lavoe, Blades couldn't claim the degree of authenticity granted Lavoe. Besides having a devastatingly effective behind-the-beat style, Lavoe's brassy and nasal voice signaled both streetwise know-how and a direct link to the Puerto Rican countryside traditions of *jíbaro* music that the Panamanian could not have. As a critic put it, "[Lavoe] never really crossed over from Puerto Rico to the US; he always nurtured that *jíbaro* connection."[209] The same critic placed Blades in the category of "great voices" of salsa, all the same. We might say that for this critic, Lavoe's voice was "ethical" and Blades's "aesthetic."

As representative voices of salsa, Lavoe's and Blades's together partake in a further distribution of the sensible in relation to the literary that inflects the politics of voice in the music. As Ochoa Gautier puts it, if the literary denotes a space for and of critical thinking, music appears to lie outside critical scrutiny and is thus ignored, undervalued, or praised.[210] Nonetheless, given a proper linguistic linkage, music may become a means to establish relations between the inner mind and the body that can figure "an appropriate moral subject."[211] The singing voice emerges then as the medium to produce "historical modes of audibility" by the way it gathers and explores relations between speech, song, and written word, which requires some "systematization of popular expressivity." By these lights, Blades's voice would actively participate in one such systematization, linking speech and written word in highly literate songs. Lavoe's voice would likewise do so, by embodying the lexicon and modes of speech of the Puerto Rican diaspora in New York City. Both participate in the public sphere insofar as they possess communicative capacities and share a language through which they enter the space of representation as acoustic beings. Voice offers ideals of acoustic communion and corollary values of unity, spontaneity, a relation to the past and place, and heightened expressive powers.[212] The singing voice goes a long way toward variously suturing the inherited distributions of music and literature.

A quandary appears: a genre such as salsa, historically tethered to popular expression, is politically representative of a community but aesthetically devalued in relation to other forms. Or, if it is aesthetically valued, it is rendered politically separate from a community. It follows that political subjectivity needs either to mask the popular voice or to become an expressive subject that masks rationality.[213] From this analytic perspective, Blades circles around this binary by distributing his agency throughout popular knowledge—the words of "Navaja" come from the people—rather than only "give" people their "voice." This distribution of agency might erode (but not erase) the individual/collective distinction, distributing whatever sovereignty may be required of a proper political subject. The relations established between spoken, sung, and written word by way of voice do not, then, constitute a practice of representation (of the people by giving them voice), but neither does it constitute only a practice. These relations beget "different conceptions of voice," to cite Ochoa Gautier, to the degree that they enact and embody ongoing processes of literarization, literization, and literarity every time "Navaja" sounds, plays, or otherwise manifests as an acoustic event.[214]

Conclusion

With "Navaja," salsa intervenes "in the sharing of the perceptible" that helps define and compose the worlds that Latino and Latin American audiences, publics, and people live in, how those worlds become audible, and how what is audible can be assembled in words, music, and voice as song.

"Illiterate in two languages," immigrant lumpen, lettered men, continental migration, a sanctioned transculturalist, dancers, audiences, publics, "el pueblo," a "new cultural past"—these are some of the actors and actants linked in and by the political aesthetics of a salsa hit. They come into relation through acts of experimentation and translation that result in heterogeneous and often contradictory modalities of listening. Words—as much as voice and song—play a key role in these politics. If Blades self-consciously chose to play the role of pedagogue, asserting the hierarchical position he held as a relatively privileged Latin American immigrant to an ethno-cultural minority setting in the US (the predominantly Nuyorican circles of salsa), I have made the case of how his pedagogy also enacted a principle of equality. Recall that Blades and Ortiz were adamant about the fact that they could give listeners *and* dancers what they (Blades and Ortiz) felt they could understand, no matter how complex or novel, because "the people know." We have seen how Blades believed in audiences' critical engagement and recognized the need to widen salsa's thematic field. Blades worked under the assumption of a radical "equality of intelligence" among all existing and potential audiences. "I didn't invent those words [in 'Navaja'], they belong to the quotidian popular speech of our people."[215]

Politics resides in "Navaja" in the confrontation of egalitarian inequality (that only those whose function is to think and write can think and write) and egalitarian equality (that anyone who thinks—that is to say, everybody—thinks). As Rancière writes, "Inequality could not be explained to the unequal without an assumption that the unequal possesses an equal power to understand."[216] But because we also saw how Blades's pedagogical and poetic experiments backfired by turning audiences away, the assumption of a fundamental translatability reveals the song's capacity to both affirm *and* question that translatability.[217] This simultaneity of affirmation and questioning constitutes what I call syncopation.

Latino Latin Americanism helps reveal the heterogeneous and divergent political arrangements that musically entangle audiences, publics, and peoples. Song may be ethical, poetic, or aesthetic; it might be a beacon of affirmation for some, a force of bringing audiences into historical consciousness (e.g., Blades's argument for Latin America), or an index of the fundamentally sonic character of letters. While for some, Blades was nearly apostolic, and for others he galvanized a revolutionary conscience, we cannot overlook a simpler fact: his song and his work constitute exemplary performances of interlocution. Interlocution produces interlocutors.

Such production forms part of Blades's musical Latin Americanism, the instantiation of a public assembled from heterogeneous elements, from de la Nuez's polemical "illiterate in two languages," to lettered elites vying for a connection with the musical truth of the people, to anyone between. Despite his pedagogical project's shortcomings, Blades's project of making the argument for Latin America in New York City constitutes an "act of historical solidarity."[218] For Blades, "writing" unfolds against a particular historical horizon and tradition (e.g., the lettered tradition or vernacular poetics). Writing is the necessary mediation of its author's biography. But most fundamentally, writing is a value more than a fact, a possibility more than a determined outcome, a disposition more than an object. I thus understand "Pedro Navaja" less as an object—a song or hit—and more as a disposition toward writing that traverses the layers of Latin American tradition, politics, and aesthetics I have considered so far. This traversal shapes Blades's Latino Latin Americanism.

Blades's writing traverses the relation between language produced and language consumed. His project expresses no singular solidarity in favor of either, but instead literally takes place in the relations between the production and consumption of language. Barthes distinguishes between the community that values writing because it is "freely consumed language" and the community that values writing because it is language "freely produced."[219] In Blades's Latino Latin Americanism, writing happens in the relation between production and consumption, where "consumption" refers to the general field of aesthetic perception and not merely economic purchase. This relation, which gives as much as it demands, is another name for syncopation; the general historical horizon against which it takes place and that it helps produce is that of a Latin American modernity.

Syncopation is constitutive to Latin Americanism's necessary commitments to particular notions of time and temporality, of space, location, and place. When Blades argues for Latin America from the Latino world of New York City salsa, he postulates a classical Latin Americanism that addresses the entire continent. This Latin Americanism necessarily assumes two conditions of possibility: first, a synchrony that "regards anything Latin American [lo latinoamericano], despite its impasses . . . in its whole ensemble within a single epoch, that of the modern."[220] Second, a syn-topia or "heterogeneous cultural construction that is nonetheless uniform in its orientation."[221] For Blades's Latino Latin Americanism, simultaneity operates as a temporal dimension that conglomerates the social and makes the political body cohere, and similitude operates as a spatial dimension of representation.[222]

The specific situation of the dis-encounters with Latin America of the

Latino world of salsa that Blades describes, however, manifests that any such synchrony and syn-topia is never full; it may be impossible. In other words, Blades's project exposed the salsa community's absence of attunement (Sp. *sintonía*), its lack of coincidence in the sonorous as signal of recognition. Blades's intervention adopts several strategies. One attenuates the chronicle's fidelity to the local, wagering instead on an imaginary space that, though less faithful to place, might carry out the classical Latin Americanist project of regional integration. To enable this wager, Blades can count as one of his main resources New York City's singularity as a modern space in Latin American symbolic geography. At the same time and by means of the word, he must abstract enough from this geography and unmoor it to allow its circulation. "Navaja" renders the metropolis as both archetype and concrete referent, interchangeable, potentially displaceable to any urban location in the Caribbean and Latin America. It makes the metropolis a node in a network of possible interchanges, via capitalist phonography, that are not reducible to "the city" or "*el barrio*." This network of possible interchanges shares with the capitalist market that makes it possible a mechanism according to which all participants assume a relation of potential reciprocity in the absence of any specific relation other than their co-participation in the abstract relations that capital enables and even encourages.[223]

This analytical conjuncture is crucial to better grasp what I propose we understand as "re-socialization"[224]: a return of things (in the broadest sense) to the irreducible network of relations constituting the social where things are made at the same time that they make the social what it is, particularly, in our case, when they have not been recognized as such. Hence my interest in Monsiváis's proposal and in the corollary defense of a profoundly creative lettered practice at the heart of so many musical vernaculars. But this practice is also a part of this process that Blades's salsa—by excavating the lettered in its (the music's) modes of communication and asserting a constitutive intermediality between music and letters—refuses a discontinuity between bodies dancing, bodies listening, and bodies thinking, and thus expresses an ongoing conflict between words and listening.[225] Latino Latin Americanism embodies this conflict as it travels North, as it returns South in the form of a hit song, and as it provokes subtle epistemic shifts in the simultaneous divergence and convergence between the so-called Latin American and Latino cultural fields. It makes of words a matter of listening and of listening a matter of attending to words.

Re-socialization, then, involves the return of the word to the acoustic, where it never ceased to dwell. There, in this tense but productive coexistence, song distributes the sensible such that it can reformulate possible ties between saying and living, telling and experience, singing and rendering meaningful. It does so while traversing traditional socio-economic stratifications that have underwritten—all too often—Latin Americanist aesthetic and political practices. In this way, "Navaja" is particular for how it links the singable and the audible, the sayable and the intelligible—and for how it fails to do so. The traversals of "Navaja" create a living index of both convergence and divergence, rendering sensible how Latino Latin Americanist social fragmentation is immanent to the Latin Americanist project itself, how at the moment of its emergence and from the listening perspective of an immigrant to the North—at once proximal and remote—it became possible to open up new spaces within the domain of representation, to push representation against itself to reveal gaps intrinsic to the temporality of late modernity.

2 * Crossing Under (and Beyond)

At the turn of the new millennium, Rubén Blades released two extraordinary recordings, *Tiempos* (Times, 1999), and *Mundo* (World, 2002). In these, the singer-songwriter both continued and recommenced his decades-long project of addressing Latin America. At the same time, the music took an unexpected turn for someone so profoundly marked by the perspective afforded him by working predominantly in and from the US; that is, by what we saw to constitute the Latino Latin Americanism of salsa. To better represent what he called "the feeling of Latin America" and "what we [Latin Americans] are," Blades employed, in *Tiempos*, a predominantly Costa Rican group of musicians and offered a heterogeneous repertoire encompassing a diversity of genres such as Argentine *chacarera*, Afro-Cuban *guaguancó*, and Afro-Brazilian *baião*, many of them in novel hybrid combinations.[1] *Mundo* cast an even wider net, showcasing an international crew along the Costa Rican musicians from *Tiempos* and featuring Irish traditional song, Afro-Cuban *son*, and flamenco-salsa mixtures, alongside other genres. The cross-cultural collaborations in *Mundo* celebrated the shared "ancestral memory latent inside all beings" given in the "common source" of all human life[2]—here Blades appealed to then recently published scientific findings of genetic traits tracking the beginning of the human species to Africa. In an extraordinary move, these recordings were produced and recorded in San José, Costa Rica, a relatively quiet (but remarkably productive, as it turned out) musical location, even in an increasingly globalized musical industry; it was an intriguing choice for such ambitious transnational productions.[3] All of this signaled an unexpected shift in the character of Latin Americanism, marking new pathways for aesthetic circulation in the Americas.

By shifting his "locus of enunciation," Blades seemed to have sought a renewal of the potential for his own brand of Latin Americanism, *crossing under* to the actual place he had long addressed from the US. The "locus of enunciation" was a contested issue for Latin Americanism. Nelly Richard, for example, argued that at the center of tensions of Latin Americanism in academic contexts lay the relationships "convened by different

geographical-cultural contexts and institutional locations where we situ-
ate ourselves to speak 'about' or 'from' Latin America though complex
systems of representation and politics of signs."[4] Debates about enunciation could be summed up in the contrasting positions of Walter Mignolo
and Alberto Moreiras. Mignolo conceived it as a *sine qua non* for any
decolonial Latin Americanism that it might yet voice the subaltern subject.[5] Moreiras explicitly argued that "no thinking exhausts itself in its
conditions of enunciation."[6] Blades might have seemed to "intersect"
Latin America with Latin Americanism, to use Richard's quip, enunciating a Latin Americanism both from and about Latin America, and aiming
to attenuate the view from the center that his earlier Latin Americanism, anchored in New York City, inevitably entailed. As I will argue, the
"mixed appropriations, translations, and reconversions" in his albums
yielded "an ambiguous map of shifted localities between center and periphery," which, as George Yúdice would put it, produced a "de-centered
centrality."[7]

Blades's shifts recast his career-long relation to the affective, communicative, creative, economic, expressive, and political possibilities of salsa.
Salsa had been a soundtrack for over three decades that heard him develop a highly regarded body of socially conscious and politically charged
songs. These songs, as I argued in chapter 1, convoked new modes of aurality in which word and song seemed to operate in equidistance from either
literature or music while sharing in both. In these turn-of-the-millennium
releases none of the political verve was gone;[8] if anything, it was drastically emboldened by a critique of the spread of neoliberalism across the
American continent and its irremediable blurring of left and right politics
in the name of free-market economies, as well as of the intensified forms
of social violence these had spun, including the consolidation of drug trafficking. Blades had been listening in to the continent. At the same time,
the fluid labor practices and intricate cross-cultural production, marketing, and distribution strategies increasingly enabled and demanded by
transnational interactions in the time of globalization constituted both
the material condition of possibility for these musical projects and the
ideological ground against which to critique these conditions. That he
was now recording for Sony International was no longer a novelty as
had been, for example, his much-debated move (or, to some, abandonment) from Fania Records to Elektra Records in the early 1980s, when he
became a central figure in *crossover* arguments.[9] Although embedded in
the higher echelons of the music industry (and more than a fleeting film
career, to boot), Blades remained an outsider, aware that the recordings
would constitute a problem for retailers and radio broadcasters.

Tiempos and *Mundo* would be notable concept albums on the basis of their musical accomplishments alone: the sonic imprint is impeccable throughout, the musicianship everywhere in abundant evidence. Blades's lyrical inventiveness shows no signs of exhaustion. His uncanny sense to render visual images in tightly woven narrative threads is nowhere attenuated. Both albums received critical acclaim in the US and Latin America (each garnered Grammy Award honors: *Tiempos* won the Grammy for Best Latin Pop Album, while *Mundo* won the Grammy for Best World Music Album and the Latin Grammy for Best Contemporary Tropical Album, and both albums included the Costa Rican trio Éditus as co-recipients).[10]

Blades had grand designs. He noted explicitly that sonic representations of Latin America and Latinity in the US, his own included, had long been monopolized by Afro-Cuban idioms. He may have been overstating the case, but not without some basis. After all, among Latin music produced in the US during the 1970s and 1980s, salsa had most ambitiously embodied and mediated the desire to address Latin America. As we saw in chapter 1, a well-known and widely embraced trope in salsa had been that of "Latin," "Latino," or "Pan-Latin" "unity," usually cast as a call to people from various Latin American and Spanish Caribbean nations, at home and abroad, into transnational solidarity on the basis of shared or at least overlapping cultural practices.[11]

This chapter takes as a point of departure the notion of "unity" as a historically contingent form of Latin Americanism. Three caveats, all related to *representation* as an ordering principle, underwrite this form: (1) I invoke as a general frame Moreiras's description of Latin Americanism as "the set or the sum total of engaged representations providing a viable knowledge of the Latin American object of enunciation."[12] This "object of enunciation" acquires a degree of objectification in the sense of being something beholden and "enunciated"; but it is best understood as an assemblage with material and symbolic dimensions. In keeping with the analytic stance from the preceding chapter, I am concerned with a distributed object whose constitutive relations do not exclude the possibility of experiencing these relations as a thing that gathers, an object in a robust sense of something that calls upon, convokes, and even demands care and thought.[13] (2) Representation also refers to forms and processes of mediation that identify, categorize, explain, and organize the "object of enunciation" into a body of variously communicable and presumably shareable knowledge—that is, affectively and corporeally, but equally intellectually and rationally. I distinguish representation from *representability*. Representability designates a political understanding of representation as a set of constraints and possibilities given in the socioeconomic relations of actual people and mediation networks (sonic creation, production, distribution, dissemination), as well as analytically, as the capacity representation may have to enunciate its object.[14] (3) Because "Latin America" is an ever-transforming geo-historical complex, Latin Americanism is not reducible to a discursive phenomenon that presupposes a ground in relation to which discourse is articulated. What this ground *is* and what it can *do* (and for whom) remain open questions, ones that Blades insists on answering at this late stage of the Latin Americanist tradition.

I take the representational function Blades assigned to salsa as a particular form of musical *Latino* Latin Americanism, enunciated with US-based Latino musicians. Salsa's Latino Latin Americanism replicates neither an imperial Latin Americanism (i.e., a constitutive representation of Latin America by and from the "First World," "the North") nor a colonial Latin Americanism (i.e., a representation within Latin America dictated by the designs of local and national elite sectors).[15] The new recordings, however, spring from an emerging sector at century's end: a creative class in Latin American societies that, without being necessarily in control of the means of production, constitutes a central node in its operation. This sector includes well-traveled musicians with digital literacy and broad musical tastes. In the case of Costa Rica, this training is subsidized by the state's investment in arts education for the youth.[16] This situation raises questions about the suppositions and functions of salsa's Latino Latin Americanism and about the conceptual challenges it encounters along diverse positions that unavoidably emerge in the context of determined historical junctures and circumstances.

This chapter asks: What sorts of relational forces attend to salsa's Latino Latin Americanisms, which Blades seems so intent on moving away from? From this point, it examines the politics at stake in his recent shifts. Besides the critical positions it reads in Blades's shifts (i.e., as a critique of Latin Americanisms within salsa, his own included), the chapter considers *Tiempos* and *Mundo* as broader critiques of the conditions of possibility for Latin Americanist representation along the coordinates of time and history (*Tiempos*) and space and place (*Mundo*)—the former also alluding to deep time. I consider what happens in the displacement of the locus of enunciation of Latin Americanisms from the US to Latin America.[17] If Blades's shifts do register an emerging transformation of the poetics and politics of musical Latin Americanism, his representational practice begs two questions: (1) What effects do shifts in the calculus of differences and identities, equalities and inequalities, and solidarities have for a Latin Americanism that begins to question the very limits of sonically thinking and knowing "Latin America"? (2) What becomes of "Latin America" when the very idea of it emerges from the intersection of sonically enunciated, spatial-temporal processes? Blades's extraordinary millennial projects afford a broad examination of political possibilities and limitations of musical Latin Americanism. From his work emerges a *Latin American Latin Americanism,* a Latin Americanism produced on Latin American soil just when the very notion of soil as location is challenged by intensified global circulations.

This chapter critically examines various analytics that might account for the dynamics of Blades's Latin American Latin Americanism. The two projects have as conditions of possibility heterogeneity (a plurality of genres better represents Latin America), hybridity (mixtures mark a fundamental Latin American character), ontopology (music's being, and therefore Latin American being, is grounded in specific places), and audiotopia (a musically produced virtual space where one can reimagine the sociopolitical). These analytics help clarify two syncopations in the projects: One, Blades's modern commitment to Latin Americanist representation moves toward a heterogeneous, atopic, world-encompassing of its musicking, but at the same time this atopic perspective requires an ontological grounding in place, or ontopology; two, as Blades crosses under the South, publics appear to have moved beyond representational Latin Americanism. First, a brief overview of the two recordings.

TIEMPOS (1999)

The overall instrumental sound of *Tiempos* is anchored by a *sui generis* ensemble within the Latin American popular music tradition: a trio of acoustic guitar, violin, and percussion learnedly called Éditus (Lat. sublime, elevated).[18] Added to this core group of Costa Rican musicians (Ricardo Ramírez on violin, Edín Solís on guitar, and Carlos "Tapado" Vargas on percussion) are piano and keyboards, electric bass, reeds, and additional percussion, identified as the "Latin Jazz Sextet." A string orchestra appears in some tracks, its members drawn from San José's rich classical music scene. The tone of the sound is generally characterized by soft edges, a color palette that is as muted as it is deeply expressive, a departure from ensembles associated with Blades, including his trademark brass-less sextet of the 1980s and early 1990s, Seis del Solar.

The mixture of genres in *Tiempos* has been characterized as Latin folklore meets new age, classical, and jazz. The recording is exacting, with a clear sheen across the sonic spectrum, a broad sense of aural space, and high resolution in the final mix. The inventive musical writing, mainly by the Costa Rican arranger Walter Flores (pianist and keyboardist of the "Sextet" and musical director of Blades's projects in Costa Rica), exudes erudition; the music explicitly affirms these musicians' expansive and intimate exploration of music from around the world and from various historical periods of the Western art music tradition. The arrangements demand rigorous precision in their execution, with multiple parts super-imposed in the style of baroque counterpoint, while at the same time leaving ample space for improvisation. Figure 2.1 shows a representative passage.

"Hipocresía" [Hypocrisy] voices a searing indictment of the blurring, today, of ideological distinctions across the political spectrum and of the submission to neoliberal policies. This passage comes from the cli-mactic end to the song in which Blades angrily repeats the denuncia-tion of the song's title over an accumulating contrapuntal layer of three parts by the soprano saxophone (improvising), violin, and guitar (play-ing what appear to be written-out parts). Beneath, dank low and middle strings play closed-voiced chords on every quarter note and a ponderous rhythm section groove locks in an ostinato on the upbeats that provides the track with its basic rhythmic blueprint. Heterogeneity governs the musical texture. In its baroque allusions, the string ostinato simultane-ously contrasts and supplements a groove that can best be defined as a distillation of the basic structure of Afro-Brazilian rhythms that ac-cent the second half of the measure. Handclaps, an increasingly pres-ent feature of Blades's music at this time, are redolent of flamenco, al-beit rather generally. This song resists classification in terms of a single, identifiable genre.

Tiempos has been described as cinematic, in the context of Blades's well-established ability to paint scenes with words, as in "Pedro Navaja." Journalist Neil Strauss heard the album as "a record with an evocative world-embracing sweep often reminiscent of film music."[19] Strauss's in-tuitions resonate with the musicians'. Éditus guitarist Edín Solís: "we felt that the final result was like the recreation of a soundtrack for a kind of film narrating several stories with his [Blades's] lyrics."[20] Much in *Tiem-pos* is evocative of place, of moments, and events. Sound effects index, for example, rain, the sea, the running engine of a for-hire gunman's motorbike on the prowl, or artillery during the 1989 invasion of Panama by US troops. The songs' stories cover a variety of subject matters, includ-ing nostalgia for childhood, the travails of divorce (Blades's), Panama's role as a "bridge" for the world, decaying politics, imperial power, and spiritual faith. Blades displays characteristic creativity in lyric writing and abiding interest in lettered forms like chronicle, reportage, and short story. From first-person confessional mode to third-person narration, the viewpoints, too, are varied. In all, the album reports on the contemporary state of affairs in Latin America—economic, political, social, spiritual. Its title could be taken to mean "estos tiempos" (these times).

Figure 2.1. Rubén Blades, "Hipocresía," arranged by Walter Flores, ending

The album marks a time of personal and political reckoning. Here Blades describes the underlying ethos of the project:

> The reflective and melancholy tone of *Tiempos* was strengthened by the union of the classical, the popular, and the folkloric and by the percussive support of rhythms from the Caribbean, Central, and South America. These combinations have produced a musical equilibrium not found in my past musical productions, and is [*sic*] culturally more representative of the feeling of Latin America. From the violin to the *Bombo Legüero*, from the accordion to the *Caja Peruana*, from the berimbau to the Cuban conga, from the guitar to the soprano saxophone, from the piano to the maracas and from the string quartet to the timbale, the diversity of instruments, the sensibility and technical knowledge of their executants, all these allowed giving to each theme a treatment that respects and adopts the intention of the lyrics.[21]

Tone colors and rhythms are marked as indexes for territorial associations that, to take Blades at his word, combine to form an inclusive sonic representation of Latin America. This sonic cartography moves swiftly from the

Pan American to the national. But his synecdoche—by which an instrument's sound or a rhythmic configuration (related to but not identical to a groove, and an echo of the widespread practice among musicians in Latin America to use "ritmo" to refer to a genre) stands in for broader national identification—is as unmistakable as its semiotics are elusive.

Blades's lyrics are ordered by a tidier taxonomy of affect through his choices to set certain lyrics to certain genres. This constitutes both a generic territorialization of affect, as well as an affective territorialization of genre: simply, affect is tied to some characteristic given in genres associated with actual territories and vice versa. For example, "Tú y mi Ciudad," a haunting song about absence and personal loss, is set to the *chacarera* rhythm (which has a number of territorial affiliations within the Southern Cone). Sung to this rhythm, Blades says, the song "acquires a dimension that would be irreproducible under the implacable demand of Cuban 'clave.'"[22] By contrast, another title, "20 de Diciembre," commemorating the deaths of Panamanians during the 1989 US invasion, "finds in the groove of Cuban *güagüancó* [*sic*] the energy and majesty that this genre alone produces."[23] In "Sicarios," a brilliantly chilling chronicle of a day in the radical anonymity and cold brutality of young professional gunmen, the sound of accordion and a modified *cumbia* rhythm indexes Colombia, which listeners may intuit as the narrative's location. A video release for this song, however, places the action in a Latin American metropolis shorn of any distinctive signposts: the events could take place anywhere on the continent. The semiotics are as elusive as they are allusive.

Such semiotics of genre, rhythm, and tone color are bound to be more or less formal, particularly because individual tracks present various sonic indexes in hybrid mixtures. For example, in "Sicarios," the berimbau provides a fundamental element for the musical texture, but its sound does not localize the story somewhere in northeastern Brazil, for instance. One might well say that its distinctive sound, *qua* sound, materially embodies the process of hybridization itself. I shall return to a detailed analysis of hybridization and of why this is no longer the sort of transculturation that Blades had pioneered since the 1970s in relation to lettered practices. For now, it warrants noting that the heterogeneity underlying the Latin Americanism of *Tiempos* had an additional and seemingly simpler explanation. Asked about his shift in musical direction, Blades declared straightforwardly that "I was actually very bored with repeating the same sort of formats. I felt that the necessity to write within the constraints of Afro-Cuban music, and the instrumentation I was using, was not allowing the songs to expand."[24] As Jan Fairley notes, in spite of the perceived increase in globalized musical exchanges, "musicians have always tried to keep up with the times, not just to please their audiences, but also to rejuvenate their own playing, to experiment and out of curiosity."[25] Ed Morales, the widely read Cuban-American author and journalist, labeled *Tiempos* a "reinvention."[26] And Strauss described the singer of *Tiempos* as a "musician who constantly challenges his audience with his artistic twists and turns," going against character vis-à-vis his earlier music and in a way from concomitant Latin pop trends exploding in the US—for example, Ricky Martin, Marc Anthony, and Jennifer Lopez.[27]

The questions remain, then: What disciplinary formations and practices produce and regulate such "rejuvenation" and "reinvention," and what unheard force structures the parameters and limits a musician's reimagining of his or her work? Fairley, Morales, and Strauss remain caught within a politics of an intentional subject, which though not fully absent here is, I think, ultimately insufficient to explain creative shifts such as Blades's.

MUNDO (2002)

Like *Tiempos*, *Mundo* exudes musical ambition. It too constitutes a musically expansive reinvention, a move from the Latin American Latin Americanism of *Tiempos* to a cosmopolitan Latin American vision of the world's music—or of the Western world's "World Music," without, however, being an outright and explicit attempt to capitalize on World Music trends.[28] There is in *Mundo* a rethinking of the place of clave-based rhythmic structures, though far less in straight-ahead salsa contexts than in the search for music where clave may function as a kind of rhythmic DNA. Instead, the album explores Northern African–sounding mixtures along with what Blades calls "gypsy" music, including, among other things, *cante hondo*, "Asiatic rhythms," melodies that invoke Northeastern Brazil, Celtic World Music sound (which Blades traces back to the Galician and Basque connection to the Celts), a traditional song from Mali, songs by Gilberto Gil, popular jazz musicians Pat Metheny and Lyle Mays, and, memorably, a version of "Danny Boy" that begins traditionally, bagpipes and all, and ends with a Cuban *rumba* beat. Songs are sung in Spanish and English without much ado about the album's bilingual character. The top-notch musical basis of Éditus and arranger and musical director Walter Flores remains, but there is a brass section and notable guests perform on Latin percussion, Irish flute and bagpipe, and Aboriginal Australian didgeridoo. Collaboration and parities of all kinds are the new name of the game: two vocal groups, the Brazilian male quartet Boca Livre and the Argentine female quartet De Boca en Boca, make prominent solo appearances. This consolidates the practice, already heard in *Tiempos*, of having tracks performed solely by the supporting or guest musicians. The CD cover prominently showcases all the Costa Rican musicians involved, with Éditus and Flores sharing the front cover with Blades.

The music combines an airy quality with more dense textures. The production, realized mostly in Costa Rica but also in Brazil, is glossy, with an abundance of overdubs and carefully crafted production values. Suitably, the writing is highly polished throughout, as shown in the excerpt in figure 2.2.

Ripe with sonic orientalisms such as a certain kind of ornamental figuration (in the instrumental hook that begins at m. 10 and the bass line, beginning at m. 11), the use of tone colors such as the bouzouki, and the melodic preference for augmented intervals, both "Middle Eastern music" clichés, this passage also incorporates a straightforward clave structure (here a 2:3 pattern). The percussion in the main body of the track is audibly "Latin," characterized by busy stop-time breaks after the fashion of 1990s New York City salsa studio sessions (the invited percussionists, Bobby Allende and Marc Quiñones, are first-call musicians from that scene). The vocal line is delivered in the tight and throaty style of flamenco *cante hondo*, suited to but also straining Blades's vocal register. Different from most tracks in *Tiempos*, this and the majority of *Mundo*'s tracks are danceable.

Significantly, no longer are rhythms, grooves, colors, and so forth bounded by the *sonic representation* of Latin America. Instead, in the project's sonic heterogeneity, Blades enjoins us to listen at a planetary scale and in terms of deep time—history is no longer a main concern. As he put it,

> Earth was not originally created with political divisions. Nature is impervious to where a country begins or ends. Spirit is universal. Life comes from a common source. Supported by these premises, We—artists from Argentina, Brazil, Costa Rica, US, Mexico, Panama, and Puerto Rico—have collaborated in the creation of this project. We believe that music is an ideal spokesperson to express the best possibilities of the human character. In celebration, and united in the hope that we all share to that ancestral memory that is latent inside all beings, we offer MUNDO.[29]

In keeping with this ambitious agenda, songs address the fundamental interconnection of various musical cultures, which Blades explains in brief program notes preceding the lyrics of each track.

There are new and unusual elements. Science now provides Blades an alibi. The work of British neuroscientist Bryan Sykes compels references throughout the lyrics to an idea of human unity and kinship. According to

Figure 2.2. Rubén Blades, "Bochinches," arranged by Walter Florés, introduction

Sykes, all human life has a genetic origin traceable to one group, the clan Lara, in present-day Africa.[30] This shares space with songs of unrepentant personal nostalgia, character sketches, literary adaptations, and love songs. This might be a Latin Americanism with a twist, at once cosmopolitan, globalized, personal, and planetary. It inches toward a naturalistic critique of cultural difference.

Crossing Over

Blades had explored a diversity of musical genres in one album prior to *Tiempos* and *Mundo*. In 1996, he recorded *Rosa de los Vientos* (Sony International) in Panama, with Panamanian musicians, and performing songs exclusively by Panamanian composers. Evan C. Gutierrez called it "more full [*sic*] of mystery and folklore than any previous project," highlighting "a healthy dose of cumbia" in addition to Blades's "trademark rhumba-fusion, super-literate salsa, and even a little funk for fun."[31] Although the album earned Blades a Grammy (Best Tropical Latin Performance, 1997), the recording solidified the sense that, even when playing mainly Afro-Cuban–oriented music, the singer was on to other things.

The project's production and realization in Panama was important and part of a broader reorientation South by Blades. In 1994, he had run for the Panamanian presidency with the center-left party he founded the year before, Movimiento Papa Egoró, coming in third, despite a very brief campaign (five months) and a refusal to ally itself with preexisting parties.[32] The party garnered 17 percent of the vote. Eventually, the party would dissolve in 1999, in good part due to conflicts with the fact that Blades was directing the political project from the US, where he continued to pursue his artistic career. That career involved, among other activities, a guest performance on an album by Little Steven where he sang in English, appearances in the films *Color of Night* (1994) and *The Devil's Own* (1997) and in the hit TV show *The X-Files* (1997), and, notably, playing a lead part in Paul Simon's short-lived but much discussed and critically panned Broadway musical *The Capeman* (1997).[33]

Much before the era of personal branding, Blades seems to have been fully aware of the power granted by visibility and recognition abroad as a spokesperson for Latin America. "Right now," he had said in 1986, "I am doing everything I can to be understood by people who have traditionally ignored Latin America. And as a musician who's going to return eventually to Panama, I know the power of the media: I too need that cultural blessing."[34] Part of that "power" and its corollary "blessing" included what was then regarded as visibility and participation in mainstream US media, a process dating to his move, in 1982, to Elektra Records, a first-ever for a salsa musician and a signal case for the possibilities of musical crossover from the peripheral Latin music market.[35]

Blades's move to Elektra included a change from the traditional salsa ensemble. The singer opted for a lean sextet, which he called Seis del Solar.[36] The new group paid homage to the sound of the boogaloo era, particularly the great Joe Cuba Sextet, from the early 1960s, which prominently featured the vibraphone (alongside the piano) and eliminated the brass section altogether. The resulting sound was considerably cooler, closer in spirit to what would have been the signature colors of West Coast Latin Jazz (one thinks of Carl Tjader and Willie Bobo here). The new ensemble would fit the Panamanian's nasal tenor.

The group's debut album, *Buscando América* (Elektra, 1984), made a strong musical impression, but it immediately thrust Blades into heated debates about cultural loyalty under the label of crossover. It was named among the year's top albums by the *Village Voice* and earned Blades his first Grammy nomination for Best Tropical Latin Performance. Commenters regarded the move from a "Latin" to an "American" record label as an example of crossover, one represented in the 1985 film *Crossover Dreams*, in which Blades played the lead character, "Rudy Veloz."[37] Deborah Pacini Hernandez summarizes: "[Veloz] fleetingly achieves mainstream success after abandoning salsa aesthetics in favor of a more eclectic and world beat–inflected style. . . . Despite being fully bilingual, bicultural, and bimusical (Rudy's record collection pointedly contains rock 'n' roll records), he is unable to sustain his mainstream success and ends up returning to the barrio and his musical roots, a culturally wiser, if economically poorer, man."[38] For Pacini Hernandez, the film raises the question of "why Rudy believes he has to alter his musical and performance style at all to gain mainstream acceptance at a time when so many non-Latino consumers were favorably disposed to dance music of diasporic origins."[39] The "achievement of mainstream success" of which Pacini Hernandez writes corresponds to what Reebee Garofalo had described as the "process whereby an artist or a recording from a 'secondary' marketing category like country and western, Latin, or rhythm and blues achieves hit status in the mainstream or 'pop' market . . . its most common usage in popular music history clearly connotes movement from margin to mainstream," as good a definition of crossover as any.[40] In general, "crossover" mobilized a spatial metaphor to describe attempts by a recording artist to engage in genres and styles not previously associated with him or her.[41]

The film, along with the artistic success of *Buscando América*, placed Blades on the industry's critical radar. On *Billboard*, Nelson George, a vocal critic of crossover in Black music, compared the Panamanian's challenge to debates among "black musicians and record people," and noting a tension between the possibility for market expansion at the expense of diluting "black music traditions," which "would hurt artists."[42] George referred to *Crossover Dreams*, in which a "Latin star" tries to "cross over to the white audience"; "the music may be different, but the experiences of the character Blades portrays will strike home with many Afro-Americans."[43] Blades would seem to agree; George cites a 1984 *New York Times* article where the musician had expressed that "I find the whole idea of crossover dangerous, because it implies the abandonment of one base for another. I'd rather talk about convergence—the idea of two sides meeting in the middle of a bridge."[44] "Convergence" here is not what George had in mind, crossover dynamics and politics being quite different when both "culture" *and* language are at stake, as they were for Blades.[45]

Reviewing *Buscando América*, Robert Palmer, the renowned pop music critic for the *New York Times*, put the matter in stark terms:

> Whenever a pop musician who appeals to a limited audience gets to the top in his field, the chimera of "crossover" begins to beckon. The field may be salsa or reggae, blues or gospel music or rap. Each music has its core of artists and supporters who have had similar upbringings and share an identity that is separate and distinct from the cultural mainstream.
>
> How does such an artist "cross over"—win a share of the mainstream audience—without losing the loyalty of his original fans? The history of such attempts is usually a history of failure, especially in the salsa field, which presents the mainstream pop music fan with two barriers to understanding, one of language, the other of culture. Salsa stars who want to cross over tend to dilute their music, either by singing in English or by dabbling in rock and other mainstream styles. Neither of these approaches has been successful for most performers.[46]

Palmer's comments home in on the core dilemma of crossover. The dilemma emerges between seemingly incompatible alternatives: either maintaining a sociocultural commitment to forceful ideas of truth to and of a community, audience, and fans or embarking on an effort to broaden the artistic and commercial reach of a musical genre and style and a marketing category, perceived to "dilute" the truth-value of the sociocultural commitment.[47] Crossover constitutes a movement across musical categories, each one originally marketed to different consumers and having varying budgets for production and promotion. According to David Brackett, in the early to mid-1980s, "the concept . . . had a particular valence and expressive power," epitomized in the Ichaso film: "Little else could explain the appearance of a movie such as *Crossover Dreams* that thematized the struggles over genre and identity . . . by the time of the release of *Crossover Dreams* it had become that what had been a dream for some had turned into a nightmare for others."[48]

Blades seemed to disavow crossover as such or to link his move to Elektra to it. Instead, he referred to earlier ideas about his brand of salsa as "urban music," to which he now added the key and ambiguous adjective "American." He also recalled his perennial experimentation with musical form:

> The basic elements in any successful crossover would have to be honesty and quality. . . . I would never want to lose my audience by trying to present a salad of an album, with one or two songs in English, to appeal to whom exactly? I'll always keep the basics of the music, the Afro-Cuban structure, the language. But I'll give the music little twists; I've never subscribed to the idea that the music will disappear if you change it a bit. When I signed with Elektra, my ambition wasn't to make a crossover album. I wanted to make an urban American album that can be appreciated by any American city dweller and may bring people who haven't identified with salsa a bit closer to us.[49]

Blades envisioned a different kind of crossover, one in which new audiences, basically urban, would come to his music. It is hard to say what audience he might have had in mind. Perhaps English-speaking, relatively well-educated and sufficiently cosmopolitan audiences, curious about other "cultures"? And would these be monolingual, for whom the English translations of the lyrics included in the album would be useful? Could they be a "predominantly English-speaking audience for mainstream American popular music"?[50] Or could it be instead the "growing size of an audience that increasingly negotiates both cultures," "Hispanic *and* Anglo," as Panamanian-born musicologist Don Michael Randel suggested?[51] For Randel, Blades's music from the 1980s moves away from the pastoral ethos of more traditional salsa—it is more complex, with irregular rhyme schemes, an embrace of irony-tinged humor, Spanish vernacular diction at one moment and parodies of legalistic Spanish the next, a reference to prayer ("Hail Mary") juxtaposed with one to James Bond, multiple music-genre references (doo wop, church music tropes, salsa). "Blades," he concludes, "is not crossing over *to* a new audience so much as he is crossing over *with* a new audience whose culture is profoundly Hispanic but increasingly imbued with Anglo culture and energized by its very own political and economic aspirations."[52] For Randel, the matter was socioeconomic, a new demographic of upwardly mobile Hispanic people representing the expanding but core public that made it possible and necessary for Blades to push further the lyrical and musical experiments that audiences of "Pedro Navaja" would have recognized.

Three factors complicate the idea of an emerging new audience. One, it is unclear how "complex and intersecting social codes" emerge in Blades's new musical production that might have spoken to an upwardly mobile audience. Songs about historical events such as the 1980 assassination of Monsignor Óscar Arnulfo Romero, the archbishop of El Salvador, which Blades allegorizes in "El Padre Antonio y el Monaguillo Andrés," might have made some in these audiences less interested in the travails of the continent. The same could be asked of the titular track in *Buscando América*, a wrenching account of a search for an America that has been made to disappear, in reference to Latin American dictatorships during the 1970s and 1980s.[53] These and other songs fit within the reportorial mission that Blades had embraced since the 1970s. The "social codes" Randel refers to were not new but rather ingrained in the continent's troubled history. Two, although purchases among "Latin" consumers increased during the 1980s and 1990s, as Arlene Dávila notes, the distribution of this share was unevenly distributed in favor of dominant groups in particular regions. Cuban-Americans in Florida had, in the main, a greater purchase on their local economies including mass media such as radio than, say, Puerto Ricans had in New York.[54] Dávila argues how cultural representation (e.g., greater visibility in the mainstream media and press), the kind embodied by Blades, did not translate into political enfranchisement. For example, one thinks of the reactionary position of Cuban-American groups in Miami and Florida who boycotted Blades's earlier hit "Tiburón" for its sharp denunciation of US imperialism. Three, some of Blades's experiments, particularly his all-English-language album *Nothing but the Truth* (Elektra, 1988), featuring an all-star lineup (Sting, Lou Reed, and Elvis Costello), were met with indifference—Blades's songs in this project remained fully committed to urgent topical matters. *Agua de Luna* (Elektra, 1987), perhaps his most lettered album, featuring adapted short stories by Gabriel García Márquez, was heard as a disavowal of popular salsa audiences.[55] The historical, economic, and experimental dimensions in Blades's work pushed audiences in different and often incompatible directions.

Randel is correct that US critics found Blades's crossover successful. But audiences, which may have crossed over with the singer, never materialized into a public in the way that occurred with his music from the 1970s. Eventually, the singer objected to the term, calling it a "racist label": "Musicians from the Third World do not need a Green Card to be allowed to play in the First [World]. They are talented, nobody has to discover them."[56] He chose to operate within a space of aesthetic experimentation that included work in two languages, artistic collaborations, ongoing interest in literary practices, and, perhaps most consistently of all, a continuing commitment to working with various musical forms, styles, and genres. This translated into a pursuit of heterogeneity as a value and as an index of the complexity of thinking of Latin America and indeed America.

Here a key distinction appears between the expectations in the US that, as critics almost inevitably put it, musical production from the peripheries remains faithful to identitarian interests, an expectation perfectly understandable within a space of often radical separation among groups on the basis of race and ethnicity. As Brackett, Garofalo, and others note, this expectation, which operates at the level of musical style and form, recording, marketing, and distribution networks, and audience reception, constitutes a condition of possibility for "crossover" to exist and for it to be experienced as either assimilation and loss or transformation and gain. Language, as Blades made clear in comments to John Rockwell, marked a delimiting line for which "crossover" had no clear precedents, the many Spanish-tinged hits in the past notwithstanding (e.g., Ritchie Valens's "La Bamba" or Nat King Cole's recordings of Latin classics).[57] Given that his thematic content, declamatory style, and commitment to Afro-Caribbean (Cuban, Puerto Rican, and Nuyorican) forms remained constant throughout most of his post-*Siembra* music, it is at the level of musical genres (and "ritmos" as their avatars) where we can hear Blades's efforts to amplify and recalibrate, if not redouble, his earlier Latin Americanism. The increasing musical heterogeneity of his 1999 and 2000 projects indexes these efforts. This heterogeneity sounds Latin America, going beyond arguing on its behalf, as he claimed to have done in the 1970s. As he trains his sights on a new locus of enunciation, "crossover" loses much of its explanatory capacity.

HETEROGENEITY: BETWEEN APPROPRIATION AND RESTITUTION

The concept of heterogeneity may help clarify Blades's mobilization of diverse genres (or "ritmos"), their affective reach ("feeling," in his words), and the local histories and social milieux that these might embody. The millennial projects perform their Latin Americanism through the display of diversity of what he reclaims as rightfully Latin American musical practices.[58] The degree to which *Tiempos*, for instance, displays formal, generic, and stylistic heterogeneity would measure the adequacy of its representation of Latin America's "feeling." By embracing Latin America's musical heterogeneity, Blades affirms what makes Latin America unique. Heterogeneity discloses "[a] kind of intra-Latin American singularity," compelling a new mapping of musical Latin Americanism.[59]

There were resonances to this position in debates in the US roughly contemporary with Blades's albums. These debates revolved around how to think of Latin Americanism when three of its classic *values*—the nation, literature, and the people—were perceived to have reached their limits. Kate Jenckes identified a "New Latin Americanism"[60] that interrogated the role of hegemonic *operations* in gathering a sense of proprietary cultural identity and any kind of multicultural recognition of the Other within, as well as notions of regional coherence and even of cartographic criteria for Latin Americanist delimitations. As critic and philosopher Federico Galende put it, "any thinking of emancipation must always be a thinking without cartography."[61] The debates were important also for how they addressed one powerful response to the attenuation of those values and operations: in an increasingly interconnected world and under the homogenizing threats of neoliberal governance, Latin American singularity called for renewal via the reaffirmation of its heterogeneity.

In Blades, then, heterogeneity goes beyond a certain stylistic eclecticism, a managed plurality of musical choices, or a hybridization of diverse musical genres within the time-space of a recording. Rather, heterogeneity entails a process of recuperation, a political stance vis-à-vis homogeneity, an evaluative position before its objects, and a remapping of previously established sonic geographies. At stake is the *restitution* of something unacknowledged, be it musical genres or marginalized identities. Restitution renders heterogeneity as a conceptual border with the epistemic function of demarcating salsa's homogenizing Latino Latin Americanism. Heterogeneity sounds out a supposedly as-of-yet-unheard plurality of music that makes up the rich musical world of the continent, its sonic "singularity," and a truer Latin Americanism. Restitution fosters an analytic relation to its objects, for a restituted work becomes a "recovered" object, understood and evaluated as much or even more than it is experienced.[62] Within Blades's conceptualization of Latin America in *Tiempos*, recovery informs the restitution of a certain resonance of various musical genres and styles heard in close juxtaposition—for example, a Cuban *guaguancó* here, an Argentinian *chacarera* there, and so on. Blades produces a novel Latin Americanism in which the force of his words and the forms of his music overcome what otherwise could be a potpourri of genres from the Americas. The reason is that restitutive heterogeneity creates relations where none might have necessarily existed, establishing for the singer-songwriter and for his audiences potentially novel "points of inscription" into the greater Latin American sonic geography, a cartography in which new "cognitive mappings" might be necessary for the aurality that heterogeneity demands.[63] One might well imagine musical heterogeneity in Blades's projects supplanting literature, disrupting national boundaries, and shaping a new and more fully interconnected people, to cite the three Latin Americanist values Jenckes mentions.

In *Tiempos* and *Mundo*, Blades retraces his immigrant trajectory with consequential effects. As Walter Mignolo observes, migratory movements raise the possibility and need for "alternative sites of enunciation."[64] This happened when Latino Latin Americanism served as the hegemonic medium for Blades to "[make] the case for Latin America." With his return to Central America, we hear what alternative sites of enunciation compel him to say. The importance, beginning with *Rosa de los Vientos* and culminating with the millennial projects, of recording in Panama and Costa Rica and performing with local musicians, expresses Blades's belief in the importance of where he speaks for redrawing his musical geography of the continent. Latin America could not be something to be sounded; it was a concrete location from which to sound.

"Alternative sites of enunciation," however, is not a fancy name for processes of returning to the specific and the local that relocate a Latin Americanism previously enunciated from the North to its proper place in the South. There is an important corollary to the idea. Namely, that its unity-in-heterogeneity makes Latin America different from other regional assemblies. For Moreiras, the tension between this claim to heterogeneity-within and difference-without expressed a dualistic logic juxtaposing internal ("endotopic") and external ("exotopic") knowledge. In turn, heterogeneity constituted an *appropriative* operation. That is, the proposal for a heterogeneity as a fundamental representation of Latin America auto-appropriated an aspect of regional reality (endotopic knowledge) *and* elaborated it as an explanatory model (and thus generalizing, exotopic knowledge) for that reality's singularity. This operation rendered auto-appropriation into something legible as "difference" for an-Other. Moreiras calls this legibility from without "restitution": the placing-again (or restitution) of Latin America back into the globe by making its difference (i.e., its singularity) legible to the rest of the world, giving it a place in the world market of intelligible identities. Appropriation, like heterogeneity, demands this universal validation.

Under Moreiras's analytic, relocating what was sounded *as* "Latin America" *to* Latin America requires careful evaluation. Here, for example, is how the singularity-in-heterogeneity in Blades's projects necessitates some form of universal validation. In *Tiempos*, the positive value of heterogeneity would reside in its being preferable to homogeneity, a restitution grounded in the universalist struggle between the One and the Many. In its worldly aims, *Mundo* may well toil "not in the name of the marginal subject, but in the name of truth in its Western form, or in the name of the multiplicity that, in this model, represents truth: represents the *nature* of the global."[65]

There is another knot in the tension between appropriation and restitution—that is, between Latin American Latin Americanist particularism and the universals it requires. Namely, that unlike other forms of regional representation (e.g., Orientalism), it is articulated from and by "Latin Americans" *and* by immigrant Latin Americans. Moreiras calls this Latin Americanism's "dissymmetrical gaze," for, different from asymmetry (a lack of symmetry), dissymmetry lacks the elements necessary to achieve symmetry. This helps explain the need for the exotopic operation of restitution and for the articulation of appropriation to "endotopic representation."[66] Any symmetry that might be achieved by speaking from the South is the result of the fact that the object "Latin America" cannot be other than the outcome of the operations enabling representation, on the condition that we overlook the persistence of dissymmetry at the heart of these operations: appropriation and restitution, and exotopic and endotopic knowledge. Representation is shot through by the "double injunction" of Latin Americanism to claims of radical singularity (e.g., its unique heterogeneity) and participation in a global system of differences, in general. This double injunction shares in a Western (and epistemically masculine) anxiety over engaged representation and totalization.[67]

Blades is not immune to these tensions. Placing this analytic within the context of Blades's move from New York City–based musicking to Costa Rica reveals the political stakes of appropriation and restitution. Together, Blades's shift in locus of enunciation and the mobilization of genres and styles previously not associated with his music represent an effort to redress the *asymmetry* of salsa's Latino Latin Americanism. Of course, the impetus of appropriation propelled the earlier Latin Americanism, with his declared intention of making a case for Latin America being its quintessential move. To be clear, I am not affirming that the earlier Latin Americanism reflected a completely *a*symmetrical and exotopic perspective of Latin America from without; the presence of a veritable society of Caribbean and Latin American immigrants in the US would have already been endotopic. Rather, I am suggesting that *dis*symmetry is constitutive to Latin Americanism: representation's need for some universal value means that it could never achieve symmetry, whether from within or without. The appeal to a new locus of enunciation and to musical heterogeneity seems to deflect this constitutive aporia but cannot. In fact, the production of a representation of Latin America in Costa Rica—by musicians there, using all the apparatuses of musical production available there, and by a figure long associated with Latin Americanism—only accentuates dissymmetry. Nonetheless, if restitution/appropriation offers an "opportunity . . . to address historical conditions of production and redress some of its social and political determinations,"[68] heterogeneity accrues value as a perspective through which listeners can hear the continent in relation to a globalized world that threatens to blur all regional distinctions.

ÉDITUS LISTENS

The musicians from Éditus had their own perspective on this globalized world. For them, there was not a sense of restitution or of the contradictions inherent to Latin Americanism's "dissymmetrical gaze." Instead, heterogeneity constituted their musical experience of the world, which was itself conditioned by self-awareness of connection to that world. As percussionist Carlos Vargas affirmed, "what is happening is that there are no borders. One notes this when listening to many musicians' productions. Everybody is taking elements from here and there. Pat Metheny is searching his roots in Irish music but continues with jazz and looks for musicians who can handle all things related to ethnic percussion . . . [the] *Kronos* [string quartet] gives a classical treatment to Piazzolla's themes or traditional African songs . . . this is socially important because it brings us all together and integrates us."[69] Guitarist Solís echoed the sentiment: "The facility that exists today to connect and to be up to date with what is going on in every last corner of the world enables one to have a clearer vision of what happens and helps one define which route to go on through."[70] Their discourse was marked by an ethos of aural and virtual connectivity and free circulation of musical forms in their listening practices.

There are two sides to connectivity. On the one hand, listening does not necessarily occur on an even plane, for it is likely that such practices "make us feel near to others without having to understand them."[71] Similarly, "privileged interlocutors" in the periphery may be compelled to think like their metropolitan interlocutors and to anticipate how they might be listened to.[72] On the other hand, connectivity can reaffirm situatedness and contribute to the resignification of place and locality. As Jesús Martín-Barbero remarks, "the movement of globalization" intersects with "the reinvention of citizenship" in the "diaspora that mobilizes networked knowledge," where "diaspora" refers to what he calls a "de-centered modernity" that dislocates linear information to create "transit spaces: a multiplicity of senses—directions and meanings—and figures."[73] Éditus violinist Ricardo Ramírez echoes: "Costa Rica has always been a country that is very open to music, to all currents, and we as musicians, in particular, have been very open to listen to all kinds of music. We three [Éditus] have had in common the desire to mix and interpret these things."[74] Embodying a new "communicational reason," this statement affirms "transit spaces." As Martín-Barbero puts it, "creative experience" corresponds with the attainment of "communicative competence" in the service of experimentation.[75] Asked about the role of Costa Rica's "atypical condition" in Central America (i.e., a nation-state without an army, with relative political and economic stability, and by then internationally renowned for its ecological projects), Vargas noted that

> Costa Rica is very young culturally, there isn't a strong tradition here in the way there is in Brazil, Cuba, and Argentina; and because there is no tradition, we construct it, receiving influences from every which way . . . indeed, we live in a country that is like an island within the region; for a variety of reasons, the sociocultural level is a bit higher than its neighbors' and this produces a greater artistic opening, the possibility of being better informed of what goes on in the world.[76]

The Costa Rican musicians' expressions of optimism and openness recall Ulrich Beck's pithy observation that "There is no memory of the global past, but there is an imagination of a globally shared future."[77] Beck avoids absolute distinctions between nationalism, the classic locus for a robust sense of a shared past, and cosmopolitanism, which offers a future-oriented imagination. Though both "are past- and future orientated," nationalism wagers that the future is grounded in a shared past, while cosmopolitanism wagers that "it is the future, not the past, which 'integrates' the cosmopolitan age."[78] Another distinction emerges between the integration that partakes in a consciousness of the global and its cosmopolitan dimensions, on the one hand, and on the other, effective actions taken to seize on that consciousness, particularly in the absence of institutional means other than markets to carry out actions in the name of this cosmopolitan consciousness. In this sense, actions entail a modicum of risk and experimentation, with the corollary that they offer no guarantees that they will have produced or at least promoted an experience of a "globally shared future."[79] For Beck, an advocate of cosmopolitanism, "in the dimension of space we talk and reflect upon the de-territorialization of the social, the political, and the economic," and "in the dimension of time we have to reflect upon the *retraditionalization*' of the social, political and cultural through a globally collective future."[80] This constitutes a sort of inversion of tradition's location in the past, for "re-traditionalization" now "takes the position of tradition and memory in the past-orientated national imagination."[81]

We might interpret Vargas's statement about the "greater artistic opening" afforded by Costa Rica in Beck's terms. An ecumenical musicking, although channeled through the institutional networks of global musical production, offers an opportunity to enact a future. In this future, the loose relation to a tradition constitutes a case of "re-traditionalization," and like it, Éditus's music a wager on experimentation. Similarly, their musicking might embody "cosmopolitanization," which Beck proposes as "a frame of reference for empirical exploration for globalization *from within*, globalization internalized."[82] This offers "a descriptive analysis of social structure" that does not, however, eschew "conflicts of globalized social worlds" that emerge out of the challenges in relating novel experiences of space and place to temporality.[83]

These "conflicts" do not emerge from the practices of musical experimentation of Vargas and his colleagues. To the contrary, the ease with which they traversed musical genres and styles was received positively. And neither do conflicts appear from the thematic content of Blades's new songs, designed as expressive affordances given by musical heterogeneity. Rather, conflicts appear in the counterpoint between the spatial dimension of an interconnected Latin America in which national territories were traversed as if unimpeded, on the one hand, and on the other a temporal dimension which, for Blades, could only be a domain of redemption of a past Latin Americanism that he sought to broaden, if not rectify, while at the same time envisioning what was yet to come. Speaking of *La Rosa de Los Vientos* and *Tiempos*, Blades said, "these albums point not only to where I'm going, but to where we [the Latin music community] could go in the future."[84] And yet, what new boundaries may emerge and what relational transformations within and across those boundaries does Blades's renewed Latin Americanism entail? To address these queries, I consider an analytic designed to interrogate rigid boundaries: hybridity.

HYBRIDITY

A music analyst might describe the excerpts in figures 2.1 and 2.2 as textbook cases of hybridity—provisionally, a combinatory aggregation into a single composition of elements of diverse but identifiable provenance.[85] However, there is more at stake than formal identification of stylistic traits associated with and dependent upon the logic of musical genres; namely, there are temporal, emplaced, and spatial stakes in hybridity.

Present in the minds of theorists of Latin Americanism throughout the 1980s and 1990s, hybridity names emplaced forms of knowledge production and their resignification processes. It recognizes that multiple systems (of knowledge, meaning and signification, temporality and historicity) coexist that produce particular spaces (aesthetic, cultural, social, historical, economical, geopolitical) precisely because these spaces and the places where they occur are themselves multiple.

Néstor García Canclini described the production of these new aesthetic spaces in Latin America as "hybrid transformations generated by the horizontal coexistence of a number of symbolic systems [that] enable the conservatory musician to use the knowledge of classical or contemporary harmony to produce erudite experiments in rock, jazz, or salsa."[86] This could well describe the work of Éditus. Blades is no stranger to hybrid experimentation; García Canclini singles out his work from the 1980s as an example of particularly successful hybridization.[87] In either case, García Canclini, after Bourdieu's notion of aesthetics as a means of class distinction, conceives musical hybridity in terms of high and low encounters and their new spaces of interaction and experimentation within an otherwise regimented and segmented modern Latin American society.

Five basic tenets I draw from hybridization inform my analysis:[88]

1. Hybridization requires that its materials circulate as part of discrete and/or disparate symbolic and market systems, and thus that they remain ready-at-hand for actors (e.g., market forces, technologies, media and communications networks, state and civil society institutions, individuals) to transform or "reconvert" them.[89] This risks that someone's hybridization may be someone else's extraction or appropriation, among other possible cross-relations.

2. The materiality of objects is supplemented by an ideological field within which they are located by those who use or claim them as properly theirs. This field carries sociocultural traces, including tradition, custom, technologies of reproduction, and associations with discrete and usually opposing and stratified categories of modernity (high/low, elite/mass, center/periphery, lettered/oral, urban/rural, traditional/modern, state/private, local/global, identical/different, developed/underdeveloped).

3. Hybridization is inherently dynamic. It is intersectional and disruptive of norms by recourse to a broad spectrum of strategies, from agonistic transgression of dominant symbolic systems to their coherentist resignification. This speaks to the intrinsic

ambivalence of hybridity and is one of the reasons that critics insisted that hybridization could occlude Latin America's constitutive asymmetries of power and incommensurable cultural fields.[90]

4. Hybridization speaks to the co-presence, within sociopolitical spaces such as the nation, of various temporalities and historicities, horizontally unfolding streams that cannot be subsumed under the binaries of vertically layered and opposing strata enumerated above in 2.[91]

5. Existing discrete domains, ready to be hybridized, within the social field is a presupposition originating from the strategies of purification that constitute modernity. In Bruno Latour's well-known argument, modernity is the sum of operations by which society produces radically separate spheres for what is cultivated (culture) and what is objectively given and only discovered (nature), which distinction helps organize other binary oppositions such as tradition and modernity.[92] In the increasing awareness of these legacies of modernity, Ernesto Laclau could affirm that "hybridization is not a marginal phenomenon but the very terrain in which contemporary political identities are constructed."[93] The corollary—that if hybridization is everything, then nothing is hybrid—would fail to take seriously the actually existing processes by which the powers of purification continue to exercise their effectivity in Latin American societies, lest we reduce the dynamics to the very binary opposition that begets the matter in the first place: pure/hybrid.

Like heterogeneity, hybridization presupposes a culturally plural field. But whereas heterogeneity functions as a restitutive dispersion of hitherto underrepresented cultural practices, hybridization mediates the partial integration between the materiality and temporality of those practices.[94] Temporality here designates how a group or individual might conceive, construct, and experience the present, past, and future, and how these modalities are related to one another. More specifically, it refers to how actions in the present are thought to be able to intervene in the past and future. Temporality here encompasses both long-span projects and everyday life. Why temporality? Because the ideological claims (tenet 2) hinge on the intersection of hybridization's materiality (tenet 1) and temporality (tenet 4), and this intersection also supports the capacity it may have to transgress, resignify, or otherwise transform the cultural practices it engages (tenets 3 and 5).

As examples of the material-temporal relation in hybridization, consider the two excerpts from figures 2.1 and 2.2. In the first are the aesthetic verities of the baroque-like counterpoint between guitar, violin, and saxophone an artful and erudite foil to the contemporaneity of Blades's cries against the neoliberalization of all social domains? Or, is the truth of that present-day reclamation temporally amplified or even elevated by appeal to some historical transcendence of European art music? In figure 2.2, are the orientalist turns of phrase to be heard as timeless sonic evocations in the context of an intercultural sonic lingua franca that Latin American musicians now too claim as a kind of cosmopolitan right to sound? Or, are those turns of phrase sonic alibis for the fact that no matter how cosmopolitan musicians may have become, the exoticizing ear remains a difficult thing to overcome, even when the intent is to celebrate the others' music and its impact on one's own?[95] (The music, written by pianist Walter Flores, was originally titled "Un Tico [national colloquial for Costa Rican person] en el Oriente" ["A Costa Rican in the Orient"].)

Rather than wallow in endless semiotic interpretations, I ask: What are the conditions of possibility for these temporalities to coincide, coexist, and collide—to enter into syncopated relation? In Costa Rica, there appear to be processes of structural modernization constituted by a sense of an open tradition, technical innovations transforming musical competences and modes of musical production, and a mobilization of a present pregnant with possibilities for an unforeseen future. In *Tiempos*, Blades specifically addressed his sense of changing times: personal upheaval, on the one hand, and on the other the awareness of an exhaustion of earlier forms of Latin Americanist musical expression, as well as the bitter realization that changing sociopolitical structures demanded a different mode of (musical) address. The weight of past musical traditions, a knotted-up present, and the uncertainty of what was to come constituted conflicted temporalities that he decided to address.

And so, the question of why it becomes possible (even necessary) to take charge of these multiple temporalities may seem clear enough. Less clear is the idea of a subjectivity whose agency "takes charge" of them. To put it simply, I think of the temporalities of two main parties here, Blades and Éditus. Their juxtaposition comes into a formation that, at least from a musicological perspective, includes contemporary Latin America and recent Latino American music, as well as the archives of Western art music historiography and Western sonic ethnography. These archives exercise their own kind of agency, as does the thorough musical education of the Éditus musicians under their government's financial benefaction. This agency derives, in part, from their aural experience as voracious listeners and dedicated music students from across Latin America and the globe, to say nothing of their complex sense of territorial and sonic interlacings, or of their self-positioning as advocates of indigenous musical traditions and of an ecological sensibility in Costa Rica.

Hybridization is at play in the coming together, in *Tiempos*, of these temporalities, of some sense of preexisting materials, of various ideologies of ownership, borrowing, and abandonment of these materials. It is also at play in strategies for leaving behind forms of musical Latin Americanism tethered to, say, presumed purities of Afro-Cuban forms' capacity to address Latin America. We have traces of four of the tenets outlined above, except for tenet 3. This tenet addressed the ambivalence of hybridization processes. Yes, there is the unbearable obviousness that a music record partakes in the instrumentalization of culture industries. More important in this case is the ambivalence between Blades's agonistic recasting of his new Latin Americanism (i.e., leaving behind his earlier, salsa-grounded efforts to make the case for Latin America) and the coherentist resignification of musical genres in an inclusive cartography of Latin American genres. Furthermore, this ambivalence is of a different order from that through which it gains sounding form in the musical hybridization of the Éditus musicians and collaborators. If Blades's new Latin Americanism can be best understood through the analytic of heterogeneity and the dynamics of restitution and appropriation, the Costa Rican musicians' processes of intermixing better correspond to the dynamics of hybridization. For the latter, these dynamics form part of how they construct subjectivities in virtue of their local situation. The way they put it, these local situations constitute them as hybridizing subjects in the first place. If, for the Blades of *Tiempos*, Latin America remained an enclosure still graspable through the reach of heterogeneous inclusivity, then for Vargas and his colleagues the tendency is toward the assemblage of a quasi-totality (the world of musicking in which everyone knows what everyone else might be doing) without a musical origin.

Blades's millennial projects resonate with rich ambivalences in contemporary Latin Americanist relations of hybridity as well as the quasi-assemblages afforded the Éditus musicians. For one, global networks reconfigure relations between and among peoples according to a "logic of inclusion and exclusion" given in the condition of being either "connected or disconnected."[96] From this perspective, the projects are not only a form of restitution of configurations such as musical genres, they are an enactment of a form of inclusion and participation of actual people; and the same goes for hybridization. Éditus and the musicians and technicians associated with them enter into and are included in a network of transnational Latin Americanist musical practices. But those musicians and technicians themselves, as much as, if not more than, Blades, had already engaged in elective connections. Availing themselves of the historically deep, territorially vast, and ethnographically complex sonic archives at hand today, they thus gained some of the cultural capital that accrues from either expert or experimental knowledge of those archives. It was they who, having the material means and the necessary information at their disposal, chose to become competent in a number of musical styles, but also not to connect themselves to other available forms.[97] We are talking about the potential to construct intertexts with any number of innumerable musical texts circulating today. This bewildering possibility demands an increased consciousness about what to weave into this intertext, how to do it, and in whose company. This is both a unique opportunity and a demanding challenge: (1) this intertextuality obeys an unpredictable calculus of identities and differences; and (2) in the act of constituting the intertext, the actors themselves are constituted by it.

Hybridity, alas, is a capacious idea. It encompasses two general topologies, one shaking off the rigidity of Blades's own Latin Americanism and the other enabling the hybrid intermixes in each of the tracks that, combined, animate his heterogeneous project—and with it the unresolved tensions between restitution and appropriation, inclusion and exclusion. With *Mundo*, then, one can envision Blades's Latin American Latin Americanism taking both his restitutive and appropriational apparatus as well as the musicians' hybridizing creativities and competences to their nearly logical conclusion: the opening of Latin Americanism to encompass the world, quite literally.[98]

Ontopology/Audiotopia

Heterogeneity and hybridity, their multiplicative and synthetic aesthetics, and their traversal of the singular-universal relation all offer useful ways to assess and evaluate how Blades expands the reach of his Latin Americanism. In them, however, the relation of place to the sonic and musical goes troublingly without saying. *Mundo* broadens the Latin Americanist sonic field by reaching deeply into past times and widely across spaces. The resulting chronotope bespeaks equally of music's immense ability to world and of the power of those who have the means to thus world. This power to world should not be automatic cause for celebration: *Mundo* instantiates forms of temporal singularity and uniformity, particularly in the movement toward a kind of sonic planetary in which archaisms effectively suspend or circumvent the laborious processes of histories. Baroque and orientalist allusions in *Mundo* and *Tiempos* turn into timeless expressions of places. Blades renders these places with astonishing musical facility through sonic imprints that have an origin but no history. These sonic imprints are pressed nonetheless in the service of a planetary Latin Americanist *telos* grounded in the shared bio-evolutionary beginning of humankind. The deep history of this origin displaces the local histories that spurred on Latin Americanism in the first place. And yet those particular histories reach out for a world beyond Latin American borders. And so, the kernel of this chapter's argument comes into view: if *Tiempos* marks a *crossing under*, a traveling South and a return to Latin America, *Mundo* marks a *crossing beyond*, a remapping of the continent both as a site for global listening and as the locus of enunciation of this capacity.

Understanding this "beyond" compels two final analytics: ontopology and audiotopia. An ontology tethered to place (*topos*), an ontopology, grounds Blades's move "beyond." The sonic is conceived, constructed, and valued on the basis of a relation to *topos*: "By *ontopology* we mean an axiomatics linking indissociably the ontological value of present-being to its *situation*, to the stable and presentable determination of a locality, the *topos* of territory, native soil, city, body in general."[99] This entails first, that cardinality—the capacity for understanding and knowing one's spatial position—defines our being by situatedness and confirmed by one's self-presence to that situatedness. Second, however natural the link between cardinality and being may be posited, ontology demands sustenance. Two sets of tensions emerge out of the dis-placements, replacements of Blades's move "beyond": (1) between the sedentarism with which he grounds genres and the musical nomadism they encourage; and (2) between the regulating ideals of representational adequacy and genre singularity as a means to achieve such adequacy, on the one hand, and the empirical density of the musical practices of Éditus, on the other. Crossing beyond remains ensnared in these tensions.

Politically, ontopology is axiomatic. It has no essential relation of being to place, no intrinsic unassailable truth to the logic of propriety that subtends that relation, and no transhistorically binding force to guarantee its permanence. It demands cultivation. One only needs to note the constant effort needed to tie neighborhood to nation, *oikos* to *polis*, and self to body, to sense ontopology's demands. Blades's relocation of creative addresses to various senses of "Latin America" exemplifies these demands. Such precariousness turns the permanence of ontopological links into arduous processes of identity reproduction and difference maintenance. We see this in the establishment of figures of the outside, but also in the latent threat of dislocation and displacement that supplements location and placement. Locality may be materially grounded and intuitively privileged by a phenomenology of everyday situatedness within a more or less demarcated territorial *ambitus* and a socio-affective *habitus*. But locality, in modernity, is constituted, in Arjun Appadurai's words, "as series of links between the sense of social immediacy, the technologies of interactivity, and the relativity of contexts."[100] Thus, ontopology invites cathecting locality to somewhere beyond, compelling homologies between an actual *topos* and a virtual one. These homologies produce experiences of contact in an increasingly delocalized world. From this perspective, globalization constitutes as much a historically bound process of cultural, economic, and political character as it does an episode in the long history of ontopological mediations of local/global relations. Ontopology is an axiom with real consequences.

The coming together of ontopology with musicking's materiality reconfigures creative, cognitive, corporeal, and affective possibilities. Toward the end of the long twentieth century, musicians and listeners became ever more conscious of how they choose to enact and rearticulate relations of music to place.[101] Ontopology, I argue, serves as a constitutive logic and affective force for such choices. These relations do not entail only a radical ontological heterogeneity (as I argued happened with Blades's millennial projects) but also their virtualization. Enter audiotopia. Couched in late twentieth-century US cultural studies' adaptation of postmodern slogans (e.g., "shifting geographies, crossed borders, and transnational imaginings")[102] and advanced as both interpretive grid and resource for mobility and identitarian flexibility as a political praxis afforded by musical sound, "audiotopia" provides an analytic for this virtualization: "the space within and produced by a musical element that offers the listener and/or the musician new maps for re-imagining the present social world."[103] Audiotopia is rooted in the logic of *topos* (place and space are considered to be cognitively and affectively equivalent) but pressed into the service of uprooting any and all *topoi* established by authority, be it nation, culture, or geography: "audiotopia . . . are both sonic and social spaces where disparate identity-formations, cultures, *and* geographies historically kept apart and mapped separately are allowed to interact with each other as well as enter into relationships whose consequences for cultural identification are never predetermined."[104] Blades's projects could be mapped as efforts to audio-topologically deterritorialize previous Latin Americanisms through the traversal of new pathways of sonic circulation. But, as is often remarked, similarly to hybridization and heterogeneity, any and all counter-hegemonic deterritorialization all too often entails a hegemonic reterritorialization.[105] His ontological commitment underwrites such reterritorialization.

Ontopology and audiotopia pair up like the real and the virtual. While the real contains today much which is virtual, neither domain can be unduly privileged without considering mobility. For example, although music is particularly effective to create senses of place and "space . . . that we can inhabit," there must be a place in this space for critique of the transnational division of labor in Blades's projects, which enables those projects while at the same time relying on the more sedentary existence of the Costa Rican musicians relative to the nomadism of Blades himself or the mobility of the US-based musicians (in *Mundo*).[106] Any interculturalist optimism that music may generate cannot erase existing material inequalities across various *topoi*, nor can it smooth out differences that go hand in hand with those inequalities or ensure that communication does not misfire. In the end, too, ontopology is not merely a tool for deconstruction of audiotopia's allure or of the call that place makes of people or of their heeding this call: differences and inequalities remain *situated*, particularly when those sites are mobilized through sonic circulation and aural connectivity, and their effects remain material.

Blades's millennial projects juxtapose the materiality of ontopology to the virtuality of audiotopia. This is the aporetic conclusion of his Latin American Latin Americanism, which strives to move beyond the dynamics of regional representation while maintaining the unalienable right, the foundational impulse to speak from, of, and for a region.

WHAT POLITICS?

Tiempos and *Mundo* instantiate two types of listening, cartographic and planetary, respectively. One might say that *Tiempos* does not recognize how a politics of representation based in musical genre reinscribes taxonomies of cartographic hearing that are themselves constitutive of Latin Americanist representation. Such mapping is a central mechanism of colonial and imperial representation.[107] By "crossing beyond" this mapping, *Mundo*'s planetary Latin Americanism brackets off the grids of geopolitical localization that compose the globe or what Gayatri Spivak calls "that abstract ball covered in latitudes and longitudes, cut by virtual lines, on the equator and the tropics and so on."[108] "Crossing beyond" might constitute a form of restitution, provided one shifts the focus from musical genres to relations among people, and in a way the same can be said of "crossing under." As Spivak puts it, nobody lives on the globe, but we all inhabit the planet. However, the planet cannot be represented as an "undivided 'natural' space," an abstraction that too "can work in the interest of . . . globalization"; it is an "underived intuition," meaning that it does not offer a priori models for its total cognition.[109] Unlike *Tiempos*'s cartographic Latin Americanism, *Mundo*'s planetary-scale sonic Latin Americanism poses formidable challenges to representation and its politics.

Mundo's planetary politics is complicated by its effort to enunciate a Latin Americanism beyond Latin America. In transcending previously existing signification boundaries, *Mundo*'s planetarity produces an "empty signifier."[110] As Laclau explains, in a system of signification (e.g., "Latin American musical genres"), each element has an identity and a positive value insofar as it is different from other elements. Within that system "*chacarera*" is different from "*son*," "*son*" different from "*baião*," and so on. But in order to signify "Latin American feeling" as a whole, each difference between elements in the system must be considered equivalent. The system's elements are thus split between the logics of difference and equivalence that guarantee signification. Not only that, the system requires exclusions that both delimit it as a system and whose own elements lie beyond its range of signification. Those limits (and the beyond they demarcate) cannot be signified from within the system using its terms. This is important for the analysis of the possibility of systems (in the plural), for example Latin American Latin Americanism, Latino Latin Americanism, or Planetarity. Here, the latter two cannot be signified using elements from the first, unless the former's structure of signification is subverted. How? By erasing the structure of difference in favor of the structure of equivalence across systems: the differential relation between Latin American Latin Americanism, Latino Latin Americanism, and Planetarity becomes a series of equivalent differences, which is to say no differences at all. What were former exclusions in the form of "pure negativity" (i.e., the ignorance of the system of signification "Latin America" by "American Latins," as Blades referred to 1970s immigrant and migrant Latino communities in New York City) or in the form of "pure being"[111] (i.e., something beyond the limits of the system of signification, as for instance a wordliness thought to be inaccessible to Latin American modernity) become part of a total system of signification: "Planet," "*Mundo*," "cultural integration," or "worldwide genetic cross-relations."

These totalizing signifiers are "empty signifiers," signifiers with no attached signifieds. These aren't signifiers that can be attached to signifieds according to different contexts (equivocal or floating signifiers) or that are not fixed (ambiguous signifiers). Nor is it the case that these empty signifiers are of no use whatsoever to signification processes. In fact, they are fundamental to the struggles over the politics of signification. They introduce a cornerstone of politics, namely that in the face of inequalities in distribution of resources and power differentials that maintain those inequalities there are things that must be demanded precisely because they are now unavailable. As part of a political demand, then, a project of total integration such as *Mundo*'s is a symptom of the necessary insufficiency of sonic distribution as it currently exists. As a demand the "beyond" is disquieting, unfamiliar, out of reach. Because of that, it is grounds for contention. In contrast, as a political realization the "beyond" assumes the form of a totality and embraces yet another transcendental figuration—the fundamental unity of all sonic cultures across the world. A politics of "beyond" ends up as a politics of self-fulfillment, one that believes to have reached its transcendental goal and thus spells the end of politics.

We reach a place that offers no vantage point from which to determine what the terrain traversed in crossing beyond has been, or to survey the space it now occupies. We reach a moment in which there is no future. *Mundo's* sonic planetarity, like all totalizations, becomes an immanence attending to musicking. Its location becomes a place "outside measure (the immeasurable)" with a value "beyond measure (the virtual)."[112] A fulfilled empty signifier is not just empty, it is also blind (or, in our case, deaf) to all limits. It leaves no room for further demands, for further desires and the possibility of struggling to satisfy them. For all its promises of boundlessness, the beyond, it might seem, becomes a dead end. What then? Can a politics of encounter suffice? Or must musical Latin Americanisms, as Blades enacted them from the 1970s until the turn of the century, come to an end?

Conclusion

There is much to admire in the unrelenting creativity and enduring will to aurality of Blades's millennial projects. Their significant political wagers include the displacement of locus of enunciation, democratization of participation and agency by others, and questioning the ossification of musical Latin Americanisms. And yet, despite their emphasis on heterogeneity, exclusions remain: of indigenous voices, of women, of the body by the attenuation of dance-oriented music, and notably of Afro-Latin agency at a time when Afro-Latin movements in Latin America were gaining momentum. There is a sense of loss throughout. Blades's projects emanate from a particular socioeconomic stratum: the intellectual, mostly creole, and metropolitan Latin American middle class. Besieged from above by neoliberal policies benefiting the creole elite and from below by social movements making demands of the society as a whole, this stratum experiences the disintegration of the "idea of Latin America" as a loss of a sense of belonging and identity. And there are the promises of heterogeneity. If, in Adorno's words, "as the heterogeneous collides with its limit it exceeds itself," then Blades's commitment to heterogeneity pushes his Latin Americanist representation to impossible limits.[113]

Blades remains committed to *representation as politics,* an idea based on ontopology confronting an increasingly fugitive and nomadic music whose powers to effectively anchor sounds and rhythms to places and spaces became attenuated. Éditus might have been partaking in a *politics of encounters* based on alliances that may recognize conflict but also forge participatory solidarities and occasions for integration. Encounters speak to a "politics of space that could put the local or the process that establishes locality to work, not as a fixed point or as a familiar territory, but rather as the mobile site of tactical articulations of the relation between contextual situations, code mediations, and discursive positions."[114] Non-totalizing, modest, and open-ended, a politics of encounters do not necessarily translate into the transcendental figurations at play in appropriation and restitution, and in heterogeneity and hybridity.

Much of what I said about the passage from homogeneity through heterogeneity and hybridization could be rephrased in temporal terms. By rearticulating Latin American tradition to a musically innovative project, Éditus might engage the engine of a Latin American modernity for which what is at stake is "more a question of establishing new relationships with tradition than surpassing it."[115] They equally might seem to conjugate a future-oriented re-traditionalization, in Beck's argument, which, on the basis of the analysis of temporal multiplying singularities offered earlier, poses as many questions as it gives answers. The intersection of Latin Americanism with Latin America propagates temporal syncopations. The temporality of sonic interventions constitutes at once a destabilization of their political potential and the impetus for their constant reformulation. This destabilization and the corollary impetus for renewal are a mark of their fugitive political agency and momentary interpretive force, a mark embodied, in the terms I conceptualize syncopation, in the point of encounter and collision of their syncopation that reveals an unthought at the heart of the possibility for encounter. Syncopation marks immigrant imaginaries, itineraries of migration, and returning, crossing over, crossing under, and crossing beyond. For these, as well as for the analytics introduced in this chapter (heterogeneity; hybridization; crossing over/under/beyond), time remains out of joint. The shift toward intersecting salsa's earlier Latino Latin Americanism with Latin America adumbrates an excess of possibilities for a future that, like the present, can only be thought of as a future imperfect. In that future, a new "beyond" might appear.

An ethos of search marks Blades's millennial projects that resonate another contemporary concern for Latin Americanism, namely, Latin Americans' search for a place in the new century.[116] This search seeks to resolve a tension between place and time by locating a home in time, in this new century.[117] But, like the location of the collision of syncopation, this home in time feels like a displacement, not a resolution to the aporias of Latin American multi-temporality: this home in time is dispersed throughout the world, in *Mundo*. Perhaps we hear in Blades's musical Latin American Latin Americanisms the limits of any generalized knowledge of and relation to "Latin America." We may hear in them the nagging tone of an excess that neither crossing under nor beyond can quite quell.

Next, we encounter a related but wholly different phenomenon: the rise of Colombian-born Shakira to global superstardom. Any excess that the musical genres and global reach of *Mundo* might have sounded as the music poured over hemispheric borders will be rendered into a cosmopolitanism.

3 ⁎ Shakira's Cosmopolitanisms

Shakira, universal Colombian.

Reydeltiempo, comment on "Así fue el concierto
de Shakira," Casa Editorial *El Tiempo*[1]

Capital is becoming more and more cosmopolitan.

John Stuart Mill, *Principles of Political Economy*

Self. "People know me and love me all over the world, and that makes
me feel like a citizen of the entire planet." Thus affirmed Shakira, the
Colombian singer-songwriter and pop superstar in a 2003 interview.[2] She
has expressed interest in learning about the places she visits on tour and
reading up on local histories. Her knowledge of multiple languages—
English, Italian, French, Portuguese, and Catalan—is well known. In
2007, news came that she had taken a summer course on the "History of
Western Civilization" at the University of California, Los Angeles.[3] Both as
an expression of her self's constitution as an open individual with a will
to connect outwardly to the world (i.e., Shakira Isabel Mebarak Ripoli,
born in Barranquilla, Colombia, February 2, 1977) and as a global media
persona and brand ("Shakira"), such expressions of worldliness signal an
interrelation between sentiment, subjectivity, and commerce. They blur
distinctions that attend formations of the self, individual, persona, as well
as the various characters she embodies in songs, live performances, and
videos. Biographer Katherine Krohn writes that "[Shakira] is also passionate about her humanitarian causes to help people. She cares about the
world." Krohn highlights the Colombian's work as a goodwill ambassador
for UNICEF (the youngest ever appointed to this position); as a fundraiser
for the Association for Latin American Solidarity (ALAS), which imple-
ments integrated early childhood public policies; and the foundation she
began, Pies Descalzos (Barefeet), to support children's—especially young
girls'—education in her hometown. One glimpses the breathless pace at
which the singer traverses various spheres in contemporary global space,

exercising several forms of authority subtended by her status as pop superstar.[4]

City. On November 15, 2006, the people of Barranquilla—a city of about two million on Colombia's Atlantic coast—eagerly awaited its most famous citizen's triumphal return to the stage. The city was one of only three included in the Colombian leg of the singer's world tour in support of *Fijación Oral Volume 1* and *Oral Fixation Volume 2*, a two-volume bilingual album that had by then sold over twelve million copies worldwide.[5] Hours before the concert, the city had unveiled a sixteen-foot, six-ton statue of the performer: clad in adorned jeans, guitar in hand, it was redolent of her *rockera* (female rocker) style from around 1995. Built with Colombian iron but designed and made in Germany by sculptor Dieter Patt (a wealthy fan who donated the piece), the monument bears an aspirational inscription by Shakira herself: "when you look at me, think that you too can accomplish what you set out to do" (*"Cuando me mires, piensa que tú también puedes lograr lo que te propongas"*). "What you can do," indeed: two weeks prior, she had won an unprecedented five awards at the Latin Grammy Awards ceremony. Upon returning home, she reportedly declared, "Barranquilla is the large breast that fed and nurtured me as a human being, a woman and an artist. Returning is a chance to be with all the people from whom I learned and to pay homage to my roots."[6]

As the inaugural host city to the Latin American portion of Shakira's world tour, Barranquilla got to play its once undisputed role as the port of entry of worldly cultural trends to Colombia. This time, in 2006, the world came in the form and sound of a native daughter, but with a crucial difference: Barranquilleros felt that they had somehow, through her music, shaped the contemporary world.[7] Everyone around the world, it seemed, was listening to Shakira's music, to her voice and her songs.[8]

Although Barranquilla is today ranked as the fourth most important Colombian city, the city had long thought of itself as its most cosmopolitan metropolis. For one, it had a well-documented record of hospitality to musical trends arriving from abroad. As the largest maritime port on the Atlantic coast and the main gateway to the country's interior until the early twentieth century, the city had been first to experience the impact of record players in the 1910s.[9] Gramophone companies such as Victor, Columbia, and Brunswick all had agents in the city. Cuban, Argentine, Mexican, and US music was widely consumed by Barranquilla's middle and upper classes throughout the 1920s into the midcentury.[10] Peter Wade reports a Jazz Band Barranquilla in 1927, with a repertoire of "foxtrot, pasodoble, tango, danza, waltz, and pasillo."[11] Local musicians traveled overseas to record. The pianist Angel María Camacho y Cano recorded in New York City for Brunswick in 1929, and in 1930 with Columbia; his music would be marketed back in Colombia as "music that is genuinely ours."[12] Still, all this music was being produced, marketed, and distributed alongside other international Latin American hits. And it could be taken as being "genuine" or not, or something in between. All the same, it circulated and was consumed, in the broadest sense of the word.

Country. Worldly musical forms had long been inscribed in the sound of the Colombian state and nation. In 1887, one Oreste Sindici (1828–1904), an Italian-born musician living in Colombia—where he arrived in 1862 and then settled after the small opera troupe that brought him to the tropics disbanded in 1865—would set to music a poem of then president Rafael Núñez, a native from the Caribbean coastal city of Cartagena (some 133 kilometers south of Barranquilla). Sindici's setting had the confident stride of martial music and the appealing air of the lighter Italian operatic fare then in fashion, a style that might reasonably be called an international lingua franca for anthems across the Americas during the post-independence period.[13] Holding it all together was the formal organization of the decidedly European musical logic of tonality.

By 1890 Sindici's setting had been heard in official government gatherings in Rome, Mexico City, Caracas, Curaçao, and Lima. New York City was the site of its initial 1910 recording; just four years later, when recording was virtually nonexistent in the country, another version was recorded in Bogotá. Although nothing is known of the dissemination and audience reception of these recordings, the relatively early date for inscribing this music might reflect how the 1910s were a decade of accelerated concentration of mass media enterprises. In 1920, the Colombian Congress officially decreed Sindici's setting as the national anthem, "¡Oh Gloria Inmarcesible!" (Oh, Indestructible Glory!).

In some sense, the Colombian anthem found its way home from abroad. At the same time, it made itself at home in the world of anthems, for local lore held it to be among the two most beautiful national anthems ever written, second only to "La Marseillaise." Never mind that Núñez's Spanish prosody fit somewhat uncomfortably into the phraseology of Sindici's operatic *verismo* chorus; it mattered more that citizens came to think that it belonged properly in a worldwide sonic community of anthems as the nation's proper and unique sonorous symbol. For decades heard nightly at the beginning and end of national radio and television broadcasts, the anthem would become ingrained in millions of casual listeners and viewers, becoming a small but persistent sonic element of their everyday sonic life as Colombians.[14]

World. In a broad consideration of Latin American musical cosmopolitanism, Thomas Turino proposes that national anthems, in which "the best of local traditional culture combined with the best of the foreign and the modern, that is cosmopolitan culture," create "iconicity with other nation-states."[15] In this account, modernity originates abroad, and cosmopolitanism—"cosmopolitan culture"—expresses a kind of centrifugal movement of the domestic out to the foreign, of the nation to the world of nations, abetted by national elites seeking to be and feel part of that wider world. That Núñez was the architect of the modern constitution of the Colombian republic only solidified the anthem as a musical emblem of the shift from postcolonial nation to fully independent nation-state.[16]

Modernity, nationalism, and cosmopolitanism were of a piece at Colombia's inception. And in the late nineteenth century, for local elites and others like traveling musicians, relations among these three forces were grounded in Colombians' sense of what was local and what wasn't. This sense was a condition for an equally strong sense that the local could partake in what wasn't, a sense of being at home in the world and with the world at home. In the end, the world depended equally on a dialectic in which the nations it spawned (i.e., modernity, in conjunction with capitalism as its material sphere and cosmopolitanism as its "affective" sphere) needed to validate it. For the time being, the world remained within the sphere of a modernity not yet at home in a country like Colombia.

I exaggerate, of course, but only a little. Colombian elites (economic, intellectual, literary, political) had long felt at home abroad. Consider José María Torres Caicedo (1830–1889), the Francophile Colombian diplomat who first proposed the expression "Latin America," while residing in Paris, where he died.[17] Or consider Baldomero Sanín Cano (1861–1957), the Colombian critic who was "the author of the most systematic cosmopolitan discourse on the literatures of the world and the relation that Latin American and Spanish writers should establish with them."[18]

Music from abroad being heard *in* the nation and *as* the nation, national music being recorded abroad *before* it becomes a State's music, national music *heard* abroad—although of unique trajectories and outcomes and fueled by different cultural, economic, and geopolitical contingencies and needs, such sonic circulations somehow fall within the analytics of cosmopolitanism. Cosmopolitanism may be broadly understood to name the ongoing expansion of the local's ambitus and the corollary compression of the global. On first impression, in its capacious signification, cosmopolitanism appears to account for the many possible, imaginable, and actual relations between some corporate polity and whatever that polity considers to be "the world at large." That polity is not—cannot be—static, and neither are notions and lived perceptions of what that "world" is.

Echoing a common criticism, Ackbar Abbas observes that "in the modern era, which corresponds to the economic and political dominance of Western nations, cosmopolitanism by and large meant being versed in Western ways, and the vision of 'one world' culture was only a sometimes unconscious, sometimes unconscionable, euphemism for 'First World' culture."[19] Cosmopolitanism observes directions: the center demands that the world be made in its image, what we might call "hegemonic cosmopolitanism," the periphery wishes recognition and participation in the "world," what Abbas calls "cosmopolitanism of dependency," but its people desire and practice a certain openness to the outside, what Abbas calls "cosmopolitanism of extraterritoriality."[20] Most everyone in nineteenth-century Colombia had little or no access to the means needed to feel part of that "World," let alone to be inserted into its emergent cosmopolitan networks. Turn-of-the-century dynamics, including increasing foreign capital investment, would only contribute to the population's growing contact with a world already ever more present in Colombia's territories. There, as in other Latin American nations, a rapidly growing merchant class would gain access to goods, information, and sensibilities developed elsewhere; merchants were themselves key disseminators of such things via commerce. And the coastal region of Colombia's north, earlier than the rest of the country, would play a central role in these developments.[21] Music and the phonographic industry would mediate the circulation, transmission, adoption, and transformation of various forms of individual and collective play, embodiment, knowledge, and experimentation.[22] A century later, Shakira's triumphal return home marked a particularly intense expression of this mediation, except that she was now herself medium *and* mediation of a world long heard at home, a world that now heard that home in the figure of the singer, songwriter, and brand.

The phenomena that I elaborate in this chapter under the rubric of "cosmopolitanisms" involve multiple actors unevenly distributed across an open network of heterogeneous elements irreducible to the idea or practice of a creative mixture of local and imported elements.[23] In the case of the Colombian national anthem, this network included: the transit of knowledge and creative labor in the form of Sindici's musical training at the Rome Conservatory; the efforts by an amateur Colombian comedian, José Domingo Torres, in persuading Sindici to set Núñez's middling poetic work; Nuñez's own lettered condition steeped in Western literary and poetic traditions; technologies of musical notation and inscription, including phonography; the metropolitan environment and cosmopolitan aspirations of Colombian civil, ecclesiastic, military, and diplomatic sectors at the turn of the century; the circulation of capital throughout the

Americas; and the development of mass media. What we may call creative cosmopolitanism inflected political life.

Shakira's own participation in such a network constitutes an expression of its continued presence, proliferation, and radical transformation in advanced capitalism; it is the subject of this chapter.[24] She too partakes of an important movement in the circulation of music throughout the long twentieth century—namely, the cosmopolitan achievements of tango and samba, which, as Florencia Garramuño argues, traveled abroad before their return home as celebrated and sanctioned national musics, or the various traversals promoted by the Cuban and Mexican musical industries such as rhumba, cha-cha-cha, and mambo. Similarly, Laura Putnam's insightful analysis of the cosmopolitan lives of workers in the circum-Caribbean during the "jazz age" fits this description.[25] Fernando Ortiz's boast in the 1960s about the "cosmopolitan triumph of the Cuban drum" forms part of a related cosmopolitan sphere, echoing Alejo Carpentier's declaration two decades earlier that "the island of Cuba had an ability to create music with its own distinctive form that from the earliest times found an extraordinary success abroad."[26] "Cuban music . . . covers the planet," Carpentier claimed; "it is listened to in Moscow as in Mexico, in Paris, as in Egypt."[27] This network would include the US.

In this chapter, Latin America syncs with the US and syncopation might seem to fade out in the cosmopolitanism of late capitalism and, indeed, neoliberalism. We have a musical complex, Shakira's, that—partly initiated by shifts in the mass consumption and firm embrace of rock and pop in Latin America toward the end of the twentieth century and partly spurred by the elaboration of local musical resources—finds its way into the world as being both of the world and of a place that must place itself under erasure while retaining the potential to be visible and audible to that world.[28] Attaining a cosmopolitan Latin Americanism entails a paradox—namely, that Latin America be both less and more of what it presumably has been. Here, the contradictions of particular universals and universal particulars—keystones for various logics of modernity, globalization, transnationalism, and cosmopolitanism—become affectively powerful, at once palpable and elusive. From the North, these logics become necessary but often disquieting keywords, for they challenge self-normative understandings of what the US might be and do in the world. "Shakira" and Shakira, I argue, embody this paradox and its networks, often rendering her sense of cosmopolitanism as a cosmopolitics. Here's how Shakira responds to the question of political participation: "this does not mean to occupy a political job but instead the need every citizen has to participate in the destiny of its nation, of the world, of the polis. But the polis has overgrown us and not only Barranquilla or

Colombia: for everyone it is the world, and we should worry about the destiny of humankind, where ecology is going, what is going to happen to the 75 million children who do not receive any education in so many places in the world."[29]

Home, World

The year 1999 was a signal moment for "Latin American music"; the Latin American market became the recording industry's fastest-growing sector.[30] In this year, a number of artists of Latino and/or Caribbean background achieved mainstream success in the US pop music scene, a phenomenon the media dubbed the "Latin Explosion."[31] Few anticipated at the time that the most celebrated and successful popular music figure of the new millennium, not just in the US but also worldwide, would be Shakira, the Colombian-born singer, then regarded as an up-and-coming figure but marginal to the "Explosion." Instead, the "Explosion" celebrated Puerto Rican idol Ricky Martin and Nuyoricans Jennifer Lopez and Marc Anthony—performers closer to the metropolitan center than was the new immigrant.

Following the 2001 release of her first English-language album, *Laundry Service*, Jennifer Lopez said, "Shakira is Colombia." Mexican Paulina Rubio—who herself would be part of concerted but ultimately failed efforts to crossover to the US English-speaking market—prognosticated that "Shakira will be the first truly Latin American artist to make a crossover to the market." Christina Aguilera praised the Colombian as being "different" and "unique," and was impressed by her full assimilation of rock despite being Latin American; the US-born Aguilera is herself half-Ecuadorian, and efforts were made to exploit this connection.[32]

Outside of music circles, the two globally best-known Colombian artists spoke. Nobel Prize winner Gabriel García Márquez (long a resident of Mexico), an early and vocal admirer, affirmed portentously that "nothing that could be said or not said about Shakira will be able to alter the direction of a great and unstoppable artist." The painter and sculptor Fernando Botero delighted that "I am fortunate to be in Shakira's words and to be one among millions of Colombians who, thanks to each one of her songs, are in the words of the rest of the world. More Grammy and Billboard awards will come, and, what is more important, the heartfelt applause of all those who admire you [Shakira]."[33] For Colombian president Andrés Pastrana (1998–2002), Shakira represented an emblem of "a new national era," and he later festooned her with the title of "national goodwill ambassador."[34]

Back in the US, as the original enthusiasm about the "Latin Explosion" tapered off throughout 2000, increasing references to Shakira in US media identified her as an intriguing Latin American Alanis Morrissette, given the Colombian's public appearance at the time (long dark hair, relatively unadorned after the fashion of alternative rockers) and musical style (pop-rock combining soft acoustic passages with bombastic rock, wide vocal range, assertive voice, and the use of distinctive yodel-like shadings).[35] By 2006 Rubio's, García Márquez's, and Botero's forecasts had long become reality. Comparisons had stopped; suddenly Shakira was her own style.

As table 3.1 shows, with 30 million records sold, her statistics were comparable to those of a selected group of pop superstars, none of them "Latin."[36] Indeed, as table 3.2 summarizes, by the end of summer 2006, the singer had established notable benchmarks. Potent symbolic accomplishments bolstered the hard figures that delighted industry executives and producers. She accrued a number of momentous performances: at the World Cup finals in Berlin (July 2006); in concert before the Giza pyramids in Egypt; at a free concert in Mexico City's El Zócalo (May 2007) that broke all attendance records; headlining the German concert during

Table 3.1. Shakira's global album sales compared to those of contemporary stars

Artist	Individual world album sales (1993–2006)	Total world album sales (through 2006)
Shakira	*Pies Descalzos* (1996): 3,700,000 *¿Dónde Están los Ladrones?* (1998): 4,380,000 *MTV Unplugged* (2000): 1,780,000 *Laundry Service* (2001): 12,630,000 *Fijación Oral, Vol. 1* (2005): 3,590,000 *Oral Fixation, Vol. 2* (2005): 5,000,000	31,080,000
Christina Aguilera	*Christina Aguilera* (1999): 12,800,000 *Mi Reflejo* (2000): 1,500,000 *My Kind of Christmas* (2000): 1,400,000 *Stripped* (2002): 9,550,000 *Back to Basics* (2006): 4,000,000	29,250,000
Marc Anthony	*Otra Nota* (1993): 300,000 *Todo a Su Tiempo* (1995): 800,000 *Contra la Corriente* (1997): 400,000 *Marc Anthony* (1999): 3,000,000* *Libre* (2001): 500,000* *Mended* (2002): 500,000* *Amar Sin Mentiras* (2004): 200,000* *Valió la Pena* (2004): 200,000*	5,900,000

*Denotes numbers for US sales only

Table 3.2. Benchmarks in Shakira's career

Date	Accomplishment
August 1996	*Pies Descalzos* certified Platinum in Venezuela, Peru, Chile, Mexico, and Central America, certified 5× Platinum in Colombia
April 1997	*Pies Descalzos* receives RIAA Gold Certification in the United States
September 1998	*¿Dónde Están los Ladrones?* is released, holds number 1 spot on the US Billboard Latin chart for 11 weeks
January 1999	First Grammy nomination, for *¿Dónde Están los Ladrones?* (Best Latin Rock, Urban or Alternative Album)
December 1999	*Pies Descalzos* and *¿Dónde Están los Ladrones?* receive RIAA Platinum Certification
February 2001	First Grammy win, for *MTV Unplugged* (Best Latin Pop Album)
December 2001	*Laundry Service* hits number 3 on the Billboard 200 chart, while the single "Wherever, Whenever" reaches number 6 on the Billboard Hot 100
June 2005	*Fijación Oral, Vol. 1* has highest-selling debut for a Spanish-language album in the United States, hits number 4 on the Billboard 200
August 2005	First artist to perform in Spanish at the MTV Music Awards
February 2006	Wins second Grammy for *Fijación Oral, Vol. 1* (Best Latin Rock, Urban, or Alternative Album), performs with Aerosmith on ceremony telecast
June 2006	Single "Hips Don't Lie" tops the Billboard Hot 100
June/July 2006	Performs at opening ceremony and before final game of World Cup in Berlin, Germany
December 2006	"Hips Don't Lie" becomes top-selling single in Europe for 2006
March 2007	Performs for 100,000 at the Pyramids at Giza in Egypt
May 2007	Performs for 210,000 in Mexico City's Zócalo
July 2007	Headlines Live Earth climate change benefit concert in Hamburg, Germany

Live Earth, the set of climate change awareness concerts worldwide (July 2007); her World Cup performance in South Africa (2010), where her "Waka Waka (This Time for Africa)" served as the official musical theme of the world's largest sporting event; headlining the 2014 World Cup in Brazil. Such performances left little doubt about the reach and scale of the Colombian's popularity.

Even seemingly "distant" achievements such as becoming number one in Thailand or Korea were registered with gleeful pride in the Colombian general press—as if unaccustomed to such visibility by a Colombian—and in industry press releases in the US—as if trying to make sense of such unprecedented crossover success. Arguably, and no doubt under the aegis of the long arm of a globalized culture industry, no Colombian, let alone a

Colombian woman, had ever reached such degree of audibility, visibility, and recognition. In the eyes of many she had far surpassed lettered luminaries García Márquez and Botero on the world stage.[37]

Colombian news media had closely tracked the singer's fortunes since her work first appeared in the world market in 1995 with *Pies Descalzos*, a hit in Latin America and Spain, number one in eight countries, and, despite minimal promotion, platinum in the US. The staggering achievements of a decade later became regular and frequent front-page news as well as fodder for intense discussion locally about what it all could mean. In the midst of the excitement, it appeared as if the scale of Shakira's success presented an interpretive challenge at home. Did she represent a unique opportunity to boost the country's tarnished image abroad, or, as a form of collateral damage, was there a threat of being spectacularly reduced to images, sounds, and stories built around a pop mega-celebrity, marginalizing other equally deserving but far less popular figures in the arts and sciences? At a time when, as Ana María Ochoa Gautier notes, the sonic had emerged as the predominant sphere for Latin American identification and recognition in the world, with music displacing literature from that role, and promoting the formation of an "aural region,"[38] what did it mean for a Colombian woman singing in a pop-rock style and in Spanish and English to embody that emergence so iconically? In other words, what had she listened to and how, so that now she was listened to everywhere? Could this not be a form of seeking aural equality?

Some responses to Shakira's success tended to emphasize continuity between country and world. The move was expansive. Following Shakira's 2006 sweep of the Latin Grammy Awards, journalist Agustín Gurza commended the singer for her unique ability to simultaneously sustain her popularity in Latin America and overseas. Alejandro Sanz, the Spanish pop singer and duet partner with Shakira on the 2005 megahit "La Tortura," regarded her "greatness" as the ability to remain "very faithful" to her "roots"—the nature of which he did not detail—and to be "very innovative."[39] For Gurza and Sanz, these were positive developments, in line with a celebratory transnationality (Gurza) or a "rooted" practice of musical innovation (Sanz). For these commenters, hers was a smooth transition from Colombia to Latin America and from there to the world, most importantly, one that folded each one of these planes into the other without making any of them disappear.

The public sphere in Colombia, however, was more markedly contentious, even antagonistic. When it came to analyzing her music's nationalist dimension, responses were sharply pointed. Rupture of "traditional" Colombian indexes (linguistic, musical, sartorial, etc.) was interpreted either positively or negatively, but not in terms of continuity, let alone in terms of a sustained dialectic of continuity within change. Colombian journalist Eduardo Arias bluntly declared her "the most important Colombian popular artist in the last two decades," adding, in a barely disguised barb toward Colombian vallenato-pop and Tropipop star Carlos Vives, that she didn't need to wear typical garb or write patriotic lyrics in order to win over Colombian audiences.[40] Vives himself would later declare, in a bizarre critique of her Anglo-American rock and pop stylistic allegiances, that he wished Shakira were more attentive to the Magdalena River (Colombia's largest and the geo-cultural axis for a number of important folk music genres) and less to the Mississippi.[41] That Vives enunciated his Hispanist critique at the Congreso Internacional de la Lengua Española (International Congress of the Spanish Language)—attended, among others, by the king and queen of Spain—turned the issue toward a politics of monolingualism: singing in a language other than that of the former crown was tantamount to betraying Colombian identity.[42]

In 2006, it had been three years since Shakira last performed in Colombia. Her concerts there in November 2006, part of her world tour supporting *Fijación Oral Volume 1* and *Oral Fixation Volume 2*, stirred heightened expectations and feverish interest. Media reports fixated on the tour's enormous operation: an entourage of nearly eighty people, a private plane, and a moving logistic nightmare, even for a country by then accustomed to staging large-scale concerts and hosting pop and rock superstars since the 1990s. Widespread too were reports that despite such logistic complexity the star kept an air of simplicity about her, without the trappings of other visiting stars, most of whom routinely made impossible-to-meet demands about accommodations, security, and the like.

Audiences had their own ideas—and they should be considered a public, given the discursive networks they produced and the reflection of their understanding of the place of the nation in relation to the figure of "Shakira." As part of the intense public attention to the concerts, fans and detractors alike submitted copious comments to *El Tiempo*.[43] To illustrate the reactions' relative intensity, there were 253 comments sent to *El Tiempo* immediately after Shakira's concert in Bogotá (Nov. 17, 2006), compared to 110 comments when Gabriel García Marquez returned on May 30, 2007, to his hometown of Aracataca for the first time in twenty-five years.

Commenters' dominant concern was representation: Shakira served as an informal ambassador for Colombia, offering to the world an overwhelmingly positive image of the country. She offered proof that the country—mired as it had been by internal armed conflict, extreme violence, and social crises related to corruption and drug trafficking—could and indeed had produced a talent valued by millions worldwide. One commenter observed that, as an artist, Shakira must have been interested in other cultures, plus she did not choose which culture to be born into.[44] Another noted that Colombians have long been influenced by international music but remain fully Colombian (a textbook definition of cosmopolitanism in Turino's sense).[45]

A majority expressed pride in the accomplishments by a compatriot, often extending that pride to claims of Colombian creative singularity, peppered with occasional unfavorable comments on other Latin American female pop stars. Others listed the widely disseminated statistics of the singer's success abroad in order to counter critics of the singer's vocal style; if people outside the country could clearly appreciate her talent, the argument went, anybody not doing the same locally would be at best deaf, at worst unpatriotic. Included too were Colombian expatriates reporting their firsthand overseas accounts of how British, Dutch, Russian, or Spanish audiences, for example, were unconditionally won over by the singer. To some, only overseas could the most intense nationalist pride be felt in the wake of the country's largest migration wave in its history.[46] To others, the experience of being abroad meant that their first affiliation was with the country as a whole and only secondarily with the particular region where they came from—Colombia's divisive regionalism is constitutive to the nation, and the Caribbean Coast, where Shakira hails from, has long been considered to be the national antagonist of the Andean region where the capital lies. There too were a few readers from other Latin American countries who scaled out national pride to include the continent. The week of November 21, 2006, Shakira would go on to perform sold-out shows in Santiago de Chile (Nov. 21 and 22), Buenos Aires (Nov. 24 and 25), and Lima (Nov. 28). All across the printed media would dote on the singer, complimenting her at every stop.

Fewer commenters occupied a middle ground, adopting a more critical, albeit positive, interpretation while cautiously avoiding the projection of an individual onto a national totality. One wrote, "Yes, Shakira has ended up becoming an ambassador for Colombia before the entire world . . . but Shakira is neither Colombia nor is she who she is because of Colombia, Shakira is simply SHAKIRA, a Colombian artist who has reached the entire world because of her music."[47] Somebody else noted that it is a country's society as a whole that best represents it, not an individual citizen. To think otherwise, this reader pointed out, would reflect a needful anxiety over icons and would constitute a form of ineffectual fetishism. Those adopting this position, however, tended to reduce the singer's accomplishment to the purely musical, an aestheticization that left little room for other forms of mediation of her success.

And inevitably, there were detractors. Complaints were issued on nu-

merous accounts: that Shakira cannot sing; that her English is poor; that
even though she may sing in Spanish, she "thinks" in Lebanese; that she
develops her talent in foreign cultures and that even though she carries
the name of Colombia across the globe (the singer names Colombia in
virtually all her live performances), the culture she enacts in concert is
not Colombian;[48] that her rock-pop stylings reflect her succumbing to
North American tastes and industry pressures; that no matter how mixed
they may be with national flavors, those musical genres are not local; that
the pop elements in her music constitute a betrayal of her true roots as a
"rockera" (female rocker); that she confuses dancing for music making;
that she cannot represent true Colombian musical creativity; that she has
been transformed into a semi-exotic faux blonde in order to make images
of Latin Americans more palatable in the US and Europe; that in spite of
fabrications of personal simplicity and spontaneity by the press and industry, she spends a fortune on hair care—yes, $12,000 dollars a month
(35 million Colombian pesos)—and clothing (400 million pesos); and that
her own contributions to her foundation on behalf of uneducated children
in Colombia are not enough.

A particularly strong indictment read: "SHAKIRA, SHAKIRA, as CO-
LOMBIAN as her ARGENTINE accent . . . as HUMBLE as her mansion in
MIAMI . . . as PATRIOTIC as her ARABIC dance . . . c'mon WAKE UP . . .
it is not 'envy,' as all those furiously infatuated with her say, it is REAL-
ISM . . . not magical realism, just realism, plain and simple."[49] The charges
were factual. The singer's speech carried none of the distinct accent of
Colombia's Atlantic coast where she was born and grew up; instead, she
spoke with a light Argentine accent (the so-called Porteño accent, from
Buenos Aires), reflecting her then-long romantic relationship with the son
of Fernando de la Rúa, Argentina's disgraced president (1999–2001). The
singer's permanent residence was in the Bahamas, with residences in Miami, New York, Uruguay, and the Dominican Republic. Her belly dancing
routines originated from a widely publicized early interest in her father's
Lebanese culture; indeed, since the nineteenth century, communities with
roots in Lebanon have had a large presence across the area where she was
born. As another reader commented, "the Atlantic coast is a cosmopolitan
region, one that opens its doors to all its visitors with great pleasure." No
matter, for the scathing critic, Shakira's internationalism constituted a
problematic breach of the nation's proper boundaries.[50]

Supporters and detractors were generally not naïve about the economics of worldwide success. Many acknowledged the fundamental role of
the US-based recording multinationals and the culture industry. The cost
of concert tickets at home, on the other hand, caused serious concern.

With tickets going as high as $500,000 Colombian pesos (approximately US$229 or €172 at the time), higher than the cost of comparable seats in New York or London, many felt that such money was deserved by acts like U2 or the Rolling Stones, but not by a relative newcomer to the world stage. Many wondered why there were no subsidies to help defray ticket costs, since the artist would have known the expense for regular Colombian fans. Others countered that there was no reason why Shakira ought to charge less simply because she is a Colombian-born artist. To think so, they maintained, was to be trapped in a *"mentalidad de regalado"* (a mindset of self-worthlessness). One person went as far as thanking neoliberal, far-right Colombian president Álvaro Uribe Vélez (2002–2010) for fostering an economy that made it viable for concertgoers to afford such prices. (Another praised the president for making it safe for people to attend such large-scale events.)

Still others wondered if all the polemics weren't evidence of the continuing provincialism of a country still uncomfortable with success abroad or unaccustomed to a global-level concert life at home. In an unusual turn to the academic, a reader invoked Malcolm Deas, the noted Irish historian and Colombia specialist who, the reader summarized, "has concluded that the greatest evils besetting Colombians derive from our lack of a common objective, that we lack collective projects, as confirmed by the senseless comments of so many people in this forum." "If as Colombians we cannot celebrate or at least tolerate the success of an exemplar compatriot like Shakira," the reader continued, "nothing will be able to unite us." This reader addresses stigma, a major worry for Colombia's image abroad throughout the 1980s and 1990s: "Shakira satisfactorily fulfills the desire that we Colombians have to be seen from a different perspective in the world stage."[51] "Congratulations to Shakira for her patriotism and love for her homeland," wrote another; "overseas there are no regionalisms that create frictions [among us] . . . we all are COLOMBIANS . . . and if asked 'where are you from?' we answer 'COLOMBIANS.' What is most interesting about Colombia is the variety of people and cultures, that identity is what makes us different."[52]

As expressed in these diverging responses, nationalism was alive and well, but so was a sense of both a traditional internationalism and an impending transnationalism. These reflected cosmopolitanism's contradictory character, the modalities in which it exists, and the various spheres and pathways of connection and disconnection across which it is experienced. Cosmopolitanisms are uneven and unequal, and even more so in relation to the increasing globalization of the culture industry that made "Shakira."

BECOMING GLOBAL

None of the polemics accompanying Shakira's visit to Colombia could have perturbed industry executives in the US reeling from the excitement of one of the few unqualified business successes of 2005. Commenting on the decision to closely stagger the release of *Fijación Oral, Volume 1*, and *Oral Fixation, Volume 2*, Spanish- and English-language records, marketing vice president for Epic Records Lee Stimmel claimed that "We did not see audiences as if they were divided. . . . We said: this music is way too important and fantastic to be marginalized."[53] Stimmel was referring to the fact that the Spanish-language version of the record was released worldwide, not just in Spanish-speaking markets, as was done likewise with the English-language record. Epic president Steven Barnett had been more direct about the high expectations for Shakira's 2005 releases: "Sometimes with great artists you have to reinvent the way you do business. Often, record companies talk about global plans for a record. This is a global plan for two records." Ceci Kurzman, Stimmel's predecessor at Epic and Shakira's manager, had also affirmed before the 2006 windfall that "we're going to work both records completely around the world."[54]

In reality, the industry's strategy represented the culmination of a set of risky tactical decisions, beginning in 1999 with the recording of the singer's Spanish-language *MTV Unplugged* (released in 2000), to gradually introduce her to audiences broader than what industry reporters and analysts identified as her "fan base": at the time mainly Spanish-speaking Latin American and Iberian audiences. This experiment widened in 2001, with the release of her first English-language record, *Laundry Service*. Only four of thirteen tracks were sung in Spanish, including "Suerte," a version of the first single hit "Whenever, Wherever." Both versions appeared as part of MTV's regular rotation.

In what would become a standard line of action as well as a source of deep anxiety by media and recording industry executives, Tom Calderone, MTV's senior vice president of music and talent programming, commented that with such moves they sought to cross the artist over into English while "maintaining her heritage by playing the Spanish version"[55]—this despite the fact that the single had already held the top of Billboard's Hot Latin Tracks for five weeks. A surrogate for a marked division between Spanish- and English-speaking audiences in the eyes of recording executives and producers, the issue of bilingualism would occupy much of Shakira's media reception; bilingualism would worry a music industry struggling to comprehend rapid transformations in how audiences negotiated music's relation to language. Long the lingua franca of global pop, could English now be joined by Spanish?

In a much-publicized move, it was widely reported that the Colombian had mastered the English language in very little time, which to some made her "the first true major crossover into the English market by a Spanish-speaking artist."[56] Her penchant for mentioning Colombia in live performances, especially on national TV in the US, constituted an element that, as Epic Records president Polly Anthony said, "lends to the intrigue and the exotic nature of the whole campaign."[57]

This "whole campaign" consisted in mobilizing all divisions of Sony Music worldwide to create, in the industry's jargon, the "highest awareness level" for the bilingual release of *Fijación Oral 1, Volume 1*, and *Oral Fixation, Volume 2*. Sony Discos chair Oscar Llord revealed that his division's objective was to support Epic's initiative to release a two-language record by focusing on Shakira's Spanish fan base, meaning Spanish-speaking audiences in the US. Sony Music Latin America coordinated all efforts across Latin America, and Epic concentrated on the English-speaking market in the US. Meanwhile at Sony, TV, radio, and media executives from twenty-four countries gathered in Madrid, Spain, early in January 2002 to attend a "world showcase" by the Colombian, only the second one of its kind ever at the corporation. *Laundry Service* had been released in Spain (as *Servicio de Lavandería*) concurrently with the US release, selling 400,000 units in just ten weeks. According to Sony-Columbia managing director Raul Lopez, Shakira had an established fan base in Spain. Throughout February and March, the album would be released in staggered fashion in Canada, the UK, and the rest of the world. By July *Billboard* confirmed the album's "global smash" status, with three hit singles. By December, ten million copies had been sold, with four million in Europe alone. So great was the success that Julie Borchard, Sony Music Europe's senior vice president of marketing, would half-jokingly complain of having a hard time getting the singles off airplay so as to make room for other records. Throughout that month, Shakira had completed the European leg of her world tour, sponsored by Pepsi and Reebok. This would go on to constitute one of the most successful branding projects ever undertaken by the industry. The gamble had paid off—in two languages.

The unquestionable success of *Laundry Service* did not dissipate anxieties, especially among US executives, over alienating a core audience of Spanish speakers. However, in a rare recognition that there might have been ongoing changes in the way audiences related to pop artists, the president for touring at Clear Channel Entertainment, Arthur Fogel, noted that "music fans of the world and music fans of North America" were increasingly "allowing themselves to open up to different artists." Fogel would have known; Clear Channel, the largest radio broadcast monopoly in the US, was involved in promoting Shakira's tour there.[58] Nonetheless,

Fogel echoed a common concern within the music industry: "it's hard to move in a different direction and keep that fan base satisfied."[59]

Sustaining the successful business and musical structure of *Laundry Service* was a major challenge. After all, several of the same people behind Shakira's world campaign had famously failed to sustain the popularity of the original model—Ricky Martin's—for this scale of production. With diminishing sales across the board and shrinking budgets for production and promotion, by 2004 the industry's fears and hopes for "crossover" artists appeared to have reached an apex. Explanations abounded. "The Latin market, from radio to media to the public, feels abandoned; they feel betrayed," volunteered an anonymous executive, who added that "there are artists who do nothing with the Spanish media [when promoting an English album]. And everyone who made the artist into a star in the first place feels pushed aside."[60] Indeed, serving two masters, as journalist Leila Cobo from *Billboard* pointedly noted, was not just affectively complicated but prohibitively expensive and time consuming. For Miami-based music mogul Emilio Estefan, the chief engineer of Shakira's move to the US, the risk was as simple as having to double all costs (i.e., two recordings, two videos, two separate promotion campaigns), which, if done poorly—that is, allowing the core base to feel that efforts were not evenly distributed—could hurt the entire process.

In reality, the actual recording and promotion structure was not symmetrically arranged. Reflecting the binary logic behind the very idea of crossover, the business model had a two-tier structure that strictly exercised a division of labor across languages, so to speak. The mainstream label assumed costs, collecting sales revenues or assuming losses for English recordings, and the Latin affiliate did the same for Spanish recordings. For projects like *Laundry Service*, the mainstream label provided local subsidiaries with a budget to promote Spanish-language songs, but it did not share the profits with them. That structure would be challenged in 2005, as Epic planned the release of *Fijación Oral, Volume 1*, and *Oral Fixation, Volume 2*.

With simultaneous releases in one hundred countries, Epic took an enormous but calculated risk: first releasing the Spanish album, premiering its first single, "La Tortura," in a now-famous MTV video (without subtitles or an English-language counterpart and featuring a duet with Spanish singer Alejandro Sanz), simultaneously releasing that track to radio stations worldwide (using special digital technology to prevent copying), and embarking the singer first on promotional visits to Mexico, Argentina, Colombia, and Spain, and only then to England, Germany, and the US. Gone were concerns about language as a barrier in itself. As Helena Verellen, senior marketing director for Epic International, put it, "even in countries in Asia, where there is no Spanish market at all, there is potential to sell a Shakira album, whatever it is."[61] In the age of branding, marketing, and distribution synergies, Swedish customers of mobile phone company Three could download the video for "La Tortura," and Korean phone users of a particular provider would watch and hear the same video in a commercial for designer jeans. The goal? To set up in those places (and others) the then-upcoming release of the English album.

In light of 2006's successes, the singer's confident prescience in a 2001 statement seems all the more remarkable: "my Latin market is as important, or more [so], than others. It's not that I'm abandoning one territory for the other. On the contrary: I'm expanding."[62] Hers was not quite the same logic as that of the industry anxious about real or imagined differences across audiences and consumers, nor that of Colombian fans worried about her leaving the country behind. It was, however, the logic of the contemporary market, one that follows John Stuart Mill's observation over a century and a half earlier that "capital is becoming more cosmopolitan."[63] But combine this statement with the singer-songwriter's more humanistic claims to world citizenship and we have cosmopolitanism in one of its clearest forms. Perhaps, then, the Colombian fan that wrote "Shakira, universal Colombian" may have been on to something by essaying a pithy formulation for a complex phenomenon. The apparent paradox of a universal particular might well represent an effort to make sense of something for which there is neither a simple affective nor cognitive blueprint. What I wish to suggest is that the dialectic universal/particular in the fan's quip theorizes a practice—a set of actions, a mode of thinking, and a feeling—that is neither universal nor particular—or, more precisely, that is both universal and particular but in incommensurable ways. In order to better understand this relation of practice to theory, I will outline a genealogy of cosmopolitanism, tracing those strands that come together in the phenomenon "Shakira" and that, as affirmed by the public and the industry, she renders possible.

Cosmopolitanisms

Cosmopolitanism begins with an assumption: the preexistence of an all-encompassing domain that extends beyond any locality, the cosmos (Gr. *kosmos*, orderly arrangement). There follows an aspiration: because humans are *of* this domain and rightfully dwell *in* it, anyone can participate in it. But in the Greek context from which it arose, there is a particular form of communal and political organization with preexisting norms and filial practices that grounds this aspiration, the polis. As Hannah Arendt explains, the polis displaced previous forms of kinship, "the *phratria* and

the *phyle*," such that a properly defined citizen now belonged to "two orders of existence; and there is a distinction in his life between what is his
own (*idion*) and what is communal (*koinon*)."[64] The polis is fundamentally
relational. It introduces an expansive sense of political belonging: "the
polis . . . is the organization of the people as it arises out of acting and
speaking together, and its true space lies between people living together
for this purpose, no matter where they happen to be."[65]

Cosmopolitanism's allure emanates from two dialectical moves. First,
the polis introduces a notion of citizenship that distinguishes natives from
foreigners. The citizen (*politēs* = citizen) constitutes itself in the relations of a community that publicly attests to and guarantees its deeds and
words. Expanding this citizenship out to the cosmos, however, requires
that the polis be conceived as the earthly reflection (a particular) of cosmic harmonious orders (a universal). In a second dialectic, the universal
informs the particular such that the particular must necessarily invoke
this universal. The political validity of the particular enables the expansion of citizenship to the cosmos in the figure of the cosmopolitan (*kosmos*
+ *politēs* = cosmopolitan).

The tensions in this universal-particular relationship take many forms.
The Cynic philosopher Diogenes of Sinope engaged in a self-conscious and
principled detachment from local allegiances, rejecting the polis's conventions and laws in order to embrace an encompassing model of natural
citizenship in which everyone is equal.[66] Diogenes's actual embodiment
of the notion was subtractive, effectively rejecting his Sinopean-ness; he
is said to have lived in a barrel, which he placed in the public space of
the agora, for the community to see and attest to his deed and word. Only
by disavowing the local could he arrogate the claim to be a citizen of
the cosmos, critically collapsing the political formulation of community
within the polis. Cosmopolitanism does not entail leaving local soil, but it
implies that one might as well.

This ancient episode helps reveal a set of dimensions of cosmopolitanism: (1) its claims (in deed and word) are necessarily rooted; (2) material conditions coexist with actions, feelings, thoughts, and words often
classified as imaginary or symbolic and compelled by ambitions, desires, and fantasies: cosmopolitanisms are both material and ideational;
(3) rootedness, materiality, and the imaginary inform a set of binary
oppositions (particular-universal; material-symbolic; concrete-abstract;
real-imaginary; global-local; exterior-interior; periphery-center; world-
nation), rendering cosmopolitanisms stubbornly dualistic; and (4) the
subject of cosmopolitanism raises questions of entitlement and privilege—
here, a male philosopher arrogates to himself the right to leave behind

(and below) the polis's compulsory obedient citizens. Despite egalitarian claims, cosmopolitanisms are potentially elitist and individualistic.

Under imperial campaigns, cosmopolitanism comes to encompass war, territorial conquest, and commerce alongside possibilities for cultural intercourse and ethical responsibilities to remote others. Here appears what Amanda Anderson calls an early form of "cultural fusion."[67] For their part, Stoic philosophers conceptualize this spatial expansion in a political geometry of ever-expanding concentric circles (individual, polis, world, cosmos) and formalize this new possibility of long-distance affiliation and potential exchange as "cosmopolitanism." As Plutarch wrote, "we should regard all human beings as our fellow citizens and neighbors."[68] The allure of these economic imperatives and forms of long-distance intimacy is obvious.[69] But it also introduces dangerous surrogates for "imperial apologetics" that continue to this day.[70]

Our analytic of cosmopolitanism renders a politically constituted sense of spatial relations, assuming a shared temporality that goes unsaid. This entails the material and ideational traversal of a set of *reference points* (individual, community, city, state, humankind, world) with two domains, local and global, as a central axis. It also entails *frames of intelligibility* undergirded by values such as the ethical responsibility to strangers, an expansive sentiment of filiation beyond blood kinship, an interest in others' activities, and a corollary desire for engaging them.[71] *Commercial intercourse* and *communicational dynamics* are put into play, as are senses of belonging and connecting, contact and isolation, practices of circulation and exchange, and notions of political expansion and contraction. *Ideological forms* include notions of sameness and difference, inclusion and exclusion, homogeneity and heterogeneity, outwardness and inwardness, alongside the possibility of reparative linkages to the wider world, operations of world-making, and ideas of what the global and the universal are. *Institutions* of all kinds—technological, cultural, financial, and governmental—are involved. Its *operations* can appropriate, expropriate, and ex-appropriate, dislocate, compare, and translate: cosmopolitan politics encompass the entire spectrum from antagonism to hospitality.[72]

Empire makes of cosmopolitanism an earthly affair. Heterophilia becomes a political reality (material and ideational), and a horizon for normative economics. Feelings and actions motivated by "cultural" filiation with strangers may now coexist with unsurmountable "physical" distance. Cosmopolitan geometry may be conceptually recursive across its points of reference, but expansion is dissimilar for those involved. Cosmopolitanism retains a relational but uneven character through which societies disclose constitutive tensions in the politics of belonging.

Latin America's (Lettered) Cosmopolitanism

The intense debates around Shakira fit all too well within perspectives on cosmopolitanism, modernity, and colonialism.[73] Cosmopolitanism played an important role in Latin America and even more so in Latin Americanism. That Latin America has been made sense of by Latin Americans abroad is intrinsic to the roots of nineteenth-century Latin Americanism—the term was articulated in Paris and, partly, as a presumed relation of "Latin" America with other parts of the world, whether French imperialism (and a corollary Hispanism) or anti-American imperialism. Both, nations and the continent, as a possible set of interrelations among nations that exceed their "sum," gain shape from this particular perspective. Latin Americanism is dialectical. "Throughout the nineteenth century and good part of the twentieth century," notes Néstor García Canclini, "each person belonged to a nation and from there imagined its relationships with the others." Some relationships, however, had another point of reference. "The experience of estrangement served writers and plastic artists to see their countries of origin otherwise. A good part of the literary 'constitutions' of Latin American nations were written from abroad . . . [by] pilgrims thinking from afar the sense of their homes."[74] Shakira, it might seem, and under a wholly other sense of Latin America, embodied these two vectors of Latin Americanism's dialectic.

Most vividly felt in the world of letters and the increasingly urgent question of the continent's place in the world of literature, nineteenth-century debates in Latin America strongly differentiate cosmopolitans—that is, intellectuals and diplomats advocating a broader engagement with other European traditions—from Creole nationalists insisting on the Hispanic tradition. That nationalists could remain enthralled by the incorporated Other of the Hispanic tradition reminds us that, as Sheldon Pollock argues, autochthony results from a particular political effort and disposition involving the self-conscious renouncement of ties with a larger world on which the autochthon actually depends.[75] Nineteenth-century cosmopolitanism helps reveal ongoing dynamics of imperial difference; some prefer the heritage of the old Spanish colonial order and others—José Martí, most famously—would encourage encountering the new empire, the US, even and particularly in order to know the Latin American Other.[76]

These debates "articulate the normative demand according to which Latin America defines itself within a universal geography of Literature instead of in relation to itself and to any single individualized foreign literatures."[77] Cosmopolitans share "a common epistemological structure" that constitutes a "desire for the world" expressed as aesthetic preferences as well as critiques of what they see as parochial nationalism. The nationalists' "foreign" is the cosmopolitans' "worldly." As Mariano Siskind adds, "cosmopolitan intellectuals invoked the world alternatively as a signifier of abstract universality or a concrete and finite set of global trajectories traveled by writers and books."[78] The Communist Manifesto's prophecies for a "world literature" constitute a surrogate "for the material, dynamic formation of a global field of symbolic and material exchange, where Latin American writers and texts actively negotiate the terms of their participation in this world-historical process."[79]

These cosmopolitanisms will produce self-conscious identifications of Latin American literature as fully embedded in Western culture (Borges's famous mid-twentieth-century claim) or as laying on a periphery that, as Brazilian Joaquim Nabuco thought, was made palpable by the reliance on long-distance technological mediation.[80] Both positions uphold the enduring cosmopolitan geometry in order to place Latin America *in* the world (Nabuco) or *with* the (Western) world (Borges).

A PHONOGRAPHIC WORLD

But "Literature" is not "music." For although the Marxian cosmopolitan telos for capital travels through technical dispositives to yield a "World Literature"—that is, through print technologies, print journalism, the telegraph, and the constitution of new reading publics—the forms and materials that accompany the early stirrings of a world music operate in another sphere. Michael Denning has shown how phonographic capitalism first sought to capture local vernacular forms in order to sell phonographs to a growing middle- and upper-class consuming public.[81] The phenomenon that Denning identifies relates to the early interest phonograph companies (Victor and Columbia) had in selling equipment to local markets by recording local and regional musicians, as happened in Barranquilla in the early twentieth century or in recordings made by Colombian musicians in New York City.[82] The musicians Denning documents themselves did not first express a sense of self-consciousness of their place in the world, or the development of their forms in relation to forms elsewhere. In other words, in this case only phonographic capitalism was "cosmopolitan," its cosmopolitanism material, while musicians remained unconcerned with participating in "a global field of symbolic exchange," let alone part of a "world-historical process" of the kind lettered figures expressed.[83]

As Denning details, the onset of electrical recording ushered in a period of extraordinary capture of musical vernaculars worldwide between 1925 and 1930. "Thousands of inexpensive discs made from shellac (a resin secreted by the female lac bug, a colonial product harvested in the forests of South Asia) were released, disseminating musical idioms which have since reverberated around the globe under a riot of new names: son, rumba, samba, tango, jazz, calypso, beguine, fado, flamenco, tzigane, rebetika, tarab, marabi, kroncong, hula."[84] "Unlike modern novels, paintings, theater, or even film, which 'represented' the modern 'masses,' these discs circulated the voices of those masses," Denning argues.[85] This "musical revolution," as he calls it, "inaugurated the world musical-space of the century to follow," and set into motion "a remarkable dialectic between musicking and recording, between the everyday practices of music culture and the schizophonic circulation of musical performances on shellac discs."[86] All this enabled "music" to forcefully reconfigure social orders and redistribute sonic allocations across many societies, including Colombia's. This redistribution constituted a fundamentally political matter in which the capture, storage, and transmission of sound formed new modalities of communication; music refigured the place of bodies and dance, and remapped societies' musical territories in which particular forms were tethered to—in some cases untethered from—particular places or sectors of the national population.[87]

If this period may not have constituted a cosmopolitanism in the manner that Siskind analyzes in relation to literature, it may reflect the material dimension of cosmopolitanism that Marx and Engels foresaw. In the instances of tango and samba, these "local" musics went on to become "national" musics in large part after they had traveled overseas and received foreign audiences' and dancers' validation.[88] Many of the grand projects to nationalize music across the continent developed under the aegis of new recording technologies and the laborious classificatory enterprise of folklorists. Ochoa Gautier affirms: "In Latin America, the history is a little more complex [than the 'discovery' of traditional music by the World Music movement] because one of the crucial aspects for the birth of mass popular music was the realization of local music recordings at the beginning of the [twentieth] century." For this reason, "some musics that reached significant commercial diffusion never lost their association with the idea of folklore altogether."[89]

Ortiz's and Carpentier's quips about the worldwide acceptance and cosmopolitanism of Cuban music sum up these dynamics. In its material and symbolic dimensions, musical cosmopolitanism retains not just the allure of contact, the powers of affecting others with one's sounds, and the imperatives of global capitalism, for it too illustrates the local, regional, and national need for sonic validation of and by others. As James Ferguson argues, global capital is decidedly nonlinear (and non-scalar), "it hops, neatly skipping over much of what lies in between," often bypassing crucial nodes such as the national, the regional, or the local.[90] Although not a central preoccupation of traditional cosmopolitan aspiration, temporality now appears to play a key role. In Denning's assessment—namely, that musical vernaculars impact the future of music and the world—that impact occurs because the traversal and trajectories of this new cosmopolitanism literally appear *as* the music is heard, listened to, and experienced around the world. End-of-twentieth-century globalization, however, puts a different spin on musical cosmopolitanism.

Discontents of Music in/as Globalization

Cosmopolitan frames of intelligibility become reconfigured nowhere more strongly than at the institutional level of technologies, finance, metropolitan infrastructures, and migration. The impact of technological acceleration and availability of new migratory movements cannot be underestimated. Thus on one hand, technological interconnection and the access to deep music archives online give rise to a sense of expanded possibilities for experimentation: metropolitan young musicians in Colombia beginning roughly during the 1990s operate with an awareness that hardly any music remains unavailable to them and, in turn, new recording initiatives there bring these musicians closer to vernaculars previously unavailable or in the hands of people associated with the State—for example, folklorists.[91] On the other hand, because of the radical reconfiguration of the materiality of musical communication in the digital era (what Timothy Taylor calls the most radical change in the West since the invention of musical notation in the ninth century), "our era," as Steven Feld remarks, "is increasingly dominated by fantasies and realizations of sonic virtuality," and "as sonic virtuality is increasingly naturalized, everyone's musical world will be felt and experienced as both more definite and more vague, specific yet blurred, particular but general, in place and in motion."[92]

As the debates among Colombian fans and detractors around Shakira reflect, new tensions explode concerning the erosion and reconfiguration of subjectivities. Attention to these other dimensions of a globalized musical modernity constitutes an attitude that Martin Stokes calls "critical."[93] This perspective affords seeing the tense dynamics between "small" and "big" musics, how global finance has an oversize impact on musical circulation and on the spatial and temporal configurations that music helps define. The fate of the "local" interrelates to "times of globalization," in Ochoa Gautier's expression, and in a complexly changing environment in which, as Stokes reckons, "the future cannot be read from the past," and in which, in Erlmann's analysis, synchronicity rules the day.[94]

The political economy of musical globalization demands careful evaluation, equally in the stirrings of world music during the 1980s and 1990s as in the emergence of Shakira as a global figure in the first decade of the twenty-first century. Music's role as a "designated space of fantasy in the Western imagination" works too well for a celebratory popular consensus too eager to indulge in and to identify in technology a kind of "base" on which the cultural "superstructure" of novel experimentations, fusions, and hybrids relies.[95] Furthermore, these global senses of belonging are central to the political repertoire of empires.[96] A problematic "art of the possible" consists in expanding such sense to the widest sphere imaginable.[97] Enter cosmopolitanism.

In this economy, colonial and imperial differences, old, new, and renewed, share in their status as conditions of possibility for modernity.[98] Thus, the legacies of Spanish coloniality (colonial difference) coincide and collide with the ongoing impact of US imperialism (imperial difference), something which, in the case of literature, renders Latin America as a subsystem with the capacity to influence the literature from the metropolitan center.[99] Questions of scale that we find in cosmopolitanism reappear in which various notions and experiences of location and belonging are challenged in which real and imagined forms of displacement take place that can be either agonistic, antagonistic, or of accommodation. Along the way, the old scalable Stoic geometry, which undergirds the notion of world system with its order of center and peripheries, is reconfigured, its topology rendered obsolete. Not only do cores, peripheries, and semi-peripheries emerge, but so do new and unheard linkages resulting from unpredictable contacts and outcomes that blur any presumed clarity of the world system.

In this context, Stokes's call for a critical attitude toward cosmopolitanism, even a certain reticence, holds considerable appeal: to understand the world (or this world) less in terms of a single system with a dominant macro-socioeconomical structure than as a "set of projects with cultural and institutional specificity." This set of projects constructs, refers to, dreams of, and fantasizes about a world that does not rob humans of their agency, particularly the agency in which they assert their rootedness, and of the ineradicable located character of their ambitions, desires, and dreams that situates music making (listening, performing, dancing, etc.) *in* a world.[100] Or, as Feld puts it, musical cosmopolitanisms embody "the agency of desire for enlarged spatial participation, performance and imaginaries of connectedness," swaying toward "'diasporic intimacy,' the uncanny closeness that unites dispersal and displacement with reclamation and replacement through surprising loops of material and echo feedback."[101] Unlike the globe of "globalization," this world of musical cosmopolitanism doesn't compress space or time, reflecting the active role people play in "making worlds" in which they struggle for a place while embracing or loving "the music of others."[102]

And so, like other cosmopolitanisms, someone's musical cosmopolitanism takes place because it is possible, despite its impossibilities.[103] Provided we avoid regarding the world of cosmopolitanism as an abstract universal totality, a signifier of an exterior whole that would suture lacks that necessarily attend to the local, or a system with clearly defined centers to which the periphery and semi-periphery may tether its creative and expressive fortunes, cosmopolitanism should help us understand the messy interplay of rooted localities with something beyond (e.g., "a world") that these localities constitute for themselves in the connections they imagine and pursue. One could say that cosmopolitanism's ancient ideals of acting, feeling, and thinking outwardly from a rooted location retain their allure, except that now, in the maelstrom of globalization, these become a necessity, or at least the better alternative.

ACTUALLY EXISTING COSMOPOLITAN LATIN AMERICANISM

How then to put the capacious mode of cosmopolitanism to work analytically in the case of Shakira? Despite her own claims to feeling like a citizen of the world and acting on behalf of global institutions with cosmopolitan aspirations such as UNICEF and her own Fundación ALAS, and despite the claims to universality such as that cited in this chapter's epigraph ("Shakira, universal Colombian"), doesn't cosmopolitanism risk being everything everywhere—and thus nothing and nowhere at all? Let's address this question by considering two material elements: new migratory patterns and the transformation of certain metropolises into nodal points in global musical networks.

"Fifteen percent of Ecuadorians and approximately one tenth of Argentinians, Cubans, Mexicans, Colombians, and Salvadorians live in the US, Europe, or other Latin American countries," remarks García Canclini. This means that "Latin America is not completely within Latin America. Its image returns in the mirror disseminated in the archipelago of migrations."[104] During the 1990s, Colombia experienced the largest migratory movement at any point in its history.[105] The intensification of the "armed conflict" (the undeclared civil war pitting leftist guerrilla movements against government and paramilitary forces aligned with right-wing political movements) had gradually replaced the 1980s "drug wars" as the main grounds for violence. Neoliberal policies begun in earnest under president César Gaviria's government (1990–1994) had opened the national economy to free-market policies and brought unprecedented foreign investment to the country. Standard 1990s indexes of social welfare, crime, and unemployment portray a country that many had reason to leave.[106]

And leave they did.[107] Leading up to the new millennium, Spain enjoyed years of political opening and economic growth, now as part of the European Community.[108] Combined with flexible migratory policies and a shared language, this growth made Spain a magnet for Latin American migrants. Colombians arrived in large numbers.[109] Generally, these were young migrants, and the movement included many who were relatively well educated.[110] In 2000, women were a large majority.[111] The story of the growing internationalization of large numbers of Colombians owes partially to these developments; so does the fact that Spain served as the main catalyst, in Europe, for Sony's ambitious plans for Shakira's albums in 2002.

Another fundamental manifestation of the "migratory archipelago" occurs in the Americas' recording industry circuits. Although for a long time major Latin American pop stars traveled to Los Angeles to record with well-established producers and to avail themselves of its rich musical studio infrastructure, beginning in the 1990s Miami became the favored destination.[112] Miami emerged as both a global city and the main node in what George Yúdice identified as "the globalization of Latin America," one which, as Daniel Party said, produced "the *Miamization* of Latin American Pop Music."[113]

According to Yúdice, macro-economic processes such as the massive reorganization of capital in the wake of neoliberal policies and technological innovation were behind Miami's rise in the new world economy. US trade barriers were lifted, opening unprecedented opportunities for foreign investment in Latin America and prompting devaluation, privatization, and deregulation. Information services created networked modes of organization for the "transnational corporate sector and civil society" alike. Attracted by local government stimuluses, robust transportation and communications infrastructures, the largest free-trade zone in the US, a highly skilled workforce, and long-standing cultural competence with the Americas, hundreds of corporations made Miami their base. They left regional offices in Mexico City, Bogotá, Buenos Aires, and San Juan, among other "minor world cities," for the Florida gateway, centrally located relative to the rest of the US and also to Europe and Latin America.[114]

Shifting demographics of US immigration had a direct impact on the culture industries. "Latin Miami is no longer an exclusively Cuban city, there are hundreds of immigrants from Nicaragua, the Dominican Republic, Colombia, Venezuela, Argentina, Brazil, and other countries," writes

Yúdice, remarking that "quite a few have come to work in the entertainment and new media industries."[115] Yúdice's analysis captured the centrality of these industries for the making of the new Miami.

For many, the Miami Sound Machine, the immensely successful group led by Cuban-American musicians and entrepreneurs Emilio and Gloria Estefan, constituted one of three phenomena responsible for the rise in the city's international profile during the 1980s.[116] The effects were concrete. "By the early 1990s, the major music multinational corporations like Sony and Warner reestablished offices there and throughout the 1990s all majors had their regional headquarters [there]."[117] To record in Miami became a guarantee of the highest production values available anywhere in the world, the city a veritable musical cosmopolis. And, as Party notes, the centralization of production and distribution in Miami formed a crucial step toward reaching the largest possible audience in Latin America.[118] Ochoa Gautier places the phenomenon within twin processes of monopolization by the so-called majors (Universal, Sony, EMI, Warner, and BMG)—which came to control 90 percent of global music production in the 1990s—and of the "transterritorialization" of musical production to Miami.[119]

Shakira settled in Miami in 1997, with all the advantages a contract with manager and executive producer Emilio Estefan could offer. By then the Estefans had a virtual monopoly on Latin music production in Miami. After all, the musical aesthetic of their Miami Sound Machine was chart-topping. The Estefans effectively crossed over to the US market with highly crafted and catchy musical hybrids, besides their more straightforward American pop tunes, all produced in Miami. Shakira, however, offered Estefan's emporium something more by having already been groomed and proven in the Colombian and Latin American markets. Gloria Estefan was to share writing duties with the Colombian, including translating and adapting Shakira's Spanish songs to English.[120] For Emilio Estefan, the Colombian was going to be "the biggest crossover in history."[121]

Estefan proved correct. Shakira's first project in Miami, the Spanish-language *¿Dónde Están los Ladrones?* (1998), reached the top of the Billboard Latin and Latin Pop charts in the US and was a major hit in Latin America, despite disappointing European sales. Recorded over nine months with an extensive producing team drawn from Estefan's vast roster of engineers, producers, arrangers, musicians, and video directors, the album sold half a million copies by the end of the year in the US and one and a half million worldwide. The album combined Latin Pop and Latin Rock styles and was memorably laced with a "Middle Eastern" feel and Arabic words (the singer's and a male chorus) in "Ojos Así," the album's fifth single and most successful track. The singer performed it to acclaim in Los Angeles, during the inaugural show for the first ever Latin Grammy Awards in 2000.

Shakira shared writing and producing credits for "Ojos Así" with two veteran members of Estefan's team—Javier Garza, a Florida-born engineer, and Pablo Flores, a Puerto Rican DJ and producer. Estefan was the executive producer and directed one video himself. Much would be made of the leading role that she played in the making of her music, tinkering with sound details as much as writing the songs: "the track," as Licia Fiol-Matta has observed, had traditionally been the space of the male producer and "the all-important hallmark of modern musical creativity" in pop music.[122] In this, Shakira had a disruptive role. But, as became the norm for production values in this and subsequent albums, the song expressed a Miami musical-cultural aesthetic: sounding at once like everywhere and nowhere in particular. "Ojos Así" was at once the apotheosis of commercially marketed World Music and its dissolution as a category. The song was not an earnest tribute to the "East" such as in Blades's *Tiempos*. In "Ojos Así," the "Middle East" was simply at hand, a more or less generic sound and musical "feel" from among the near infinite archive of sounds available to Miami production teams and used as a deliberate projection and amplification of the singer's identification with her Lebanese heritage, notably in the video's and live concerts' "belly dancing," which would eventually lead to her immense popularity in Lebanon and Egypt.

The juxtaposition of traces of authenticity (i.e., anything that could be linked to the singer's biographical background) and commerce (i.e., anything that wasn't "authentic") would be an asset for the shifting images the performer would adopt. At the same time, in the context of US xenophobia in the aftermath of the September 11, 2001, attack, the singer's embodiment of the belly dancer was taken as an index of her political daring and/or the perpetuation of an Orientalist gaze.[123] Elsewhere, the impact Shakira's dancing had was nothing short of remarkable, the media reporting how it helped renew interest in the form in countries where it had fallen out of fashion.[124] Back in the US, her embrace of worldly images and sounds, with its ambiguities and ambivalences, all key to her crossover success, were overlooked. Ann Powers, the highly regarded pop music critic for the *Los Angeles Times*, wrote,

> Shakira is one of the most successful musicians of Lebanese descent on the planet. The Colombian-born singer is also Latin pop's defining crossover artist; call her the most charismatic rock star of the new century and you wouldn't be wrong, either. Nobody has more of a right to claim the overused honorific "polyglot" than this 29-year-old child of a half-Italian mother and an Arabic father. Wowing the predominantly Latino crowd

at Staples Center . . . she showed that she's absorbed every lesson Robert Plant, Madonna and Selena had to offer and still managed to completely distinguish herself. . . . In a set that reached back to her first Spanish-language hits and concluded with this summer's monster hit "Hips Don't Lie," Shakira demonstrated what genuinely multicultural stardom looks and sounds like. It means proudly displaying your roots, demonstrated by a set list full of Spanish lyrics and choreography based around the belly-dancing that Shakira learned as a child, and assuming that it's not a problem to integrate those influences with whatever else moves your spirit. It also requires projecting an individuality that's stronger than any one influence. That's not an issue for this radiantly self-assured artist, whose only apparent flaw is the lack of a substantial dark side.[125]

Latin American crossovers, which Powers celebrates in Shakira, are never a straightforward process. Party proposes a twofold crossover model for music produced in Miami during this time.[126] In the first model, producers sought to expand to Latin American markets the music of artists who had a mainly national following. Sung in Spanish, a homogenized Latin Pop aesthetic marked the musical styles, yielding in essence richly produced pop ballads equivalent to the "Adult Contemporary" genre in the US.[127] "Abundantly exemplified in the Latin American and Spanish market of the 1970s and 1980s, the pop ballad," manufactured in Madrid during the late 1960s and 1970s, was "an international genre" lacking "local traits." A second crossover model aimed specifically to enter the "American mainstream pop market."[128] Again, the Miami Sound Machine offered a blueprint: although sung in English, their hit "Conga," which charted in the Dance, Latin, R&B, and Pop Billboard lists, was a Latin-funk number characterized by its montuno pattern and Latin percussion rhythm tracks. Shakira's *¿Dónde Están los Ladrones?* sat comfortably within both these crossover models, although her music carefully avoided "Latin" music clichés. Latin American markets appeared to be eager to embrace her expansive stylistic repertoire.

The cultural field on which such "Miamization"[129] takes place is more complex when one considers contingencies given in the US. According to Yúdice, Miami's "terrain suited the particular brand of multiculturalism the city came to embody," which is not to be confused with "the same multiculturalism [*pace* Powers] found throughout the United States": "The Latin-based entertainment-led boom in Miami has contributed features of Latin American discourses of mestizaje and hybridity, which are generally thought to be more inclusive than US identity politics." Yúdice concluded, "Latinness or Latinoness is undergoing a transformation in Miami; it is less rooted to a specific or minority identity. Perhaps this is because of all US cities (indeed, all cities in the Americas), Miami is the only one from which a generalized international Latin identity is possible."[130] Or, as María Cepeda put it, someone like Shakira would occupy "the interstices between the Latin American and the US Latino contained within the rubric of *Latinidad*."[131]

Ochoa Gautier remarks on the musical and affective resonances of such "transterritorialization." She writes of Carlos Vives—Colombian singer, actor, and erstwhile critic of Shakira's English-language singing. Vives achieved unprecedented success at home with a modern album that recreated classic vallenato for the Colombian label Sonolux and later signed with Estefan. Vives's case is emblematic:

> The move of Carlos Vives . . . to the production machinery of the Estefans in Miami is clearly manifested in the redefinition of his musical style that now appeals to a "Latin" sound, minimizing some of the vallenato elements that ground him more strongly in the sphere of Colombian consumption. This tension between the "Latin" and the "Latin American" is reflected clearly in the polemics surrounding the Latin Grammy Awards (created in 2000) and signals contradictory trends between the transnationalization of music and its adaptation to a global market. That is, the "transterritorialization and capitalization of a Latin American cultural *feeling*" are increasingly linked to the construction of a global pan-Latin sound that while it appears to affirm the national by giving presence to Latin American artists, on the other hand does this by means of a stylistic adaptation to the transnational postulates of the industry of the Latin American/Latino.[132]

Party's proposal—that "Latin Pop needs to be understood as the result of postnational modes of production that successfully hybridize Latin and North American elements"[133]—might be tempered with Ochoa Gautier's analytic of transterritorialization. Ochoa Gautier perceives transterritorialization to redraw existing musical territories while nations and localities remain in place, as in a musical palimpsest. This is closer to Cepeda's reading of Shakira as an "idealized transnational citizen."

When the link between sound and place—long a trademark of modernity's musical aspirations—is inoperative or is only partially operative, the industry may more adequately be called transnational, while the music itself may be understood as sometimes transnational and sometimes transterritorial. For example, different from Vives's initial exploitation of regional forms, Shakira entered the industry not through commercial exaltations of local forms but through pop confections, gradually incorporating a broader range of music. One might regard these incorporated repertoires, which were part of pop and rock's global circulation since the 1960s, to be so tightly woven into the musical sensibilities of many listeners of her generation in Colombia that they render ineffective the view that only music made there was proper to the nation. This is an old critique of autochthony. It is less frequent, however, to regard those musics to be "Colombian" to the degree that they are listened to there, and listened to carefully, with an ear on its details, expressive potential, and possibilities for experimentation. Listening and dancing, rather than composing and performing, becomes the index of propriety.

One might also consider Shakira and Vives as instances of a new extractivism within the culture industries. Within this view, Colombia provides musical resources on behalf of the continent to world markets.[134] Why should Colombia become the source of new musical trends, a site for a worldly, post–World Music music? As Yúdice suggests of Latin America as a whole, is this music an effect of the fact that hybridity, mestizaje, and transculturation had long been constitutive of cultural practices in the continent? Or has the accelerated opening of markets there moved cultural industries from the international to the transnational during the 1980s and 1990s?[135] Is Colombia—a country in which the deep sociopolitical crisis "of the late 1990s and early twenty-first century has profoundly shaped, if not outrightly provoked, a veritable popular music renaissance"—a particular case within the "Latin-music boom"?[136]

From the relative historical privilege of Barranquilla's cosmopolitan aspirations to her capacity and desire to embrace musical styles from an early age, numerous factors were in play in Shakira's case. Professional networking, of the kind emerging already during the 1980s, meant a record contract with Sony Music Colombia at age thirteen, her first major release appearing when she was fourteen. Two records aimed at the local public were considered flops. In the then typical combination of pop-rock ballads and dance numbers with 1980s synthesizer-dominated tracks, the first of these sold 1,200 copies outside of Colombia—an inauspicious beginning. And yet, what would tank most artists' careers was actually the first step toward Latin American stardom; stories of her personal resilience since have become standard in media coverage. A third release, with Sony Music and Columbia Records, *Pies Descalzos* (1995), brought on board US-born Colombian producer Luis Fernando Ochoa and a more substantial budget of US$100,000. The record presented a mixture of pop-rock originals, heartfelt ballads, "dancehall-lite," and crucially, a new image as a female rocker (rockera).[137] According to *Rolling Stone*, the album represented "a giant leap forward from the synthesized pop of her first two discs," with influences that included rock acts like Aerosmith and Tom Petty, grunge supergroup Nirvana, and Alanis Morrissette, with whom critics heard close parallels. By 2001, already an established superstar, she could perform "cookie-cutter pop" that put her in the same league as Britney Spears and Christina Aguilera, although as *Rolling Stone* noted, "the stylistic breadth of Shakira's music—elements of folk, Middle Eastern and traditional Latin styles over a foundation of rock and pop—gave her a degree of credibility the American teen queens lacked."[138] This ever-expanding musical range described what was possible in Miami *in relation to* what had happened in Colombia and Latin America and expressed a will-to-the-world (and a will-to-world) that characterized the artist's aesthetic outlook and cultural competence.

The hybridity, transnationalism, postnationalism, and transterritorialization that characterize the worldly work Shakira produced in Miami constitute symptoms of a transcultural process that had already taken root at home. This "home" encompasses the heterogeneous cultural space of the nation, and within that the region, city, and self; such would be a classical Latin Americanist interpretation. But because "home" also refers to "Miami," it compels a slightly different topology from classical Latin Americanism's network—namely, something like a spiral replacing the old concentric model of cosmopolitanism. For this topology, cosmopolitanism affords a multidimensional picture of the phenomenon "Shakira" and "Miami," but also of the lingering powers of "Colombia" to anchor important relations and affinities at play in such phenomena. Of course, in this assembly's symbolic and material elements, there is strong evidence of Latour's argument that cosmopolitanism operates as an uneven and unequal network of accesses and agencies, of Marx's and Engels's prognosis for capitalism and a bourgeoisie chasing resources and reselling them, and of Stokes's position that we cannot dismiss the powerful musical affinities bringing people in touch with the music of "others." But closer analysis of the contemporary embodiment of the affinities that audiences experience as consumers reveals a paradigmatic expression of radical transformations of subjectivity—namely, cosmopolitanism's center of gravity, the self shifts decisively toward a new pole: the brand.

The Branded Self

Much of what is at stake in contemporary claims to cosmopolitanism pertains to questions of consumer choice, forms of identification, and cultural practices brought into unprecedented synergistic relations under neoliberalism.[139] Key to such relations are notions of freedom within which "freedom to believe oneself to be the sole author of one's individuality" is particularly symptomatic of the present conjuncture. The paradox is telling: the proliferation of choices, including that of identification, compels the individual's capacity to assert and choose her own individuality amid dizzying proliferation, even and particularly if that assertion and choice consists in rehearsing an endless parade of personae. Music emerges out of this force field as a singularly capacious mode of self-definition, as a mechanism of identity formation, and as an object of consumption.[140] Shakira's relation to the forces of marketing embodies the complex entanglements of contemporary musicking. Out of these entanglements she too emerges as a brand.

But music alone does not perform this labor. For the figure of the pop superstar, the self that this figure always already entails, the personae that it most publicly assumes, and the characters that her music appears to embody become refracted through a specific formation in music making in advanced capitalism—namely, the brand. One can only half dismiss, if at all, the claim that under the practices of advanced capitalism enhanced by neoliberalism "brand is everything, and everything is brand," as Dan Pallotta, founder of the unironically named "Advertising for Humanity," declared in 2011.[141] Right at the turn of the century, Naomi Klein dramatically encapsulated the conjuncture thus: "[corporate] logos, by the force of *ubiquity, have become* the *closest* thing that *we have* to an *international language.*"[142]

Like consumption and consumerism, brands express "capital socialized to the extent of transpiring the minute relations of everyday life, to the point of becoming a context for life," a phenomenon that draws its appeal and power from the capacity to establish "relations between products in time" and to appear as "a mode of organising activities in time and space."[143] A partial lexicon of this crowded world might include "'public brands' (civic institutions), 'brand extensions' (new products from existing brands) . . . and 'brand leaders' (the very best brands)."[144] No mere object, tag, or hashtag attached to a persona, the brand constitutes a matrix of social relations, a locus of both uniqueness and distinctiveness as well as of a saturating ubiquity in which an assemblage of features congeal in an instantly recognizable form. In our case, the name "Shakira" and the images, sounds, and multiple associations it may convoke. Taylor explains: "brands aren't simply names of objects, but objects that carry meaning for people as things that make sense to them and communicate their sense of who they are to others."[145] Brand building aims for broad likability ("brand equity") by cultivating "brandface" (or "the way the consumer sees herself when she engages with the brand)"; marketing what Amanda Hess calls "an entire way of being"; and selling ideas, not just things, as Klein put it.[146] Or, in the case of cosmopolitanism, selling the idea of an aspirational idea, not merely reinforcing nationalism via consumption. Brands often emerge in synergistic relation (called "co-branding") to actual objects, such as the jeans and phones that Shakira's mid-2000s releases were linked to. Her image formed part of a long advertising campaign by Pepsi harking back to 1999, during the exciting aftermath of *¿Dónde Están los Ladrones?*, the album that solidified her status as a star throughout Latin America.[147]

The Pepsi campaign is telling. When in November 2002, Pepsi signed a deal with Sony Music Entertainment (SME), the drink company sought to promote "co-branded sale efforts at nonmusic retail outlets." Under the arrangement, the company "would advertise 'sneak previews' of new music from Sony artists while sponsoring television specials and using its retail muscle to get Sony music CDs into places like gas stations and convenience stores."[148] According to Dawn Hudson, head of Pepsi North America, "nothing connects with young people like music, and with its dedicated focus on developing the very best artists from around the world, no one is better suited to help us intensify that connection [than Sony]." For Thomas Mottola, CEO of Sony Music, Pepsi was a "natural choice for this one-of-a-kind co-branding campaign."[149]

Although Pepsi had long used pop stars in advertising campaigns, Shakira was once again ahead of others in co-branding herself. As William Spain reported, "Pepsi and Sony are already involved in a successful co-promotion involving Shakira under which Pepsi sponsored the Latin star singer's tour and even plastered her face on beverage cups."[150] Antonio Lucio, chief marketing officer of PepsiCo Beverages International, outlined the singer's importance to the campaign thus: "Our involvement with Sony Music and their artists has been a real win for Pepsi brands over the years, and this next step is a natural extension. Having worked with Shakira internationally since 1999, we've been successful in making SME artists a key part of Pepsi's music programs to better connect music fans with their heroes and us."[151] And part of that "natural extension," it seems, was a contradictory move both to broaden the Latino market and to blur ethnic boundaries in advertising. Thus, according to PepsiCo client director of multicultural marketing Giuseppe D'Alessandro, "we adapt the campaigns to the way the market is feeling. The Latino market is exploding and is very young and they feel this is the time for a huge Latino movement." D'Alessandro added that "Shakira, a Grammy winner, is an ideal representative of the brand essence for all youth. She has done Spanish- and English-language commercials for Pepsi over the past year."[152] On the other hand, as Laurel Wentz remarks, Shakira, alongside Beyoncé, was a key part of Pepsi's multicultural appeal: "over a much longer period than most marketers—Pepsi did its first African American ad in 1948—the cola giant has evolved from the ethnic segmentation most companies still use, to looking at young ethnic consumers more as tribes bound by shared interests than ethnicity."[153] As with Sony, Pepsi's co-branding campaign had global objectives, the cosmopolitan character of the enterprise being a suitable (non)enclosure for accentuating the Latino connection of Shakira and her appeal to such "tribes." The byline for the announcement of the entertainer's Tour of the Mongoose (2002–2003) read "This fall Pepsi will bring Shakira's passion for music and thirst for life to fans across the world." The form of the brand and the dynamics of branding gain particular force in how these emerge in connection to pop music stars. Brands and branding are tethered to a subject: the figure around which self, individual, persona, and character congeal. Part abstraction and part radically material entity, the subject enables the personification of the brand and the branding of the persona. It also enables the self to be folded into the branding operations. The mutuality between corporate humanization and the corporatization of humans is fundamental to brands; the same goes for personification (corporations and personae) and personalization (corporations and selves).

Corporate interests maintain overwhelming power over branding. But it would be wrong to reduce branding's dynamics to consumers as merely duped, corporations as dupers, and performers as the half dupers, half-duped mediating figures between them. Instead, enduring debates about citizenship complicate these dynamics. Thus, we find conflicting experiences of (mis)recognition when "Shakira" is said by supporters to remain a proper Colombian. And the peculiar experiences of individual intimacy with brands prompts Shakira's detractors to suspect that the mobility of her public image (her persona) betrays a hollowed-out self behind the image. The female body then becomes a locus of identification, critics obsessing about the singer's changing appearance. As Pier Dominguez notes, "*Time* chose her as the cover star for their Era of the Rockera issue, signaling her pan-ethnic Latinx transcendence, but also the way her performance and visual style adhered to a minimalist rocker ethos. She wore leather pants and offbeat hairstyles and colors (such as multi-colored braids)." "But this image," Dominguez continues, "was reshaped after the emergence of a crossover Shakira, soon dismissed by some as a sexualized gringa sellout. . . . Some said this project moved her into an American, whitened, blonde, and artificially thin direction. On the *Laundry Service* album cover, she appears to have washed herself clean of her previous rockera identity: the newly blonde Shakira is also newly nude—or so she suggests by posing with naked shoulders, parted lips, a hint of a leg on which she rests her hand." Looks and sounds are of a piece:

These blends of pop, rock, and Latin American genres have kept audiences guessing about which version of Shakira is coming next. Thanks to that unpredictability and her widely eclectic musical vocabulary, she transcended her instant as the spicy flavor of the month. Creating multiple sonic personae, responding to and playing with public fantasies about her sounds, she continues to cross over, arguably more than any other artists from supposed Latin music booms over the last few decades.[154]

In a succinct statement about her brand's changing appearance, Shakira stated that "Pop always gives you the opportunity to metamorphose."[155] Pop, yes; and so do the branding synergies behind it allow, enable, and promote such metamorphoses. Even so, not all kinds of pop promote metamorphosis. Recall audiences' relative indifference to Rubén Blades's efforts to reinvent himself (chapter 2). Modernity may have achieved a liquid state, but for some musical genres and for some musical subjects, it remained rock solid. Those who celebrated Shakira for her adaptability interpreted her lack of conformity as a significant dimension of her brand, while others decried her as a sellout for the same reason.[156] Through it all, and as an effect of contemporary digital fandom politics, the boundaries between public discourse and private sentiments became blurred.

This blurring works in tandem with one of branding's most striking features—namely, that the brand operates as a matrix of production itself, an effect of global cultural industries' will-to-consolidation. The successful colonization of subjectivity by the brand means that the brand is distributed and distributable across a range of other things (products, identities, etc.) such that it acquires memory as it helps forge memories. In short, the brand constitutes a remarkable actor in the production of relations.[157] In the context of globalized cultural industries and music branding, consumers become loyal audiences and audiences become loyal consumers, willing and ready to fight over their passions at a keystroke.

The whole might be understood as a symptom of a larger political moment which fundamentally renders all social relations profitable, endlessly networked activities that are experienced as freedom to fashion and curate the self, and translates them into information-gathering algorithms. This amounts to the biopolitical dimension of the "society of control."[158] As Jeffrey T. Nealon summarizes, "today the dominant mode of economic production entails producing identical objects; in fact, niche-market consumption is oftentimes ideally refined to a market of one. . . . Lifestyle purchasing is the primary economic driver in a neoliberal finance economy, and that form of hyper-consumption is dependent on constant biopolitical innovation." Nealon, in fact, proposes that music embodies this order particularly well: "if biopower strives to connect individual lives and identities seamlessly to mass demographic patterns, then we can see more easily music's privileged status as a kind of operating system for biopower."[159] As Gilles Deleuze puts it, "the self does not undergo modifications, it is itself a modification."[160]

In order to better understand the work music does, one must still press pause on the endless proliferation of figures that branding enables in order to consider how a song itself constitutes a relational matrix. We might explain the process as a semiotic-affective relay for which music's sonic features provide a nearly perfect medium: a song featuring Shakira's unique and powerful voice, singing the chorus "Whenever, wherever, we're meant to be together; I'll be there and you'll be near, and that's the deal, my dear," may interpellate a listener for the assertive and straight-forwardly transactional character it gives a romantic pop tune. Add to that the sonic iconicity of the *siku* (panpipes; Sp. *zampoña*) that provides a short interlude after this chorus—an "Andean" sound not heard in pop music since Simon and Garfunkel's 1970 "El Cóndor Pasa (If I Could)," here playing a repetitive pentatonic (and irresistibly catchy) rhythmic riff. Add also the bouncing rhythm track's four on-the-beat bass drum hits; a *dumbek* (the goblet-shaped drum associated with Middle Eastern music) playing underlying syncopations and a modified Ayoub rhythm (fig. 3.1); and a charango (another "Andean" sonic icon) replacing what would be a rhythm acoustic guitar part—add all of these elements, and one has a pseudo-global sonorous assembly ("Latin American" and "Worldbeat") that, as the locales shown in the song's video suggests, could happen nowhere and everywhere: the singer rises from the seas, on a desert, atop snow-capped mountains.[161]

"Whenever, Wherever" provides, in sonic form, elements for a pro-liferation of significations. It is as if the track itself were tasked with producing curatorial fodder for manifold subjectivities. As pop music ana-lysts know too well, rather than merely conveying particular meanings, the song as vehicle allows for multiple articulations. The track's music is particularly effective in its capture of embodied gestures. The lead vocal part divides the beats into even parts while the rhythm track maintains its syncopated Ayoub character throughout, creating a delectable ten-sion between the parts; carefully placed "drops" allow the vocal part to return with greater impact on the verse. "Whenever, Wherever" is, as Alex Henderson wrote, "infectious," a suitable expression for its affective power, bodily and immediate.[162] This affective experience marks both the

Figure 3.1. Ayoub "rhythm"

endpoint of the listening and viewing experience—to which dancing and moving to the music are intrinsic—and the origin of the loyalties that the brand convokes. It may relay back to the sense that drinking from a can of Pepsi stamped with the singer's likeness may somehow draw one closer to both what she stands for and what one in turn is; it may relay back to the feeling that one is part of a global assembly communing in the irrepressible experience of "Whenever, Wherever," or that one is part of the idea that the world may be one, after all, at least sometimes, some places, under certain conditions and in some situations. With this, audiences might have been ready and desiring of whatever song Shakira might share next: "Whenever, Wherever," one of the all-time bestselling singles, was to be surpassed by "Hips Don't Lie" (2006), which cemented her place in global pop stardom.

At that juncture, the semiotic-affective relay between audience and consumer loyalty encompassed a bewildering number of spheres. This in turn helped ensure a modicum of expectation that the experience may be both repeatable and expanded. Dividuals (the favored unit of social intelligibility here) might themselves expand while remaining loyal to the brand that they constitute as it, in turn, helps constitute them in sounds, images, moves, styles, and flavors. Such "expansionary individualism"— which in my account fits the idea, ideals, and actually existing practices of cosmopolitanism uncomfortably well—allows and even demands that identities may be adopted without losing a grounded "self." Perfectly at home in a "liquid modernity," in a postmodern subjectivity and indi-viduality, and in the dividual subjectivity of the society of control, the semiotic-affective relay works well in a world in which individuals value the right to "alter the cultural categories that define him or her."[163] It remains to be seen if this right to change constitutes a new phenomenon or the intensification of an already existing, quasi-immanent potentiality for choice by a Latin American musician embedded in and productive of the continent's transcultural matrix.

THE ECONOMIES OF A COSMOPOLITAN SELF

Recall Shakira's manifest sense that returning to her hometown—besides embodying contemporary musical migrancy, movement, and circulation— implied a distributive (and redistributive) operation. Such an operation entailed both giving something back to the place that nurtured her and, as many commenters remarked—from anonymous people responding to newspaper reports to illustrious lettered Colombian figures like Botero and García Márquez, who lionized her—giving Colombians something to be proud of. In this case the gift and the commodity cannot be separated: Shakira's gift is a commodity—herself—as well as the expression of an idea and a feeling—Colombian-ness—in terms of its marketability. Following Anna Lowenhaupt Tsing's argument that global circulation has long entailed the interpenetration of forms of interchange and exchange, we can think how the social relations produced by the brand share in forms of relation that, though irreducible to it, have capitalism as a condition of possibility and which partake in novel networks of contemporary interconnection.

Cosmopolitanism is itself a sphere of possible (and to some, "available") interconnectedness. For example, while a fan may receive what "Shakira" gives, this fan in turn gives back in an uneven interchange of this hybrid commodity-gift form: the fan's use value may always become an exchange value for the interests that benefit most monetarily from the brand Shakira, herself included. In other words, similar to "affect" in the regime of affective labor, use value becomes subject to exchange itself. But if capitalism becomes increasingly cosmopolitan, as Marx and Engels and Mill predicted, cosmopolitanism participates in capitalism's production of inequality and uneven accumulation from which the question of class emerges. The poor may inhabit the worlds the global and the cosmopolitan offer, but both at a cost and with only a partial admission to their bounties. The cosmopolitan, on the other hand, may inhabit virtually any world. But fans' affective labor, though always productive for the brand, is marked by profoundly unequal access to a brand that seems ever so accessible to all those who listen to radio, watch TV, or use digital media.[164]

Recall Feld's caution about virtual encounters within the global musical system: Shakira's pervasive media presence makes her "available" to legions of fans who feel intimately connected with her songs, images, and "personal" narratives. Recall those who wondered why she wouldn't use her personal fortune to subsidize concert tickets in Bogotá, and those who, pleased with president Uribe Vélez's neoliberal policies, claimed that the new free-market economy directly made her appearances in Colombia possible. Consider the opinion of two highly respected Colombian musicians based in Bogotá: bassist and composer Juan Sebastián Monsalve, and percussionist and cultural activist Urián Sarmiento, who in 2008 expressed to me that it had been a long time since musicians there cared whether Shakira might call on local talent; for them, Shakira had long disappeared from Colombian musicians' horizon.[165] Of course, there are Colombian musicians based in Miami, such as Gustavo Patiño, who built a career in his hometown of Cali as an expert on Andean folkloric music and was called to play the iconic *siku* part on "Whenever, Wherever." At the same time, Monsalve and Sarmiento themselves had traveled to India in 1998 in search of new musical horizons. Although differently for each, given their economic background and musical preferences, much of their projects of musical renovation and innovation in Colombia are intrinsically linked to these worldly experiences.

The many ways in which "Shakira" comes to be what she is—and she is as many things to as many nodes in the vast network over which "she" travels and helps build, from individual fans to the global entertainment industry—configure a set of economies of the figure of the cosmopolitan self. Meanings do not cease to matter, whether they're the possible semiotic relays of a song manufactured in Miami and heard the world over, or the anxieties over identification among Colombian fans or among US-based recording industry executives confronting the possibility of mass-market, bilingual pop productions. The brand is inextricable from these economies; Taylor cites Alina Wheeler, who observes that "brand identity . . . makes big ideas and meaning accessible."[166] By accessible, Wheeler means partly that the brand is a multi-sensorial phenomenon that can be seen, heard, and watched as much as it can be touched and held. Small wonder that notions such as "emotional branding" and "brand personality" surface, blurring boundaries between self, individual, persona, and character in a way redolent of the conflation that Tsing names.[167]

Emerging from the spheres of advertising and marketing, "brand," "branding," "co-branding," "brand identity," and "the branded self," among other buzzwords, express the radical permeation of commercial exchanges into virtually all aspects of contemporary pop musical experience. Being immanent to neoliberal economics, such notions embody, often literally, the unceasing character of affective labor. In an early definition of affective labor, Maurizio Lazzarato wrote of "labor that produces the informational and cultural content of the commodity," where cultural content involves "the kinds of activities involved in defining and fixing cultural and artistic standards, fashions, tastes, consumer norms, and, more strategically, public opinion."[168] Michael Hardt and Antonio Negri elaborate on the notion, outlining three spheres of such "immaterial labor": "the communicative labor of industrial production that has newly become linked in informational networks, the interactive labor of symbolic analysis and problem solving, and the labor of production and manipulation of affects."[169] Within this regime, everyone labors: from the individual who, in our case, writes songs; to the panoply of musicians and music producers that render her songs into the finished product; to the armies of workers needed to pull off any given performance; to the anonymous *El Tiempo* commenters who generate disputes, producing with each log-in an additional click to add to the millions that account for digital newspaper circulation; to the teenage fan decorating her or his walls with images of the artist; and so on. The passive consumer—if this figure ever existed—becomes an active producer or "prosumer," often creating content for the global feedback of the phenomenon "Shakira," producing a new public sphere within which circulate strong feelings of attachment and detachment, and new reconfigurations of some of modernity's most valued items, such as the nation. The lexical constellation around brand constitutes what Wheeler calls "an intangible asset,"[170] which is a dimension of affective labor, the heterogeneous but palpable relations it requires, produces, and compels.

Within the Latin Americanist frame that I pursue, we witness the possibility that the cosmopolitanism at stake in "Shakira" partakes in what Gerard Delanty identifies as a "cultural contestation in which the logic of translation plays a central role."[171] I take the "logic of translation" to mean different things. It includes the traditional notion that there is a one-to-one rendering of a source into a target: for example, the global figure of Shakira might translate into a new kind of Colombian being in the world, or a single song may or may not be rendered with similar enough poetics in two languages. It includes the idea that a foreign-born entertainer may fully cross over into the US market—even rendering the idea of "crossover" moot—in which case "translation" means adaptation and transformation, making the target the main event, attenuating the centrality of the source in traditional notions of translation and easily inviting charges of "assimilation." It also includes Benjamin's intuition that any translation entails a sense of an incomplete whole and the embodying of something shattered, which is all there is from the get-go. And it includes the Babelian chattering among all involved, which does not just accompany the emergence of "Shakira" the "social reality" but that, in my argument, constitutes her (it). Thus understood, the very definition of the "logic of translation" is at stake. So too is determining its effectiveness, operationality, and the terms of what is translated—in short, the "emergent social realities" of cosmopolitanism.

THE LANGUAGE IN QUESTION

Following up on the "logic of translation," I end by exploring how Shakira's bilingual musical production and approach to language constitute fundamental elements of the economies of the cosmopolitan self. To begin, the commercialization of bilingual musical production appears today as an unqualified success.[172] Recall how radio executives' fears about airing Shakira's breakthrough bilingual album *Fijación Oral, Vol. 1 / Oral Fixation, Vol. 2* came to naught. Rather than fragmenting audiences by language, the industry ended up benefiting from an expanded market. Of course, we might adduce such fears to an aversion to new risks in an industry riddled by failure; major hits are not the norm in an industry with massive overhead costs for introducing and promoting novel acts in the mainstream. This fear, in turn, reflects US society's perniciously stubborn monolingualism.[173] Consumers for whom Shakira's bilingual productions constitute a new social experience form not just a new market sector but also a new public. Their musical investments contribute to an emerging "alternative public sphere," as Juan Flores and George Yúdice propose.[174] This may well translate into an expanded sense of citizenship or social belonging for Spanish-speaking immigrants: gains in a political sphere that regards market consumption as a fundamental form of social belonging.

How does language operate as a political or commercial dispositive? The notion of an alternative public sphere suggests that these aren't mutually negating alternatives. Nonetheless, language in the US is a "surrogate terrain" for struggles over defining Latino communities' role in determining what "America" is. As Flores and Yúdice observe, defining this role entails understanding "the conditions under which [Latinos] enter the political arena," which includes, importantly, "the permeation of representation by the consumer market and the media." This permeation renders language "the terrain on which the heterogeneous constituencies of Latinos are rallied not only as consumers but also as cultural subjects." Recall the Pepsi-Shakira advertising campaigns' duality that de-emphasized ethnic alliances while expanding the Latino market. This market—and its corollary consumerism—operates as "an integrative force" that cannot, however, be reduced to the production of assimilated "Americans." Why? Because "the force of consumption, understood in its broadest sense, holds sway in the culture of experience," such that it is not enough to simply translate an advertisement slogan from English into Spanish. When producing spots for the Spanish-speaking market, advertisers acknowledge the need to capture in Spanish "the spirit of the English copy." Flores and Yúdice call this "trans-creation": a traversal across two poles demanding that cultural agents "be positioned there, with ready and simultaneous access to both sides."[175] "There" in this phrase means "a border."

With the theoretical concept of the border, Flores and Yúdice appeal to the shifting constitution of what "America" becomes under constant migration from the South to refer to "America as a 'living border.'"[176] Hybrid forms as such do not express this living border; rather, the living border manifests through a poetics of multiple access that, like Spanglish, embodies expressive and communicative needs both in everyday life and in aesthetic forms.[177] In Gloria Anzaldúa's signal political and theoretical contribution, the border entails seizing upon language as a means for self-affirmation and to recognize that language matters socially and poetically: socially because language relates to others and occurs under specific social conditions, and poetically because it not only expresses but helps constitute a self.[178] "Continual creative motion" is how Anzaldúa describes the border's counter-hegemonic work, which disrupts "the unitary aspect of each new paradigm."[179] Shakira's entanglements with two languages put her in contact with the disruptive potential of the border.

The living border of language, the alternative social sphere it produces, and the entanglement of economic and political spheres it generates all prioritize cultural remapping over political geography, its subjects coming to experience not an existential split but an affirmative amplification via the poetics of multiple access. Driving this affirmation is not only the power of agency and intentionality of a figure like Shakira, but also the hegemonic entertainment industry that recognized the need to redraw the pop industry's boundaries (recall the Sony showcase in Madrid). And so, to the question of language as a political or commercial dispositive, we answer that both sides (i.e., the singer-songwriter and her audiences, and the industry) share similar needs: for one, to change cultural maps by exercising a degree of linguistic self-determination, and for the other, to tap into a greater consumer market. Thus, it is not that Shakira's bilingual experimentation is wholly mediated by an industry indifferent to the cultural effects of such experimentation. For the industry also finds itself mediated by these experimentations. This is precisely the kind of co-imbricated public sphere where institutional settings like the media extend into a horizon of social experience and social experience occurs in such media.

If language constitutes a surrogate terrain for political demands, and if these political demands emerge in the alternative social sphere where the commercial and the expressive commingle, translation's dynamic role in all this remains to be discussed. After all, the critique that Flores and Yúdice offer has a model in the interlingual character of Spanglish, specifically that of Nuyoricans and Chicanos, but not necessarily of Spanish-speaking Latin American immigrants to Miami who might more typically represent Shakira's US public. Bilingualism and translation into English are the linguistic terrains in which the singer-songwriter dwells.

In her encomium on US bilingualism's productive risks, Doris Sommer writes that "more than one language is a supplement, not a deficiency. It is a dangerous supplement to monolingualism. . . . Bilingualism overloads mono systems, and multilingualism does it more. But in principle bi- and multilingualism make similar mischief with meaning." She adds that "[mistakes] mark communication with a cut or a tear that comes close to producing an aesthetic effect," and that "democracy depends on

constructing those miraculous and precarious points of contact from mismatches among codes and peoples."[180] Communication, aesthetics, and
democracy, no less, might be added to the "emerging social realities" of
cosmopolitan translation, the creation of an "alternative public sphere,"
and politics of access of the border.

These claims might be approached by identifying where such "precarious points of contact" take place. Consider, for example, the often
remarked upon "quirks" of Shakira's English lyrics as instances of "contact from mismatches among codes." Given that in her first US-produced
records she wrote lyrics in Spanish first, the English lyrics are literally
a translation. In this regard, remember that the singer-songwriter ada-
mantly refused to compromise when writing lyrics in her adopted language, deciding against the original plan to work with Gloria Estefan, a
bilingual performer with far more experience and proven success working
in English. These translations have been heard as idiosyncratic English.
The following remark, by Jon Pareles, about a 2014 record, epitomizes
these hearings:

> But the endearing parts of "Shakira" are the quirks that still separate her
> from North American pop singers: the warbles and breaks in her voice
> that make her professions of love sound both innocent and obsessive, and
> the idiosyncrasies of her English lyrics: "You looked at me with your blue
> eyes / And my agnosticism turned into dust." They keep her from getting
> entirely swallowed by the Anglo pop machine.[181]

Pareles posits these words as a mark of distinction (in relation to other
pop singers) and as a means to a qualified inclusion in the "Anglo pop machine" that allows the singer to remain partially outside of it.[182] Consider
also what Ed Morales—one of the first critics in the US to review Shakira's
Spanish-language music—wrote of *¿Dónde Están los Ladrones?* in 1999:

> Take the opening lines from "Ciega, sorda, muda" (Blind, Deaf, and Dumb):
> "My argument / And methodology is over / Every part of your anatomy
> / Appears in front of me." Suddenly Shakira sounds like she likes her sex
> with a side of semiotics. Instead of imposing some lame Jon Secada aes-
> thetic on her, Emilio Estefan lets Shakira, listed as "artistic producer,"
> ply her mariachi-horns cum tropical-Fleetwood Mac bounce to kick the
> songs into reasonable listenability. So what if "No creo"'s listing of Marx,
> Sartre, and New Age guru Brian Weiss sounds suspiciously like John Len-
> non's "Time is a concept by which we measure pain"—she sings it like
> she owns the idea of self-reflection. . . . but if transcending her roots to

become a player in Miami necessitates some concessions to not-ready-for-salsa listeners, a cleverly embedded poetry still manages to peek through in Shakira's worldview.[183]

Such cross-linguistic phenomena—here I agree with Sommer—constitute a healthy supplement. Their "slips" compel particular aesthetic effects; they tear through otherwise predictable lyrical clichés, like when "agnosticism" shows up and somehow manages to not sound pretentious but rather unique, even inventive. And if Sommer is correct, in some way this would enhance democracy's negotiation of linguistic differences, amplified by pop music's wide circulation. This certainly would be consonant with an understanding of the political that is concerned less with the organization of social blocs that might resist or refuse hegemonic power and more with the appearance in the public arena of the new. It is similar to Arendtian politics of action and appearance and to Rancièrian dissensual politics of distributions of the sensible. In the latter case, singing the line "my agnosticism turns into dust" would challenge preexisting conditions of possibility of what can be said, heard, seen, by whom, how, where, and when, such that it asserts the intelligibility of the singer's words. As a corollary, it asserts her equality in relation to others as a singer-songwriter in a borrowed tongue. At its most basic, this understanding signifies the reclamation of a share in the communal distribution of the sensible, making those practices previously considered supernumerary but counted nonetheless within the *demos*, at least as shaped in terms of pop culture consumption. And one would have to regard the question of accent in relation to sense as expressions of what Steven Connor calls the location of "the plastic tangibility of sound"—namely, the mouth itself. As he suggests, the mouth can produce mingled senses as a collision between culture and communication.[184]

This account of the politics of translation would correspond to Pareles's sense that Shakira's lyrical idiosyncrasies afford her to be both within and without the "Anglo pop machine." Typically, claims to equality or to participation arise in the context of someone being included within a larger configuration but actually excluded from full participation—what Rancière would call "the part with no part." By Pareles's analytic, however, Shakira appears to both be a part of a milieu ("Anglo pop machine") and exceed it, a sort of part extra-part in which the "extra-part" would be a "positive" exclusion, from the critic's perspective, given by her linguistic specificity.

The mismatch that leads Pareles and others to perceive an "aesthetic effect" raises two issues. First, Shakira's English is, like others' before her, such that she can sing "many un-English things in English."[185] Second, this would place her in a wider—and typically literary—constellation of figures such as Conrad and Nabokov, among many others, who, as Mauricio Tenorio-Trillo notes, "have used English as their vehicle of prose, though with many other languages in the background of their thoughts."[186] And would it not also be possible to think in terms of a musical version of "minor literature" in which "a minority constructs in a major language"?[187] Paraphrasing Gilles Deleuze and Félix Guattari, mutatis mutandis, wouldn't Shakira embody the impasse that might bar access to songwriting for Latin American immigrants only to then act on that impasse by making it into a peculiar impossibility—the impossibility of not writing songs, the impossibility of not writing in English, the impossibility of songwriting otherwise?[188] A certain tension between linguistic affirmation and dissent would result: an affirmation because it is the major language still, and dissent because it is made to do what it is not supposed to (i.e., sing "un-English things in English"). This dissent/affirmation would be transferred to the overtly commercial milieu in which those words do deterritorializing work to the degree that they may open up to those who might listen. At the same time, it is that milieu which reterritorializes this minor songwriting, restricting it to brief moments in otherwise straightforward English usage.

But pop music is not literature. And this is precisely the point. Song, in the US of the early aughts, forges small disruptive spaces in a way that literature does not anymore. Overt trans-creation—of the kind characterizing Nuyorican literature and poetry in the late 1960s and early 1970s, the works of Sandra Cisneros or Julia Alvarez, and Chicano literature—did not have the same purchase in the contemporary alternative public sphere that pop songs do. Nor did Latin American writers working in English, like Peruvian-born Daniel Alarcón (b. 1977), have the broad readership that might have compelled critical responses to their use of English.[189] Alarcón's debut short-story collection, *War by Candlelight*, was published in 2005 by HarperCollins, a major house, and was a finalist for the PEN/Hemingway Foundation Award (2006). His first novel, *Lost City Radio* (2007), has been translated into ten languages, including Spanish. In 2011, he created NPR's first non-English podcast, *Radio Ambulante*, which he co-hosts. Consider also the runaway success of Junot Díaz, whose work is indelibly stamped with the experience of the Dominican diaspora in New York City. At the same time, pop songs' political returns might be small; after all, we're talking about a few words here and there, not sustained efforts of the kind novelists, essayists, and poets might have afforded. And yet, along these lines and together with her "un-English songs in English," we could read Shakira as the initiator of the practice of defamiliarizing the strangeness of hearing Spanish in the US (and global) pop culture.

Ed Vulliamy writes that "everyone knows English is the lingua franca of pop music. Less widely acknowledged is that the gyre is turning, that other languages, especially Spanish, are eroding the hegemony of pop and other genres." According to Sebastian Krys, a producer for Shakira, "You simply can't have a global No 1 any more without a hit in Mexico and Spain"; and for Tim Ingham, "not only is non-English language repertoire dominating key territories today—it's also taking over the world." In 2018, eight of YouTube's ten most-viewed songs were by Spanish-speaking acts. Vulliamy himself describes Shakira (and Enrique Iglesias) as "an avant garde [*sic*] of pop music from outside the Anglo weave seeping into and fraying it."[190] Years earlier, Tommy Mottola, then head of Sony Music, had said of Shakira that "she is absolutely brilliant as an artist," and went on to predict with uncanny prescience that "Latin music is the reservoir of talent that can be the crossover pop stars and the global pop stars of the future."[191]

All these things are expressions of the emerging social realities afforded by the "logic of translation" as the corollary of a cosmopolitanism experienced and enacted by Shakira. This maps out the political topography of the question of language in Shakira and "Shakira": translation (which renders certain phrases idiosyncratic) and bilingualism (which asserts a certain equality to intelligibility) in the US constitute operations that produce the partially outside insider. Does this render anyone who, like Shakira, sings partly in Spanish or moves across two or more tongues, into a dissensual figure? This raises further questions about a politics of the subject, for, *pace* Arendt, it is not the individual whose actions carry the weight of distribution. Much as industry types like Estefan and Mottola might have singled out Shakira as an agent for such reconfigurations, they work only to the degree that they are heard and listened to. Here we cannot forget the commenter's acid words about the singer-songwriter's Argentine accent, nor Carlos Vives's complaints about her English singing, nor García Márquez's pride, whatever the language.

If Shakira's work signals the attainment of aural equality, the listening that shaped her music and her singing now transforming how she (and Latin America) is listened to, and if that attainment signals a powerful moment in the history of migrant creativity, how does syncopation come to bear on all this? We may essay two possibilities. In one, the old division between center and (cosmopolitan) periphery dissolves, the latter breaking through the ramparts of monolingualism. Here, at last, Latin America syncs with the US and syncopation might seem to fade out in the cosmopolitanism of late capitalism. "We're all cosmopolitans" would

be the operating motto. In another, the US becomes the site of dislocation, falling behind the beat of the times, largely unable to come to
terms with shifting cultural boundaries that its own version of capitalism
provoked. But in the end, and to echo Ochoa Gautier, it is not the case
from the perspective of the US that it is now all over for Latin America
(the apocalyptic vision); nor is it the case, from the perspective of Latin
America, that it is now integrated, much as "its image returns in the mirror disseminated in the archipelago of migrations," as García Canclíni put
it; nor is it the case that, as Feld observed, relations under the present
technological regime remain at the level of the merely virtual. The circuits of a cosmopolitanism unevenly linking individuals, cities, countries,
musical passions, capitalist ambitions, brazen technologies and marketing
epistemes, languages, and translations constitute the pathways by which
modernity unfolds. Such circuits demand that things be at once present,
behind, and ahead of themselves. In both networked and concentric cosmopolitanisms, the syncopations of modernity persist. So do their often
unexpected rhythms, even and particularly when these cosmopolitanisms
seem to propel Latin America into a present that somehow seems out of
reach but that, once "here," accentuates its tumultuousness.

Modernity, then, as condition of possibility for Shakira's (and "Shakira's") cosmopolitanisms, that includes the promise to move beyond modernity? Perhaps aesthetics, in its quintessential modern capacity, hovers over these processes and phenomena in the sense Jacques Rancière
understands it: "the multiplicity of connections and disconnections that
reframe the relation between bodies, the world they live in and the way
in which they are 'equipped' to adapt to it."[192] As Rancière argues, the aesthetic closes in on life—that is, it addresses life so directly that it seems to
close the gap between its main avatar, art, and life itself—at a particular
moment (ca. 1800) in Western history well within European modernity's
temporal sphere. Accordingly, neither the forms nor the contents make
art more or less political, for art's political force is immanent to the emergence of the aesthetic as a privileged embodiment of the political. "Art,"
Rancière writes,

> is not, in the first instance, political because of the messages and senti-
> ments it conveys regarding the state of the world. Neither is it political
> because of the manner in which it might choose to represent society's
> structures, or social groups, their conflicts or identities. It is political be-
> cause of the very distance it takes with respect to these functions, because
> of the type of space and time that it institutes, and the manner in which it
> frames this time and peoples this space.[193]

How then to evaluate Argentine icon Fito Páez's declaration that Shakira's music is made in "a very technical and calculated fashion," yielding "a hybrid genre that has no history," and concluding "that [her] music is more of a product" than his own much-vaunted brand of rock en Español?[194] Páez wears his modernity on his sleeves—and doesn't even know it. He holds on to exhausted notions of "political art" on the one hand, and on the other fails to perceive that just like his own brand of rock, the pop confections spun out of Miami studios, for example, speak to musicking as a mode of production, one which, in the latter case, consists in "linking disparate sounds" as a form of "creating connections."[195] Furthermore, the Argentine remains desensitized to the fact that there is no music without history and to the very real possibility that globalization either demands new ways of thinking history or is itself a way of (re)thinking history. Not to mention the gendered connotations of his jabs. But perhaps Páez's complaint registers a possible experience of rootlessness in cosmopolitanism, which he translates or mistranslates into a lack of temporal rootedness—a lack of history. For time (and its corollaries of memory, archives, experience) and its relation to place (and space) remain those dimensions of modernity—or at least the versions of time and place that it enforces—where syncopation is most audibly felt but most difficultly perceived.

4 * Histories and Economies of Afro-Latin Jazz

If you see me coming, better open up your door;
If you see me coming, better open up your door;
I ain't no stranger, I been here before.

Traditional Blues, in Houston A. Baker Jr., *Blues, Ideology,*
and Afro-American Literature: A Vernacular Theory

Given the extreme reflexivity of late modernity, the future does not just consist of the
expectation of events yet to come. Futures are organized reflexively in the present
in terms of the chronic flow of knowledge into the environments about which such
knowledge was developed.

Anthony Giddens, *Modernity and Self-Identity: Self*
and Society in the Late Modern Age

Twenty-six miles southeast of Havana, Cuba, lies San José de las Lajas, a town of about 70,000 people. In December 2010, townspeople gathered in a plaza in front of the central cathedral to hear Arturo O'Farrill (b. 1960, Mexico City) leading his NYC-based Afro Latin Jazz Orchestra (ALJO). The "Afro-Cuban Jazz Suite," a multi-part, 18-minute-long composition written in 1950 by O'Farrill's father, Arturo "Chico" O'Farrill (1921–2001), was the featured closing piece that evening.

Prominent in Cuba, the O'Farrill family had first arrived in San José from County Longford, Ireland, by way of Montserrat in the seventeenth century and went on to become among the Island's wealthiest; merchants with commercial interests in sugar, they had been slave traders, and went on to prominent positions in administrative, political, and cultural affairs.[1] Today, a luxury hotel in Havana bears the family name. In San José, Chico's ancestors had built the cathedral in front of which the ALJO performed.

That evening in San José, ALJO's drummer, Vince Cherico, who had played the "Suite" countless times under the direction of both O'Farrills, recalls looking out to an audience in deep reverie and concentration, utterly transfixed by this music, rarely heard on the Island despite Chico's legendary status.[2] Cherico, a first-call musician in New York City and a veteran with many miles on the road the world over, soon found tears welling up in his eyes, nearly falling on the borrowed drum set.[3] Most in the band were overcome with emotion, as were O'Farrill, his mother, his wife, and his two teenaged sons who accompanied him on this trip.

Since his father's death in 2001 and following his first trip to the Island in 2002, O'Farrill had imagined "how to return him to Cuba, somehow, through his music, playing it here with my mother in the audience. It would be a way to close the spiritual, artistic, and familial circle of re-encounter."[4] By O'Farrill's account, his father "died with a broken heart, acknowledging that he would never return to his beloved island. It was the only emotion that made him cry, his emotional pain. Since I was a child and afterwards, as a young man, I felt my father's pain."[5] O'Farrill's familial attachments mean that there is no choice in electing one's dead. But repatriation of his father's remains means also making a place for his dead and making history as well, setting the return to Cuba in relation to the time that his father's musical creativity helped make a central Cuban contribution to jazz. Something begins when someone dies. As Arturo affirms, the trip inextricably linked personal and cultural economies:

> It also implied paying a cultural debt, because if you listen to Chico O'Farrill's music, you discover that much of what has helped the world of jazz evolve is Cuban music. Some aspects of this music can only come from rhythms, textures, and compositional schemas with Afrocuban [*sic*] influence. I dove in those waters but never had the opportunities to return them, to bring them home. For me, the opportunity to interpret this music is a way of saying: Thanks to the Cuban people and to its culture in general for its fecund influence. Of course, the other part is to acknowledge that Cuban music is still not comprehended as a source of jazz, as it should be.[6]

The "Suite" constitutes the first extended-form composition in the style variously known in the US as Afro-Cuban Jazz, Latin Jazz, and, more recently, Afro-Latin Jazz. At first, its musical surface might not seem to stereotypically compel the kind of contemplation that Cherico observed in the Cuban audience in San José. The sound is assertive, even defiant in the confidence of its musical matter—instrumentation, harmony, melody, counterpoint, rhythm, texture, and overall development. The "Suite" embodies O'Farrill's intimate knowledge of and will to experiment with the modernism of serial techniques, the implacable laws of clave, the pliant tenderness of bolero, and the then still perceived tartness of Stravinsky's harmonies. The whole affirms that the best of jazz coexists with the best of Afro-Cuban music, either music embedded in the other with uncanny comfort, rendering moot a categorical generic distinction. In the "Suite," O'Farrill's exquisite conception of Cuban big-band music is filtered through the ears of modern jazz, and modern jazz is heard anew as Afro-Cuban music: harmonically complex, densely layered counterpoint and challenging but memorable melodies unfold over the precise and combustible churning of a three-member percussion section. He wrote the "Afro-Cuban Jazz Suite" at the relatively early age of twenty-nine, only two years after his first trip to New York City in 1948.[7] The original recording session, produced by Norman Granz for Machito and His Afro-Cubans, featured a veritable who's who of the jazz scene at the time: Charlie Parker was the alto sax soloist, with Buddy Rich at the drums and tenor saxophonist Flip Phillips and trumpeter Harry "Sweets" Edison playing important roles.

But that was 1950. In 2010, many other things resounded in this re-markable music, that plaza, those listeners, those New York City–based musicians (then shuttling back and forth to Cuba with relative ease),[8] perhaps none more arresting than the story and history of irreparable exile. The "Suite" may have uncannily incorporated the spirit of Cuba's past in the sound and the letter of cultural rapprochement, but the form and scale of the relations it expresses couldn't be overcome with its return. Nor could the political specters on both sides of the Cuba-US divide be put to rest. That 2010 evening, much unfurled: that concert, that piece, that audience, the institutions inextricably bound to them, the musicians, down to their tears—all within histories of musical migration and human immigration. Tracing these associations entails identifying their temporalities and analyzing their attenuating, enduring, transient, or disappearing features. Chico O'Farrill's embrace of jazz, his son's embrace of his father's embrace of jazz, and the now historical incorporation of those embraces into the unprecedented cultural politics and cultural policy of jazz in the US—Jazz at Lincoln Center (JALC), where the ALJO was resident ensemble from 2002 until 2007, under the leadership of Wynton Marsalis—all constitute "beginnings repeatedly begun."[9] That is, events that continuously but in varying forms and at different scales demand a constant reckoning with a present that cannot but map and remap the past in order to compel uncertain but necessary wagers on the future.[10]

Why must beginnings be repeated? Why can't they constitute momentous emergences of new forms that break through existing norms, appear in and to the world,[11] and subsist on the strength of their creative and social virtues? These beginnings fold into one another to create what we might take to be histories of Latin Jazz (a provisional and barely adequate placeholder).[12] Such histories play out in multiple locations at once and display—with an intensity perhaps not felt in the cases of salsa and pop music from the previous chapters—the forces that time and temporality unleash in hearing the relations in the Americas as an expression of their "syncopated modernities" and on the claims that migrant creativity makes on behalf of aural equality. As I elaborate here, these forces obey economies of exchange and accumulation, of giving and taking, and of credit and debt, in which the ontological status of the dead—or rather of their specters—are real wagers on the capacity of music to make worlds.[13] These spectral economies and their corollary histories stage the syncopation's power to fold a general mode of musicking—jazz—inside and outside itself, all under the imperatives of the Americas' ethno-racial and imperial disorder. Although musicians from various "cultural" backgrounds imagine themselves to expand jazz and thus to participate in building a common in which the music is what's shared across "cultures," national imperatives and competing logics of cultural belonging and ownership get in the way of this common. A musical common, once begun, cannot accept new beginnings.

This chapter tells a story of a shared commitment to the past by O'Farrill and Marsalis, their ensembles and institutions, that differs in how they conceived and enacted the relation of time and space to place, two contrasting but intertwined modes of making history out of a tradition. In this, each figure redeems the past, but their affordances, given along the coordinates of race and citizenship in the US, yield different outcomes. For Marsalis and JALC, the past remained open because of the perverse view of the jazz tradition by white critics. For O'Farrill, his father's past—in the entanglement of migration, institutions, musical practices and creativity, and shifting political winds in the complicated history of US-Cuba relations—remained unredeemed. In at least some small way, as Michael Taussig suggests, redemption entails giving an object "another lease on life[,] breaking through the shell of its [the object's] conceptualizations so as to change life itself."[14] Walter Benjamin lends a beautiful addendum: "there is a secret agreement between past generations and the present one. Our coming was expected on earth."[15] But, as he soberly continues, "like every generation that preceded us, we have been endowed with a weak Messianic power, a power to which the past has a claim. That claim cannot be settled cheaply."[16] This weak Messianic power constitutes what Pablo Oyarzún calls "the index of the tension towards the redemption [of the past]."[17] No generation can ever fully redeem the past; it remains ever open, unceasingly calling on us. This in turn begs the questions: From what can that which has already happened be redeemed: oblivion, untimeliness, exclusion? By what operative logic would it be redeemed: salvation, deliverance, restoration? Whatever the operation may be, what futures emerge from it? Can a musical common truly emerge? Must the "stranger" always knock on the door and remind those inside that they were always already here, as the blues lyrics in the epigraph beautifully assert and plea? The story too, then, is centrally about those who hold the key to that door.

Making Place for Time

"We're truly prepared to take on the music of the twenty-first century." Thus said Arturo O'Farrill in an early promotional video for the ALJA (the not-for-profit organization O'Farrill began in 2007 upon leaving Jazz at Lincoln Center),[18] registering a pivotal moment in which his orchestra's musical multilingualism constituted the *sine qua non* for musical innovation. They project a future characterized by heterogeneity and a pluralist vision for jazz. But as Scott DeVeaux observes, "looking both ways is the favorite stance of the neoclassicist: a careful balance between the modernist ideology of continuous innovation and an insistence on the priority of tradition."[19] The ALJA's mission statement proudly nodded toward a past embodied by now canonic figures from the world of big-band Latin music: "The Afro Latin Jazz Orchestra was founded in 2002 to perform compositions by masters such as Machito, Tito Puente, Chico O'Farrill . . . and others."[20]

Speaking in 2012 on the occasion of the Orchestra's ten-year anniversary, ALJO's musicians echoed O'Farrill's outlook. Rolando Guerrero, a much-in-demand Afro-Honduran percussionist: "what we are doing is maintaining history and creating history."[21] As Michael Rodriguez, a Florida-born trumpeter of Ecuadorian parents, put it, "it's a special occasion because we are keeping the music alive in this genre, this setting, this situation, you know, big band Latin jazz, one of the few bands that are keeping the torch." In trumpeter John Walsh's words, "it's an honor to be a part of a continuing tradition, but it is exciting and challenging to be part of a tradition that is moving forward." Veteran jazz trombonist Earl McIntyre: "one of the things that is important about the organization is that many times when you join organizations like this they specialize in music of the past, or they have an agenda for the present, or they feel they're blazing roads into the future; this organization is doing all three. And that is an incredibly ambitious undertaking, especially when you take into account the wide variety of cultures that we're talking about." "Any band that just plays repertoire music," asserted saxophonist David DeJesus, a New Yorker of Puerto Rican background, "is forgetting the purpose of music, which is to kind of push things forward, and any band that is just playing original compositions is sort of forgetting the roots . . .

we've found a good balance of doing it all."[22] Tradition and innovation stood in careful balance.

The Orchestra began as a repertoire ensemble with the explicitly stated mission to recreate music of the golden era of big-band jazz associated with the ballrooms of New York City during the 1940s and 1950s.[23] The Orchestra's archival foundation in a recognizably accomplished past plays a central role in constructing the future of what O'Farrill gathered under the neologism "Afro-Latin Jazz." This new archive held the sounds that others in another historical moment had called Afro-Cuban Jazz and what others still call Latin Jazz. These musics had been new in past decades. The institutional founding, first of the ALJO and second of the ALJA, marked an unprecedented event in these musics' trajectories—namely, a new beginning, a making place for time; it was also a beginning repeatedly begun.

And there were further beginnings. Only following a period in which this older repertoire became canonized as part of the larger cultural project of Jazz at Lincoln Center (JALC), its formal parent institution, did O'Farrill adopt a wider purview on "Latin" music. Starting in 2007, this shift was evident in a turn toward a late-day Pan Americanism embracing musical traditions beyond the hegemonic triad of Cuba, the US, and Puerto Rico. I asked O'Farrill in 2015 why it was that the repertoire of his orchestra seemed conservative at first. According to him, the repertoire was largely left to his choice, although special concerts would need to be discussed with JALC director Wynton Marsalis and the Center's administration. But as he put it, "when you are based on someone else's idea, you are not encouraged to experiment." In the end, he believed that Marsalis gave Afro-Latin music merely "cursory recognition." Following his departure from the Center in 2007, he said, "fuck it, we're free; let's go back to find what this music is about."

This shift had everything to do with its institutional setting and its cultural politics. The Orchestra served as the resident ensemble at JALC, where it initially functioned as a "Latin" version of that performed by the much-debated jazz neoclassicism of the Center's musical director, Wynton Marsalis. As O'Farrill put it, "while we were there, we had to work within the constraints of the institution, which meant adhering strictly to a narrow definition of the music. A canon: that was what I initially proposed and that is all they wanted. When you feel like your survival within an institution is at stake, you do what you need to do, but you don't feel free."[24] In this context, what is "tradition" and what is "history"?

What was remarkable about the formation of the Orchestra, its institutional basis, its historiographic perspective, and its eventual shift toward a broader repertoire lies in this new archive's capacity to offer Afro-Latin music a place for the time that it had existed, existed in O'Farrill's present, and would have existed in the future he envisioned. But tradition and history—the "past," in short—have a way of troubling place and time. The relation of shared but discrepant accounts of the past between Marsalis's African American historiography and O'Farrill's fundamentally migrant historiography shapes the Latin Americanism of Afro-Latin Jazz. The JALC project warrants a prolonged look.

Making Place for History

Much excitement and renewed expectations for the future of jazz greeted the arrival of a remarkable number of unusually talented young musicians to New York City in the 1980s, Marsalis (b. 1961, New Orleans) prominently included. Predominantly Black, together these musicians showed great respect for and precocious command of the musical complexities of bebop and so-called hard-bop idioms and their creators.[25] Baptized "Young Lions" by the media and recording industry, they were seen to revive general interest in music that—according to many critics, journalists, and musicians—had during the previous two decades lost its way.[26] Such critics had two primary concerns. If the 1960s free jazz and avant-garde experimentation were heard as having fostered an extremely permissible set of musical values that made it possible to define jazz by distorting its form and emptying its content in the name of freedom, the 1970s jazz/rock fusions were heard as having pruned jazz by simplifying its rhythmic and harmonic content in the name of mass popularity and commercial appeal. The heroic redemptive powers of the young musicians in the 1980s derived not solely from their musicianship; these powers were part and parcel of their commitment to a particular version of the jazz tradition that defined a form of musicianship grounded in absolute virtuosity, a commitment that some of them expressed by giving their musical ideals and social and cultural expectations highly charged rhetorical form.

The amalgamation of this rhetoric with musical practice yielded discursive and material formations with the potential to recast jazz history. Such projects aimed not only to reposition jazz within the US's larger institutional networks but also to relocate a venerable aesthetics of Blackness in the national imaginary. The public sphere soon became the site of polemical debates in critical, intellectual, and media circles about the proper charting of jazz's future. Along with its canonizing logic, this moment's alleged neoconservatism might have marked a pivotal turn—for many, *the* pivotal turn—for late twentieth-century developments in the jazz world in the US.

Propelled by the artistic vision of the by then most vocal and visible member of the "Young Lions," Marsalis—together with the cultural, social, and political platform of his principal mentors, Black intellectuals Stanley Crouch and Albert Murray—by the early 1990s jazz came to share a place of prominence alongside the classical arts at Lincoln Center for the Performing Arts on Manhattan's Upper West Side.[27] The focus on musical creativity as a fundamental cultural attribute of and means of representation for Black peoples in the US was taken as self-evident, as was the discursive elaboration of a nationalist program defining "America" with Black music as a central component expressing the inextricable but unique sense of belonging in the nation that Murray called "Omni-Americans."[28] This cultural attribute's capacity to restructure social relations was powerfully realized via the institutional performance network at Lincoln Center. The Center provided the infrastructure to reorganize and redistribute aesthetic and material resources including a formidable pedagogical apparatus at Juilliard, teaching outlets throughout local school programs, and coordination of the State Department jazz tour programs, which would provide Latin Jazz musicians with expansive touring opportunities.[29]

By 2004, the project Marsalis came to represent, initially a performance series begun in 1987 first entitled Classical Jazz at Lincoln Center and eventually renamed Jazz at Lincoln Center in 1991, would move to its own location at the Time Warner complex, a luxury shopping, dining, hotel, and residential complex, in addition to the location for a multi-theater set for JALC, on Columbus Circle, New York City, at a cost of $131 million.[30] We might say that this project—quite literally—helped make a place for time, for a particular historical vision of the past in the present, or what I call "making history for time."

MAKING HISTORY FOR TIME

Sparking JALC's immense public success was the 2001 broadcast of the ten-part documentary series *Jazz: A Film by Ken Burns*. The film plotted a canonic narrative according to the dicta of JALC, including a near erasure of music making from most of the 1960s and 1970s, and offered to millions of viewers a multimedia presentation of Marsalis's version of the jazz tradition.[31] The series consolidated jazz as "America's classical music" and at the same time advanced the idea that the music embodied the best of democratic values, placing it as a locus of the intrinsic relation between race and nation.[32] This narrative was sometimes supported and critiqued in a single breath. For example, noted cultural studies scholar George Lipsitz conceded that the canonic narrative of *Jazz* was understandable, reflecting claims of "a central place for African Americans in the history of modernism."[33] Tempering this concession, he observed how "in the version of modernity described in *Jazz*, art becomes a specialized and autonomous activity detached from tradition, something created by alienated individuals rather than historical communities."[34] The series' traditionalist aesthetics were equally polemical. George E. Lewis argued that JALC's conservative stance helped it secure funding and garner mainstream media attention and coverage. He noted, after Krin Gabbard, that despite Marsalis's complaints about artists selling out (e.g., the electric Miles Davis), many of the young musicians associated with JALC "happened to be" those with major record label contracts; for him, Burns's *Jazz* simply transplanted to music history the so-called synergies of contemporary corporate branding.[35]

The network of values organizing the discourse and practice at JALC resists easy summary.[36] Much energy was invested in reestablishing an unbroken continuity between the early 1960s and the 1980s. In order to legitimize this elision, Marsalis would outline strict boundaries for what jazz was and, most importantly, for what it wasn't.[37] This helped establish a heroic jazz historiography with founding fathers Louis Armstrong and Duke Ellington defining the tradition: Marsalis got to elect his dead. It also consolidated their core repertoire as the center of the jazz canon. Armstrong and Ellington provided the blueprint for the dual elevation of solo (Armstrong), orchestral, and compositional (Ellington) virtuosity that Marsalis would come to embody. Tellingly, Marsalis sought to clear a related historiographical ground and to assert control, as a musician and as a Black American, of the music's narrative:

> My generation finds itself wedged between two opposing traditions. One is the tradition we know in such wonderful detail from the enormous recorded legacy that tells anyone who will listen that jazz broke the rules of European conventions and created rules of its own that were so specific, so thorough, and so demanding that a great art resulted. This art has had such universal appeal and application that it has changed the conventions of American music as well as those of the world at large.
>
> The other tradition, which was born early and stubbornly refuses to die, despite all evidence to the contrary, regards jazz merely as a product of noble savages—music produced by untutored, unbuttoned semiliterates [*sic*]—for whom jazz history does not exist. This myth was invented by early jazz writers who, in attempting to escape their American prejudices, turned out a whole world of new clichés based on the myth of the innate ability of early jazz musicians.[38]

What does Marsalis mean by "tradition"? It is now a cliché that the humanities and interpretive social sciences hold traditions to be the product of "invention" or "construction."[39] This constructivist perspective gives way to a more "compositional" outlook that sees tradition-production processes as expressions of world-making for societies, although there remains in society a set of relationships (movements, moments, and tendencies) that are "residual," "emergent," or "dominant."[40] Further, tradition carries performative functions. It is a "mode of discourse that is diagnostic of the past," called "discursive," and a classificatory mode that differentiates past from present; it is also a "mediating force" that emphasizes "the intertextually constituted continuum of reiterations" by which "the past survives in the present."[41]

Appealing to Marsalis's notions of tradition and history, I seek to rethink their relationship in terms of tensions between temporal and spatial continuities and discontinuities. I thus view tradition as discursive and mediating performatives in the production of history. Together, such tensions between tradition and history express modernity's dynamics. Departing from the general constructivist position, I analyze the relationship between that which is made (or invented) and that which appears to be given (or received from the past). This query—which transposes to Marsalis's "cultural" plane the dialectic relationship between the invented (i.e., "culture") and the given (i.e., "nature")[42]—challenges his concern with myth as ideological critique of a problematic representation of the "proper" past toward questions of what I have called the ontological composition of not just music, but of a world—Marsalis's and others'.

In Marsalis's culturalist argument, one tradition (his) emerges as *the given*. The critics' tradition, on the other hand, appears as a vulgar racist ideological fabrication, an invention in the worst sense. Historiography offers the way out of this dualism, on condition that tradition be rendered as history. Given the historiographic investment at stake in JALC, the passage from tradition to history will be seen as a mode of management of the past that redoubles the relationship of the given (i.e., "tradition") to the made (i.e., "history").

WHITHER TRADITION?

Arjun Appadurai notes a "widespread though tacit assumption that the past is a limitless, plastic symbolic resource, susceptible to the whims of contemporary interest and the distortions of contemporary ideology."[43] Instead, he argues, the past must be so transformed. Two forms emerge. The first is the *ritual past*, a *social charter* with non-durational and quasi-transcendent form accessible through ritualized performance.[44] A society calling upon the ritual past experiences it like an inexhaustible resource. The second is the *empirical past,* a mode of temporal management that is durational and material.[45] The empirical past corresponds to the proven actions of the society that claims them as theirs.

A set of mediating forms constitute the *debatable past,* which links the ritual and empirical past: *authority,* with regard to source, origin, and guarantor of pasts; *continuity,* with regard to the acceptance or rejection of breaks that might enforce or impair a charter's credibility; *depth,* with regard to the relative valuation of time spans; and *interdependence,* with regard to the past needs to be interweaved with other pasts that serve as an alibi ensuring credibility to a charter.[46] The success of the ritual and empirical past rides on the ability of these forms to manage the stability of a charter and to establish and preserve its material archive. These forms, however, remain debatable, making them immanent to internal and external social antagonisms and factionalisms.

A social charter, the material archive, and a corporate body are co-constituted. For instance, the charter and the archive trace a corporate body's temporal itinerary and map its spatial dispersion.[47] The inscriptions of the debatable past are thus not representations of this body; they compose that body. The inscriptions also provide immunity to a corporate body, as for example when Marsalis forges a historical narrative to undermine the false narrative of the white critics.

Let's consider the forms of the debatable past Marsalis deploys. To locate authority, he calls on the deeds of heroic figures such as Armstrong and Ellington, placing them as the origin of modern jazz.[48] Two interrelated operations shore up their status as authorities: *phonography* and a corollary *mode of listening.* Phonography becomes an audible register of what jazz *is.* As inscription, phonography is both material—in Friedrich Kittler's sense of an absolute and historically indifferent etching of pure sound in recording—and sensory-semiotic—in Lisa Gitelman's sense of offering a "legible representation of auditory experience."[49] "Genealogies of inscription," writes Gitelman, "allow what anthropologist Michael Taussig calls 'particular' histories of the senses, as different media and varied forms, genres, and styles of representation act as brokers among accultured practices of seeing, hearing, speaking, and writing."[50] In our case, Marsalis brokers the material and sensory-semiotic relations via music analysis, a prescriptive *mode of listening* that selects, categorizes, harnesses, and channels jazz phonography.[51] Listening, a living act, animates authority.

And so does live performance.[52] Figurations such as "Blues," "swing," "collective improvisation," "syncopation," "call and response," and "vocal effects," which Marsalis famously lists as defining "What Is Jazz," stage in live performance what is aurally demonstrable from a music-analytic standpoint.[53] Reordering Gitelman's intuition of inscription, auditory experience is here rendered as a legible representation—subject of discursive enunciation and of aural experience, the figurations become shared codes that make communication about the tradition possible. As repertoire becomes living history, reproduction incorporates a set of auditory reckonings; these reckonings become coextensive with the tradition from which Marsalis draws the figurations; and their enduring audibility guarantees the *continuity* of the past. Listening, then, constitutes a dynamic mechanism for rendering the empirical past of the jazz tradition as an equally empirical (i.e., material and sensory-semiotic) history of jazz. To know this history is to be able to hear it and experience it in the event of performance.

Marsalis's figurations link the ritual and empirical past but do not operate on a temporal field as such. Rather, they displace temporal origins, authority, and continuity to an aural terrain. The source of the jazz tradition and of its corollary history lie in the elements it assembles, the correlate mode of listening it compels, and the particular interactional performance practices it generates. Add to this the claim that these figurations coalesce at a particular place and time—New Orleans, during roughly the first two decades of the twentieth century—and we see why the aural, as embodied in music, attenuates and gives specificity to the potential temporal distensions of the ritual past.

One figuration in Marsalis's list, "worldliness," stands out for being the sole nonmusical one. It performs double duty. First, it names the *interdependence* of the tradition with the world at large and the world's engagement with jazz, each strengthening the other.[54] The point is that the tradition, in order to become history, requires other places and other times. The problem is that this entanglement is asymmetrical. Marsalis glosses over other spheres of interdependence such as imperialism, neocolonialism, and global capitalism. "Worldliness" is inextricable from "world history" and so evokes other pasts, not just other places.[55] Second, the figuration renders the world as an anonymous space. This space offers its *depth* to the debatable past at the expense of addressing the multiple temporalities of the wild yonder beyond US borders.

And within US borders: interdependence is significant to understanding the fortunes of Afro-Latin Jazz given the allure of jazz for musicians from the Caribbean and the Americas[56] who have migrated to the US in order to partake in the music's forms. Authority and continuity, however, impose boundaries in these musicians' participation in the "tradition." The tradition cannot be let to unravel, as it threatened to do during the

1960s and 1970s; that moment plays a merely negative part in the music's history. "Latin Jazz" from the 1950s, however, receives a dispensation, provided that its degrees of closeness and distance from the tradition be established and thus partake in the history of jazz—but only in an ancillary role. Marsalis's figurations regulate questions of "musical" kinship. Race-based ancestry adjudicates the modes of belonging to the tradition:[57] Arturo O'Farrill's dead cannot be Marsalis's own. Marsalis emerges as a remarkable redeemer of his dead.[58] O'Farrill's redemptory efforts will require something other, something more. In the end, the beginning of "Latin Jazz" harbors this impropriety, its debt to another tradition, which is why the advent of the ALJO must be a beginning repeatedly begun. Its musical innovations may be *in* jazz history but are not *of* it. "Latin Jazz" exists as the syncopation of "Jazz."

RACE, RACIALIZATION, *RACECRAFT*

Although "Afro-Americans," in Marsalis's expression, are central to the tradition, he sought a formulation not reducible to race; "I don't speak of 'black' Louis Armstrong," he bluntly remarked.[59] As Eric Porter notes, "Marsalis refuted the assumption that musical excellence was biologically based but also claimed that prescribed modes of artistic behavior pertained to cultural, if not racial, identity."[60] Porter goes on to identify a "struggle to link the artistry of jazz to African American exceptionalism while simultaneously rejecting the racially deterministic belief that black accomplishment in jazz was innate."[61] The force of the logic of cultural expression can be felt in this comment: "For Marsalis, then, jazz is the expression of the highest ideals of the black cultural (as opposed to racial) imagination. Jazz emerged out of a traceable past, structured by a formal set of elements, and practiced by a recognizable group of composers and performers."[62] The expression "black cultural imagination," however, glosses over the internal contradictions in the economy that transform the past into property funded by the coin of the partly empirical and partly transcendental character of the "formal set of elements" of Marsalis's analysis. This section unpacks these contradictions.

On US soil and across its national space, the double logic of property and the proper, of ownership, along with the appropriation of the common, form part of a network of a priori liaisons of ethnic and, *pace* Marsalis, racial affiliation and belonging. If not race, perhaps racialization—"those instances where social relations between people have been structured by the signification of human biological characteristics in such a way as to define and construct different social collectivities"[63]—ought to be critical for understanding the passage from the common to culture and ethnicity. Such passage occurs via a historical narrative drawn from both the ritual past and the empirical past of the jazz tradition peopled by African American musicians. Racialization made bodies visible as part of the process of formally recognizing jazz within the space of the nation.[64] It was a mode of self-management that linked jazz's proper musical elements with a legitimate historical narrative, the aurality it compelled (attentive, serious, respectful, and participatory), and the racial specificity of bodies performing faithful versions of Ellington's and others' music. And so, despite claims to the contrary (e.g., "I don't speak of 'black' Louis Armstrong"), Marsalis's work at JALC asserted the centrality of Black bodies and Black experiences to the jazz tradition and of their present and future as a historical phenomenon.[65]

Taking a long view of the vitality of bodies and performance in the making of Black diasporic cultures, Stuart Hall notes how, given their radical exclusion from mainstream culture wherever they arrived, Black people's cultural repertoires—especially musical practices—were among the rare performative spaces available.[66] He details two intertwined directions of overdetermination for inhabiting those spaces: the first deals with Black inheritance, and the second deals with diasporic connections across cultures. By this account, JALC initially took the first direction with relation to performers' visibility and audibility, while Marsalis followed the second direction when addressing music's "worldliness." Generally, such displays inevitably result in "a kind of carefully regulated, segregated visibility."[67]

This constellation of race, bodies, and spectrality within an economy of tradition and history, along with Marsalis's counter-technology of modernity, constitutes a problem for a foremost critic of Black modernity, Paul Gilroy. For Gilroy, Marsalis abandons modern "conjuring"—a more allusive and alluring relation to Black musicking in modernity than Marsalis's reproductive aesthetics—and signs a pact with postmodern (and postmortem) "iconizing and muting."[68] The "simple recycling of ideas which looks superficially like the continuation of a vital tradition," he adds, is "the Marsalis or Lincoln Center option. It fetishizes technique to produce a sham authenticity from the hard labour of mastering the preferred techniques and approved vocabularies."[69] Embracing one's dead has its risks: Gilroy describes Marsalis's attitude as the equivalent to dancing on past masters' graves.[70] The dispute over the spectral character of the Black music tradition could hardly be made more explicit.

Despite their sharp differences, Marsalis and Gilroy share an abiding commitment to notions of musical Blackness for which the allure both of the past and of ancestry is constitutive, and which, although constructed and non-essentialist, is fundamentally cultural. Gilroy's "conjuring" and

Marsalis's "Negro tradition" might be understood in terms of what Karen E. Fields and Barbara J. Fields call "racecraft."[71] For Fields and Fields, where "*race* stands for the conception or the doctrine that nature produced humankind in distinct groups," and "*racism* refers to the theory and the practice of applying a social, civic, or legal double standard based on ancestry, and to the ideology surrounding such a double standard," racecraft "does not refer to groups or to ideas about groups' traits . . . [and] refers instead to mental terrain and to pervasive belief." Racecraft "originates not in nature but in human action and imagination."[72]

Like witchcraft, in comparison to which Fields and Fields develop the notion, racecraft is a thoroughly rational practice born from and sustained by belief and imagination. Belief and imagination, however, are easily associated with the irrational, as they put it.[73] In the use of the word "craft," however, they shift the focus from the merely ideological and toward the "constitution" or "making"—what I call composition—of "a social world whose inhabitants experience (and act on) a marrow-deep certainty that racial differences are real and consequential."[74] The critical task becomes showing the problematic and unjust rationality of such beliefs in shaping racist thinking—for example, in the critics whom Marsalis excoriates—*and* the rationality of the same belief in anti-racist thinking—for example, in Marsalis's promulgation of "the Negro tradition." In other words, politically, racecraft opens up the question of the better choice of anti-racist thinking and of the constitutional possibilities that such choice opens up.

The challenge as well as the possibility for redirecting the power of belief lies in the centrality of the sensorial in racecraft. Praxis is essential to this redirection: "practices . . . make beliefs available to the senses through real-world doing."[75] A key element of these practices is an "invisible ontology"; that is, the presupposition of "invisible, spiritual qualities underlying, and continually acting upon, the material real of beings and events."[76] This "invisible ontology" implies that visible ontologies, for instance, those associated with racial phenotypes, are of a different character, an unfortunate effect of their ocularcentrism. For those interested in music, this "invisible ontology" might affirm a seemingly inextricable and eminently audible link between Black bodies and minds and the expressive power of their musicking; but the same logic also constrains possible critiques of this link.[77] From this, one concludes that when it comes to the audible, in general, and music, in particular, racecraft gets a free pass. Or better, one concludes that the invisible ontology of Black musical powers complements and amplifies the visible ontologies of Black bodies in performance.

Indeed, music is not only audible. Fields and Fields remark how, in order to ward off doubts about the actual existence of those things that it upholds, the invisible ontology of belief demands that rituals be repeated, keeping "the evidence ubiquitous."[78] But rituals, as Renato Rosaldo wittily put it, are "busy intersections."[79] Repeated performance constitutes the ritual past discussed before, for it expresses the need to reinscribe this past in the embodied performances of the musical present. Importantly, ritual repetition renders belief as "an effect of the relation between peoples."[80]

Racecraft offers a compelling notion anchored in belief and practice that highlights the existential density of social construction and helps explain the endurance of racial logics. It aims at displacing "race" as an empirical datum, showing how, for instance, ancestry and phenotypical traits that may group people together are not in themselves "racial" but are made so by the crafting capacity of belief. Race subsists because of the kind of magical thinking (hence the connection with witchcraft) that transforms, say, ancestry—the link of people across generations—into a racial matter. The craft in racecraft resides in racial thinking's power to make a world in its image, to make it possible to believe in and live by (i.e., "compose") what doesn't exist. Here Fields and Fields take their constructivist argument to its final consequences: race does not exist, only racecraft does.

Racecraft complicates the relationship between the given and the made, or what Fields and Fields call the "empirical" and "belief," respectively. Racecraft is made, but is operative as an actual existence given in and by belief. Within a "society" (the US), the space that opens up between these competing versions of the given and the made creates the conditions of possibility for the "invention of culture," as elaborated by Roy Wagner. Culture is the terrain over which Marsalis develops his critique both of white critics' ideology and of the corollary validation of the proper jazz tradition. Wagner remits the question of "invention" to an issue of symbols and production of meaning in a broad semiotic sense not limited to linguistic symbols. Any society engages two kinds of symbols. First, there are conventional symbols (i.e., agreed upon by convention) that draw a contrast between themselves and the things they symbolize; these are made. Second, there are symbols that assimilate the things they symbolize, with no apparent gap between symbol and thing; these are given. In Wagner's words, "The unique experiences, people, objects, and places of everyday life all correspond, in those features that render them distinct, to this second mode of symbolization—as 'symbols,' they stand for themselves."[81] While Fields and Fields allow for a distinction between these two modes and of their relation as the space where race-craft emerges, Marsalis emphasizes the second mode, while rightly denouncing the critics' conflation of the two.

Every culture or significant cultural class in a society, Wagner argues, favors one symbolic mode over the other as being most appropriate for human action. But differentiating symbols compels disputes over meaning—recall the debatable past. Such a dispute emerges between what "early jazz writers" and Marsalis himself consider the given: for the former, it is the "noble Negro musician" that is given, while for Marsalis, it is the virtuoso innovator. The given, in short, is not as self-evident as it may seem; it is always the result of intense ideological investment. At stake is nothing less than social transformation—that is, "invention"—and the subsequent management and administration of such transformation for the benefit of the winners in the contest over differentiating symbols.

Marsalis's efforts to render tradition (the given) into history (the made) represent just this struggle. To do so, however, Marsalis needs to retain a kernel of the given in the made, evidenced by the appeal to proper names, places, and experience. The main consequence of this—and the reason for my pursuit of the relationship between "racecraft" and "invention"—is that even when constituted as the made, the given remains *a given* (without a gap between itself and experience) and so cannot *be given* (in the sense of a gift).

But there is an important difference in Wagner's proposal. It is less the case that culture is invented, as in the purely constructivist model, than that culture is a system of invention in which invention is a constitutive performative of culture: invention is what culture *does* and culture *is* what it is because of what it does. This invites a revision of racecraft epistemics. "Belief," in Fields and Fields's proposal, appears now as a Durkheimian gloss in the form of a "social allegory."[82] This allegory lends "belief" an epistemic credibility it may not have in itself. Recall that Fields and Fields posit the ontological as a belief in the invisible. The analytic consequences are significant, for, as Wagner puts it in reference to his discipline, "an anthropology that . . . reduces meaning to belief . . . is forced into the trap of having to believe either the native meanings or our own."[83] Operating within the singular space of "culture" in the US, this either/or option would translate into what I called a matter of choice between the true belief (Marsalis's tradition) and the false belief (the early jazz writers' mythology). Both operate within the logic of racecraft, Marsalis's protestations to the contrary notwithstanding, except that one belief would be racist (the early writers') and the other would not (his). With Wagner, we might be compelled to accept that both choices constitute productions of

meaning from specific perspectives. This is not to say that they are politically equivalent, but rather that each must signify ("compose") some
differentiating criteria for belief and its opposite, or between the given
and the made.

This is an unsatisfactory conclusion: showing the given-ness and the
made-ness of what are clearly two sides in an uneven hegemonic arrangement does not open a new politics of jazz in the late twentieth-century
US. It merely registers how regressive and progressive positions are made
from the same cloth and how they make a similar investment in the relation of tradition to history within the nation. My wager, however, is to
show how such mutual investment comes under question precisely with
the arrival of other interested parties (i.e., "Afro-Latin" Jazz) that end up
altering this national configuration.

In the constitution of JALC, we find a set of complex operations that
marshal the past's elasticity, a mobilization of tradition in the service of
a history. This history, told from one perspective alone, emerges out of a
capacious maneuvering of the tensions between the given (tradition, the
deep temporality of the ritualized past, sensu Appadurai) and the made
(history, the debatable past). Neither the given nor the made is what it
seems (or is made to seem). And yet, the conflation of the given and the
made remains remarkably operational. If JALC makes place for time, its
effectivity depends on the particular political and cultural conjuncture out
of which it emerges. In Raymond Williams's mapping, *tradition* requires
institutions—educational, state, media—that publicly inscribe knowledge
in society members' private experience. Williams's third element, *formations*, are "conscious movements and tendencies (literary, artistic, philosophical or scientific) which can usually be readily discerned after their
formative productions." Formations help describe the various and divergent practices of "jazz." Such particular formations "are articulations of
much wider effective formations, which can by no means be wholly identified with formal institutions, or their formal meanings and values."[84] In
considering JALC as an institution, two such "wider effective formations"
were decisive—namely, its cultural politics and cultural policy.

Jazz, Culture, Politics

The unprecedented investment by JALC in rendering tradition into history, managing the meaning of time and of cultural ownership, all tied to
a binary racialized social order in the US, constituted a *politics of culture*,
a mobilization of *cultural policy*, and an affirmation of *cultural citizenship*.
Altogether, this was a classic exercise in the politics of aesthetics pre-

sented in the book's introduction: a distribution of the sensible, of what could be said, heard, seen, in spaces and by those previously excluded from the polity's wider discursive field.

Two interrelated notions underlie this conjuncture of aesthetics, culture, and politics. The first is "cultural reconversion," the increased promotion toward the end of the last century of culture across the state, culture industries, and social movements for the advancement, inclusion, and recognition of underrepresented minorities.[85] Reconversion, here, transforms a musical tradition into the embodiment of democratic values, universalizes a vernacular, and makes of its forms American classical music. Reconversion works within a second notion: "the expedience of culture," the increased interaction and dependence between the state and civil society around "minority rights" and their political agency that places culture as its main mechanism.[86]

The importance of cultural policy comes into focus as "the institutional supports that channel both aesthetic creativity and collective ways of life—a bridge between the two registers . . . [It] is embodied in systematic, regulatory guides to action that are adopted by organizations to achieve their goals."[87] Within a general alignment of citizenship with economic, social, and cultural practices,[88] cultural policy regulates the very notions of creativity it underwrites and polices the actions taken on behalf of and through the aesthetic. Cultural policy institutes, transforms, and regulates sociocultural spaces and subjectivities. It aims to facilitate the smooth functioning of civil society and promotes new conversations in the public sphere. It has the power both to transform the very meaning of the cultural forms it circulates and to steer their core values. Cultural policy constitutes an imminently performative endeavor, strategically deploying culture as an ideological and practical force field within institutional settings with broad societal reach. In the case of JALC, prior to its institution, only the Western Art Music tradition was worthy of public, private, and state investment. Jazz would now partake of this privilege, an economy whose currency is culture and whose exchange protocols are subject to struggles over historical ownership and representation.

Cultural policy mobilizes the notion of "cultural citizenship," "the right to know and speak."[89] Cultural citizenship promotes "new forms of civic life"[90] and complements and enhances forms of citizenship long refused to Black Americans: political ("the right to reside and vote") and economic ("the right to work and prosper") citizenship.[91] This helps us understand why JALC necessarily represented an institutionalization of race for which "culture" served as a surrogate.[92] Citizenship indexes proper belonging and authenticity.

Music's demand for embodied performance works all too well with the needs of racecraft. Its endless renewability via improvisation in performance makes it inexhaustible, qualities that fit the expediency of culture episteme to a tee. Recall also Veit Erlmann's quip: "music becomes a medium that mediates . . . a mediation," where mediation is the organization of social interaction and the medium an "interactive social context."[93] In our case, cultural policy meets the ritual past, empowering a turn to "mythologies, tonalities, and rhythms of nation, race and ethnicity"— "memories," he remarks, "of a time that never was."[94] One might say that JALC's cultural policy exploits music's mediation to create connections between "activity, practice, value, and meaning" that produce particular senses of time.[95]

The cultural politics of JALC and corollary affirmation, recognition, and inclusion of Black culture might suggest a reconstitution of notions of citizenship and culture. But they mean instead the deployment of already existent understandings of citizenship and culture in order to resituate minorities within the grid of intelligibility of a nation.[96] This depends largely on which minority is involved. For Black culture, JALC both reconstitutes citizenship and culture under cultural citizenship and must necessarily do so within the grid of a racist society. In terms of my previous analysis, the tension between tradition and historiography becomes manifest in a tension between the need for social *reproduction* of Black culture and the aspiration for *transformation* of the social order precisely by the incorporation of Black culture.[97] It also depends on the contingencies of "political, economic, and media capacities" that shape the potency of any cultural policy project.[98] As a result, we find the emergence of an elision at the heart of this massive and hugely successful project: another minority knocking at the doors of an already privileged minority. The reproduction of Black culture enters into conflict with a public sphere increasingly transformed by other historical perspectives. This is JALC's syncopation, and O'Farrill's claims to historical inclusion and equity make it manifest.

Making Place for Time (Again)

In its public constitution, the ALJO began with a historiography based on big-band Latin Jazz 1940s origins and its canonic figures. If, for Marsalis, New Orleans cradled jazz into existence, New York City, for O'Farrill, bore Afro-Latin Jazz. And if Louis Armstrong and Duke Ellington served as paradigms in Marsalis's heroic narrative of modern jazz, then O'Farrill (father), Mario Bauzá, Chano Pozo, and Tito Rodríguez played a parallel role in O'Farrill's—to the degree he conjured figures other than his father, O'Farrill too was electing his dead. The differences between these narratives, however, are significant. Emerging out of situations of migration to the US by Caribbean and Latin American musicians in the earlier part of the twentieth century, these origins were "beginnings repeatedly begun." That is, these musicians constantly reconstituted a certain Latin Americanism upon arriving in the US for which music constituted a fundamental resource to reckon with where they had come from and at what time. This is what I call "making place for time," because these migratory reckonings raise questions of space as much as they do of time, history, and tradition.

Experimentation with jazz and Latin music by these musicians served as a technology for producing a *lieu de mémoire* and accumulating time and memory.[99] With its founding in 2002, the ALJO reactivated that technology, indexing thereby the absence of the *milieux de mémoire* that jazz and Latin music once composed.[100] Music served as a focalizing dispositive for how O'Farrill, the Orchestra (ALJO), the Alliance (ALJA), JALC and its cultural politics, and the concentrated artistic and economic scenes of New York City all composed differently viewed and heard worlds.

Further examining the shifts and recalibrations in the Latin Americanist musical production at stake between JALC and the ALJO shows how, despite their shared commitment to the past, they differ in how they conceived and enacted the relation of time and space to place. I identify a set of figures—including but irreducible to historical characters—that contemporary actors consistently invoked to create symbolic and material economies grounded less in a tradition than in the differing relations that the living held with their specters—past, present, and future. I propose to understand these relations and the asymmetries they produce in order to rethink another relation—namely, that between *cultural-epistemic* modalities of representation as depictions of the world and an *ontological* sphere that intervenes into the composition of worlds.

¿DE DÓNDE SON LOS CANTANTES?

An ever-relevant Cuban *son* refrain asks: *¿De dónde son los cantantes?* (Where are the singers from?). The query concerns both the singers' place of origin (*¿de dónde?*) and affirms their ontology as being tethered to a place (*de donde son*).[101] This witty refrain captures the importance of the relation of place to musical origin. The *son* goes further: the singer wants to know the answer to this question in order to affirm the fact that she wants to learn their songs, their art and craft. To place and origin we add memory and musical knowledge. These matters are of the essence to the relation of O'Farrill to Marsalis.

Where did O'Farrill come from? O'Farrill's most important professional musical experience, prior to his involvement in Marsalis's projects, had been with the left-of-center composer and bandleader Carla Bley. As the heir of a pioneer musician in the development of Afro-Cuban and jazz music, raising the profile of his own immediate, familial past and inscribing it into the canonic account of jazz was central to his first institutional project, the ALJO. The Orchestra emerged out of the renewed interest in Chico O'Farrill's work when he began a weekly engagement at New York City's Birdland with his Afro-Cuban Jazz Orchestra and was further resuscitated in the album *Pure Emotion* (1995), produced by veteran jazz promoter and manager Todd Barkan (who would become ALJO's manager and JALC's artistic administrator).[102]

In November 1995, Wynton Marsalis invited O'Farrill, father, to be part of a concert with the Jazz at Lincoln Center Orchestra entitled "Afro-Cuban Jazz: Chico O'Farrill's Afro-Cuban Jazz Orchestra." Arturo O'Farrill recounts:

When he [Marsalis] invited Chico to perform at Alice Tully Hall with his orchestra, it occurred to me that we have a beautiful big band tradition that is wholly and completely based on Latin music. But we didn't have a repertoire orchestra of our own that could begin to canonize and represent a more institutional overview of the history of our music. I talked to Wynton's assistant [April Smith] and I said, "I'm really impressed with what Wynton is doing. Maybe you could ask him if he could help direct us to an institution that might embrace and fund an exploration into our big band tradition." She mentioned this to Wynton; he indicated to her that it was a very interesting topic and that he would think about it.[103]

The rest is history: "Over the years, Wynton and I kept in touch, and we would play together periodically. One day we played a Christmas tree lighting in front of Lincoln Center. He turned to me and he said, 'I've decided to give your idea a home at Jazz at Lincoln Center.' I thought it was an extraordinarily magnanimous gesture—an unbelievable act of friendship and kindness that Wynton extended to me, my father, and our community."[104]

The implications were momentous. As Christopher Washburne put it, "with unprecedented institutional support, O'Farrill was thrust from the shadow of his father to what was potentially an extremely powerful position. Virtually overnight, this arena of jazz became historicized, worthy of preservation quasi on part with the repertoire played by Marsalis' LCJO."[105]

By the time the ALJO officially became part of JALC in July 2002, as Lincoln Center's Afro Latin Jazz Orchestra (LCALJO), it could only have been part of the larger cultural political project of cultural canonization. Alongside Marsalis's neoclassical vision of jazz, Afro-Latin Jazz too could now lie at the center of US aesthetics, its musicians co-contributors to the broader cultural fabric of the country, Omni-Americans partaking in the US's arguably greatest and most original contribution to modern music, the embodiment of the nation's democratic ideals of group participation and individual expression. The incorporation of the ALJO into JALC constituted the most significant expression of intercultural rapprochement in the new century and perhaps an equally unprecedented case of solidarity between two minority communities: *e pluribus unum.*

In giving Afro-Cuban Jazz—a music not fully recognized within the jazz canon—a place in US culture, Marsalis's magnanimous deed both helped constitute that music as part of a shared historiographic notion of a common past and placed it in a subordinate position within that shared history. This is fairly obvious, considering the evidence. For one, the LCALJO served a recuperative function at first, reproducing classics from the golden era of Latin big-band music. *Una Noche Inolvidable* (2005), their first and only recording during their Lincoln Center stint, was a magnificent exercise in nostalgia dedicated to great Latin vocalists such as Graciela (1915–2010), Tito Rodríguez (1923–1973), Celia Cruz (1925–2003), and Benny Moré (1919–1963).[106] According to a former manager with the LCALJO who spoke to me on condition of anonymity, O'Farrill had autonomy over the repertoire, though marquee events such as the "Una Noche Inolvidable" concert would have input from other JALC administrators and programmers.[107] Overall, these ensembles were not equals. Programming dedicated to the LCALJO was relatively scant compared to Marsalis's orchestra, although in the 2004 national broadcast of the inauguration gala concert for JALC's new complex at Columbus Circle, both ensembles shared equal time.

Polemics surrounded naming the new ensemble. As Washburne reports, Marsalis expected to keep the labels "Afro-Cuban Jazz" or "Latin Jazz," both previously used for JALC's concerts.[108] O'Farrill, however, found "Afro-Cuban Jazz" too Cuba-centric, and "Latin Jazz" to lack the proper reflection of Afro-descendent musicians' key role in that tradition.[109] And then there was the issue of race. O'Farrill recounts Marsalis asking, "Where are all the black people?" upon seeing the band's initial roster.[110] At the time, McIntyre, the trombonist, was the Orchestra's sole African American. While other band members, for example percussionist Guerrero, may have self-identified as Afro-descendent, their cultural affiliation breached the boundaries of US-defined Blackness, as Washburne points out. "Afro-Latin" was a suitable compromise. O'Farrill:

[It] more accurately describes the kinds of music worlds that we're drawing from for this orchestra. The real historical basis for this music comes from the mambo days and the Palladium days, and that music is basically rooted in Cuba. But certainly, since then Latin music has blossomed and spread out, and music from all over the continent has been recognized as Latin.[111]

In Washburne's analysis, the coinage "Afro-Latin" creates a double bind between, on the one hand, the production of "heterogeneity," "collaboration," and "commonalities" in "intercultural exchange" and, on the other, the erasure of "differences," "diversities," and "cultural specificity."[112] By this, he means both that the ALJO's ethnic and racial makeup was more diverse than Marsalis's own ensemble when it began and that, despite O'Farrill's declared Pan-Americanist perspective, its repertoire during the tenure at Lincoln Center remained firmly rooted in Afro-Cuban traditions.

The term "Afro-Latin" had precedents elsewhere. Cuban critic Leonardo Acosta used it in his work without singularizing it as a special term.[113] More locally, throughout the 1990s and most forcefully during the aughts, the term "Afro-Latin@" had gained currency in New York City circles associated with the *afro-latin@ forum*, a New York City–based nonprofit organization of which the late Juan Flores was a co-founder. Flores served on LCALJO's advisory board with James Early, a prominent African American functionary, Bob Sancho, a hospital administrator, and Rene Lopez, a leading historian and collector of Latin music. The board, according to Flores, agreed on the need for robust "outreach to the community, neighborhoods, Latino cultural institutions, and the academic community."[114] The term originated from a need to account for "a Hispanic or Latin@ pan-ethnic identity" in the wake of "the explosive demographic increase of immigrants from Latin America and the Caribbean" from 1950 to 1980, and in combination with wider transnational anti-racist movements in the 1980s.[115] "Just as in Latin America, where the prefix Afro has been critical in challenging the homogenizing effects of national and regional constructs," write Flores and Miriam Jiménez Román, "so in the United States the term 'Afro-Latin@' has surfaced as a way to signal racial, cultural, and socioeconomic contradictions within the overly vague idea of 'Latin@.'"[116] Consider the following statement that both perfectly informs ALJO's politics of the signifier (from O'Farrill's perspective) and perplexes its signifyin' politics (from Marsalis's perspective): "Afro-Latin@s belong to both groups. They are people of African descent in Mexico, Central and South America, and the Spanish-speaking Caribbean, and by extension those of African descent in the US whose origins are in Latin America and the Caribbean."[117]

Labels constrain and reduce; they also enable alliances and maintain and transform boundaries. They cannot be assumed to retain their significance across users, not just historically but also at any particular moment. In the first case, the range of signification of the term "Afro" does not hold statically from Bauzá's 1920s Havana to 1930s New York City, when he settles in the US. In the second, at the level of the individual that Washburne considers, the term constitutes neither an imposition by a dominant pole in a hegemonic arrangement nor an emancipatory dispositive for a previously unrecognized racial subject. Individuals' and institutions' relation to the term forms possible modes of managing similarities and differences. Management, however, remains caught in the explanatory grids of identitarian subject position borrowed from 1980s and 1990s social movement politics determined by more or less fixed racial categories that are then variously deployed. In other words, along with the intercultural model and the ethno-racial categories that Washburne invokes, these obey a logic in which the past and origination organize social relations, produce the possibility of culture, and determine ontological registers upon which history is produced.

When O'Farrill identifies the 1940s and 1950s as the "real historical basis of this music," he commits to the same historicist, origins-driven, and past-directed genealogy that Marsalis does.[118] In this sense, the challenge lies less in the assertion of a particular ethno-racial and cultural *ratio* (both as reason and as proportional distribution) than in how such a ratio organizes the past. Much as they try to found their accounts on a common ground, for these actors this past compels diverging duties: "Africa" for O'Farrill, and "the ancestors" for Marsalis.[119] In either case, the empirical past provides these accounts a bodily sense at the same time that each invests place with a sense of memory. Bodies and memory do the work of memorialization and, although it may seem a stretch, of mourning the dead. Like in the Cuban *son*, in learning music one honors the places where they are from, the places where they made history, and both celebrate their lives and mourn their death. To learn, O'Farrill as much as Marsalis must lend their ears, and in lending they also take something in return.

What Gives?

Recall O'Farrill's earnest recognition of Marsalis's magnanimous gesture in saying, "I've decided *to give your idea a home* at Jazz at Lincoln Center." What is given when the gift is a home built upon another gift—namely, song? What sense of home may host an idea?

The figure of the gift has an ineluctable lineage in African American thought. Nowhere is it more powerfully formulated than in W. E. B. Du

Bois's idea of music as "the gift of story and song," as, in part, Black people's offering and response to the white society that subjugated them.[120] To understand the gift at play between O'Farrill and Marsalis—the gift of giving a home to an idea at a place built on song and on Marsalis's narrative of the jazz tradition—involves more than transposing Du Bois's formulation to the present. Anthropologies of relationality offer two pairs of categories that interest me here: first, a distinction between partibles and permeables; second, a distinction between individuals and dividuals.[121] These distinctions afford novel understandings of giving and taking that, although tethered to personhood notions from a wholly other culture, help me understand what happened when Marsalis gave O'Farrill's idea a home.

Partibles, in being given or taken, break down in order to allow for new relationships. A partible entity is internally divided, with animating forces dispersed throughout its parts. Permeables, in contrast, are porous; their animating forces are replaceable—both gained and lost—throughout their existence. A key difference between partibility and permeability is that in partible relations what is given needs to be replaced, whereas in permeable relations what is given extends out from the person or collective without being separable or being constituted by identifiable partibles that must be returned.[122] With permeables, nothing is extracted or excised; only substances and codes are altered. Despite their differences, partibles and permeables may interact within a single person or collective.

Individuals are bounded and defined by possessive and oppositional relations toward the wider social field. Individuality strongly demarcates inside/outside boundaries and upholds political ideals of self-containment. Dividuals, in contrast, are microcosms of societies authored by interactions with others and inseparable from the gifts they offer. Dividuality implies greater integration with the world. Marilyn Strathern formulates the distinction as such: "Far from being regarded as unique entities, Melanesian persons are as dividually as they are individually conceived. They contain a generalized sociality within. Indeed, persons are frequently constructed as the plural and composite site of the relationships that produce them."[123]

These distinctions between partibles and permeables, and dividuals and individuals, help unpack both Du Bois's conception of Black "song and story" and the contemporary status of giving at JALC. In the context of racial orders in the US, possessive individuality becomes a necessity for racial emancipation, in no small part because individuality is the operating dispositive for white slave owners who would deny it to those they

deemed property. In the case of music, individuality *must* be given in
order to bring a modicum of concord to a discordant society. In Du Bois's
shattering formulation, Black folk offer "soft, stirring melody in an ill-
harmonized and unmelodious land."[124] In a first dialectic, music must be
had (under the logic of individual possession and partibility) and given
(under the logic of dividual integration into others and a permeability by
which white people incorporate Black sensibilities).

JALC's cultural politics were firmly anchored in the establishment of
a highly restricted sense of tradition, history, and musical culture; they
were individual. But one may take the period from 1995, the date of the
first concert, "The Latin Tinge: Jazz Music and the Influence of Latin
Rhythms," featuring Tito Puente, until 2002, when programs were dedicated to Latin and Afro-Cuban jazz, to introduce a sense of partibility,
allowing the existence within the individual history of Jazz (capital J) of
specific sites where particular animating forces of its history were lodged.
Thus, the Latin "tinge" or the Afro-Cuban aspects embodied in musical
aesthetics other than the blues or swing but dependent on them signified
that some aspects in the constitution of Jazz were ultimately non-partible,
subject only to a loan, and not to a gift. In other words, those elements
fundamental for the definition of jazz were not to be parted with.

From one perspective, giving a home to O'Farrill's idea might be understood as a shift toward permeability; the institution would be incorporating an aspect into its constitution as a whole, even though this aspect
retained a separate location within that constitution. By *making* room
for the LCALJO, Marsalis may have mobilized jazz's capacity to embrace
various tributaries of its larger tradition, affirming the tradition's interdependence and enhancing its evolutionary continuity. To have named
one of these tributaries as Afro-Latin Jazz would have been a mark of this
capacity, not of a radical differentiation, however. Further, the plasticity
and permeability of history commingles with a rigidity of JALC insofar
as jazz and Afro-Latin Jazz remained separate.[125] From the perspective of
partibles, in contrast, the institutional setting might compel the demand
that O'Farrill's idea maintain JALC's conservative historiography in return for having been *given* a home.

The coexistence of partibility and permeability, and of individuality
and dividuality, during the Orchestra's transition from occasional JALC
guest to permanent ensemble in 2002 indicates the complexities of thinking of tradition as something that can be *given* and of history as that which
is *made*, in a constructivist sense. Along these lines we find Marsalis and
O'Farrill entangled in dense relations with their pasts. The foregoing discussion presents a further dynamic that regulates the economies at stake
in giving or making room at JALC for O'Farrill's idea: debt.

SPECTERS OF CREDIT AND DEBT

Musical exchanges are fundamental for the experimentation across cultures and the emergence of new forms. Musical exchanges brought together, for example, Chano Pozo and Dizzy Gillespie, and compelled "Jelly Roll" Morton to speak of a decisive "Spanish Tinge" in the making of jazz. As the word "exchange" suggests, some sort of transaction is at stake. And such transaction entails an economy in which some give, some take, and some borrow. The fact that such borrowings are not contractually initiated does not mean that they are not susceptible to becoming due as if part of a credit/debt arrangement.[126] How and when credit/debt may be bequeathed across generations becomes a matter of central concern for any possibility O'Farrill may have had to redeem his father's deeds. Marsalis's view of the jazz tradition as a "roll-call of masters"[127] and O'Farrill's deeply personal investment in his father's intervention in the histories of Afro-Cuban and jazz music "weld [them] to particular temporal regimes as people [and] to labor to build the increment demanded by the future in exchange for actions in the past."[128] Whether in giving and taking, or in "giving a home" (Marsalis) or "paying a cultural debt" (O'Farrill), the investment in the past of Marsalis's and O'Farrill's projects constituted a lasting and productive link as well as a burden.

Here's an example. In "'Con Alma': The Latin Tinge in Big Band Jazz" (1998), Marsalis's JALC Orchestra performed 1940s and 1950s classics by iconic figures such as Bauzá, Machito, and Chico O'Farrill. Arranging and conducting were Chico O'Farrill and Ray Santos (1928–2019), a highly respected New York–born former saxophonist and arranger for Machito. Santos introduced the broadcast: "Mario and Machito, I would say, were the first band to actually get into that groove, of combining the jazz solos with the Afro-Cuban rhythms and actually getting arrangements to go with that beat and to lean over to that jazz crowd."[129] The late Ed Bradley, a distinguished African American journalist and host of JALC broadcasts, then formally intoned: "'Machito' was known as 'The Duke Ellington of Afro-Cuban Jazz.' In the 1940's [*sic*], he led New York's top 'Latin' dance band—but he also forged a new music from Afro-Cuban rhythms and jazz. The sophistication and energy of that combination took his band from the dance hall to the concert hall."[130] In a 2004 revision of Bradley's intercultural assessment, Arturo O'Farrill asserts kinship rights: "Mario Bauza [*sic*] introduced us to Latin and jazz, but Chico gave us its greatest expression. Chico gave us its intellect. Chico was often, mistakenly, called the 'Duke Ellington of Latin jazz.' He's really the Chico O'Farrill of Latin jazz."[131] Other specters return, however; introducing a performance of the ALJO during their weekly engagement at Birdland, in June 2015, Arturo

O'Farrill referred to "the conversation that Chano and Dizzy began and are still having about what this music is," embodied in two new arrangements the Orchestra was about to perform from their then-upcoming recording, *Cuba: The Conversation Continues.*

The future too remains haunted by the credit/debt relation. This is felt with particular vehemence in exchanges where the African American invocation of ancestors plays a part, as in jazz, giving a vital role to its dead generations. As Marsalis put it, "in its decades of existence, Jazz at Lincoln Center has represented this swinging music in so many contexts . . . we believe in bringing everyone with us, from the ancestors to the little bitty babies. Swing always."[132] Even in this playful appeal, one cannot ignore the echoes of the words of novelist Toni Morrison: "The ancestors are like a kind of people without time (timeless), eternal, whose relations with literary characters are benevolent, instructive, and of protection."[133] These ancestors make their presence felt in food, rituals, and music, preserving values that coexist but transcend contemporary urbanization and social mobility. In short, they transcend modernity, even as communities in the present remain steadfastly modern.[134] Following Morrison, Farah Jasmine Griffin warns that as a collective, African Americans cannot forget their ancestors, for they demand that contemporary artists be cautious in their enthusiasm for modernity's restless march toward the future. Such forgetting would risk uprooting African Americans of a past fundamental not only to guaranteeing their permanence *qua* tradition but also to safeguarding such tradition's capacity for social *reproduction* in perpetuity.[135]

Social reproduction takes form as *production.* The reproduction of the dead's legacies requires the living's constant labor, be it Morrison, Griffin, or Marsalis. In order to produce their history by animating the past in the present, they must engage in a form of spectral incorporation, engaging in those forms of collectivization most profoundly marked by dividuality and permeability. In the case of JALC's cultural policy, the past not only accrues use-value, but also partakes in an exchange system whenever that past serves to gain incorporation into the national body.

I am less interested in the hauntology of value than I am in the spectral incorporation of the dead in the production of social reproduction.[136] How does the labor of specters organize the existence of the living? Specters give a certain density to the existence of the living; specters address the living, interrogate and admonish them, help and threaten them. Most fundamentally, specters install differences in the lives of the living, and nowhere more powerfully than in proclaiming "these are *my* dead." A corollary formulation asserts in no uncertain terms and in tandem with certain nonnegotiable norms of kinship that "my dead cannot ever be truly and fully *yours*."

Because specters contribute to the formation of human collectives, a unique phenomenon emerges; namely, that it is easier to share the living than to render the dead a social common. Recall the hard work involved in rendering tradition as history on the basis of the dead discussed above, as well as the challenges in electing one's dead or being unable to do so. Eduardo Viveiros de Castro holds that while relationships among the living are experienced mainly as relative and finite, relationships between the living and the dead tend toward the absolute and infinite.[137] The dead introduce and maintain differences, but also foster inequalities among the living. Specters emerge out of these interactions as a formidable technology for the production of temporalities: finite, infinite, past, future. Like the regulative temporalities of credit/debt, such a spectral technology links past, present, and future, and can do so in perpetuity.

We arrive at an understanding of exchange where giving room to an idea and making a commingled history of jazz are defined by a speculative temporality of spectral relations. The task becomes to reconstruct the questions for which the relation between jazz and temporality offers an answer, in particular the figure of the past as an inexhaustible resource. This past, this world of the dead that returns to question and intercede on behalf of the living, introduces a classically spectral dimension to musical endeavors.[138] Related to this spectral aurality, one asks: What of the sonorous can be shared, assumed, and created when the living claim their musical endeavors as partibles, permeables, or inalienable possessions? A first response: the constitution of the jazz-temporality nexus in any historiography is given in a double relation. First, the relation some people may hold to their dead, and second, the relation that others might have with that first relation already held with the dead, a second-order relation.[139]

This double relation applies differently to Marsalis and O'Farrill. The former builds a history on a pantheon of dead heroes he elects and on the grounding idea of the ancestors. The latter builds a history on the basis of the dead he cannot elect and on the grounding idea of Africa, but he must mediate this history through the relation Marsalis has already established with the dead. Any expectation of a common spectrality reveals their incommensurable differences in this double relation. After all, the relation to the dead constitutes one of the most paradigmatic cases for the naturalization of kinship. Kinship becomes a forceful expression of the *given*. To repeat: the given cannot be given away or gifted, only given on condition that it is not really parted away from the giver. Though I am speaking of partibles, permeables might better describe the unique materiality of specters. And yet the dynamics of giving and taking, and credit/debt, inevitably unfold within the terrain of the nation and its institutions.

GIVING-BY-TAKING

The tension between credit/debt operates in a key institutional terrain: citizenship. Migrancy, immigration, and the figure of the foreign might render manifest in the sociocultural milieu of the US what I consider an *unthought* (a relation to the dead that operates at a level subjacent to actual musicmaking) and the *unthinkable* (manners of thinking and experiencing the past otherwise). In a forceful example of what I call syncopation, the relation of jazz to Afro-Latin Jazz forcefully brings out the unthought and the unthinkable in connection to the immigrant.

After leaving JALC, the ALJO embarked on an ambitious, ecumenical project of education, concerts, recordings, and commissions as part of the ALJA, housed in Manhattan's Symphony Space. Among their many critically successful programs: a tribute to the late Dominican saxophonist Mario Rivera; a critically well-received concert on the New Orleans–Caribbean connection with saxophonist Donald Harrison; explorations of Colombian and Afro-Peruvian music (with Colombian composer and arranger Pablo Mayor and harpist Edmar Castañeda, and with Peruvian composer and trumpeter Gabriel Alegría); work with Galician musicians Cristina Pato (bagpipes) and Victor Prieto (accordion); commissions and dedicated concerts with Beninese guitarist Lionel Loueke, Cuban drummer and composer Dafnis Prieto, Mexican drummer and composer Antonio Sanchez, and Puerto Rican saxophonist Miguel Zenón (all highly regarded innovators), arrangements by Croatian bandleader Sigi Fiegl, and features including Rudresh Mahanthappa, a virtuoso alto saxophonist, and pianist Vijay Iyer.

This cosmopolitan outlook would not have been easily imaginable within the original repertory function of the LCALJO, revealing the kinds of risks and experimentation O'Farrill's own institution afforded him. As Cherico put it, "Artie [O'Farrill] just goes for different things," even if that means meeting musical challenges with unfamiliar styles; on average, the ALJO has only two rehearsals and a sound check to prepare an entire concert. Greater inclusiveness yields a heterogeneous jazz cartography of the Americas, pointing to the changing sense of traditional hegemonies centered on the Caribbean and Brazil:

> The truth of the matter is that some of the best music in jazz is being created by pan-Americans. If you really just limit yourself to Cuba and Brazil,

and maybe Puerto Rico, you're doing a tremendous disservice to this music. There's some unbelievable Peruvian music, Colombian music.[140]

In chapter 2, I considered how a decentering of the hegemony of Afro-Cuban music informed Rubén Blades's turn to a number of Latin American genres. There, the singer-songwriter first disavowed Afro-Cuban hegemony only to reincorporate it in the context of a global heterogeneity in a subsequent recording project. I critiqued Blades's politics of restitution and reviewed the possibilities and limitations of his Latin American Latin Americanism: the musical platform on which he had engaged Latin America specifically addressed the continent as an aural interlocutor that was allowed only a limited response by audiences. Little of the continent's music had permeated salsa's musical forms. Moreover, Blades had to "cross under" geographically in order to cross over musically. O'Farrill's increasing opening to the continent points to an alternative trajectory of circulation. Jazz had never explicitly addressed the continent as such, but there had been important liaisons with the music throughout the twentieth century. Such liaisons had compelled, to an unprecedented degree, an increasing number of musicians to migrate North to play jazz at the turn of the century. Nonetheless, in contrast with JALC's perspective on jazz with the US first and Cuba second as the music's matrix, there appears an epistemology of restitution that, consonant with his genealogical proclivities, speaks to a broader basis for jazz as a whole. The Americas, O'Farrill says, constitute jazz's common: "jazz is a Pan-American art form, refined in the US and in Cuba, but it really comes from the Americas."[141] His language is wonderfully ambiguous; in a traditional genealogical understanding, the expression "[jazz] really comes from the Americas" could mean that *jazz came from the continent in the past,* but it could also mean that *jazz keeps on coming from the Americas* because musicians do not cease migrating.

To return to a central motif in this chapter, the ALJO's inclusive endeavors constitute less a return to some putative Pan-American origin than they do "beginnings repeatedly begun." The expression resonates now with the figure of the immigrant and the foreigner as an agent of a constant replenishing of the host nation. In this, as Bonnie Honig proposes, the foreigner constitutes not a problem but a solution.[142] Along with their heirs, the successful immigrant (e.g., Chico O'Farrill, Mario Bauzá) forms a vital part of US myths of exceptionalism: democratic legitimation, rejuvenation, affirmation of the law. The immigrant helps render the US a choice-worthy nation and, in our case, the worthiness of its music (jazz) as a cause deserving for migration and life project.[143]

And so, as part of a genealogy of immigration, O'Farrill might still constitute a problem in relation to the original racial fault line of the US.

While strengthening and complementing Marsalis's and JALC's claims to an invaluable past in the service of a proper place for Black contributions in the nation's sociocultural fabric, O'Farrill and his orchestra's acceptance of a home at Lincoln Center engages in the ultimate form of exchange: taking is what immigrants can, in return, give.[144] Alas, this exchange relies on both parties' radical impropriety, for the giver also takes by giving, binding both in credit/debt and in its constellation of temporalities.[145] That is, this relationship of giving/taking constitutes a reciprocal bind that belongs to no one in particular. Each party gives what cannot be properly theirs; the moment JALC embraces the existence of Afro-Latin Jazz it opens itself, dividually, to this internal other and so cannot exercise the autonomy it assumes when it decides to give room to the idea of Latin jazz, JALC's autonomy being most evident in its ultimate cancellation of the Afro-Latin Jazz program.[146] Whatever autonomy and individuality there may be is an effect of procedural institutionalization.

The drive to create a larger common around jazz, in its tradition-bound, neoclassical version, is shot through by a supplementary logic: immunity. Immunity demands that the community preserve itself by avoiding exhausting itself in giving as well as by acknowledging the ineluctable existence of Latin Jazz (i.e., Afro-Cuban or Afro-Latin Jazz) in order to refract its claims to being jazz.[147] Immunity enables exemption from the obligation to give (or take) and authorizes freedom from the communal obligation of those who, as Timothy Campbell writes, "enjoy an originary autonomy or successive freeing from a previously contracted debt."[148]

Immunity is never absolute. At JALC, as in the US, it remains an imperative that whatever is "Latin" (or Latino, or Latinx) remain so. This classic structure of North American Latin Americanism depends on having to give, but to give without compromising the potential claim to communal individuality; that is, without compromising the claim that there be something called a Black music or an African American culture or a music of the nation. Within the national sphere, the original debt—slavery and its corollary racism—cannot ever be redeemed and so the claim to individuality is historically necessary. And yet O'Farrill, in giving a name and a history to Latin America, engages in a Latin Americanism of his own. For this he too must conjure his dead, dead who might haunt those immigrants who, like specters, never stop showing up, returning. Here I differ with Roberto Esposito, for whom "death is our *common* impossibility of being what we endeavor to remain, namely, isolated individuals."[149] For death constitutes a radical opening to the other. But from a Latin Americanist and Afro-Caribbeanist perspective that accounts for histories of colonialism and imperialism, those arriving in the US from the subcontinent may have at once the possibility to elect their dead and to have no choice at all, more so today when few traditions remain that haven't already washed ashore South and so have already been consumed, read, heard, played, or thought about.

Conclusion

O'Farrill spoke to me about a need to "change a lot of the conversation about jazz in the US." He asserted that "we [the ALJO] create this alternative conversation."[150] Public discussion about his project, news of concerts, reviews of performances, pedagogical outreach, and recordings contribute to that "alternative conversation." Critic Ben Ratliff, unwittingly anticipating O'Farrill's assessment, prognosticated in 2002 that "jazz will become Latinized to the point of an entirely new audience emerging."[151] Ratliff might have exaggerated, but O'Farrill's projects have undoubtedly contributed toward the construction of spaces of interaction for the music in which this so-called Latinization is important.

O'Farrill's contributions, however, exceed public review and the creation of new audiences. First, the ALJA and the Orchestra have actively partaken in a "distribution of the sensible," making claims to an equality of intelligibility in relation to the hegemonic story of jazz. As O'Farrill argues, the music the Alliance embodies is not a version of a more proper "jazz" but simply a particular expression shaped by migratory circulation in the Americas of one and the same music. The amplified public sphere is one aspect of a broader "aural sphere," to use Ana María Ochoa Gautier's expression,[152] that O'Farrill might say has existed before. Second, as part of this (re)distribution, changing the conversation entails establishing an interlocutor "with whom," as Jacques Rancière writes, "not only a conflict of interests is under debate but the very situation of speaking as speaking beings."[153] According to Rancière, to address this "third person" is to lay a question at its doorstep and to establish an "I" or "we" that represents a community.[154] O'Farrill's "conversation," then, would be less a meeting of minds than the formation of "an opinion that evaluates the very manner in which people speak to each other and how much the social order has to do with the fact of speaking and its interpretation."[155] We may take "speaking" here to relay political imperatives that help reconfigure how to address musicking, its practice in the present, and both the pasts that inform it and the futures they may yet open. Any presumed inequality between two modes of linking temporality, tradition, and history—JALC's and ALJA's—would emerge because O'Farrill assumes an "equality of speaking beings." There thus exists a gap or disagreement (syncopation) within the US logos that governs the intelligibility between two parties, each a minority and each with a stake in their citizenship constituting a "cultural" gift or contribution to the good of the nation. Equal aurality names the force animating this syncopation.

Consider how, from Marsalis's perspective, the jazz tradition is undergirded by the notion that Black musicians constituted a part (of the jazz tradition) that had no part (in the nation) because it was the product of unthinking music making (as put forth by the critical tradition he scorned).[156] Marsalis's notable political move consisted in challenging and altering the social order, rendering intelligible to the nation this structure of a part with no part: Black musicians who count as musicians but not as part of the cultural making of the nation. Recall the underlying tension at the heart of Marsalis's claim: because race had been the key logic behind the establishment of this (dis)order and because upturning this logic needed to preserve that particularizing element to argue that Black musicians and culture *are* part of the nation, Marsalis had to appeal to the notion of culture to both dismiss and maintain race. The notion of racecraft helped address this tension by highlighting the primacy of performance and alluding—via Wagner's notion of culture as a practice of invention—to struggles over symbolic meaning.

This analytic approach addresses the vexing issue of freedom's relation to aesthetics. As Marsalis and many others maintain, jazz is unthinkable without the efforts of those descending from enslaved people reduced to their capacity to work and reproduce. Freedom would become not just a right but also a property of these persons by virtue of having been deprived of precisely that freedom. Free to profit and to lose for themselves and their work, however, Black Americans would still not share in what ought to be the corollary common of being an equal part of the nation's community. This shows the degree to which the elimination of the wrong given in the lack of participation in the common differs from the economic apportioning of goods and, at least in part, the reparation of the damages suffered at the hands of others. Freedom here functions as a condition of possibility for the redistribution of economic exchanges, in the form of the potential to profit and to lose. In our case, JALC becomes the embodiment of this redistribution; "jazz" is entitled to a share in the community by the good that it gives the common. This redistribution, however, conflates a logic of exchange with the logic of the common good.[157] Such conflation of the logic of exchange with the political does offer a real political payoff, since a project like JALC, by affirming how jazz embodies America's democratic ideals, makes a claim on the character of the nation's (cultural) common that exceeds mere inclusion. African American culture, for Marsalis, serves as an avatar for the inclusion of the community as a part which now has a part.

The problem with this resolution, arrived at via a logic of exchange, is that it is haunted by those who, like African Americans, emerge within the nation as another part with no part—namely, people who do not hold birthright to citizenship and are consolidated by their migration to the US. This migrant part also comes to claim direct participation in the making of something as valued a property as jazz, saying that they too offer a good to the common.[158] They may be counted in the history of jazz as being Latin, or Afro-Latin, or Latin American, or immigrants, but when it comes to partaking of the common, they can add to it but do not constitute it. Afro-Latin Jazz, the label that worked in the context of JALC, is useful for jazz, but its mere inclusion is not sufficient. This has to do with the fact that an effective transformation of the political stakes of jazz requires that the logic by which the common is determined and participation in it arbitrated be other than the logic of exchange (i.e., inclusion and recognition). This has yet to happen.

The various arguments, debates, and answers rehearsed in this chapter do not generally constitute differences over competing interests, but instead express a torsion at the heart of the common. This torsion exists because each group—and in our case JALC and ALJA—differs from itself. Rather than there being differences between groups, each differs from itself every time the common is at stake because a reconfiguration of the common implies a transformation of the social forces determining that a group be constituted under certain criteria such that the group may dissolve. The common cannot ever be truly common. And so, divergences occur on a surrogate terrain—namely, history and the temporal, spatial, and emplaced relations that constitute history.

These relations are not shared among groups, or better yet, they become key relations in the production of accounts, such as that of jazz, in which what is not shared or common is accented. Hence, the question of history remains. O'Farrill's idea of an "alternative conversation" might partially represent an alternative *history* (i.e., a heterogeneous sense of jazz's past) and also perhaps an alternative *to* history (i.e., acting in the spirit of collaboration rather than history writing). It might be an alternative to historicism and its hold on the notion of universal history, the narratability of the past, and the corollary structure in which history sides with the "winners."[159] Or he could be simply relaying the tenor of the times, one that sees an increasingly heterogeneous character for jazz today.

We may think of the notion of an "alternative conversation" in relation to what a number of decolonial historiographers identify as the need to write histories that adopt the notion of heterogeneous temporalities. But it isn't enough to address this heterogeneity. As Dipesh Chakrabarty remarks, one ought to approach the past by "staying within heterogeneities without seeking to reduce them to any overarching principle that speaks for an already given whole."[160] This would have the effect of sidestepping historicism's central concern with historical time as linear or evolutional and with "the idea that to understand anything it has to be seen both as a unity and in its historical development."[161]

When speaking of the Americas in the context of the ALJA, O'Farrill's Latin Americanism insists on jazz as something that remains open, ever susceptible to transformation—if he might have redeemed his father, there must be further need for redemption. If there is an overarching principle to his conception of jazz, in the sense that Chakrabarty warns against, it is this openness. But, in line with Chakrabarty's admonition, O'Farrill does not posit an "already given whole." Instead, to speak of "the Americas" is less to speak to an already given whole than to trace how this spatio-temporal abstraction—"the Americas"—emerges from a set of relationships produced in and through circulation itself. Jazz is here redeemed insofar as its past guarantees that it remains open, enacting Benjamin's notion of weak Messianism that I alluded to in the introduction to this chapter.

When O'Farrill turns his attention to the creativity of musicians outside of the US and toward the labor of those who have migrated here, the narrative of jazz's national foundations opens up to the multiple modalities of relating place, time, and space. As a corollary, this narrative comes to terms with the idea that jazz has been taking place elsewhere all along. With this in mind, we might rethink jazz history and the traditions that enable it. This does not necessarily mean jettisoning the idea of jazz history. For one, this chapter has addressed how making this history has been hard earned and how justifiable and necessary it is on account of the exclusion of African American musicians from the national narrative of the US. Instead, O'Farrill's vision might incorporate heterochronic and heterotopic notions of jazz into something like Chakrabarty's notion of History 2, a history in which its object cannot be managed within the framework of delimiting boundaries or as part of a conservative logic of musical reproduction, a history that cannot be reduced either to a contest between "local histories" and "global designs."[162]

And yet, within O'Farrill's vision of history there are stories of closure and correlate historical totalities more typical of History 1. This would be the case of the return to Cuba of Chico O'Farrill's remains and of his musical legacy, which would insist on a local history haunted by its own racism, which he wholly skips over. In this case, specters operate at a personal scale, yes, but also at a scale that moves to the downbeats of geopolitics, massively imposing its gargantuan rhythms on musicking. The return of his father's remains re-temporalizes O'Farrill's dead and his dead makes history for him as well, a history that necessarily tethers his musicking to a place, Cuba. These scales profoundly syncopate the many actors involved, producing for them not just the disruptions that characterize modernity but different notions of what time and temporality are. Such experiences of syncopation remain inextricably linked to the displacement between Cuba and the US (and back) that—at the same time that they acquire debts to and in both locations—becomes the source of credit tenderable to each other. Credit/debt, in short, accrues for both immigrant and host. Failure to acknowledge this mutuality gives way to the re- or even dislocation of this spatial displacement to the terrain of temporality, embodied in and entangled by claims and struggles over tradition and history.

Is there an alternative to the juxtaposition of two histories that O'Farrill engages? Is it ever possible to sidestep the impossibility of a true common defined by a dissolution of all markers of difference that yet may nonetheless maintain the indelible specificity of anyone and anything? Miguel Zenón (b. 1976), virtuoso Puerto Rican alto saxophonist and the next chapter's focus, asserts a permeable composition for which the dead make music possible but do not dictate its course yet to come.

5 * Act, Event, and Tradition: Miguel Zenón and the Aurality of the Unthinkable

Nothing appears so enigmatic today as the question of what it means to act.

Paolo Virno

The novelty of an event is expressed in the fact that it interrupts the normal regime of the description of knowledge, that always rests on the classification of the well-known, and imposes another kind of procedure on whomever admits that, right here in this place, something hitherto unnamed really and truly occurred.

Quentin Meillassoux

In 2008, the twenty-first century will sound as shown in figure 5.1. More specifically, this is how the MacArthur Foundation, in 2008, stated that jazz sounds in the "21st century":

> Miguel Zenón is a young jazz musician who is expanding the boundaries of Latin and jazz music through his elegant and innovative musical collages. As both a saxophonist and a composer, Zenón demonstrates an astonishing mastery of old and new jazz idioms, from Afro-Caribbean and Latin American rhythmical concepts to free and avant-garde jazz. This young musician and composer is at once reestablishing the artistic, cultural, and social tradition of jazz while creating an entirely new jazz language for the 21st century.[1]

High praise indeed, given jazz's inextricability from the State's claim on the music, from values of modernization, liberal ideology, and Afro-Modernism, and from the expressive practices of a minority group in the US and heard as the affirmation of creativity and participation of subordinated people in a culturally, economically, and racially segregated society.[2] And high praise, especially given that Zenón admits to having been only superficially familiar with the jazz tradition and its musical intricacies as late as 1996, the year he came to the US from Puerto Rico to study the music.[3] The excerpt in figure 5.1 comes from *Jíbaro* (2005),

Figure 5.1. Miguel Zenón, "Seis Cinco" (excerpt)

the album praised by the Foundation in which Zenón explored *música jíbara*, a Puerto Rican vernacular form that is commonly associated with the Island's countryside and its rural population of mixed ethnicity. In *Jíbaro*, Zenón set out to explore and exploit the implications of the *décima*, an octosyllabic ten-line stanza with origins in Hispanic poetics, rigorously ordering this virtuosic vernacular form; he organized every piece, for his quartet of saxophone, piano, drums, and bass, around formulas based on the numbers ten and five.

Zenón embeds clear, folkloric material within a modernist rhythmic/ harmonic milieu. In the score, the piano part is doubled by the bass, the drums playing along with their part. The counterpoint played by the piano and double bass is decidedly nontonal. The saxophone line is distinctly tonal and clearly outlines a I-IV-V harmonic progression that is typical of the "Seis Chorreao" style. Figure 5.2 outlines the harmonic progression suggested by the melody. Note the stepwise descending sequence (here, a repeated pattern that moves down a step each measure) in the second phrase, beginning at m. 18 in the score, redolent of the eighteenth-century Romanesca pattern. The track ends with a tag typical of *música jíbara* tunes.

The music made a strong impression. "I've rarely seen a jazz composer step forward with a project so impressively organized, intellectually

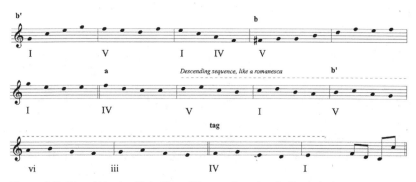

Figure 5.2. Miguel Zenón, "Seis Cinco," harmonic and melodic analysis

powerful and well played from the start," wrote Ben Ratliff in his review of
the first live performance of this project at New York City's Jazz Gallery.[4]
Tom Hull of the *Village Voice* said, "[Zenón is a] smart guy, knows his
craft inside and out . . . This is his Puerto Rican roots record—jíbaro is a
rural folk-pop style, Edwin Colon Zayas calls it his 'country music.' . . . He
writes new pieces mapping the style onto a standard acoustic sax-piano-
bass-drums jazz quartet—no cuatro, guiro, bongo, vocals. The result is
jazz centered on jíbaro roots, rather than jazzed up jíbaro or some kind
of fusion. It's exceptionally clean and clear, beguiling music."[5] Parallels
with canonic jazz figures were almost inevitable: "In comparison to Min-
gus' experimentation with Cumbia and Jazz, Zenón's approach on *Jíbaro*
proves to be vastly more intuitive," Mark Holston wrote, adding that the
project constituted "an equally rewarding departure from the jazz mainstream."[6] In his review for *All About Jazz*, John Kelman drew comparisons
to legendary saxophonist, composer, and arranger Wayne Shorter, who
was then leading arguably the most celebrated quartet in jazz. Kelman
highlights a shared intellectual approach between the two musicians but
ultimately critiques Zenón's approach. I quote him at length:

> Like Shorter, Zenon is a deep thinker, capable of taking the simplest Puerto
> Rican folk melodies—the basis of *Jíbaro*—and placing them into more har-
> monically and rhythmically complex contexts. Also, like Shorter, Zenon's
> cerebral music requires an intense focus that makes considerable demands
> on both the musicians who play it and the listeners who experience it.
> And it's possible that Zenon will ultimately achieve the same degree of
> significance as Shorter. He is, after all, still young, yet he has a remarkably
> focused conception that distinguishes both his playing and his writing.
>   But there are important differences as well. Shorter's music, as complex
> as it can get, always relies on bold experimentation from his quartet, ensur-

ing openness and a desire to let even the most challenging of constructs breathe.

Zenon, on the other hand, is nothing if not considered. In the press release for *Jíbaro*, he states, "Given my tendency to sometimes write music that is too difficult to play, I was sensitive to bringing the music to the point where it was difficult, but not impossible." Writing music that challenges its players to evolve and reach for hitherto unattainable levels of performance is not uncommon, nor is it inherently problematic; but the music on *Jíbaro* comes off as too earnest, too serious for its own good.

. . . Complex metric shifts abound, and solos appear over clearly delineated sections. While there's a certain folksy naivete about some of the melodies Zenon draws upon, the feeling gets lost in the heavily detailed arrangements . . . The beauty of Wayne Shorter's current group is that it brings a visceral quality to Shorter's heady charts; Zenon's group has equal potential to combine the head and the heart. Unfortunately, that simply doesn't happen on *Jíbaro*. But with so many of the raw materials in hand, it may be only a matter of time and maturation before Zenon develops into a truly important force.[7]

The Foundation's statement and this review might express the idea of a New World musician working in a metropolitan center, who, seeking to ground him- or herself, returns to his or her musical roots in search of resources that yield new hybrids—as the Foundation put it. The result is an increasingly mongrelized jazz, reflective of a generation of musicians for whom genre-hopping is the norm rather than the exception. Though not incorrect, this reading would only partially account for the dynamics the Foundation intimates in the question of the new and of a musical future. In its simplest version, Zenón could be said to have gone back to the future: by returning to one of the most traditional forms of Puerto Rican music, he might have been able to accentuate the capacity of the past (here, "tradition") to propel innovation. In Puerto Rico, *música jíbara* is associated with the countryside and considered a firmly tradition-bound practice, demanding strict adherence to well-established musical forms and parameters for improvisation.[8] This turn to tradition would also constitute a return, one that would help establish a temporal relation of anteriority to the contemporaneous. Also implied in the Foundation's words are notions of exteriority (periphery) and interiority (center). Namely, inherent in this review is the idea that (1) the examination, exploration, and subsequent exploitation of resources from the past demand that the musician returns to the periphery; and that (2) by contrast, the production of *Jíbaro* at the metropolitan center and through recourse to its musico-technical resources would constitute the passage to a future guaranteed by the center. This narrates a progressive sequence of events that would guarantee modernity a continuous and homogeneous temporality within which its unfurling into the future takes place. For Kelman, the maturity that time might afford him could place Zenón on an even plane with an acknowledged master such as Shorter. But not yet.

These reviews' calculus of time, space, and place reveals some of modernity's most enduring legacies. These include: maps of exteriority and interiority; narratives of temporal lag, belatedness, and supersession; the enigma of multiple unfolding temporalities; the perception of change as development; marked distinctions between tradition and innovation, the rural and the urban; the privileging of technologies and techniques; and the division of artistic, creative, and cultural labor. These temporal and spatial designs are peculiar. That global space should constitute a simultaneity (because it is an interconnected network of modernity's imperial routes) ought to be common sense within its own logic, given that the globe is an abstraction of that network. Modernity, however, transforms global space into a set of non-contemporaneous places. It establishes hierarchies determined by presumed temporal disparities. This transformation, in turn, becomes one of several commonplaces of modernity: some people and societies lag behind others depending on where in a temporal continuum they "are" and where they "happen" to be.[9]

These operations actively organize structures of classification, distribution, and the division of people according to their position vis-à-vis an alleged center of modernity: Europe or the US, which I call North Atlantic modernity.[10] A particular geographical center and epochal origin (Europe or the US) is rendered universal. And because otherness is central to the setting up of boundaries defining a center and an origin, these boundaries constitute concomitant hierarchies that rationalize and give intelligible form to difference: difference is the fundamental relation and value that emerges from the temporal and spatial designs of modernity.

Modernity and difference, I propose, are at stake in Zenón's music, and in how critics, audiences, and cultural institutions have listened to it. It could hardly be otherwise, given Puerto Rico's complex relation to the US, in general, and Zenón's sustained connection with his birthplace, in particular. This is an ongoing story, one that I argue intervenes in a musical history that is necessarily a history of listening and aurality. Thus, how to think of this nexus between modernity and difference in relation with the *Caravana Cultural*, a series Zenón founded in 2011 to present free-of-charge concerts in rural areas of Puerto Rico? The concerts introduce canonic figures such as John Coltrane and Miles Davis to audiences in small towns away from the larger metropolitan centers of the Island. What effect might result from this effort to include traditionally excluded audiences in the encounter with a music with its own tradition and history such as jazz? What can we say of how these audiences listened when the Caravana appeared to bring jazz's past to the spaces in which past he rooted *Jíbaro*?

We find two available historiographies of Zenón's creativity. One folds his breakthrough 2005 recording into a linear temporality, and another recognizes his intellectual disposition and the heterogeneity it contributes to contemporary jazz but withholds a full endorsement on an account of maturity yet to come. These deploy teleologies and narratives of progress and development. But more is at play in the relation of modern difference, the appeals to tradition, the act embodied by Zenón, and the very event of his appearance that these narratives cannot quite think of. Zenón, this chapter argues, performs an important syncopation in (but not of) modernity. He does this through an aurality of the unthinkable that is at play in: (1) the traditions in *Jíbaro*; (2) the event of the Caravan; and (3) the act of his decision not to decide on a fixed Puerto Rican identity at the forum of the National Museum of the American Latino Commission. Central to this aurality is the suspension of times and places. It is an aurality of the unhinkable because Zenón at once refuses (or is indifferent to) the terms that define the state of the situation (i.e., the field of established identities/differences within which the exercise of governance and domination comes to be experienced and the position that an element [person, time, place] in a state holds in relation to any other element). Zenón asserts an alternative unthinkable under those terms.

Critical Modernities

To understand *música jíbara* is to understand the Puerto Rican peasantry—the large agrarian proletariat that emerged from sugar plantations and manufacturing—with which it is intrinsically linked. Sidney Mintz identifies the confluence of resource extraction, exploitation of manual labor, and latent industrialization of the agrarian sector as key to the constitution of modernity in colonial Puerto Rico. The sugar complex, Mintz argues, served as a living laboratory for technologies required to discipline bodies to perform labor that Europeans would later depend on for their Industrial Revolution.[11] Mintz's work does not so much argue for the chronological primacy of the Caribbean in the development of economic modernity. Rather, it makes visible the role of an "exterior" in the formation of some of modernity's most powerful dimensions: industrial capitalism, population management technologies, and shifts in taste and consumer behavior vis-à-vis manufactured non-essential commodities. Mintz's historical materialist analysis allows us to consider that, although irreducible to it, from its inception Puerto Rican peasantry and their *música jíbara* are of and in modernity.[12]

By "critical modernity" I identify the questioning of modernity as a project of worldwide diffusion through European colonialism, first, and later through US imperialism. Where Mintz focuses on the Caribbean and the globalization of capitalist dispositives, others consider the primacy of Creole elites in the Caribbean and South America in the genealogy of the modern nation, the constitutive role of the Haitian Revolution in the realization of European political ideals, or the transformation in the relation of cultural production to forms of political contestation in the Middle Passage.[13] Critical modernity regards modernity as a "project" emerging from this ensemble of forces and as a "projection" of colonial and imperial powers onto others, which compels a thinking of modernity that minds both its complex and troubling genealogy as well as its effectivity in the present.[14]

Culture plays a central role in traditional mappings of modernity. On the face of radical economic disparities between centers and peripheries, local cultural practices in the periphery could not merely survive but thrive, either despite modernity (e.g., in vernacular forms such as *música jíbara*) or because of it (e.g., local versions of forms resulting from North Atlantic expansion). Some would locate Latin America's position within modernity as a "geographical fringe condemned in the history of civilization" and define it in terms of lag, exteriority, and difference.[15] Others would find in Latin American cultural expressions distinct and powerful contributions to an ecumenically conceived modernity.[16] Reflecting the general tenor of critical modernity, Hermann Herlinghaus writes that "the peripherical no longer signals a state of deficit but rather specific conditions and needs of decentering." He refers to

A modernity that is not situated in the midst of criteria and expectations previously rationalized; rather, a distinct modernity as an ensemble of experiences of a new cultural extension, signaled by means of topologies of the heterogeneous and the intercultural, and by anachronic temporalities. This is a modernity constituted by new crossings of the political and the cultural and by multiple articulations between the mass mediated and the popular.[17]

Herlinghaus's critical thinking of peripheries informs my analysis of critical modernity. By mapping Latin American modernity in terms of simultaneity and co-participation, critical modernity helps define the region in terms of a multiple (coexisting, coeval) modernity. The historical examination of contact between "worldly" figures and local actors is central to this critical project.[18] For Beatriz Sarlo, who coined the expression "peripheral modernity," Latin America's particular location produced sociocultural specificity as a positive value, while retaining a constitutive link to a classically defined, European lettered modernity.[19] Herlinghaus's rhetoric of decentering updates the topological reconfiguration of Sarlo's analysis.

"Difference" indexes the particularity of Latin American modernity as a place of enunciation, but recent critiques disagree as to the nature and critical power of that particularity. Alberto Moreiras speaks of "the exhaustion of difference," arguing how the insistence on difference has exhausted its critical force by circumscribing Latin America as an object of knowledge. That is, as an a priori *object* given in its difference from everything it is supposed not to be like.[20] This logic of difference in turn demands that such knowledge be cast as being properly (meaning both fully adequate and original) Latin American. Furthermore, representation's power by means of difference, Moreiras argues, has been "spent" with no apparent result other than its insistence on impossible autochthony. Taking an alternative approach, Arturo Escobar argues that in cultural encounters difference *as such* does not carry intrinsic value; instead, value circulates as "difference in effective power associated with particular cultural meanings and practices," and as whatever difference cultural "difference makes in the definition of social life."[21]

How to broker the gap between Moreiras's concern with the exhaustion of representation and Escobar's call to attend to living practices? What difference does difference make in sense-making operations propelled by creativity and innovation, as in the case of Zenón, which nonetheless are enmeshed in networks of modern representation such as the MacArthur Foundation's? Where are those differences experienced—at the level of the individual, communities, institutions of various kinds, relations of ownership, the production of subjectivity, selfhood, and personhood, knowledge—and what forms do they take—culture, economic, ideational, political?

Critical modernity advances three general ideas that, all bearing upon the modern genealogy of difference, might help address these questions. First, the movement of modernity—multifarious, chaotic, and riddled with ambiguities—destabilizes the distinction between an a priori center and a diffuse periphery onto whose shores its ideas, institutions, knowledges, and technologies have washed, are washing, or will have washed. Second, the dispersion of a sense of center and periphery makes of modernity a radically relational phenomenon, one that enables us to no longer think of modernity in the singular. The terms "alternative," "divergent," "liquid," "multiple," "peripheral," and "vernacular" constitute a small fraction of modernity's many qualifiers. Each one elaborates its local character in full recognition of what Mary Louise Pratt labeled relations of "contradiction," "complementarity," and "differentiation" of a pluralized modernity. With these terms, Pratt identifies the process by which the governed are to be made in the image of the governing power while never being quite the same. This relation is one of complementation in a dialectic that maintains a constitutive and insurmountable difference as its *raison d'être*.[22] Third, once interrogated, the mechanisms under which difference becomes intelligible reveal difference to be what separated the center from the periphery and the contemporary from the anterior, but also what separated the center from itself. The center is beset by internal differences (e.g., of class and ethnicity). But difference remains unintelligible to those engaged in its rationalization, appearing as the way things are. This operation is dialectical: modernity, like colonialism and imperialism, must uphold difference even as it needs to produce identities in its own image everywhere it "expands." Difference insinuates itself as modernity's *unthought* and as that which, in modernity, most needs being un-unthought.

Critical modernity challenges us to conceptualize both the processes of its radical plurality and the attendant de-universalization of North Atlantic modernity. It examines how a history of ideologies of superiority and inferiority, and how experiences of exteriority, have affected social and cultural structures in specific locations.[23] Its task is to study how ideas and practices drawn from the vast archive of modernity constitute the means to link everyday experiences to larger historical processes. Music pedagogies are part and parcel of these processes. With this we move to Puerto Rico and to Miguel Zenón's formative years.

MODERN MUSICAL PEDAGOGIES

Zenón relates how, growing up in the Residencial Luis Llorens Torres—the largest public housing complex in the Caribbean and one of metropolitan San Juan's most impoverished districts—a rigorous music pedagogy program with European roots marked the beginning of a long march toward "the future."[24] He recalls how Ernesto Vigoreaux, a professional musician also involved in community leadership, began offering free music instruction to young students in the neighborhood. For a full year, no one could touch an actual musical instrument. All efforts were dedicated to aural musicianship and literacy. Day in and day out, students used the nineteenth-century Spanish priest and pedagogue Hilarión Eslava's solfège manual, slowly worked their way into music notation, sang and conducted simultaneously, and took dictation. Zenón, who was then ten years old, wanted to take up the piano but had to settle for the saxophone, since only band instruments were available on loan. Eventually, Vigoreaux would take small ensembles to perform around the Island on weekends.[25] Zenón's musical education was thoroughly modern, indeed, and gaining musical knowledge this way enabled Vigoreaux to invigorate both Puerto Rico's center and the peripheries where he and his students would travel.

A more liberal but no less rigorous education followed Zenón's early musical formation when he was admitted to the Escuela Libre de Música de Puerto Rico. The purpose of the Libre, as the network of music schools is commonly known, lies in "developing and channeling the innate artistic sensibility of our people by means of a systematic plan of teaching, learning, experimenting, divulgation, and formation of musical art."[26] As its name states, education is tuition-free. It was created in 1946 by Ernesto Ramos Antonini, an Afro–Puerto Rican lawyer, musician, and legislator who was a member of the House of Representatives from 1940 to 1963. The Libre emerged from Operación Serenidad (Operation Serenity), a project initiated by Luis Muñoz Marín, who was the Island's first democratically elected governor (1949) and was known as "the father of modern Puerto Rico."

Serenidad was an early example of postwar, US-sponsored cultural policy in Puerto Rico.[27] Muñoz Marín said of this project: "[Serenidad] tries to impart to the economic efforts and political liberty objectives that are harmonious with the spirit of Man in its governing function, rather than as a servant to economic processes . . . the Puerto Rican people awaits eagerly to remain kind-hearted and peaceful in its understanding and attitudes, all the while utilizing fully and vigorously all the complex resources of modern civilization."[28] Serenidad followed the drafting of the Puerto Rican Constitution (1952), the massive industrialization of the Puerto Rican economy under the development project of Operación Manos a la Obra (Operation Bootstrap) (1947), and a wide-reaching literacy campaign (1949). In these "economic efforts" and "political liberty objectives" during this period of "modernization" to which Muñoz Marín alluded, we see one of the distributions of modernity: establishing the distinct domains of the political, the economic, the moral, and the artistic. Zenón's education from the Libre cannot be divorced from this complex of modernized institutions, being in part a symptom and realization of Ramos Antonini's and Muñoz Marín's integrative aesthetic vision. Moreover, this education, which Zenón says prepared him excellently for his eventual years as a music student in the US, embodies the correlation between modernity and modernization, itself a trademark of Caribbean and Latin American history throughout the twentieth century and a living symbol of its contradiction as a region that without being fully (or truly) modernized is nonetheless modern.

It was during his years at the Libre that Zenón developed his interest in jazz. He concentrated, however, in classical alto saxophone performance because the school did not offer a concentration in jazz. Only toward the end of his degree could he play in the school's big band. Their repertoire, he told me, consisted not of mainstream jazz but of mainly charts from well-known "Latin" bands like Tito Puente's. After finishing high school, Zenón found local gigs that familiarized him with jazz standards. By his own account, his musical language was still developing. He would later define this period by a lack of understanding of blues traditions and of musical techniques of harmony and improvisation. Nonetheless, he gained exposure to a repertoire that included modern jazz and some of Ornette Coleman's experimentations. He avidly listened to National Public Radio broadcasts and to recordings that more economically solvent peers shared with him. Speaking of his early influences, he has said: "I admired David Sánchez and Danilo Pérez, and using their music as a kind of 'North' with a Latin American touch more balanced and modern I began to find myself."[29] A year after finishing high school, he left for the US with assistance from a Pell Grant and a scholarship to the Berklee College of Music. Following his graduation in 1999, he moved to New York City. There, he first joined fellow saxophonist and Libre alumnus David Sánchez, eventually forming his own quartet. Less than a decade later he would have embodied "jazz in the 21st century."

EAR-TO-EAR WITH DIFFERENCE

Contemporary jazz circulates through markets, media, performance networks, discourse, and pedagogy.[30] What circulates, though, is not simply a set of musical forms but a vast network of values encompassing aesthetic sensibilities, predilections, and choices; cognitive technologies of teaching and learning; historical perceptions; and cultural assumptions. Within critical modernity such circulation obeys no single logic. As Dilip Parameshwar Gaonkar and Elizabeth A. Povinelli ask: "why is it that some forms move or are moved along? What limits are imposed on cultural forms as the condition of their circulation across various types of social space?"[31] One response is to consider "forms of abstraction, evaluation, and constraint, which are created by the interactions between specific types of circulating forms and the interpretive communities built around them."[32]

Zenón's exploration of Boston's performance venues is an instructive example of such limits and constraints. Systematically studying the history of the saxophone in jazz with venerable saxophonist and educator Bill Pierce, he felt increasingly prepared to join experienced players in local jam sessions. Zenón tenaciously pursued knowledge outside the classroom, querying anyone willing to talk to him about how to play something or other. From an encounter with African American students reluctant to share information, he became aware of a pivotal limit. Namely, he was confronting the constraint of acquiring intimate knowledge of a music to which he will always have been a latecomer—a music on which others had a more legitimate and immediate cultural claim and a sense of historical ownership. In particular, he realized that blues and gospel traditions, with which he had no contact growing up in Puerto Rico, were *sine qua non* conditions for proper jazz performance. Whatever those musics were, their fundamental affective constitution could not be fully codified. His social and musical interaction with African American peers was limited. "Basically, African American students played only with themselves, it was rather closed," and some often spoke of "us and the question of 'us,'" Zenón said. "It was hard to get in those circles, you know, but once you were in you began to understand that much in their attitudes had to do with where they came from, the music they heard."[33] He observed that "listening to them play, one became aware that what they brought to jazz was a language of their own . . . and then you began to try to enter into that language." For Zenón, these experiences shaped a new pedagogy focused on realizing the limits and constraints of the form "jazz" that once appeared to him to circulate in Puerto Rico simply because of its musical richness.

Though Zenón initially stumbled through these barriers and constraints, he would soon be a highly sought-after musician. For Zenón, mealtime social interaction or listening to music in a group of other students allowed for certain groupings across ethnicity and/or race, whereas the bandstand afforded others. By judiciously listening to as much blues and gospel as he could and by insisting on sitting in on sessions at Wally's—students' favored club for jamming—he felt that he had broken through the barriers he initially encountered. Danilo Pérez, the Panamanian pianist he admired during his Libre years, advised him to play with people from various cultural backgrounds in order "to get their stuff," which, Pérez said, needs to be learned through trial and error on the bandstand. Zenón recalls embarrassing moments when he was ignorant of certain tunes or unable to keep up. Before long, however, he was in constant demand. Instead of feeling that he had arrived, he relates, he felt simply that he might have been on the right track.

If the experience of the African American students Zenón recalls was fundamental to their participation in social and musical history in the US, then that experience and participation effectively had two unintended effects. First, the imposition of a cultural hierarchy on musical knowledge and information; second, the unreflective othering of someone who, seen as having a different history and experience, becomes abstracted as "different": Zenón. The coexistence of these experiences (lived, affectively powerful, and sense-giving) and those abstractions (the histories in which these experiences are inscribed) embodies ambivalences proper to critical modernity and expressed in the specificity of claims that people make in its name.

"Otherwise Modern—Yet Undoubtedly Modern"

The affirmation of difference (along lines of class, culture, ethnic, gender, generation, geopolitics, race, religion, sexuality) has in the recent past anchored analyses of participation in a world understood in pluralized terms. Difference, as William E. Connolly argues, is that in relation to which any identity is constituted. Hence a politics of difference is always a politics of identity, and vice versa.[34] Critics from various political bands have worried about the dangers of fragmentation in a social field characterized by the proliferation of multiple identities, heterogeneity, and plurality. Nonetheless the politics of identity/difference produced certain forms of coherence insofar as they shared interests in modernity: whether negating it or affirming it. If the conservatives aimed to preserve and foster the achievements of a classically defined liberal modernity, liberals were galvanized by its consensus that modernity had either rendered difference exterior to itself or universalized one particularity at the expense of all others. Liberal identity/difference politics refused modernity's normalization of exteriorizing and subsuming difference. In the name of border crossing, of the radically contingent, the contextual, the historically discontinuous, the local, the *petit récit*, and the particular, this wing of identity/difference politics pronounced, without irony, a universal derogation of universals.

This refusal, however, required more than denouncing all universalisms and categorically rejecting any and all notions of the whole or totality. As Néstor García Canclini observes, "One may forget about totality when one is interested only in the differences among people, not when one is also concerned with their inequality."[35] The critical matrix of identity/difference was itself integral to the logic of classical modernity. Or, as I put it above, modernity made difference distinctly intelligible in its peculiar temporal and spatial designs: whatever was deemed different was also exterior and anterior to modernity at the same time that modernity defined its identity in relation to difference. In an effort to renounce this logic, a liberal would also denounce, as Iain Chambers put it, "the transcendental pretensions of reason, of the Western *ratio*, that continually attempts to regulate unruly equivocations and render differences decidable."[36] The question was thus not really about the existence of difference as such but about *deciding which* differences counted and how they were valued.

These terms of engagement with difference and modernity are no longer predominant. Michel-Rolph Trouillot remarks how "modernity necessitates various readings of alterity . . . an [sic] heterology. The claim that someone—someone else—is modern is structurally and necessarily a discourse on the Other, since the intelligibility of that position—what it means to be modern—requires a relation to otherness."[37] Two interpretations are possible. First, modernity's self-imposed requirement that there be an "Other and an Elsewhere" could mean that in affirming its identity the "different" subverts the parochial universalism of European or US modernity in the name of a particular. The challenge to this first interpretation is twofold. On the one hand, if identity/difference is taken as a purely relational principle, power differentials between various identity/difference parties would remain in place in an antagonistic field that simply displaces the exclusions and exteriorizations of modernity to another terrain: that of identity/difference politics. On the other hand, if parties might enter into solidarity pacts or strategic alliances, they do so on condition of an appeal to some universal (even the claim to be against universals is itself, formally, a universal, as is the valuation of difference as such) and a concomitant, albeit partial, bracketing of the absolute particularity of identity/difference politics.[38]

Closer to the spirit of Trouillot's remark, the second interpretation falls within the overall frame of critical modernity and recognizes how its constituent elements are co-implicated. This interpretation does not merely recognize the dialectical character of identity/difference within modernity, which affirms that a party formerly excluded reclaims visibility to the degree that it asserts its difference from some excluding power. For Trouillot, modernity requires not merely an alter ego but what he calls an "alter-native," that is, an-Other which is nonetheless native to modernity: in his case, the Caribbean. Freed from a modernity that negated and subjugated them, only modern subjects remain: "*we* have always been modern, differently modern, contradictorily modern, otherwise modern—yet undoubtedly modern."[39]

The plurality of interpretation of "being modern" begs the question: Why use modernity as a critical framework at all? Trouillot's notion of "Otherwise Modern" invites common charges of radical contingency and relativity, similar to those levied against the identity/difference model. If all there is are forms of being modern, who might establish the terms for any comparison at all, and how? Conversely, don't these forms preserve a generalized, albeit tacit, idea of what modernity is—opposed to definitions of modernity as a manner of belonging—as a condition of possibility for any talk of being modern at all? Were we to have an explicit but purely formal definition of modernity, what mechanisms might give this formalism any social purchase? Why not give up on modernity as analytical framework, as so many did during the 1980s and 1990s?

Modernity enables and constrains experiences of participation and practices of comportment. These get transformed into what Foucault identified as "the permanent reactivation of an attitude . . . [an] ethos that could be described as a permanent critique of our historical era."[40] Foucault's statement is decidedly ethical: "by 'attitude,' I mean a mode of relating to contemporary reality; a voluntary choice made by certain people; in the end, a way of thinking and feeling; a way, too, of acting and behaving that at one and the same time marks a relation of belonging and presents itself as a task. A bit, no doubt, like what the Greeks called an ethos."[41] In turn, this critical attitude questions "what is given to us as universal, necessary, and obligatory." It thus asks "what place is occupied by whatever is singular contingent and the product of arbitrary constraints?" in order "to transform the critique conducted in the form of necessary limitation into a practical critique that takes the form of a possible transgression."[42] Foucault's prescriptions are grounded in the idea that modernity (and its powerful avatar, the Enlightenment) renders reality in such a manner that in order to alter that reality, one must deploy modernity's own resources. Counter-modernity is a form of modernity.

Zenón's interactions at Berklee assume the dual task of belonging to and maintaining a critical relation with modernity, as Foucault prescribes. As Gaonkar and Povinelli describe, they are constrained by forms that circulate in one way for him and another way for others. In refusing the imposition of incommensurable difference, Zenón engaged in a critical ontology; that is, by effectively recognizing the importance for some to sign their music making in the name of racial difference and cultural particularity, Zenón allowed difference to influence one's choices and the contingencies that constrain and enable participation in modernity. And yet, this Foucauldian turn can account for neither what is unique to this refusal of difference nor for what form any residual universalism and singularity might take.[43]

One is left wondering: How is a subject to transgress a structure far vaster and complex than himself? It is to this question that I turn in the second part of this chapter, introducing a conceptual vocabulary that allows us to critically engage the specificity of the refusal (not the transgression) of difference, the ethics of such refusal, and the role that universals may yet play.

DEMANDING UNIVERSALS

Critical modernity is a history of the present. As Trouillot insists, social features once thought to be European (or North Atlantic) persist "in North Atlantic narratives *now*."[44] Let's recall Foucault's idea that things experienced as counter-modern are themselves part of modernity. And let's keep in mind a truism of contemporary life under globalization: the local is hardly ever self-sufficient and is often in relation to multiple locations. These ideas enable us to think of critical modernity as an actually existing universal. This universal is qualitatively different from the vulgar and parochial procedure that transforms a particular into a universal. Instead, this actually existing universal requires "an ineradicable remainder of particularity" which itself gains intelligibility by having the universal as its own remainder; this paradox is, as Ernesto Laclau writes, "both impossible and necessary."[45] As an actually existing universal, critical modernity avoids the pitfalls of teleological historicism and transcendentalism: the dogmatic empiricism of the former and the equally dogmatic evacuation of all historical contingencies by the latter. Far from a categorical refusal, universalism demands renewed analysis. By relocating the particular, it demands ethical reconfigurations.

Gayatri Spivak and Lawrence Grossberg help encapsulate some of the tensions between modernity, difference, particularity, and singularity. In 1993, Spivak proclaimed that "an ethical position must entail universalization of the singular."[46] For Grossberg, critical modernity is powerful because it can shift modernity's *universal singular* toward a *singular universal*. In his words, "the hierarchical abstraction of the [European] particular against which all future particulars have to be measured" shifts toward "universality as movements or relations across non[-]hierarchically arranged particulars."[47] Like Spivak, Grossberg is concerned with ethics: "How might one imagine a multiplicity of singular universals, each a complex relationally constituted statement . . . of modernity? How might one think the possibility of a more ethically desirable modernity?"[48]

These authors propose alternatives for traversing the universal-singular relation as a way to think the ethical stakes in modernity. Grossberg advocates a characterless multiplicity, and expresses no less an ethical spirit than Spivak does. From her part, Spivak militates on behalf of the subaltern by means of a universalizing value granted to radical alterity, which she renders as "the singular." "Woman" is Spivak's figure of irreducible difference from which she derives the ethical position that one must always suspend oneself in attending to one's alterity. According to Spivak, the "singular" is not an individual, person, or agent. It is a category (a universal itself) that she deploys to short-circuit the dualism of universality-particularity. The problem with Spivak's injunction is that no ethical position can be derived from the singular, since it is a category without content. In other words, singularity is not a priori ethical. It needs to be rendered ethical—and in relation to a universal presumed to be a priori unethical. In Grossberg's case, he renders his "singular universals" ethical in relation to a generalized modernity that makes of "multiplicity" its core value.[49]

Spivak and Grossberg illustrate demands placed on universals and the demands universals make on those appealing to them. To do so, however, they use different pairs of antonyms: for Spivak the "particular" corresponds to the "universal" (and not the "singular"), while for Grossberg the "singular" corresponds to the "multiple" (and not the "universal"). I read this confusion as more than a semantic disagreement, one that neither the contingent universality of Spivak's nor the multiple universality of Grossberg's modernity addresses. To clarify these terms and rethink their ethical possibilities apart from identity/difference, I consider a recent episode in Miguel Zenón's trajectory rooted in the quarrels of Puerto Rican modernity.

Aesthetic Equality

Between 2011 and 2012, under the name Caravana Cultural (Cultural Caravan), Zenón dedicated monies he received from the MacArthur Foundation Fellowship (US $500,000 paid over five years) to support and conduct a series of six free concerts and pre-concert talks in municipalities across Puerto Rico.[50] Focusing on iconic figures of modern instrumental jazz (Coltrane, Davis, Ellington, Monk, and Parker), Zenón performed each concert with different quartets drawn from the New York City scene. They played in mostly small, rural towns where jazz hadn't been performed live, and where many *jíbaro* musicians come from.[51] "There are certain areas in the country which have not had an exposure [to jazz], as the metropolitan area has, perhaps because they see jazz as music from the high class," he said, "but this is not the case. We want to come to people who do not have the opportunity to go to festivals, so that they enjoy the music and learn about it without having to worry about expenses or travel."[52] In 2017, speaking at the Library of Congress, Zenón affirmed how "I've always had this idea in mind of taking jazz music and taking it to places where it's not known, you know—where people are not as accustomed to seeing it or having it around and just giving them the opportunity to be exposed. You know, I don't really see it as a way of commercializing the music or opening up the gap to one audience or anything. I just feel like it's important for people to be exposed to as much as possible and let them decide if this stuff is for them or not."[53] He called the Caravana "the most rewarding experience that I've gotten out of music, ever."[54]

The Caravana brought unexpected places and audiences into play. They presented at community centers, local music halls and theaters, and even in annex spaces to mayoral offices or a Lions Club headquarters. An anonymous writer for the popular progressive online journal *80grados* described the scene before the event: "We went to the corner pizzeria. . . . A woman who was there with her kids told another woman that at 3:00 she was going to 'the jazz' . . . it seemed as if the entire town knew about it."[55] To encourage broad participation, activities commenced at 3:00 p.m. on Sundays. "At 3:00 no more people could come in to the Annex; the place has room for 300 people. Miguel took to the microphone and began the first part of the event, a one-hour-long talk. The talk was divided into three parts: improvisation, jazz and its history, and the life and work of the featured musician, in this case Coltrane. People listened in silence. There were old people, children, youngsters."[56] In the Q&A sessions that followed, attendees asked many questions. Local student musicians were recruited to perform with the visiting musicians toward the last part of each presentation; Zenón insisted that communities take part in the project and that the Caravana leave them with a small trace.[57] The city major, Jorge Márquez, added that when he was offered the chance to host the event, he thought, "at last, thank God." The audience laughed and clapped, then he added: "we in small towns don't have a big budget for cultural activities and so that someone comes to us and brings us a project of such quality as this is a blessing"; "then," it is reported, "the people clapped thunderously."[58]

The Caravana, which began as an "abstract idea," returns to the long-nineteenth-century idea of "the music itself" and its claims to absolute autonomy from sociocultural moorings. Such a return flies in the face of musical activism in the twenty-first century. The project's main focus, Zenón declared, was "simply music." He noted that "by focusing specifically on jazz music, we have as an objective to eliminate any social or cultural stigma to which this style [genre] may be related."[59] To destigmatize jazz is to disrupt orders of history and place that determine the impropriety of a people or community and their location to a musical style. A network of relations binds a musical style, like jazz, to a specific sociocultural proper. This binding relation establishes equivalences between expressive practices, sensible affects, and classificatory systems normative to a community. These equivalences are undergirded by a further equivalence between inhabiting and ways of being (acting, feeling, thinking)—what Bourdieu called *habitus*. The result is a forceful version of ethos. Problematically, these equivalences tend to dissolve norms into facts and blur the lines between fact (what is) and law (what must be).[60] The destigmatization of a musical genre gives lie to the idea popularized by Bourdieu's theory of "distinction": that one's education and socioeconomic rank determine one's appreciation of art.[61]

The Caravana's destigmatization of jazz is thus an attempt to disrupt an ethos. It seeks to suspend the identities/differences that "distinction" enforces, and to unsettle long-standing and unquestioned hierarchies of aesthetic engagement. The Caravana is emphatically based on the presupposition of aesthetic equality. That is, it renders to perception what was imperceptible (and largely unavailable) in the name of the equality of any and all people. Aesthetic equality does not claim that the exercise of the capacity to perceive turns some forms (musical styles, performance practices) into free-flowing phenomena that may be seized by anyone as if they were theirs. Instead, its claim is much simpler, but manifold. First of all, it is more than a question of relative availability of or lack of exposure to something, like a musical practice. The stigma attached to someone's non-existing relation to a musical genre like jazz in rural Puerto Rico forms part of a history of epistemic violence. Such violence is based in the notion that inhabitants of more or less remote areas are incapable of listening to, let alone engaging with, musical forms deemed too complex, abstract, and temporally and spatially removed from their everyday life. By this account, these communities' function within Puerto Rico's economy and place in the Island's sociocultural geography curtail any potential disruption of the way things are, have been, and will be. The difference intrinsic to their subordinate position is inseparable from their "distinction." How to account for what the Caravana may have been or done?

The answer is inextricably bound to the specificities of a Puerto Rican contemporary society profoundly marked by modernity. The Caravana does not—cannot—erase these marks of epistemic violence and aesthetic exclusion. What it does do is breach this history of violence by suspending the order that sees rural Puerto Ricans as being incapable to listen. Belonging takes place in the Caravana in the form of the capacity to listen and of whatever transformation that capacity may effect. What kind of thing, then, is the Caravana? It is not any form of musical object, it is not the experience of listening, it is not the communal partaking of an aesthetic event, it is not the many relations that attend to engaging others perceptually, and it is not the comprehension of whatever might be said or learned in the process. It is rather something that sustains all these things, something I call the pure singularity of listening: people, including musicians, listened, and did so as part of an action that breached through the status quo. But here I make a cautious wager: if belonging takes place *in* this breach, it is not *of* it.[62] This breach is without content. It is the event subtracted from its empirical contingencies.

The notion of a breach without content and the idea of belonging in but not of that breach may sound like ecstatic Deleuzianism. Like an interpretation in which percepts and affects give rise to an impersonal subject traversed by the intensity of a sensorial power that may be then harnessed as a transgressive force. Like a sensorial enactment of the limits of discourse, encouraging a critique of verbal rationality and a refusal of logos for which music is often deployed. Like some version of a sense-based didacticism, disembodied romanticism, or socially therapeutic classicism. It is, however, none of these. Instead, *that* listening belongs to anyone is redolent of what Peter Hallward calls "transcendental conditions." These include the consistencies that specify humans (the raw fact of our cognitive configuration as hearers of a certain kind, the empirical contingency of disabilities notwithstanding), the categories without which human social life might be inconceivable (relationality and value), and the dynamic processes that are the human experience's condition of possibility ("agency, subjectivity . . . sexuality, [and] identification" without content).[63]

Transcendental conditions do not in themselves "govern *how* we relate to one another," and so possess no intrinsic ethical prescription.[64] This ethical force emerges instead from "unconditional principles valid for all relations, or at least relations of a certain kind." An ethics emerges from principles like equality that are "valid *for* all relations in the situation concerned." In short, ethics stem from "universalizable principles."[65] These principles are not, however, immanent to parties in a relation, or to relation itself. "They are," Hallward remarks, "imposed as if from without. They are decided, deliberated, as an external encouragement or constraint . . . [their] universality persists as a fragile *assertion* . . . it holds only insofar as its proponents are able to make it stick."[66]

Take the following expressions of the *equality in listening*'s fragile persistence. "I would like to have the expertise to speak critically about the music that took place there, on Sunday, but I don't," said the anonymous writer for *80grados*. They concluded, "I know that I liked it and that I was deeply moved by Miguel's generosity; I left thinking that this is how one constructs a country."[67] An attendee commented, "I was part of this marvelous event. Mr. Zenón's professionalism, his knowledge of jazz, on top of the simple manner in which he transmitted it, made of that afternoon a magisterial jazz lesson."[68] A spirit of inclusivity permeates these comments. Inclusivity, however, implies bringing a formerly excluded people into the normative order of society. More is at stake in the equality I have in mind. Next, I introduce an analytic to address this.

PURE MULTIPLICITY, A POSSIBILITY?

The proposals for "transcendental conditions" and "universalizable principles" introduced above mark what Alain Badiou calls a "return to the Same."[69] "The Same" is what remains when the "infinite multiplicity of differences" is subtracted, leaving what Hallward describes as "pure being qua being . . . without regard to being-this or being-that, being without reference to particular qualities or ways of being: being that simply *is*."[70] No substance undergirds this conception of being that makes possible the "Same." This austere ontology constitutes an axiom on the basis of which anyone might act, and so breach the existing differences and identities that organize the world. Such an act is indifferent to differences, negates what there is, and affirms what "comes to be" (i.e., the Same), all in regard to a truth defined as that which is the "same for all."[71] This constitutes a generic universality, "a rigorously situated project . . . [that] persists in an unending compilation of what, in the situation, is addressed 'for all,' regardless of interest or privilege, regardless of state-sanctioned distinctions (and this against those who continue to defend those privileges and distinctions)."[72] This statement requires explaining Badiou's technical terms: "state," "situation," and "One."[73]

"State" refers to the field of established identities/differences within which the exercise of control, domination, and governance comes to be experienced. The "state" is best understood as a hegemony, as the administration of power by the consent and participation of those governed. The "state" is a sense-making dispositive. It is imminently relational; it distributes, classifies, and excludes, but also includes by the logic of identity/difference: all differences among elements in the "state" operate as a function of identities ascribed to those elements that allow them to take a position or to displace to other positions within a grid drawn out of a system of differences. A "state" is known and experienced across various spatial and temporal scales: everyday, historical, local, regional, and global. Modernity, one might say, is a dispositive for the production of such a state. A "state" is that which must be disrupted and toward which an indifference to the logic of identity/difference militantly enacted.

"Situation" refers first to the position that an element (person, time, place) in a state holds in relation to any other element. Second, it refers to the elements as a pure multiplicity. This is the most fundamental formal ontological proposition at play here. All attributes of an element are subtracted, leaving the simple fact of its being. A "situation" affirms a set of pure differences as differences without any relation whatsoever, an indeterminate differentiation demanded by the fact that there is only other, and another, and another: infinite multiples with no structuring power or symbolic currency. Structuring power, nonetheless, is most effectively felt when a "situation" comes to count as "One."

This counting as "One" is the "state of the situation," and is what we encounter in commonly circulated formulations such as the "Puerto Rican people," "the audience in Barranquitas, Puerto Rico, on Sunday, February 13, 2011," or the "jazz tradition." The passage from "situation" to "state of the situation," however, is such that in the latter formulation the "situation" and its pure multiplicity appear as nothing: it is the *unthought* of the "state," a "void." In the "state of the situation," the "situation" remains that which the "state" claims to represent but cannot count or acknowledge.

Such unthought appears only exceptionally. Something suspends the logic that orders the state of the situation's elements and allows something new to appear. This is the "event." The "event" cannot be accounted for by any logic of the "state," including identity/difference; it is unpredictable and radically contingent. The fact that the "event" is unaccountable and *unthinkable* does not mean that it is the effect of some force exterior to the "state of the situation." Rather, the "event" is in fact immanent to the state and its ordering function; the *unthought* exists within the state. The "event" renders visible and audible that which the state must not count in order to constitute things as what they appear: as a set of knowable identities/differences.

The "event" renders a "truth." A truth is "an *immanent break*. 'Immanent' because a truth proceeds in the situation, and nowhere else . . . 'Break' because what enables the truth-process—the event—meant nothing according to the prevailing language and established knowledge of the situation."[74] Badiou's "break" corresponds to what I call a "breach," and "meaning nothing" to the "unthought." Truth requires an act, and takes form in four "generic procedures": love (entails individual subjects), politics (entails a collective subject), and science and art (entail individual acts with collective import). The subject in these procedures is not an intention; it is not a bundle of affect or experience, a set of perceptions, or a play of sensations. It comes into being from a procedure and a truth to the degree that such a truth induces him/her/them or it. Nothing belongs to the subject. The subject belongs to its being true *to* something. A truth, a procedure, and an act are not *in* or *of* the subject; the subject is a subject *to* them. It is an operation without content. Ethics are a function of a militant fidelity to a singularly situated act. This act has no other a priori universal than fidelity itself. Heady stuff, but helpful for thinking and acting beyond difference. Ethics here are a function of a militant fidelity to a singularly situated act divested of any a priori universal other than fidelity itself, its maxim being "Keep going!"

SINGULAR WITHOUT DIFFERENCE

On February 13, 2011, a disparate array of listeners gathered in Barranquitas, Puerto Rico—a town of 30,000 nestled in the Island's central mountains—to listen to Miles Davis's music performed by Zenón, trumpeter Michael Rodriguez (the son of Florida-based Ecuadorian parents), bassist Matt Penman (a New Zealander), pianist Aaron Goldberg (a Boston native and Harvard graduate), and drummer Nasheet Waits (the Morehouse graduate and New York City–born son of legendary jazz drummer Freddie Waits). How to explain the possibility of this event? That all elements— the people, the town, the hall, the sound system, and so on—are different and that their differences are without immanent relation is too obvious. Consider the arbitrary parenthetical descriptions: Why should it matter to cast this quintet as the apotheosis of jazz's cosmopolitanism, or as indexes of only some elements' educational and national backgrounds?

Within the state's classification systems these descriptions are identities/differences. If we insist on, say, respecting national origin or recognizing ethnicity, they acquire a universal cast. Such universals are ethically problematic. For instance, "respect" for national difference implies that "it is necessary to have first distinguished between good particularities and bad ones . . . the formal universal already [would] be included in the particularity."[75] Instead of particulars, we might consider *singulars* as a way to conceive of each of the situation's elements "as a singularity that is subtracted from identitarian predicates."[76] What I have been describing—in terms of belonging, generic universality, state, situation, one—partakes of the "event," a possibly transformative occurrence the effects of which happen *in* a situation but are not *of* it.[77]

What do such definitions—of the singular and the purely multiple, of the subject and event without content or relation—make possible? In part, they open new ethical configurations of belonging and relation that the logic of difference otherwise forecloses. Consider the Caravana: What ethical commitment does Miguel Zenón have to the event of the Caravana? Altruism is too obvious to dwell upon. Voluntarism imposes notions of free will and intention that do not tell the whole story. Singularity, I propose instead, sidesteps the ethical imperative to act on behalf of an a priori "good" and to attend to the radical alterity of the Other.[78] Singularity's ethical task is not to affirm the world as it already is—a set of differences—but as it is not. Let me be clear: singularity is absolutely without content, something that does not—cannot—*secure* the consistency of the "Same" or *guarantee* the permanence of equality. It breaches the state of the situation and affirms that which, within the state, is unthinkable.

Having clarified these terms, we can now recast the Caravana as an event. This aural event's breach cannot be described as an individual hero rupturing a dominant structure, whether the local classification of the "rural" or the imperial link binding Puerto Rico and the US. It does, however, suspend preexisting boundaries around audiences and music. In doing so, the Caravana highlights something that was inaudible and thus nonexistent within the structures of the "state of the situation"—namely, *that* everybody listens. "That was the idea [of the Caravana]," Zenón has said, "to try to break down the disconnection that exists between the popular masses and this specific type of music."[79] This actively encourages participants—or all the event's elements—to enter a minimal space and time in which what matters most is not to suspend oneself before the alterity of an Other (music, music's power, fellow attendees) but to suspend that alterity itself. What matters is to engage in a principled indifference toward any identity/difference carried out prior to the presumption that this is for the Good and that only the Good can follow from it. The event of the Caravana privileges belonging over attaining, a belonging that does not transcend the particularity of the situation. In sum, this perspective is one of radical individuation, borrowing from Hallward's conception of the "singular" in which procedures are the "self-constituent" media of their own existence. Nothing in the end might compel Zenón to perform other than his own fidelity to the event of listening.

Admittedly, the event's content-less ontology cannot account for the myriad relations in which any situation partakes. The "singular" cannot adequately analyze critical modernity, which is saturated by power relations that compel the event in the first place. Critics have remarked on Badiou's lack of concern for "relationality and historical mediation."[80] Such mediation forms part of what Hallward calls the "specific," his supplement to the "singular." Where the singular is a-relational, free of mediation, and subject to no representation, the specific is relational, mediation itself, and subject to the vagaries of representation. It pertains to any identify/difference relation. But in crucial distinction with traditional identity/difference politics, this relationality of the specific is not specified. That is, it is not determined a priori by any attributes and it does not assume that there is "an inherently . . . progressive politics of relation." In other words, there is "nothing in relationality that determines whether social relations, for instance, are to be governed by race, or caste, or wealth, any more than by principles of civic responsibility, generic equality, or collective solidarity."[81] In short, the specific does not determine a priori the ethics of a particular relation. At the same time, it is not exempt from the constraints of social relations. Relations of the specific can easily turn into abstractions, bracketing off or suppressing other relations. Mindful of this potential, the specific, nonetheless, affords my analytic to acknowledge the necessarily entangled character of modernity, while the singular preserves the potential for a difference-less event.

"None of the Above"

The state of the situation appears to demand that an immigrant musician like Zenón be constrained a priori to certain actions. With a project like *Jíbaro*, he would be burdened with the labor of cultural representation, of "arguing" for the powers of his native country's music to be both renovating in the US and renewable at home. The MacArthur Foundation's recognition of Zenón would aid this argument by including him in the national cultural sphere without granting him full political inclusion, which remains structurally precluded by the imperial situation of Puerto Rican citizens. Against this proscription stands an improper figure, the "almost-the-same-but-not-quite" imperial subject Zenón, a figure whose existence interrogates the democratic values jazz is said to embody. This figure has a corollary in the introduction of "another locus of inscription and intervention," an "'inappropriate' enunciative site," as Homi K. Bhabha put it, that opens up in the split of signification between imperial power and neo-imperial subject.[82] For Bhabha, "modernity . . . is about the historical construction of a specific position of historical enunciation and address. It privileges those who 'bear witness,' those who are 'subjected,' or . . . historically displaced."[83]

In 2011, Zenón participated in a forum of the National Museum of the American Latino Commission held in San Juan. He advocated for the inclusion of the Puerto Rican musicians he considers to have contributed nationally and internationally to affirming the Island's musical culture.[84] The Island's status as an unincorporated territory became a point of contention. "When they [the Commission] called me," said Zenón, "it was clear to me that the situation of Puerto Rico was distinct from that of any other place in the US and so it was that, with opinions in pro and con, I felt that my responsibility was with thinking about the culture and music of Puerto Rico outside of the parameters of what it means to be Puerto Rican or not."[85]

Journalist Ana Teresa Toro heard in these words that "in matters of culture—or in any other plane—[Zenón] has no problems with identity."[86] This interpretation would contradict the traditionally identitarian politics of Puerto Rican pro-independence nationalists. On second look, however, Toro's reading conceals a radical affirmation of identity closer to the singular than to the specific. In an act of self-reflection—the identitarian move *par excellence*—the musician could be heard as saying that he knows who he is before that identity enters the relational networks of the specific. His advocacy of local musicians constitutes an affirmation of their contribution to "Latino" cultural life in the US, whether or not they migrated from the unincorporated territory that Puerto Rico is.

Zenón addressed the forum: "To speak of those from here and those from there: that is an ever-existing debate, but in the case of music we must say that it belongs to everyone . . . I do not have any doubts about my identity. I am Puerto Rican, I left for the US [because] what I wanted to do I could not do in Puerto Rico."[87] Here, he marshaled music's specificity to defuse the tension between migrants and nonmigrants. His statement presents something other than the mutually exclusive options of staying or leaving. True, one of the most contentious matters in modern Puerto Rican history concerns the circulation between the Island and the US. Returning migrants, explains Juan Flores, feel and often are marginalized.[88] As Flores discusses, music has been uniquely relevant in tracing the movement of what he calls "cultural remittances," forms brought back (or sent) by migrants like Zenón or much earlier migrants who in fact have created some of the Island's most emblematic music. Music might seem to get a free pass, but the saxophonist's arguments before the American Latino Commission suggest otherwise: the distinctions marking migrants from nonmigrants revert to identitarianism in which, to cite Gaonkar and Povinelli again, "limits are imposed on cultural forms as the condition of their circulation across various types of social space."

Zenón's refusal to take sides flies in the face of national politics at home. In Puerto Rico, positions concerning identity revolve around independence from the US, statehood, or continuation of commonwealth status as Estado Libre Asociado. His position is closer to "none of the above." This option—"none of the above"—received the majority vote in the referendum on December 13, 1998, a day on which, according to a governor, "the people of Puerto Rico decided not to decide."[89] Like the referendum, Zenón's position may be taken to say little about national politics, to even affirm the status quo.[90] Against these negative interpretations, the "decision not to decide" may also embrace cynicism, neglect, or skepticism as the answer to the "unbearable ambiguity" of Puerto Rican particularity. It may amount to political performance camouflaging political response.[91] Performance, not rational deliberation, could be said to do the real political work. Both can, of course, do such work, since one does not preclude the other.

Deciding not to decide could also be understood as an exercise in principled indifference to identity/difference. This decision effectively breaches Puerto Rico's constitutive ambiguity as "foreign to the US in a domestic sense," according to the US Supreme Court.[92] We see now how within the "event" "the undecidable is decided."[93] To our earlier definition of ethics as the fidelity to "Keep going!" we add this: the ethical emerges from a "decision in the face of the undecidable," a wager whose outcome remains, as with the "event," incalculable.

I propose, then, to understand Zenón as the bearer of a decision who, by refusing to take on identity or difference, simply wagers on "presentation"—on the such-as-it-is of his being. I base this proposal both on the statements cited above and on his declared nonproprietary relation to the musical forms that he has studied and that he now insists to the Commission should be part of an institution. This operates at two registers: (1) at the individuated, non-specified, and non-redemptive register of the *singular*, where relations are suspended (not negated), and where the immanence of Being is affirmed; (2) at the register of relations—economic, sociocultural, political—of the *specific*, where decisions are made in the name of aesthetic equality which, though a universalizable principle, is nonetheless particular to its situation.

At the heart of this interpretation is the nexus of Zenón's decision and the event discussed above. To unpack this nexus requires that we shift our focus away from music as that which belongs to everybody (and thus to no one at all)—the "music is a universal language" trope—and instead turn toward "listening." Any musical tradition has a history and is *of* history; it is the epitome of the specific. And the history of our relations to musical works has an equally specific nature. But the relation that we hold to the relation that is listening cannot be determined by that specificity nor placed under alterity's deafening rumble. It can always end up breaching what we think we are. But how do we listen to Zenón's "Seis Cinco"? Can its form bear the weight of history, of the material forces that inevitably participate in its coming to be? Or rather, can anyone, in listening to it, come to bear that history? I would respond with a qualified yes, as both a matter of choice and of possibility.

Listening is imminently relational: this is the most obvious dimension of the aesthetic. From the standpoint I have adopted here, things are less obvious. True, listening most often acts as a binding force, rendering a multiplicity of individuals into a singular collective. But even in cases where listening indexes particularity under identity categories of ethnicity, class, gender, nationality, race, sexuality, and so on, the relation causally follows the relata (e.g., listeners, performers). This renders ethics a matter of making the right or wrong choice: to embrace or recognize difference is good, to reject it is bad. Either way, we are accountable to our decision, and if it is the right one we bond with others and foster community: to relate is preferable to not to relate.

Consider instead that relationality might precede the relata. That relationality is not predetermined, specific but not specified. The specific may exist outside identity/difference. In my discussion of Zenón's decision to be indifferent to difference, I made the point that such a position entails a relation precisely to the decision. That he has maintained his position can be accounted for by fidelity to a difficult decision, given the "state of the situation" of societies in the US and Puerto Rico shaped by modernity's structure of differentiation. We might say that he is faithful to being unfaithful to identity. I am aware of the performative contradiction here: that such faithfulness to unfaithfulness constitutes yet another form of identity and that I, the writer, can only relate after I identify the relata (Zenón, US politics of identity, Puerto Rican nationalism, musical progressivism, etc.). But it is one thing to exist specifically—it is after all, along with value, a transcendental condition of our species—and another to decide on that specificity. This distinction is what I have tried to clarify.

What, then, is the truth of listening? Is truth produced in listening's form or content? Is it not banal to claim that the fact of listening produces truth *in* the aesthetic? On the one hand, like Badiou, I have privileged musical art as a truth procedure. I too appear to privilege exceptional and courageous individuals who by their militant fidelity to an uncertain outcome usher in the new and transform the state of a situation. The question becomes whether such individuals constitute heroic or virtuosic figures, and how either of these might impinge on a sense of history and futurity. On the other hand, by shifting focus away from *Ethics*'s classical examples—"Haydn's invention of the classical musical style" or Berg's and Webern's faithfulness "to the musical event by the name of 'Schoenberg'"—I am not simply appealing to a "subaltern" version of those figures. I am suspending anything that resembles world history or a history of the Americas or the Caribbean. I am emphatically affirming that form, not content, produces truth. How? By means of a listening that enables time and space to act without determination, and that thus becomes a singular form. Without determining any content, listening can be new. *In* the event but never *of* it: therein lies the truth of listening.

ENDINGS REPEATEDLY BEGUN?

Listening's newness may address the past, without redeeming it, and open up the future, without predicting it. This occurs unendingly, time and time again. This differs from the institutional discourse surrounding Zenón circa 2008 that clearly situated him in relation to past and future. Can we do without this sense of past and future? Can the "singular" and the "specific" sufficiently account for the relations at play here? If within the MacArthur Foundation's discourse Zenón is "reestablishing the artistic, cultural, and social tradition of jazz while creating an entirely new jazz language for the 21st century," how do we take measure of the enigma of "what it means to act," as Virno put it in this chapter's epigraph? And how do we square that with the fact that for many in Puerto Rico, the event of the Caravana meant that "right here in this place, something hitherto unnamed really and truly occurred," as Meillassoux writes in the accompanying epigraph and as I propose we understand what happened?

In response to these questions about what is lost or gained in my analysis, I insist on its attention to both the singular and the specific. I quote Olivia Bloechl's summary of my analysis to show how it affirms that "the possibility of listening as an event opens up to what is non-existing and even unthinkable under [then] current conditions (including novel configurations of belonging)."[94] This does not mean that the actually existing conditions in which listening as an event occurs lose all purchase in my analysis. As it is manifest in relations of the Caravana to economies (cultural, political, monetary, etc.), historicity, social emplacement, personal trajectories of the musician and audiences, and so on, the *specific* plays a part precisely in making of the event a *breach* in the *state*. It is imperative that this analytic of the *specific* and the *singular* opens up to the idea of syncopation. If at one level listening necessarily occurs in relation to various economies (cultural, political), to temporalities, historicity, and emplacements, in short, *in* the specific and *in* the orders that it harbors, it also occurs in a way that it is not *of* them. Understood as collision, syncopation indexes entanglements and the specific, a being in an order. Understood as an elision and a gap, the syncope indexes the unthinkability of the singular, its coalescence in a fleeting moment that, because it always comes to an end, must be repeatedly begun.

Let us return to the relation of tradition to history (chapter 4). In chapter 4, I borrowed Paul Carter's expression "beginnings repeatedly begun" to name the constant need to reconstitute a Latin Americanism for which music was crucial. In the Afro Latin Jazz Orchestra, these beginnings aimed to make place *for* time; that is, by highlighting historically ignored Cuban and Afro-Cuban musicians in jazz historiography, they might restitute for them a place and create another sense of time (hence making place *for* time, not just *in* time). In Zenón's case, by contrast, the MacArthur Foundation makes time ("the future of jazz") for something taking place on US soil. The formula, one might say, becomes "making time for [a] place," to echo words from chapter 4. This reversal, however, does not adequately account for the Puerto Rican saxophonist's work, which seems as if it has always already been ahead of US time *and* always already behind it—at the same time.

Consider the Foundation's language that the "tradition" might be *"re*established." There are competing claims to the tradition the Foundation invokes. Given the Foundation's accent on the future ("new language"), who *will have* claimed this tradition? And when they do, how will the meanings of the "cultural" and the "social" have been transformed? How are we to understand the relation between place, region, territory, and hemisphere? For if the statement implies that Zenón's work has taken place on American soil, the proper name "America" is only implied, not stated. It repeats incantations of a veritable network of proper names: "Latin," "Afro-Caribbean," "Latin American," "Puerto Rico," and "Puerto Rican." By contrast, it offers jazz—which might be the ultimate beneficiary of the Foundation's compressed historical narrative—no specific location. Jazz is rendered a matrix that encompasses a general "artistic, cultural, and social" field and the new century. Indeed, as Zenón's saxophone teacher at Berklee put it, "jazz is everywhere."[95]

Zenón's remarkable story is partly, then, one in which he traverses an apparent lag in Puerto Rico's musical modernity only to be hailed—by the US's MacArthur Foundation—as the bearer and producer of a time beyond his own. What syncopation is this? It is one in which, as I already alluded to, listening exists *in* the event but is not *of* it and the event occurs in an order (imperiality, US perspectives of Puerto Rican modernity) but is not of it. Recall, syncopation exists in an order but becomes syncopation precisely by momentarily refusing being of it. A similar logic attends to how syncopation entangles institutions and large-scale phenomena such as "new music for the 21st century." At that level, syncopation is imaginable as being in tradition's time but not of it. It is one that is possible within an imperial historicist logic that incorporates new places into jazz's unilinear historiography.[96] It unfurls within a framework of progress, perfectibility, and unidirectional time—staples of modernity's particular brand of historicism. Walter Benjamin reminds us how such historicism follows "a straight or spiral course" that "cannot be sundered from the concept of its progression through a homogeneous empty time."[97] Benjamin describes a relentless progressivism that both dislocates the present by projecting it into a certain future (e.g., "new music for the 21st century") and condemns to oblivion the oppressed (which corresponds not to the "past" but rather to the "what-has-been").[98] Against these, Benjamin sets a present in which "every image" of the past constitutes its (the present's) own concern.[99] This crystallizes in a nontransitional present "in which time stands still"[100] and which configures a set of phenomena into a "monad . . . pregnant with tensions."[101] This crystallization gives form to a "present of the now" suspended in relation to a past. This relation constitutes an image and breaches continuity and progressivism, thereby puncturing historicism's continuum.

It is important to clarify this configuration's dialectical character. It calls for arresting time in order to grasp a notion of history that is itself not purely temporal, but also for grasping a fundamentally spatial notion of time. This arresting dialectical image suspends time in the realization that "the present of the now" is pregnant with the "what-has-been." This image "seizes hold of a memory as it flashes up at a moment of danger" as the only alternative to what already is.[102] This moment of danger "affects both the content of the tradition and its receivers," such that failing to seize this memory renders tradition and its receivers "a tool of the ruling classes" and enables the persistence of a past that either stays in the historicist's past (in the archive labeled "this happened") or falls into oblivion (as the "non-deeds" of the oppressed, a lacking modernity).[103]

By returning to the Puerto Rican past as a tradition subsisting in the present, Zenón did not move toward the future. By bringing the jazz tradition's past to rural Puerto Rico, he did not fill some lacunae in the present. *Jíbaro* does not "update" one of the Island's musical traditions. Yes, it reckons with the tradition in the present and avails itself of all manner of metropolitan musico-technical dispositives. This perspective, however, would reduce the music to technical elements that, themselves a testament to the musicians' creative powers, are valued as historical phenomena to the degree that they signify progress, change, and transformation to the Foundation. We may be tempted to understand Zenón's music as permitting the past to illuminate the present or the present the past. Instead I propose that we hold these two in dialectical suspension when bringing Zenón's appeal to the Puerto Rican *música jíbara* tradition in *Jíbaro* with the event of the Caravana into relation with his appeal to a traditional jazz historiography.

In the dialectical proposal we may regard Zenón's music as the relation between the present-of-the-now of his migratory contemporary and the what-has-been of the *música jíbara* tradition. It is as if past events—the government-sponsored recuperation of the tradition, the Serenidad project's formation of a musical pedagogy—come to dwell inside 2005 (when Zenón recorded *Jíbaro*) or inside 2008 (when the Foundation praised the album).[104] This relation's suspension of time also helps constitute a history "in spite of all."[105] This non-redemptory but nonetheless vital sense of history crystallizes in the holding-in-tension of juxtaposed temporalities; it in fact realizes these temporalities as currently coexisting. This may be what it means to act, as Virno wonders about the contemporary moment. To be clear, this is a history that suspends time in its flow so that other times can appear to offer only an alternative *to* history, not an alternative history. Like the event of the Caravana, this history can only sustain itself through the fidelity of the subject that emerges with it: "Miguel Zenón." Manifold experiences make for a conjunctural history, which in the Caravana include novel experiences for which there is no possible memory.

But can this temporal suspension arrest the impetus of a modernity that compels such suspension in the first place? Isn't the dialectical image of coexisting temporalities but a fragment in the vastness of modernity's homogeneous empty time? Could the dialectical work of Zenón's actions be paradigmatic of a chronotope beyond or other than modernity? *In* modernity but not *of* it? An emancipatory gesture susceptible to being co-opted anew by contemporary politics of the spectacle? A space for celebrating the productive syncopation of modernities, for instance rural and metropolitan Puerto Rico and imperial outpost and center?

We might rehearse first a reversal of how time is conceived. Here, the intensification of musical information, the forward-looking aesthetics, the heterogeneous and ever shifting stylistic possibilities of contemporary jazz in New York City pushes any action taken within its domain into a form of short-sighted hyperconcentration of the present. Against this, the kind of temporal horizon of the long history of social struggle of Puerto Rico under US imperialism would constitute something that, however slowly and unchanging, moves on and that offers some sense of long-range perspective. Juxtaposing these two produces, then, a syncopation—rupture, suspension, withholding—of the temporality of modernity within which the two are possible in the first place—time, indeed, appears to be incomprehensibly plastic in this view. This syncopation offers one fruitful possibility—namely, it disrupts the presumed impossibility of recounting the recent past as dwelling in some history.

Zenón's syncopation also makes time's plasticity collide with the place's immobility via an intermediary domain: space. I have related a story of a traversal of times through the recourse of spatial displacement: Zenón's experience of immigration is one of animating the spatiotemporal relation between places, of mediating the unequal distribution both of musical knowledge and of different notions of musical knowledge. The operations unfurled *in* the musician's actions (not just by them) represent an impingement of time on place. Place's immovability diminishes as new spaces are produced. Place emerges as the audible linking of spaces (between Puerto Rico's rural/metropolitan divide and the US/Puerto Rico divide) such that one dimension of time, the present, is disrupted. This is the outcome of the breach of the situation discussed above. It is also the effect of bringing the heterogeneous fragments of a schizoid "present" of dispersion into "a constellation of awakening."[106]

We have seen two narratives: one that incorporates Zenón into a linear historiography and another one that recognizes contemporary jazz's radical heterogeneity (as Ratliff does). Neither constitutes an adequate account: both are expressions of a teleological historiography, much as the latter may shatter historical coherence. I wager something else—namely, that what is at stake is an *aurality of the unthinkable*. This aurality is produced as an effect of an awareness that things do not necessarily have to be what they *are*. This "are" appears from the juxtaposition of the "presence-of-the-now" and the "what-has-been" in conjunctural history's nonhistorical temporality. This aurality, like the dialectical image, does not—cannot—redeem, reanimate, retain, replay, or regain the past. If it redeems at all, it does so "in the precious moment of its disappearance" as it crystallizes the times and histories of modernity in an instant,[107] and in that instant arrests the syncopation that made it all possible as a mirage of modernity—both in the negative sense of asserting a lagging time, the non-correspondence of place to time, and so on, as well as in the positive sense of spurring some to close the gap and in fact go beyond it toward the "future."

Conclusion

In the largely unscripted encounters presented in these chapters, immigrant musicking establishes aural contact zones (Pratt) and fosters an aural public sphere in Latin America (Ochoa Gautier) and the US. Conflict and possibility arise at every turn. Creativity and a will-to-world go hand in hand with the fact of migrancy. In turn, migrancy goes hand in hand with a claim both unremarkable and vexing: that in listening, people assemble a capacity to make and create that sets the terrain for a political contestation of equality. This contestation wagers on an equality defined in terms of a capacity to comprehend, reinvent, and transform what is musically heard. For what is musically heard will be heard by others, and in such re-hearing new bodies and archives emerge.

In the first chapter, those archives stored words and letters now scattered across all social strata, bodies came to occupy places formerly barred to them. We found, in chapter 2, how a sonic archive already South, in the ears of musicians who had been listening all along, could not simply be incorporated into the larger design of "Latin America." The tension between a politics of representation and a politics of collaboration grew with the advances of "global" logics and practices. In chapter 3, this tension reached its limit in the paradoxical cosmopolitanization of a figure whose irruption in the world demands new archives where all musics potentially commingle, linguistic hierarchies erode, local-global distinctions blur, and where the subject is affirmed but transfigured into a brand. In chapter 4, claims over kinship, the dead, the past, tradition, and history, with race as a central axis of affect and intelligibility, animated different perspectives on the relation of race, temporality, and musicking. At stake was the entrance, on equal terms, into the history of jazz, a music long held to be a signal contribution of the US and of its Black musicians to the world. Different mappings of musical traditions crisscross Miguel Zenón's innovative work as he looks to the Puerto Rican past to compose a future for jazz, and as he looks to the past of jazz to compose a present for Puerto Rico's periphery. Chapter 5 mapped these juxtapositions in terms of a modernity that sets the coordinates along which unexpected gaps appear. Zenón's musicking breaks through such gaps.

Wherever music sounds, there resonate the many entanglements that unite and separate the Americas. At the same time, such entanglements seem prescribed by the grand argument of a modernity that somehow offers values, principles, and aspirations to its involved actors. In their sounded specificity, musical forms do not escape the maelstrom of these unscripted encounters in and prescriptions of modernity: musical forms compose and are composed of all those things (values, principles, aspirations). As I have proposed, these things enter and leave assemblages that exceed any actor or element ever in a position to attain a sense of totality. I hope that even with the theoretical interventions I have staged, with a looming universalization of theory ever possible, readers do not take away the idea that I have attempted to reach any such sense. By its very nature, the notion of syncopation works through my own arguments, dislocating them as well. And this equally reflects the fact that histories and stories from the recent past remain in process, actors finding new challenges and responding to them accordingly, sometimes even shifting positions expressed in the preceding chapters.

One story I related traced the cosmopolitan reach of capitalism, a global design if there ever was one. Capitalism's expansionist character found in Shakira a treasure at a time in which Colombia, however poised it was to become a musical quarry for the global phonographic industry, was not yet a steady source of young talent. Since then, the industry's extractive practices have only intensified. Perhaps these practices are a definitive index that Colombia has arrived and consolidated itself in global musical circulation. The process that elevated a nationally successful talent like Shakira and that exploited her musical eclecticism to render her into the ultimate figure of musical cosmopolitanism—this same process has proliferated a number of other global figures. First, Juanes—a Colombian rocker whose first breakthrough album *Mi Sangre* (2004) was crafted in Los Angeles studios by veteran Argentine producer Gustavo Santaolalla— would confirm the country's status as cradle of a new archive of musical worldliness in two languages and now, with a male counterpart to Shakira, in two genders. Since then, artists such as Maluma and J Balvin form part of an elite group of Colombia-born global superstars who have become must-have guests in productions by the likes of Madonna, to give one example from the old regime, or Rosalía, from the new. Apart from the usual harangues against this or that style these artists represent, the public discussion no longer centers around conflicts about their nationality or the country's achievement of musical notoriety on the global stage. The now legendary inclusion of Justin Bieber into a mixed version of the megahit "Despacito" allegedly happened after the Canadian idol went to Bogotá and saw clubgoers' reaction to the original version of the song. We should not overlook the fact that Mauricio Rengifo and Andrés Torres— the two producers for that version by the Puerto Rican Luis Fonsi and featuring reggaeton superstar Daddy Yankee—were Colombian.

Already in the early 1980s, industry spokespersons referred to the pressure to "discover" acts with potential for worldwide development.[1] Colombia was no regular semi-periphery, however. Boasting the oldest and most stable democracy in Latin America—or so the story goes—the mid-sized country had been an early entry into neoliberal policies with the introduction of open markets to foreign goods and investment during the Gaviria government (1990–1994). Since then, in the midst of the "drug wars" and "armed conflicts"—which found the country as one of the top recipients of US military aid (under "Plan Colombia")—musicking proliferated in a peculiar but not unheard-of syncopation between "music" and social unrest. The peace accord between the government and insurgent armed groups—characterized by the ongoing slaughter of leftist activists at the hands of right-wing interests—has only strengthened a sense that anything is (musically) possible.

Social unrest has been a backing track to virtually all the sounds heard in these chapters. Recall Blades's sense that Latin America needed to be reckoned with by salsa musicians and local audiences in late 1970s and 1980s New York City. Embodying the particular historical subject of *parrhesia*, Blades wagered on song's truth-telling capacities. Less than three decades later the brand of "expansionary individualism" granted to Shakira as she reached the world did not appear to extend to Blades as he tried to broaden his sonic representation of "Latin American feeling" in his turn-of-the-century projects. Much as he remained committed to a politics of truth-telling, audiences failed to become publics. Either there was no longer a need to hear of truths in song or else truth had ceased to be a social and political imperative, as he denounced in his song "Hipocresía." This generational divide speaks to the shifting domains where redistributions of the sensible may occur. And yet, it was Blades who had a veritable political life as Panama's Minister of Tourism during the presidency of Martín Torrijos (2004–2009); his voice and likeness were seen and heard in taxi cabs in New York City in the latter aughts advertising why passengers might want to visit his home country.

The question of worlding remains. If Shakira's success on the global stage goes hand in hand with the "cultural logic" of late capitalism, with a wholly fungible sense of the world that she can call "home," what kind of world was Blades's? Music and world do not hold a direct relationship, and neither can they be fully given in advance of the assemblages they may enter. Nonetheless, we could argue that the portfolio of selves that the Colombian star accumulated was unanchored in the kind of ontopological commitments that Blades, by contrast, held. Although for many Shakira embodied an emerging new Latinity in the US, her Latin Americanism was almost incidental to her cosmopolitanism. For Blades, on the contrary, Latin Americanism even of the restitutive kind remained tethered to what he felt were actual places and histories. As Jean Franco astutely observed, the contemporary overabundance of signs stirred by economic disorder results in a maladjustment of representation, a loss of Latin Americanist categories to provide functional equilibrium to an exhausted society. Perhaps, then, we might do well by approaching the syncopation in the turn-of-the-century reception of Shakira and Blades as part of the shifts in relations of production that yield core-periphery mappings. In Immanuel Wallerstein's remark, "the more monopolized a product is, the more core-like it will be, because you can make more money on it. So, if given kinds of production spread out to more countries, that's because they have become less profitable within the original loci of production, not because these countries to which the processes spread are successfully 'developing.'"[2]

The critical verve that many experienced in Blades's music would become attenuated by the time this book closes. Franco, whose critique of the decline of the lettered city provides the most sustained account of this phenomenon, comments that as literature loses its former place of privilege, "lite" criticism "invades the novel and poetry as well as popular music," adding that "political dissidence may be more directly and forcefully expressed in rock music and rap than in the arts, even though the music industry is thoroughly commercialized."[3] The antagonists here are postmodern culturalism, with its everything-goes attitude, and neoconservative market-ism, with its everything-for-sale ethos. This argument—most vividly felt in the arc traced by chapters 1, 2, and 3—is informed by the idea that Latin American writers had successfully resignified both ways of reading and their literary genealogies. They had prompted a renovated understanding of history, and had revaluated the meaning of "contemporary culture in a way that transgressed narrow national boundaries," such that during the 1960s they "instigated the public to read as 'contemporaries of the rest of the world,'" to finally access the modern world.[4] Latin American writers' renovations overlapped with modernization projects that, however they may have helped launch literature and art into progressive roles, would also compel questions about demystification and liberation.

Blades's Latin Americanism emerges in and out of this context; it engages in a syncopated relation with it by compelling questions about aurality's compliance to the written word and vice versa; it blurs the boundary between the lettered and the aural, which in a way had always already been blurred.[5] But his own fascination with the word would place him in syncopation with some audiences, and by the time he returned to record in Costa Rica, this dislocation would be at the level of content. Between these moments, the Panamanian's 1980s songs—heard by many against the suffocating grids of "crossover" and by others as one of the most significant bodies of songs directly addressing the many travails of the continent—resonated strongly with what would come to be known as the lost decade. And just as "Pedro Navaja," that masterpiece of popular *letradismo*, introduced the lumpen proletariat as a character of Latin American modernity in the US—but not only there—and captured the often unheard and untold violence permeating everyday life at the margins, the 1980s songs would pinpoint specific historical events that voiced State-sponsored violence. In all, a remarkable achievement.

As of this writing, Blades continues to amass Grammy Awards, reclaiming his extensive catalogue from the claws of Fania Records' rapacious copyright policies by re-recording it. A stunning tango album under the musical directorship of New York City–based Argentine arranger Carlos Franzetti saw a fresh take on "Pedro Navaja." An album with Wynton Marsalis and the Jazz at Lincoln Center Orchestra presents the musicians showing their mettle in "Latin" music as the singer showcases his profound appreciation and understanding of the great American Songbook repertoire. Tours with his classic 1980s ensemble continue, often hinting at retirement. And more than ever, a brilliant band of Panamanian musicians, the Roberto Delgado Orchestra, constitute his main musical backing orchestra. Levels in skill and "feeling" in playing salsa have long equilibrated in relation to Puerto Rico's and New York City's. Salsa, in the main, has become both attenuated and relocated.[6] Crossover—that long overcome phenomenon in the cases we studied and for which Blades was once a poster boy—continues to baffle US publics perplexingly committed to notions of racial separation. Indeed, Lil Nas X, whose "Old Town Road" shocked the charts with its sticky-as-tar trap-country groove, has been called as recently as 2020 "the king of crossover."[7]

Zenón continues to produce consistently inventive and project-oriented music. *Rayuela*, a 2012 project with French pianist Laurent Coq, a musical version of Cortazar's "jazz" novel *Hopscotch*, would make for an excellent study of lettered musical translations. As he continues to explore with his usual brilliance the music of Puerto Rico, he also presents his current thinking about identity in *Identities Are Changeable* (2014), a large-ensemble recording with ample media exposure. Avoiding identitarian dualisms as much as when I interviewed him in 2008, he remains curious about what it means to reinvent the Island's rich musical archives. In a way, such projects show the degree to which the stories presented here foreclose a sense of an ending. They also show, without doubt, the limits of my analyses, which in a way exist in syncopation with the very field they try to map. For their part, the Afro Latin Jazz Orchestra continues with their innovative experimental programming and educational programs. The level of musical performance is without peer. Alas, their annual budget is far from what it needs to be and a fragment of their former host's budget at Jazz at Lincoln Center. Jazz remains a "house divided."

The debates that greeted Shakira have abated, but her status has not. The artist continues to perform at highly coveted venues; an event as "American" as the 2020 Super Bowl Halftime Show is one among many, albeit a more parochial engagement than the World Cup and its worldwide exposure. At the Super Bowl, performing solo and alongside Jennifer Lopez, the performer still proudly displayed Colombian visual emblems. Based in Spain, where her husband and children live, the Colombian remains deeply committed to social causes at home and abroad; scandals about unpaid taxes are unable to tarnish her public image as a celebrity with a conscience. Colombians, meanwhile, have moved on to other things to argue about. As I write, news comes of the superstar's pride in having completed an online course on ancient Greek (pre-Socratic) philosophy at the University of Pennsylvania, where I teach.

During the time the studies of this book unfolded, two genres have become the terrain where musicians from the Hispanophone Caribbean and elsewhere in the Americas have unprecedented presence: Dominican Bachata and various forms of Reggaeton. Both are male-dominated. The former's success is remarkable. In 2014, Romeo Santos, the Bronx-born star of the genre, sold out two engagements at Yankee Stadium, performing each concert at capacity (50,000 fans). It was the first time a solo Latino act had performed there. The only other Latin act to have performed there was the Fania All-Stars' concert performance in 1973. Reggaeton in a way bypasses the earlier centrality of a "required" US base (salsa in NYC or Latin pop in Miami, for example); it has spread from Puerto Rico to other countries and, as noted before, influenced "mainstream" popular music. The form offers a potent set of novel cognitive categories and expressive modalities for audiences across the continent. To be sure, as part of the genre's undeniable popularity, one finds resonances of recognizable Latin Americanist concerns in the music of the brilliant Puerto Rican duo of Calle 13. In 2014 National Public Radio in the US defined the duo as "politically outspoken and opinionated . . . Latin America's premier political troubadours."[8] The duo's signal influence? Rubén Blades, by their own accord.

If Latin Americanism is held to relatively determinable definitions of "Latin," or "Latino," or before that, "Hispanic," then Latinity in the US has undergone a dramatic shift. Today, Latinities proliferate.[9] Latinx, a term that tantalizingly brings the enigmatic X to the heart of "Latin" cultures in the US, has emerged as a powerful concept and practice for new generations of artists, critics, activists, and scholars. For some, the term expresses a sort of capitulation to the hegemony of English and an "Americanization" of Latino/Latina racial and ethnic strife in the US. For others, it embodies a productive way to gain a modicum of control over collective naming. Broadly encompassing, the term hasn't seized music making as one of its privileged terrains; other forms of creative endeavor and expression occupy a place in an ever more heterogeneous cultural terrain in which the former hierarchies among "Latin" or "Latin@" groups too come under pressure—my chapters admittedly focus on these established groups.

Jazz, a genre that continues to invite oversize musical talent in spite of a minuscule market share, counts an unprecedented number of musicians from the Americas among its ranks at the highest levels. Consider Chilean tenor saxophonist Melissa Aldana, who trained in her native country. In 2013, she became the first female ever to win the Thelonious Monk Competition, on saxophone. She has since launched a stellar career. Camila Mesa, also Chilean, is a formidable guitarist and singer—a rare combination in the world of jazz. The piano bench in Wayne Shorter's quartet is occupied by Panamanian Danilo Pérez, whose work as pedagogue includes a thriving music academy in Panama City. Hearing students there play in YouTube videos, one realizes that the enormous distance to jazz that Miguel Zenón might have felt before he left Puerto Rico to study at Berklee is no longer felt in the same way for a large number of talented musicians.

The sheer proliferation of musicking leaves one feeling as if no distribution of the sensible—to return one last time to this key concept—manages to achieve much. Perhaps earlier distributions look that way from the vantage point of the present. Or perhaps nearly endless multiplicities of micro-syncopations today become bits and pieces within the vast archives of big data, archives in which the more defined and sometimes better-defining syncopations of modernities themselves constitute bits and pieces. New analytics may provide much-needed insight into these multiplicities and the ways in which they inevitably—at least from a residual modern perspective—remain matters of concern in which times and temporalities, places, and spaces stubbornly assert their (dis)organizing powers North and South.

ACKNOWLEDGMENTS

I began this book too long ago. I thank everyone for never taking time to read its drafty drafts, its essaying versions; their reticence saved me a lot of shame over poorly developed ideas. That said, intellectually, socially, aesthetically, and politically, many have given something, each in a unique way, to what the book does, and thereby to what I, in a way, am: Licia Fiol-Matta; George Yúdice; Elizabeth Povinelli; Juan Carlos Heredia; César Colón-Montijo; Guthrie Ramsey; Román de la Campa; Rossana Reguillo; Timothy Brennan; David Novak; Gary Tomlinson; Peter Szendy; Roger Grant; Dylon Robbins; Denilson Lopes; Daniel Party; Michael Birenbaum Quintero; Mary Louise Pratt; Robin Moore; Roberto Dainotto; Jason Borge; Steven Feld. An early conversation with the late Ernesto Laclau proved fundamental for thinking about some aspects of the political in relation to aesthetics with greater rigor. Professor Raúl Antelo, a towering thinker of the enigma that is Latin America, generously sent, having never met me, a copy of a key but difficult to find book of his, *Crítica acéfala*. That book opened up unprecedented vistas for my thinking about the Americas.

I have tried to learn from each musician with whom I had the pleasure and honor to perform and/or record. The book, in many ways, expresses those lessons and the histories they all brought to making music happen. Each of them, whatever the instrument, whatever the musical situation, compelled me to listen. With them, every beat, every note held a world: Ray Vega; Hector Martignon; Satoshi Takeishi; Antonio Arnedo; Steve Slagle; Eddie Palmieri; Sergio George; Ricky Gonzalez; George Gonzalez; Jimmy Delgado; Eddie Montalvo; Oscar Hernandez; Chris Washburne; Barry Olsen; Vince Cherico; Adam Kolker; Michael-Philipp Mossman; Ray de la Paz; Tito Nieves; Paquito Pastor; Luis Bonilla; Horacio "Negro" Hernandez; Peter Brainin; Bruce Saunders; Ben Monder. A special note to the late Ray Barretto, a master in every sense of the word and a musician who dwelled in many of the worlds I address in this book. Nearly eight years on the road, on stages everywhere, and in studios with him taught me that the beat is always in question but never in doubt.

Warm thanks to the late Juan Flores and Miriam Jiménez Román for bringing me into insightful conversations about Afro-Latinity; at Duke to Alberto Moreiras for sage advice and to Frank Lentricchia and Jodi Mc-Auliffe for intellectual nourishing; to André Lepecki and Lytle Shaw and the Ethics of the Sensible Working Group at NYU. Generous interlocutors, vital for the content of the chapters, are Luis "Perico" Ortiz, Miguel Zenón, Billy Pierce, Arturo O'Farrill, Ed Simon, Vince Cherico, Urian Sarmiento, Juan Sebastian Monsalve, Derek Kwon, and John Walsh—I cannot thank them enough, for their words *are* this book. The collegiality I experienced during a fellowship year at the National Humanities Center was, besides formative, a set of invaluable lessons in method and ideas by historians, philosophers, literary critics, and anthropologists. Thanks, there, to Carla Nappi; Bruce Rusk; Robert Mitchell; Christopher Nelson; Pamela Long; Marcia Kupfer; Mario Klarer; Janet Browne; Sanjay Krishnan; Keren Gorodeisky; and Arata Hamawaki. And thanks to the knowledgeable and caring staff in the administration, the library, and the kitchen. Three places in Park Slope, Brooklyn, saw more of me than they should have: the now closed Ozzie's (thanks, Jason) and Venticinque (thanks, Tania), and Al di la and its extraordinary chef Anna Klinger, whose impromptu ramp risotto one spring years ago was rapture embodied. Cristina Diaz-Carrera and Michael Gallope provided early research assistance in New York City. Laurie Garriga located important sources in Puerto Rico. In Philadelphia, without the astute work of Elizabeth Bynum, the final three years of research would not have happened. And without the keen eye of Andrew Niess's editing, the book would never have been adequate. Kevin Laskey's finely tuned ears are responsible for the musical transcriptions. Maria Andrea Giraldo assisted with important migration data. My former doctoral advisees at NYU and UPenn were always within earshot during writing, their work a constant source of amazement and inspiration: Delia Casadei, Amy Cimini, Jenny Johnson, Alex Ness, Yoni Niv, Jessica Schwartz, Stephen Decatur Smith, Maria Murphy, Juan Carlos Castrillón, and Andrew Niess. Two other advisees, Daniel Villegas Vélez and Stephan Hammel, worked on topics closer to this book's; their lucid analyses helped clarify many an argument here.

Several editors invited me to publish in their projects, trusting my work-in-progress and offering me a space to essay thoughts and ideas before they made their way into this book: Liliana Gomez and Gesine Müller, in Germany; Ron Radano, a dear friend, fearless thinker, and inspiration, and the late Tejumola (Teju) Olaniyan; Jason Borge; Olivia Bloechl, Melanie Lowe, and Jeff Kallberg; Keith Chapin and Andrew Clarke; and Pablo Vila, whose support and encouragement helped me keep going.

At the University of Chicago Press, I counted my lucky stars with two shining editors: Elizabeth Branch Dyson and Mary Al-Sayed. Their guidance, knowledge, insight, and phenomenal patience with a most delinquent author made this book a reality—believe it or not, the original manuscript was twice the length of what you now hold! Fabiola Enríquez Flores and Beth Ina expertly made sure that everything worked. Phil Bohlman, series editor, trusted the project from the get-go. Thanks.

Gavin Steingo has been an intellectual partner since I met him as a graduate student; his honest, piercing critiques have kept the sails going as I cross the doldrums of academia. Phil Rupprecht, a friend among friends, has always been there, even in the long gaps between conversations. Two former colleagues and dearest of friends invited me into the art of the possible. Louise Meintjes, a wise, deeply grounded sister, intellectually, politically, and in the arts of conviviality, taught me how to trust people and put my feet on their ground. Without the presence of Ana María Ochoa Gautier, none of the ideas I explore here would have even come into being. I became a Latin Americanist in our long and intense conversations, though I'd never pretend to be anything other than her incorrigible pupil: whatever remains to be *bobadas* in this book is, *por supuesto*, entirely my responsibility.

Probing audiences at talks and conferences compelled rigor in my otherwise too eclectic a predisposition: National Humanities Center; NYU; Princeton; Case Western University; University of Chicago; Columbia University; University of North Carolina, Chapel Hill; Pontificia Universidad Católica de Chile (Santiago); Brooklyn College; Casa de las Américas and Ana Niria Albo Díaz (Havana); Romanistentag, 31 International Congress, Transatlantische Perspektiven in der Romanistik: Das kulturelle Feld in dem Karibik, University of Bonn; *II Encuentro de Latinidades*, Convenio Andrés Bello, El Colegio de la Frontera Norte, Tijuana, México; II Congreso Internacional Música, Identidad y Cultura en el Caribe, Instituto de Estudios Caribeños (INEC), Santiago de los Caballeros, República Dominicana.

Renata Pontes, a fierce mind and impossibly giving heart, accompanied the final stages of the book throughout great strife and loss with unspeakable love. She too brought me back to Latin America, from where I perhaps never really left. It couldn't be more wonderful, that site. I began thinking about this book in earnest at the time my daughter, Coco Moreno, was born, March 8, 2006. Coco left all too soon, on September 17, 2019, as I entered the final phase of the project. The joy she brought to my life and the love that I feel for her are everywhere present. To her, to her sister, the amazing, brilliant Lola, and to my beautiful younger son, Gil, this book is lovingly and madly dedicated: they are the syncope that propels one forward, theirs a time of impossible anticipation in which dwells the entire history that might yet be.

Research for this project was generously provided for by a fellowship from the American Council of Learned Societies (2009–2010) and by a fellowship from the Rockefeller Foundation at the National Humanities Center (2012–2013).

Part of an earlier version of chapter 4 appears as "Sonorous Specters: On the Histories and Economies of Afro-Latin Jazz," special dossier on Latin America, the Caribbean, and the New Jazz Studies, ed. Jason Borge, *Journal of Latin American Cultural Studies* 25, no. 3 (2016): 397–417. An earlier version of chapter 5 appears as "Difference Unthought," in *Rethinking Difference in Musical Scholarship*, ed. Olivia Bloechl, Melanie Lowe, and Jeffrey Kallberg (New York: Cambridge University Press, 2014), 382–421.

NOTES

Introduction

1. For "being in" and "becoming with," see Kember and Zylinska, *Life After New Media*, xv.

2. Rancière, *The Politics of Aesthetics*.

3. Rancière, *The Emancipated Spectator*, 72.

4. See Glasser, *My Music Is My Flag*.

5. Rancière, *Aesthetics and Its Discontents*; Rancière, "Ten Theses on Politics," 27. Other dimensions of politics appear in Rancière: "the act of political subjectivization that breaks with the police order [any form of established order]" and "the meeting ground between police procedures and the process of equality." Rockhill, "The Politics of Aesthetics," 308n5.

6. Rancière, *The Politics of Aesthetics*, 12. For detailed discussion, see Moreno and Steingo, "Rancière's Equal Music," 487–505.

7. See Lowe, *Immigrant Acts*. Charles Hiroshi Garrett addresses the question of music in *Struggling to Define a Nation*. Another key text, focused on literature, is Saldívar, *Dialectics of Our America*.

8. On sound as fathoming, see Helmreich, *Sounding the Limits of Life*, x–xi.

9. This sense of musicking builds on but departs considerably from its original formulation in Small, *Musicking*. See DeLanda, *Assemblage Theory*.

10. On modes of listening, see Kane, "*L'Objet sonore maintenant*," 18.

11. Erlmann, *Music, Modernity, and the Global Imagination*, 6.

12. Gomart and Hennion, "A Sociology of Attachment," 220–47.

13. Gomart and Hennion, "A Sociology of Attachment," 225.

14. Hennion, "Loving Music," 32.

15. "Las dos ramas, latina y germana, se han reproducido en el Nuevo Mundo. América del Sur es, como la Europa meridional, católica y latina. La América del Norte pertenece a una población protestante y anglosajona"; cited in Zea, *América latina en sus ideas*, 160–61. The adjective *latine* was pejorative: "the Spanish American seems to be nothing other than an impotent race without future, unless it receives a wave of rich and new blood coming from the North." Cited in Mignolo, *The Idea of Latin America*, 78. Ardao, *Génesis de la idea y el nombre de América Latina*. On Chevalier's adjective, see de la Campa, *Latin Americanism*; Moreiras, *Exhaustion of Difference*. Chevalier's designs were inseparable from global projections of a diminished France that nonetheless loomed large in the continent as the matrix for

its political revolutions, rational ideals, and cultural production. See Phelan, "Pan-Latinism, French Intervention in Mexico (1861–1867) and the Genesis of the Idea of Latin America," 279–98. For a counterargument, see Quijada, "Sobre el origen y difusión del nombre 'América Latina,'" 595–619.

16. "Las dos Américas," cited in McGuinness, "Searching for Latin America," 99. Others using the expression during the 1850s include Dominican Francisco Muñoz del Monte, and Chileans Santiago Arcos and Francisco Bilbao. See Ardao, *Génesis de la idea y el nombre de América Latina*.

17. Institutional projects similar to those Torres Caicedo and Bilbao proposed form part of a tradition of pursuing a southern hemisphere confederacy. These other projects did not center on Latinity as such. Simón Bolívar's "Jamaica Letter" is a foundational document. Bolívar organizes what comes to be known as the Amphictyonic Congress, or the Congress of Panama (1826), with subsequent meetings in Lima, Perú (1846–1848 and 1864), and Santiago, Chile (1856–1857). At the inaugural meeting of the Sociedad Unión Americana de Santiago (1862), Chilean liberals denounced both neocolonial efforts by Spain and France and the US "Manifest Destiny," promoting a union of republics. On the congresses, see Bushnell and Macauly, *The Emergence of Latin America in the Nineteenth Century*; on the Sociedad Unión Americana, see Lorena Ubilla Espinoza, "Pensamiento y acción americanista en los liberales chilenos: la propuesta de Benjamín Vicuña Mackenna, 1862–1868," *Estudios filológicos, no. 65* (2020), accessed January 16, 2021, https://scielo.conicyt.cl/scielo.php?script=sci_abstract&pid=S0071-17132020000100077&lng=en&nrm=isohttps://scielo.conicyt.cl/scielo.php?script=sci_abstract&pid=S0071-17132020000100077&lng=en&nrm=iso. Later in the century governmental ideas of inter-Americanism and Pan-Americanism join the two continental poles in inter-governmental institutions that survive to this day. In 1889–1890, the First International Conference of American States was held in Washington, DC, constituting the International Union of American Republics, headquartered in Washington, which later became the Pan American Union and then the Organization of American States (OAS).

18. Torres Caicedo was reacting to the US annexation of Mexican territory in the aftermath of the Mexican-American War (1846–1848) and to the American government's support for the 1856 invasion of Nicaragua by buccaneer William Walker.

19. Guerra Vilaboy and Maldonado Gallardo, *Los laberintos de la integración latinoamericana*, 33. The question of exclusion haunts the influential work of Edmundo O'Gorman: "The native cultures of the newly-founded lands could not be recognized and respected in their own right, as an original way of realizing human ideals values, but only for the meaning they might have in relation to Christian European culture." O'Gorman, *The Invention of America*, 138. Cf. Kusch, *Indigenous and Popular Thinking in América*; Mariategui, *Seven Interpretative Essays on Peruvian Reality*; and Anibal Quijano's now canonic work on decoloniality as popularized in the US by Walter Mignolo. See also Rabasa, *De la invención de América*.

20. These include Venezuelan Francisco Miranda (1750–1816), Ecuadorian Vicente Rocafuerte (1783–1847), and Mexicans José Bernardo Gutiérrez de Lara (1774–1841) and Lorenzo de Zavala y Sáenz (1788–1836).

21. Argentine writer and diplomat Juan Bautista Alberdi (1810–1884) envisioned a national pedagogy to shape the "Yankees of the South." Alberdi, *Bases y puntos de partida para la organización política de la república Argentina*. Alberdi's influential com-

patriot, writer and statesman Domingo Faustino Sarmiento (1811–1888), toured the US, writing encomia of US political figures and elevating the country's institutions to the status of models to emulate. See Faustino Sarmiento, *Argirópolis*, cited in Zea, *Dialéctica de la conciencia americana*, 59.

22. Argentine Manuel Ugarte visited the US in 1899, perceiving a radical contrast between Mexico and the US. Between 1911–1913 Ugarte traveled to every country in the Americas, including the US, promoting his ideas for a union of Latin American states. See Ugarte, *El porvenir de la América Latina*; Ugarte, *El destino de un continente*; and Degiovanni, *Vernacular Latin Americanisms*.

23. Belknap and Fernández, *José Martí's "Our America"*; Lomas, *Translating Empire*; Ramos, *Divergent Modernities*; Rotker, *The American Chronicles of José Martí*.

24. Lomas, *Translating Empire*, 37.

25. Belknap and Fernández, "Introduction," *José Martí's "Our America,"* 4.

26. This follows Ramos's influential argument in *Divergent Modernities*. See also Saldívar, *Dialectics of Our America*. Influential Cuban critic Roberto Fernández Retamar called Martí's work "the true intellectual entrance of Hispanic America to modernity," in "Modernismo, noventiocho, subdesarrollo," in *Para el perfil definitivo del hombre* (Havana: Editorial Letras Cubanas, 1981), 213.

27. Salomon, "José Martí y la toma de conciencia latinoamericana," 223–38.

28. Martí, "Nuestra América." Martí had spoken highly of US democratic ideals in his 1889 discourse *Madre América*. But unlike his predecessors, Martí insisted with unheard-of vehemence on the imperatives of self-affirmation and originality, and on the corollary necessity to actively avoid foreign models of governance. In this, his thought embodies at once an active anti-colonial, anti-imperial, and anti-racist project grounded in the valorization of the proper (i.e., autonomous, authentic) Latin American being as a built-in resistance to appropriation—cultural, economic, political, or spiritual—a capacity strengthened by his belief that "our American nations . . . are one in spirit and intent." Martí, "Nuestra América."

29. Martí, "Nuestra América." The Mexican José Vasconcelos will diagnose a constitutive multiracial society as the paradigm for Latin Americanism in *The Cosmic Race/La Raza Cósmica*.

30. Another classic Latin Americanist essay, "Ariel," by Uruguayan José Enrique Rodó (1871–1917) only intensifies the claims on behalf of the spirit. These foundational essays differ in that the Cuban's attitude was decidedly inclusive, whereas Rodó was exclusive and elitist.

31. Mignolo, *The Idea of Latin America*, x.

32. Tenorio-Trillo, *Latin America*, 1.

33. Identity goes hand in hand with the production of a proper subject in the sense of adequacy to and ownership of Latin America. This proper subject lies at the conjunction of an ontological sense of the reality of Latin America and the affective fidelity to that reality.

34. Tenorio-Trillo, *Latin America*, 2.

35. Tenorio-Trillo, *Latin America*.

36. Tenorio-Trillo, *Latin America*, 2–3.

37. Tenorio-Trillo, *Latin America*, 4.

38. Moreiras, *Exhaustion of Difference*, 32.

39. "El latinoamericanismo es de hecho un conjunto de mediaciones entre lo local

y lo universal, entre lo propio y lo extranjero, entre la particularidad de la expresión cultural y la necesidad de traducir y de hacer legible el registro local en función de la universalidad de las discusiones globales." Ramos, "Los tiempos caribeños de Amadeo Roldán y Luis Palés Matos." Many thanks to Professor Ramos for lending me a copy of his paper.

40. Tenorio-Trillo, *Latin America*, 103. Besides "idea," Tenorio-Trillo often uses "term" and "concept" as synonyms.

41. Tenorio-Trillo, *Latin America*.

42. Moreiras, *Exhaustion of Difference*, 58.

43. On Latin Americanism, see Román de la Campa, *Latin Americanism*; Moreiras, *Exhaustion of Difference*. Important work includes Levinson, *The Ends of Literature*; Williams, *The Other Side of the Popular*; and Franco, *The Decline and Fall of the Lettered City*. For "New Latin Americanism," see Jenckes, "The 'New Latin Americanism'"; and Beasley-Murray, "Introduction: Towards a New Latin Americanism." Except for Franco, these authors generally adopt a deconstructive approach, challenging cartographic logics of region and exploring the limits of the political reach of literature. More prescriptive efforts, such as the now well-known and much-debated decolonial project, exemplified in the US by the work of Walter Mignolo, also for part of a certain boom of Latin Americanist critique; I use it here sparingly. Mignolo, *The Idea of Latin America*. One may count the insightful report of Ludmer, *Aquí América Latina*. An important area for this book is the study of globalization, particularly the questioning of a place for Latin America in the global age: García Canclini and Martín-Barbero are key here. See also Beverley, *Latinamericanism after 9/11*; and Beasley-Murray, *Posthegemony*. We might read a dedicated issue of *Social Text* in a related way, as an effort to think the Americas in their interlocked rhythms of "power, violence, and place," with particular attention to spatial formations and the role of the transnational in them, distinct from globalization and migration. Sartorius and Siegel, "Introduction: Dislocations across the Americas." Driving the point home, Mary Louise Pratt remarks in her commentary to the issue that "North and South America are the only continents on the planet named in relation to each other." Pratt, "It Takes Two to Tangle," 152. See also Achugar, "Local/Global Latin Americanisms"; Montaldo, "Latin Americanism"; and García Canclini, "Anthropology." See as well dedicated issues of *Journal of Latin American Cultural Studies* 11, no. 3 (2002); and *Radical History Review* 89 (2004).

44. de la Campa, *Latin Americanism*, 1, 2.

45. Richard, "Intersecting Latin America with Latin Americanism." Richard's piece was originally published in 1977.

46. Larsen, *Reading North by South*, 1; Larsen, "Latin Americanism Without Latin America," 37.

47. Tenorio-Trillo, *Latin America*, 155.

48. Moreiras, "On Latin Americanism."

49. Moreiras, *Exhaustion of Difference*, 291; Laclau, "Why Do Empty Signifiers Matter to Politics," 36–46.

50. Palomino, *The Invention of Latin American Music*.

51. Palomino, *The Invention of Latin American Music*, 12.

52. Palomino, *The Invention of Latin American Music*, 213. Documents from the Pan-American Association of Composers (1928–1933), founded in New York City

and with membership from across the continent, address efforts "toward creating a distinctive music of the Western Hemisphere." Pan-American Association of Composers Folder, Cowell Papers, cited in Stallings, "Collective Difference," 68. Another writing speaks of "performances of Latin-American works in the United States and North-American works in southern countries" (Cowell, "Music," 501, cited in Stallings, "Collective Difference," 65). For a US optic on art music from Latin America, aesthetic solidarity, and the notions of hemispheric cohesion during the 1930s and 1940s, see Hess, *Representing the Good Neighbor*.

53. The constitution of Latin America as the cradle of a hemispheric revolution during the 1960s coincides with the affirmation of the continent's cultural identity, particularly in literature, as a constitutively transcultural region. See Rama, *Writing Across Cultures*; Fernández Retamar, "Caliban."

54. Tenorio-Trillo, *Latin America*, 103.

55. This category highlights tensions between the migrant and an established minority in the US. An important referent here is Lionnet and Shih, *Minor Transnationalism*.

56. On overcoming nobility, see Feres Júnior, *Histoire du concept d'Amérique Latine aux Etats-Unis*, 40; on "republican modernity," see Sanders, "The Vanguard of the Atlantic World."

57. On "industrial modernity," see Sanders, "The Vanguard," 109.

58. See Miller and Hart, *When Was Latin America Modern?*

59. Koselleck, *Futures Past*.

60. This idea of lag here is different from but related to Johannes Fabian's account of how hegemonic colonial powers distilled in the discipline of anthropology render relations of space into relations of time. Fabian, *Time and the Other*. See Bhabha, *The Location of Culture*; Chakrabarty, *Provincializing Europe*; Banerjee, *Politics of Time*; Jameson, "The End of Temporality"; Harootunian, "Some Thoughts on Comparability and the Space-Time Problem"; Harootunian, *History's Disquiet*; Parry, "Aspects of Peripheral Modernisms."

61. Asad, *Formations of the Secular*, 13. See Taylor, *Modern Social Imaginaries*. Taylor advocates that modernity be understood as multiple modernities, even within the "singular" character of Western modernity.

62. Sterne, *The Audible Past*, 22. Sterne draws from Berman, *All That Is Solid Melts into Air*; Călinescu, *Five Faces of Modernity*; Lefebvre, *Introduction to Modernity*; and Bauman, *Liquid Modernity*.

63. Jameson, *A Singular Modernity*. Modernity afforded alternative narratives of the past, although observing that "the only satisfactory semantic meaning of modernity lies in its association with capitalism" (13). Appeal to "alternative modernities," preferable to the "old, detestable kind," ought not to reduce everything to culture (12). That modernity remained both yet-to-arrive and already, albeit incompletely, existing and thus everywhere inescapable led to questioning its presumed singularity and to proposing multiple modernities. "To think in terms of 'alternative modernities' is to admit that modernity is inescapable." Gaonkar, "On Alternative Modernities," 1. "Alternative modernities" manifest experiences of modernity not exclusively beholden to European or North American modernity. In turn, because temporality becomes mediated by that ever compromised nineteenth-century invention, history, historical narratives carry the burden of accounting for modernity and its alterna-

tive versions. Bhabha asks, "if we contest the 'grand narratives,' then what alternative temporalities do we create to articulate the differential (Jameson), contrapuntal (Said), interruptive (Spivak) historicities of race, gender, class, nation within a growing transnational culture?" Bhabha, *Location of Culture*, 174. On "multiple modernities," see the dedicated issue of *Daedalus* 129, no. 1 (2000).

64. This question and the points in this paragraph are adapted from Povinelli, *Empire of Love*, 16.

65. Pratt, "Modernity and Periphery," 22.

66. Pratt, "Modernity and Periphery," 23.

67. Sarlo, *Una modernidad periférica*.

68. Schouten, Theory Talk #13.

69. Herlinghaus and Moraña, *Fronteras de la modernidad en América Latina*, 11.

70. Herlinghaus and Moraña, *Fronteras de la modernidad en América Latina*, 11.

71. Herlinghaus and Moraña, *Fronteras de la modernidad en América Latina*, 11.

72. Music scholarship often engages with questions of aesthetic modernism in Europe and the US but is generally less interested in the question of modernity. Modernity is discussed in, among others, Bohlman, *Jewish Music and Modernity*; Erlmann, *Music, Modernity, and the Global Imagination*, an important referent for this book; Gutkin, "The Modernities of H. Lawrence Freeman"; Johnson, *Out of Time*; and Madrid, *Sounds of the Modern Nation*. The field of sound studies addresses modernity more directly. See Erlmann, *Hearing Cultures*; Sterne, *The Audible Past*; and Thompson, *The Soundscape of Modernity*.

73. Trigo, "General Introduction," 11.

74. Sarlo, *Una modernidad periférica*; García Canclini, *Hybrid Cultures*; Larraín Ibañez, *Modernidad, razón e identidad en América Latina*; Ramos, *Divergent Modernities*; Herlinghaus and Moraña, *Fronteras de la modernidad en América Latina*; Monsiváis, "Penetración Cultural y Nacionalismo"; Martín-Barbero, "Between Technology and Culture: Communication and Modernity in Latin America"; Quijano, "Coloniality and Modernity/Rationality"; Quijano, "Coloniality of Power, Eurocentrism and Social Classification"; Mignolo, *The Idea of Latin America*; Calderón, Hopenhayn, and Ottone, *Esa esquiva modernidad*; Oyarzún, *La desazón de lo moderno*; Garramuño, *Primitive Modernities*. For general discussion, see Brunner, "América Latina en la encrucijada de la modernidad"; Brunner, "Notes on Modernity and Postmodernity in Latin American Culture"; and Herlinghaus and Moraña, *Fronteras de la modernidad en América Latina*. Martin Hopenhayn articulated a related concern: whether the crisis of modernity in Latin America would lead to its coming apart or to assimilation into broader global designs. Hopenhayn, *No Apocalypse, No Integration*.

75. Sterne, *The Audible Past*, 2.

76. Ochoa Gautier, *Aurality*.

77. Novak, *Japanoise*, 20.

78. On race and gender, music and modernity, see Kheshti, *Modernity's Ear*.

79. See Pacini Hernandez, *Oye Como Va!*; Wade, *Music, Race, and Nation*; Madrid, *Sounds of the Modern Nation*; Madrid, *Nor-tec Rifa!*; Borge, *Tropical Riffs*; Karush, *Musicians in Transit*; Corti, *Jazz Argentino*; Acosta, *Otra vision de la música popular cubana*; Acosta, *Descarga cubana*; Acosta, *Descarga número dos*; and Acosta, *Raices del jazz latino*.

80. Clément, *Syncope*, 119–20.

81. Brossard, "Syncope," 148. I have modernized the French spelling.

82. Brossard, "Syncope," 150.

83. Nancy, *The Discourse of the Syncope*, 10. See also Didi-Huberman, *Confronting Images*.

84. Landes, "Le Toucher and the Corpus of Tact," 89.

85. Compare with Appadurai's notion of "disjuncture," which addresses a modernity rushing everywhere under globalization. Appadurai, "Disjuncture and Difference in the Global Cultural Economy." See also Appadurai, *Modernity at Large*. The signal Latin American contribution to these debates used the notion of hybridity. See García Canclini, *Hybrid Cultures*.

86. Moten, *In the Break*, esp. 85, 87–88; Baraka, "Apple Cores #6." Paul Gilroy speaks of "syncopated temporality," "a different rhythm of living and being." Gilroy, *The Black Atlantic*, 57–58.

87. Gilroy, *The Black Atlantic*, 57, 58.

88. Gilroy, *The Black Atlantic*, 58.

89. Quintero Rivera, *¡Salsa, sabor y control! Sociología de la música "tropical,"* 189.

90. Quintero Rivera, *¡Salsa, sabor y control!*, 203.

91. Quintero Rivera, *¡Salsa, sabor y control!*, 207.

92. Quintero Rivera, "Sensibilidades y comunicación en las músicas populares Afro Latinoamericanas." (Unless noted, all translations are mine.) Lara Ivette López de Jesús studies the relation of music and literature in the Caribbean under the framework of syncopation. López de Jesús, *Encuentros sincopados*.

93. See Perkinson, "Constructing the Break"; Bruce, "Interludes in Madtime: Black Music, Madness, and Metaphysical Syncopation." In general, this critical optic follows in the wake of the influential work on music and Blackness of W. E. B. Du Bois, Leroi Jones (Amiri Baraka), Richard Wright, Ralph Ellison, and more recently, Gilroy, Moten, and Alexander G. Weheliye. Weheliye: "[It] is not sound as an idealized, authentically vernacular, or discrete sphere that distinguishes Afro-diasporic cultural production in/as Western modernity but the use of the sonic to both create and recalibrate some of its central topoi, such as the equation of script with reason and humanity, narratives of unmitigated progress." Weheliye, *Phonographies*, 45.

94. Tsing, *Friction*.

95. Andrade, *Ensaio sobre a música brasileira*, 31. I adopt the standard Brazilian academic practice of using the first name to refer to Andrade.

96. Andrade, *Ensaio sobre a música brasileira*, 31.

97. Pérez Villalón, 224. Pérez Villalón, a literary critic, offers textual readings of Mário's poetry where he identifies mentions of the syncope and reads them as indexes of disruptions of regularities in the order of the State and the Republic, regularities that he identifies with Brazilian modernity. I do not engage hermeneutics of this kind. I formulated the notion of syncopated modernities before learning of Pérez Villalón's essay. Thanks to Dr. Renata Pontes de Queiroz for bringing this article to my attention.

98. Pérez Villalón, "Modernidad sincopada," 232. "Una clave de entrada a las relaciones entre lo nacional, la modernidad, lo popular y la estética, una clave que puede servirnos además para pensar la temporalidad del modernismo brasileño, tensionado entre las atracciones de lo primitivo y lo contemporáneo, de lo regional y lo cosmopolita, de la máquina y de lo ritual, lo popular y lo erudito."

99. Moten, *In the Break*, 85.

100. Moten, *In the Break*, 87–88.

101. Dylon Robbins proposes a broader conception of Afro-Diasporic musicking, including Brazilian forms, Afro-American funk, and salsa, on the basis of polyrhythm. For Robbins, the syncope is a "frame of reference" that "organizes time" and "situates beats," but ultimately obeys a regular and monorhythmic order against which disruptions are understood. Polyrhythm captures the "undercurrent of overlapping rhythms" of Afro-diasporic musics and "maps out an audible geography of movement and migration coinciding with the successive arrivals of Sub-Saharan Africans of different ethnicities to the Americas." Robbins, "Polyrhythm and the Valorization of Time in Three Movements," 84. Influenced by Mário, Robbins juxtaposes the Brazilian's ideas about rhythm to those of Cuban Antonio Benitez Rojo, who famously marshaled polyrhythm to conceive of an underlying order beneath apparent chaos, its proliferation an expression of the Caribbean "cultural machine." Benitez Rojo, *The Repeating Island*.

Counterpoint offers another possible heuristic that, however, lacks a thinking of gaps and elisions that syncopation provides. The term tracks a temporal phenomenon of "intertwined and overlapping histories" out of colonial and imperial encounters. See Said, *Culture and Imperialism*. Cuban Fernando Ortiz famously used the notion of "counterpoint" to understand Caribbean modernity in terms of the collisions of colonial (and imperial) domination, "the making and unmaking of cultural formations," in Fernando Coronil's words. Ortiz, *Cuban Counterpoint*, xiv.

Chapter One

1. De la Nuez, "Mis diez personajes."

2. For a discussion on "a people" and its complexities, see Badiou et al., *What Is a People?*

3. Glissant, *Caribbean Discourse*, 258–59. According to Glissant, reggae originates and returns to the Caribbean but does not traverse the continental US in its formation, making its route via the North Black Atlantic of the UK. I am profoundly grateful to the late Juan Flores for his support of my work and for our shared conversations. On music's role in the Puerto Rican diaspora, see Flores, *Divided Borders*; Flores, *The Diaspora Strikes Back*; and Flores, *Salsa Rising*.

4. One might nuance Glissant's macropolitical diagram with Lara Putnam's lucid mapping of workers' diasporic routes from the British West Indies into coastal Central America and to North America during the "jazz age." See Putnam, *Radical Moves*.

5. "Salsa," although produced in New York City, is unconceivable without the foundation of Cuban *son* and *guaracha*. The Cold War hovers over the whole enterprise, about which both de la Nuez and Glissant are eerily silent. My own relative silence over the Cuban connection to salsa is related to how Cold War politics in Latin America inform much of what Blades does and says he does. On the importance of Cuban music for salsa during the 1960s and 1970s, see Flores, *Salsa Rising*; García, *Arsenio Rodríguez*. On salsa's Cuban origins, see Manuel, "Puerto Rican Music"; Salazar, "Salsa Music Rivalries"; Salazar, "Pioneers of Salsa"; Acosta, "Perspectives on 'Salsa'"; and Ulloa, "La salsa."

6. Quintero Rivera, "Salsa, entre la globalización."

7. Quintero Rivera, "Salsa, entre la globalización," 100.

8. On Latin Americanism, see Moreno, "Tropical Discourses"; and Pimentel-Otero, "Latin Americanism."

9. Tablante, *El dólar*, 44–45.

10. For the original, writing-focused formulation of "lettered city," see Rama, *The Lettered City*. Critiques appear in Rappaport and Cummins, *Beyond the Lettered City*; and Spitta, *Más allá*. For an influential analysis of the fortunes of the idea, see Franco, *Decline and Fall*. For a mapping of the lettered city's sonic domain, audile techniques, and administrative claims on nineteenth-century Colombia, see Ochoa Gautier, *Aurality*.

11. Broadly, transculturation refers to the mode by which cultures with dissimilar powers meet and in which conflicts emerge in the establishment of new cultural forms. Heterogeneous and dialogic, transculturation speaks to the "non-synchronous development of peripheral modern . . . societies"; de la Campa, *Latin Americanism*, 83. Its analytic provides a preferred optic into Latin American particularity. For its socioeconomic and anthropological articulation, see Ortiz, *Cuban Counterpoint*. For transculturation in Latin American literature as one of its signal achievements, see the influential work of Rama, *Writing Across Cultures*. Ana María Ochoa Gautier develops the idea of transculturation, with a focus on relations between the work of folklorists and the music industry in the creation of national and international spheres, all of which contribute to the creation of an "aural modernity in Latin America." See her "Sonic Transculturation, Epistemologies of Purification and the Aural Public Sphere in Latin America." Ochoa Gautier offers an in-depth genealogy of the role of music in literature in "García Márquez, Macondismo, and the Soundscapes of Vallenato." One could read the novelist's comments on Blades as an expression of a reverse operation by which the Panamanian takes literature "back" to the popular music—and in Ochoa Gautier's perspicacious insight, the mode of aesthetic encounter—where it came from.

12. In an assemblage, emergence is the shared property that is proper to neither its parts nor a whole. In short, its relations "precede" the relata. See DeLanda, *New Philosophy of Society*.

13. Regrettable as de la Nuez's tone may appear, he might conceivably aim to denounce US imperialism's effects on actual people. There is an unresolvable tension between illiteracy's negative effects and bilingualism's positive aspects. On Nuyorican, Chicano, and Latin American immigrant inter-lingualism, see Flores and Yúdice, "Living Borders."

14. Fiol-Matta, *Great Woman Singer*, 79.

15. Hyon B. Shin and Rosalind Bruno, "Census 2000 Brief: Language Use and English-Speaking Ability: 2000," October 2003, https://www.census.gov/library/publications/2003/dec/c2kbr-29.html.

16. Otero Garabís, *Nación y ritmo*, 138.

17. See Díaz-Quiñones, "Puerto Rico."

18. Flores, *Divided Borders*, 147.

19. Duany, *La nación en vaivén*, 83. Helen Safa reports different figures: between 1950 and 1970, some 606,550 Puerto Ricans (27.4 percent of the Island's population) moved to New York City. Safa, "Social Cost," 81.

20. Duany, *La nación en vaivén*, 84.

21. Duany, *La nación en vaivén*, 87.

22. Duany, *Blurred Borders*, 7.

23. Flores, *Divided Borders*, 147.

24. On mono- and bilingualism in US electoral politics and the idea of a "common language," see Bauman and Briggs, *Voices of Modernity*, 302–3.

25. For an astute analysis of Nuyorican literature as a "minority" or "noncanonical" literature in the US, see Flores, *Divided Borders*, 152.

26. Blades's politics are confirmed by the critical reception of his work as a "salsa with conscience" capable of expressing the realities of the Latino and the Latin American urban condition. On salsa music and Latino identity, see Berrios-Miranda, "Significance of Salsa Music"; Cruz, *Rubén Blades*; Espinoza Agurto, "Una Sola Casa"; Flores, *Salsa Rising*; Flores, *Bomba to Hip-Hop*; Glasser, *My Music*; Janson Pérez, "Political Facets"; Padilla, "Salsa: Puerto Rican"; Padilla, "Salsa Music"; Padura Fuentes, "Salsa y conciencia"; Randel, "Crossing Over"; Singer, "Puerto Rican Music"; and Washburne, *Sounding Salsa*. Padilla discusses the following artists as part of a trend of conscious salsa in the fifteen years prior to 1989: Celia Cruz ("Soy Antillana" and "Latinos en Estados Unidos"); Rubén Blades ("María Lionza," "Plástico," and "Pablo Pueblo"); Ismael Miranda ("Americano Latino"); Raphy Leavitt ("Somos el Son"); Conjunto Clasico ("Somos Iguales"); Ray Barretto ("Fuerza Gigante"); and El Gran Combo de Puerto Rico ("Prosigue"). See also Moreno, "Corpus Delicti."

27. Rama, *Writing Across Cultures*. For a spirited argument against these "impulses," see Volpi Escalante, *El insomnio*. For a critique of Latin Americanist literature, see Moreiras, *Exhaustion of Difference*; Shellhorse, *Anti-Literature*. For the most comprehensive analysis of Latin Americanism as an academic discourse, see de la Campa, *Latin Americanism*.

28. With his orchestra La Perfecta, Eddie Palmieri pioneered the use of chordal voicings in fourths and parallel motion, along with the use of a brass section of trombones. Ortiz's approach, which includes contrary motion (the piano and bass move against the trombones), sounds different here, closer to jazz idioms than Palmieri's style does.

29. As legendary salsa sound engineer Jon Fausty described it, city sounds were captured by placing a microphone outside the windows of La Tierra Sound Studios, where *Siembra* was recorded, at 1440 Broadway in Midtown Manhattan. García, *Liner Notes*.

30. New York City–style dance strictly upholds regularity in the clave, and Puerto Rican and Nuyorican musicians avoid "crossing" or "turning" the clave; they never consecutively repeat one "side." Cuban musicians, particularly in the modern "timba" style, often "turn" the clave, appealing to what they call "clave license." For more on "turning the clave," see "Beyond Salsa," accessed June 13, 2018, http://beyondsalsa.info/; Peñalosa, *Clave Matrix*.

31. Quintero-Herencia, *La máquina de la salsa*, 289.

32. Interview with Rubén Blades in Panama City, interview by César Colón-Montijo, October 14, 2015. In the full excerpt, Blades mentions "Ojos de Perro Azul," his setting of a García Márquez short story, and how, even with its authorial weight, it was the arrangement by Oscar Hernandez that made the track memorable. "El arreglo es un tema muy importante, que muy poca gente considera, porque en la mayoría de los casos las personas que escribimos los temas no temenos conocimiento

de orquestación y el arreglista se convierte en parte en compositor. . . . El arreglista te puede hacer o deshacer un número. Mira, 'Ojos de Perro Azul,' creo que Oscar Hernández hizo el arreglo. Independientemente de la letra, independientemente de la interpretación de un cuento de Gabriel García Márquez, [en] 'Ojos de Perro Azul' es el arreglista el que hace que ese número sea memorable, para mí . . . Entonces el arreglista agarra una canción que puede tener cierto nivel de importancia y la transforma en una cosa especial o la destruye." I thank Dr. Colón-Montijo for sharing this excerpt.

33. Interview with Luis Ortiz, phone interview by Jairo Moreno, July 20, 2015. Unless otherwise noted, Ortiz's commentaries are from a phone interview with the author, July 20, 2015.

34. This is not to be confused with *son urbano* as a dancing style contrasting the *son montuno*—both forms of dancing Cuban *son*. See Pietrobruno, *Salsa and Its Transnational Moves.*

35. Blades observed how "the basis of all salsa music maintains its Afro Cuban roots: there is an introduction, there is a vocal part, then a mambo, then an improvisation, then a chorus, etc." Santana Archbold, *Yo, Rubén Blades.*

36. Quintero-Herencia, *La máquina de la salsa,* 289.

37. The relation between these characters could be understood as that between a male anti-hero and a female heroine. In 1982, Blades noted that in an earlier draft, Navaja simply killed the woman. He found this "too easy" and "unjust," in part because of what he knew about contemporary US feminism. "Thus, I placed the female character as an equal, not only in the tragedy of the two characters, but in her response to the attack: it is not uncommon that a man kills a woman but it is uncommon that she surprises him." Santana Archbold, *Yo, Rubén Blades,* 55.

38. Blades's official website offers a different translation: "I saw him turn the corner of the old neighborhood / Walking the walk of the cool and slick dudes." See Rubén Blades, "8-Pedro Navaja," Rubenblades.com (2011), http://rubenblades .com/lyrics/2011/1/12/8-pedro-navaja.html.

39. Benjamin, "The Storyteller," 92.

40. Santana Archbold, *Yo, Rubén Blades,* 54.

41. Blades might have been engaging Brechtian *gestus,* in which detailed description of behavior expresses social relations through the attitude of the character. See Viselli, "In Possession."

42. Another interpretation of this passage is as a more standard jazz progression in a chromatic circle of fifths in the key of F, starting on its raised fourth scale degree (B half-diminished): B half-diminished to E7/Bbm7 to Eb7/Ab maj.7 to Db 6/9/ Gm7-C7 add 13th.

43. Otero Garabís, "Esquinas." The Alexandrine verse had been popularized by Rubén Darío, the signal modernist Nicaraguan poet; see his "Caupolicán" (1888) and his other sonnets.

44. Quintero Rivera, ¡*Salsa, sabor y control!,* 182; Aparicio, *Listening to Salsa,* 86, 85.

45. Santana Archbold, *Yo, Rubén Blades,* 37.

46. González, *La Crónica Modernista Hispanoamericana,* 120.

47. Rotker, *La invención.*

48. Santana Archbold, *Yo, Rubén Blades,* 65.

49. Santana Archbold, *Yo, Rubén Blades*, 52.

50. Villoro, *Tiempo transcurrido*, 13.

51. "[Jazz] progressively records the history of the community, its confrontation with reality, the gaps into which it inserts itself, the walls it too often comes up against. The universalization of jazz arises from the fact that at no point is it an abstract [*en l'air*] music, but the expression of a specific situation." Glissant, *Caribbean Discourse*, 110.

52. White, "Fictions of Factual Representation," 121–34.

53. White, "Fictions of Factual Representation," 122.

54. Quintero Rivera, *¡Salsa, sabor y control!* As Juan Flores and George Yúdice—following Stanley Aronowitz—affirm, culturally defined social movements enter the political arena by "address[ing] power itself as an antagonist." Flores and Yúdice, "Living Borders," 59.

55. See Laclau and Mouffe, *Hegemony*; Mouffe, *Democratic Paradox*.

56. Rancière, *Politics of Literature*, 4.

57. González, *Companion*; Ramos, *Divergent Modernities*; Rotker, *La invención*. "By the end of the nineteenth century, journalistic production per capita in Spanish American urban centers was among the largest in the world. Argentina . . . ranked third globally in terms of periodicals per inhabitant, and by 1882 there were already 224 newspapers in the country." Reynolds, *Spanish American Crónica Modernista*, 4, cited in Prieto, *El discurso criollista*, 35.

58. Rama, *Writing Across Cultures*, 5.

59. Reynolds, *Spanish American Crónica Modernista*.

60. Rama, *La crítica de la cultura*, 84. See also Ramos, *Divergent Modernities*.

61. Written during his exile in the US for journals and dailies such as *La Opinión Nacional* (Caracas) and *La Nación* (Buenos Aires) but published also in Mexico's *El Partido Liberal*, *La Revista Ilustrada* (New York City), and *La Patria* (Havana), "Martí's *crónicas* presupposed an underlying order to the often chaotic events being described . . . the teeming masses in New York, the conquest of the West . . . the criminals, the intellectuals, the civic celebrations, the public controversies . . . all the myriad characters of the events of life . . . are seen as part of a single, coherent historical process": *modernity*. González, *Companion*, 34. See also Rotker, *American Chronicles*; Ramos, *Divergent Modernities*.

62. Rama, *Writing Across Cultures*.

63. Among the best-known examples are the Cuban José Martí (1853–1895), Mexican Manuel Gutiérrez Nájera (1859–1895), and Nicaraguan Rubén Darío (1867–1916). See González, *Companion*; Ramos, *Divergent Modernities*; Rotker, *La invención*.

64. Rotker, *American Chronicles*, 47.

65. Egan, *Carlos Monsiváis*, 86.

66. Warner, *Publics and Counterpublics*, 67.

67. Monsiváis, *A ustedes les consta*. Cited in Rotker, *American Chronicles*, 48. See also Martín-Barbero, *De Los Medios*.

68. De Man, "Literary History," 384.

69. Quintero Rivera, *¡Salsa, sabor y control!*

70. Quintero-Herencia, *La máquina de la salsa*, 289.

71. Otero Garabís, *Nación y ritmo*, 108–9; Díaz Quiñones, *La memoria rota*, 131; Santos-Febres, "Salsa as Translocation"; Washburne, *Sounding Salsa*.

72. Mimetic fidelity correlates with authenticity, on which see Brennan, *Secular Devotion*, 84–85. On the distinction between an identitarian notion of the people and a notion that deals with the people as a "political subject," or "the very name of the political subject," see Marchart, "In the Name," 3.

73. Saldívar, *Dialectics*, 152.

74. Saldívar, *Dialectics*, 151. On popular musicians' use of commercial means, see Lipsitz, *Time Passages*.

75. Saldívar, *Dialectics*, 152.

76. Quintero-Herencia, *La máquina de la salsa*, 290.

77. Quintero-Herencia, *La máquina de la salsa*, 290.

78. Quintero-Herencia, *La máquina de la salsa*, 289.

79. Quintero-Herencia, *La máquina de la salsa*, 290–91.

80. Quintero-Herencia, *La máquina de la salsa*, 290.

81. Quintero-Herencia, *La máquina de la salsa*, 290.

82. Rama, *La crítica*, 366.

83. Benjamin, "Storyteller," 84.

84. Ong, *Orality and Literacy*.

85. Bauman, "Remediation of Storytelling."

86. Benjamin, "Storyteller," 106.

87. The Cuban *son* and the Puerto Rican *plena* and *bomba* entailed traditions of machismo and exaggerated swagger that often addressed the social strata from which many musicians came. See Manuel, "Representations of New York City," 38.

88. Duany, "Popular Music in Puerto Rico," 201.

89. Benjamin, "Storyteller," 89.

90. Santana Archbold, *Yo, Rubén Blades*, 65.

91. Benjamin, "Storyteller," 91.

92. Consider the following examples. In Puerto Rico: Katherine Martos, RUBEN BLADES Pedro Navaja—En Vivo Puerto Rico HD. Avi, accessed June 13, 2018, https://www.youtube.com/watch?v=NOSrMg67FwU; in the US: gardenmartha, Rubén Blades—Pedro Navaja, accessed June 13, 2018, https://www.youtube.com/watch?v=Lhu-Y1ztFCc; and in Mexico: microchinto, Rubén Blades—Pedro Navajas (En Vivo Cumbre Tajín 2010), accessed June 13, 2018, https://www.youtube.com/watch?v=_Z6LMdKzQy8.

93. Benjamin, "Storyteller," 100.

94. Benjamin, "Storyteller," 97.

95. Benjamin, "Storyteller," 101.

96. Santana Archbold, *Yo, Rubén Blades*, 29–30.

97. Martín-Barbero, *Communication, Culture and Hegemony*, 157. See also Hoggart, *Uses of Literacy*; Frye, *Anatomy of Criticism*.

98. Benjamin, "Storyteller," 86.

99. Benjamin, "Storyteller," 90.

100. Quintero-Herencia, *La máquina de la salsa*, 290.

101. Quintero-Herencia, *La máquina de la salsa*, 290.

102. Quintero-Herencia, *La máquina de la salsa*, 290.

103. Rama, *La crítica*, 379.

104. Pier, "Metalepsis."

105. Rimmon-Kenan, *Narrative Fiction*, 93.

106. McHale, *Postmodernist Fiction*.

107. Bauman and Briggs, *Voices of Modernity*; citing from Pollock, "India in the Vernacular Millennium"; Pollock, "Cosmopolitan Vernacular,"; Pollock, "Cosmopolitanism and Vernacular."

108. Monsiváis's "high" and "low culture" partially function as avatars of what Rama conceptualized as the "lettered" and "real" city. In his prologue for the 2004 edition of Rama's *La ciudad letrada*, Monsiváis casts its demise as the result of the rise of a technocratic private sector, the incessant proliferation of images, and popular culture's "hatred of rationality." "The great epoch of the Lettered City has lapsed," he declares. Rama, *La ciudad letrada*, 24.

109. Monsiváis, "Ídolos populares," 56.

110. Monsiváis, "Ídolos populares," 52.

111. Monsiváis, "Ídolos populares," 53.

112. Monsiváis, "Ídolos populares," 54.

113. Monsiváis, "Ídolos populares," 55.

114. Monsiváis, "Ídolos populares," 55.

115. Monsiváis, "Ídolos populares," 55, 56. For an insightful study of the role of voice in Puerto Rican song, see Fiol-Matta, *Great Woman Singer*.

116. Monsiváis, "Ídolos populares," 56, 57.

117. Rama, *Writing Across Cultures*, 43. Argentine musicologist Carlos Vega coined the expression "mesomúsica" to describe "the set of [musical] creations functionally dedicated to leisure (melodies with or without text), salon dance, spectacles, ceremonies, acts, games, classroom, etc. accepted or adopted by listeners in culturally modern nations." Vega, "Mesomúsica," 5.

118. Vega, "Mesomúsica," 5.

119. Moreiras, *Exhaustion of Difference*.

120. Franco, *Decline and Fall*, 194.

121. Franco, *Decline and Fall*, 194.

122. Franco, *Decline and Fall*, 194.

123. Franco, *Decline and Fall*, 194; citing from Lyotard, *Postmodern Condition*, 22. Lyotard voices an aesthetic theory linked to thanatology and not to performative re-iteration: "Art is the vow the soul makes in exchange for escaping the death promised to it by the sensible, but in celebrating in this same sensible what drags the soul out of inexistence." Lyotard, *Postmodern Fables*, 244–45.

124. "Timbre, language, and subtlety are not requested . . . by the sense that the body and culture ascribe them. They [bodies, cultures] must remain as worn out witnesses of a delayed and imminent disaster . . . and there is no poetic possible to regulate this manner of being a witness, and neither is there an aesthetic that might tell us how it [this disaster] must be received." Lyotard, *Postmodern Fables*, 245.

125. Franco, *Decline and Fall*, 17.

126. As of this writing, on YouTube one finds impressive figures for a salsa tune from 1979: over 15.5 million views here (https://www.youtube.com/watch?v = ACD _wuxuMzg) and over 20 million here (https://www.youtube.com/watch?v = UibAE _x6NM8), from a 2014 concert with Wynton Marsalis's Jazz at Lincoln Center Orchestra, posted in 2018.

127. Pollock, *Language of the Gods*, 4.

128. Pollock, *Language of the Gods*, 4–5.

129. Pollock, *Language of the Gods*, 4. See Bauman and Briggs, *Voices of Modernity*, 15.

130. Moreiras, "Introduction," 129. On the link to primitive accumulation, see Ortiz, *Contrapunteo cubano*.

131. Monsiváis, "Ídolos populares," 54.

132. Moreiras, "Introduction," 129.

133. Ochoa Gautier, "Sonic Transculturation," 17.

134. Avelar, "Transculturation and Nationhood," 251.

135. Avelar, "Transculturation and Nationhood," 256.

136. Moraña, "Boom of the Subaltern," 645.

137. Dominguez, "Las mujeres."

138. The job entailed carting mail from 57th Street and Broadway to 52nd Street every day. Asked about his work there, Blades said, "the complexes and conditionings are so great that anyone who has studied at the university and comes from a popular neighborhood (*barrio*) is regarded by people from the neighborhood as a person that comes from a different social milieu" ("*Los complejos son tan grandes, los condicionamientos son tan grandes que cualquiera persona que tenga un estudio universitario y venga de un barrio es considerado en muchos casos por la propia gente del barrio como si fuera una persona que viniera de una condición social distinta*"). Interview with César Cólon Montijo, Panama City, October 14, 2015. I thank Dr. Cólon Montijo for informing me of this interview and sharing it with me.

139. Fania had 70 percent of the salsa market in 1975, equivalent to $8 million. Tablante, *El dólar*, 206. In the 1970s, Venezuela became a particularly important market for the label, coinciding with the country's years of economic prosperity (214). In the 1990s, the Colombian market accounted for a much more significant portion of the label's Latin American sales (221). However, a shift in marketing came in the form of anthologized catalogs that allowed them to make a much cheaper product (231). While some, like Jerry Masucci (Fania's polemical co-founder), attempted to place salsa on an equal footing with Anglo-American pop music, others tried to make salsa competitive by selling discs at a discount, allowing the genre to have larger global reach. Still, although in 1977 Fania had only 3 percent of the Latin music marketed in the US, in the salsa genre, it occupied the top spot, with 34.1 percent (15 discs) in the market (209), but in the salsa world the label had 68.6 percent of the total market, with the 46 most popular titles. For a broader discussion of genres, including salsa, and the music industry, see Negus, *Music Genres*.

140. The song served as the basis for a biopic of Lavoe, *El Cantante*, directed by Leon Ichaso and starring salsa and pop idol Marc Anthony.

141. Borges, *Vínculos*.

142. "Antes de Siembra, la salsa era identificada con solo el ritmo y el baile. Con este disco, producido por Fania Records y cuyo mayor éxito fue Pedro Navaja, Willie Colón y Rubén Blades probaron la inteligencia de sus seguidores, que tuvieron que pararse a escuchar lo que decían." "Vuelve a Editarse 'Siembra.'" On the co-constitution of the intellectual-artist, the collective, and Latin American cultural particularity, see Franco in *Modern Culture*, updated in Jean Franco, "Latin American Intellectuals."

On the links between intellectuality, mass culture, commodification, and industrialization and the emergence of new cultural spaces, see García Liendo, *El intelec-*

tual. This idea has important precedents. Avelar offers an insightful analysis of the great Brazilian writer Machado de Assis's nineteenth-century staging of the tensions between erudite, popular, and mass music in his "Ritmos do popular no erudito."

143. Tablante, *El dólar*, 211.

144. A key referent here is Chico Buarque's epochal 1971 *Construção*, a concept album with groundbreaking musical, literary, and political ambitions.

145. Rondón, *El libro*, 276, 281 (italics original).

146. The performance can be seen here: Willie Colón y Hector Lavoe Vivo En Panama Timbalero (Panama), accessed June 7, 2018, https://www.youtube.com/watch?v = CJV0fKEddIo.

147. Polin, "Visit with Ruben Blades."

148. Curet Alonso, "Memoirs," 199.

149. This citation originally appeared on Blades's now defunct website. It is, however, consonant with his other pronouncements.

150. Santana Archbold, *Yo, Rubén Blades*, 35.

151. Santana Archbold, *Yo, Rubén Blades*, 35.

152. Hamill, "Hey, It's Rubén Blades," 45.

153. Moreno, "Tropical Discourses."

154. Sanabria, "Ruben Blades," 34. "Cuentas del alma," "Ligia Elena," and "Decisiones," among others from the 1980s, all adopt an increasingly melodramatic character to represent personal relations while keeping a humorous undertone in their characterization of social archetypes. Other songs from that decade such as "Buscando América," "Desaparecidos," and "El padre Arnulfo y el monaguillo Andrés" take a denunciatory posture, reporting on the consequences of dictatorships, military takeovers, and related right-wing injustices in Latin America.

155. Sagramoso, "Rubén Blades."

156. "'Pedro Navaja' representaba lo que él realmente hubiera deseado escribir." Cited in Quintero Rivera, *¡Salsa, sabor y control!*, 186; Rondón, *El libro*.

157. Celis Albán, "Blades." The Hay Festival in Cartagena is considered one of the most important literary festivals in the Spanish-speaking world, with 52,000 reported attendees in 2015. "Festival Report: Hay Festival Cartagena de Indias, 29 January–1 February 2015" (Cartagena: Hay Festival, 2015).

158. "Había historias urbanas pendientes de ser contadas, historias de la calle, de la esquina, del barrio, que podían suceder en los ambientes latinos de Nueva York o en una calle de Buenos Aires, Ciudad de México o Caracas. Eran historias que reproducían, hacían vívido, en sus arreglos, todo el escenario auditivo que contaban, toda una nueva realidad encubierta. . . . Era la visión de un narrador y a la vez un músico sofisticado, culto, que con herencias de lo Caribe y del jazz introducía cuentos inéditos en la canción popular latina. No era tarea fácil en el ambiente politizado latinoamericano de los setenta, cuando se les pedía a los escritores no solo de canciones un 'compromiso revolucionario' que Blades supo dilucidar inteligentemente. Lo suyo fue otra forma de decir lo político." Celis Albán, "Blades."

159. Rondón, *El libro*, 288.

160. Rondón, *El libro*, 280.

161. Schwarz, "Altos e baixos," 116; Diana Taylor, "Brecht."

162. Beverley, *Subalternity and Representation*, 10.

163. Santana Archbold, *Yo, Rubén Blades*, 57–58. Antonio Viselli suggests that

Blades had no direct connection with Brecht's ideas, although he presents a good case for a comparison between Brechtian theatre and "Navaja." Viselli, "In Possession."

164. Ribeiro de Oliveira, *De mendigos e malandros*; Ribeiro de Oliveira, "Musical Comedy"; Saona, "Orden y progreso"; Sartinger, "Rewriting"; Thomaz, de Souza, and Fernando de Lima, "Categorias sociais"; Webb, "Masculinities at the Margins." Buarque's play was made into a movie in 1985 (*Opera do Malandro*, dir. Ruy Guerra) and has seen repeated productions in Brazil. Newsweek Staff, "Way, Way Off-Broadway."

165. As registered in the legal case concerning the play's authorship, "During one of Blades's public concerts in Puerto Rico, [Idalia] Pérez-Garay's sister listened to the 'Pedro Navaja' song and considered it an excellent theme for a musical play. She shared the idea with her sister, and the two continued to discuss the idea of presenting a production using Blades's song and an adaptation of Brecht's play" (transcript, July 29, 1994, pp. 26–27, 121). Pérez-Garay was a member of Teatro since 1967 and its artistic director in 1989. See *Cabrera vs. Teatro del Sesenta* (United States District Court, District of Puerto Rico, March 31, 1995).

166. Schwarz, "Relevance of Brecht," 34.

167. Augusto Boal develops a Theatre of the Oppressed (Teatro do oprimido) in 1960s and 1970s Brazil. Diana Taylor, "Brecht."

168. Pianca, "De Brecht," 94.

169. Diana Taylor, "Brecht."

170. Buenaventura, "De Stanislavski a Brecht"; De Toro, *Brecht*; García, "Brecht y América Latina"; Peixoto, "Brecht, nuestro compañero"; Pianca, "De Brecht"; Posada, *Lukács*; Schwarz, "Relevance of Brecht"; Diana Taylor, "Brecht." There are competing accounts of the earliest Latin American performance of *Threepenny Opera*: in Buenos Aires (1957) and Mexico City (1943), with one alleged early staging in Buenos Aires (1930). Pellettieri, "Brecht," 49. Brecht himself used Neruda's *Canto General* in his *Friedenslied* (1951).

171. Pianca, "De Brecht"; Diana Taylor, "Brecht."

172. García, "Brecht y América Latina"; Posada, *Lukács*; Diana Taylor, "Brecht."

173. Posada, *Lukács.*

174. Benjamin, "Author as Producer," 236 (italics in original).

175. Brecht, "Against Georg Lukács," 82.

176. Benjamin, "Author as Producer," 225.

177. Benjamin, "Author as Producer," 222.

178. García, "Brecht y América Latina." In Brecht's commentary on the lawsuit concerning the filming of *Dreigroschenoper*, he writes that "in the decisive extension of literature's social obligations, which follows from the refunctioning of art into a pedagogical discipline, the means of representation must be multiplied or constantly changed . . . The socialization of these means of production is vital for art." Brecht, *Werke*, 465–66.

179. Thompson and Schwartz, *Concert Life in Puerto Rico*, 312.

180. According to the World Encyclopedia, it was adapted in Puerto Rico by Pablo Cabrera in 1980 and then revived in 1984 and 1994. Holmberg and Solorzano, *World Encyclopedia of Contemporary Theatre*. The production has also been staged in New York; in Havana, Cuba; in Venezuela in 1986; and in Puerto Rico and Miami in the early 2000s by Lolyn Paz. Shepard, "Stage"; Bruckner, "Stage"; "Otro edificio"; Palamides, "Compañía Nacional"; "La verdadera historia."

181. Versényi, "1985 Festival Latino," 112.

182. Versényi, "Brecht," 42; Brecht, *On Theatre*, 180–81.

183. Boal, *Teatro del oprimido*, 24; García, "Brecht y América Latina," 81.

184. Brecht, *On Theatre*, 186.

185. Rancière, *Politics of Literature*, 100–101.

186. Rancière, *Politics of Literature*, 103.

187. Rancière, *Politics of Literature*, 102.

188. Rancière, *Philosopher and His Poor*, 12.

189. Bourdieu, "Outline."

190. Viselli, "In Possession," 51; Figueroa, "Ruben Blades."

191. Nancy, "Communism," 147.

192. Rancière, *Philosopher and His Poor*, 13.

193. Moreno and Steingo, "Rancière's Equal Music."

194. Rancière, *Aesthetics and Its Discontents*, 24.

195. Quintero Rivera, *¡Salsa, sabor y control!*; Quintero-Herencia, *La máquina de la salsa*.

196. Santana Archbold, *Yo, Rubén Blades*, 37.

197. Santana Archbold, *Yo, Rubén Blades*, 55.

198. Curet Alonso, "Memoirs," 199.

199. Santana Archbold, *Yo, Rubén Blades*, 52.

200. Randel, "Crossing Over."

201. Santana Archbold, *Yo, Rubén Blades*, 45.

202. Santana Archbold, *Yo, Rubén Blades*, 51. In 1979, Blades referred to the allusion to Kafka in "Pedro Navaja" as partly a hero and partly a bandit archetype of the nineteenth-century Latin American hero who rebelled against Spanish rule.

203. On the foundational role of Colombian Vallenato music in the writing of García Márquez, who nowhere insisted on a dichotomy between song, voice, words, and dancing, see Ochoa Gautier, "García Márquez." Cf. critics who more often posit an irreparable rupture between body and logos, for example, Quintero Rivera, *Cuerpo y cultura.*

204. Rancière, *Politics of Literature*, 9.

205. Rancière, *Politics of Literature*, 7.

206. This formulation is borrowed from Rancière, *Disagreement.*

207. Archipolitics consists of the repeated affirmation of a community's origin (*arkhê*) and resistance to change; parapolitics consists of the maintenance of democratic order so long as people remain in their place according to specific social functions they must carry. See Rancière, *Disagreement*; Moreno and Steingo, "Rancière's Equal Music."

208. See *Latin Music USA: The Salsa Revolution*, Public Broadcasting Service (PBS), accessed September 4, 2018, https://www.pbs.org/wgbh/latinmusicusa/episodes/episode-2-salsa-revolution/ (48:22) [inactive link].

209. Newton, "Waiting for Lavoe," *Broward Palm Beach New Times*, August 9, 2007, accessed December 30, 2020, https://www.browardpalmbeach.com/music/waiting-for-lavoe-6310461.

210. Ochoa Gautier, *Aurality*, 202; Nancy and Lacoue-Labarthe, *Literary Absolute.*

211. Ochoa Gautier, *Aurality*, 202.

212. Ochoa Gautier, *Aurality*, 167, 171.

213. Ochoa Gautier, "Silence."

214. Ochoa Gautier, *Aurality*, 173.

215. Santiago, "Ruben Blades."

216. Rancière, "What Intellectual Might Mean," 66.

217. On translatability, see Hansen, "Mass Production of the Senses."

218. Barthes, *Writing Degree Zero*, 14.

219. Barthes, *Writing Degree Zero*, 16.

220. Raúl Antelo, "Una crítica acéfala para la modernidad latinoamericana," *Iberoamericana* 8 (30): 129.

221. Antelo, *Crítica acéfala*, 129.

222. Antelo, *Crítica acéfala*, 130, citing Agamben, "Messiah and the Sovereign."

223. Charles Taylor, *Modern Social Imaginaries*; Flores and Yudice, "Living Borders"; Dávila, *El Mall*; Dávila, *Culture Works*; Dávila, *Latinos, Inc.* For a genealogy of the category "Hispanic" in early advertising campaigns, see Mora, *Making Hispanics*.

224. See Ortiz, "Introduction" of *Cuban Counterpoint*.

225. Ochoa Gautier, "Sonic Transculturation"; Ochoa Gautier, "García Márquez."

Chapter Two

1. Rubén Blades, *Tiempos*, liner notes; Jorge Chino, "Rubén Blades: La Vanguardia Musical de Fin de Siglo," *El Andar*, 1999.

2. Rubén Blades, *Mundo*, liner notes.

3. Blades had previously recorded outside the US. *La Rosa de Los Vientos* was produced in his native Panama with local musicians. The musical emphasis, however, he later noted, had remained "slanted towards the afrocuban [*sic*]." Losilla, "Ruben Blades."

4. Richard, "Intersecting Latin America with Latin Americanism," 686.

5. Mignolo, *Local Histories/Global Designs*.

6. Moreiras, *Exhaustion of Difference*, 25.

7. Richard, "Intersecting Latin America with Latin Americanism," 687; George Yúdice, "Estudios Culturales y Sociedad Civil," 44, cited in Richard, "Intersecting Latin America with Latin Americanism," 689.

8. Reviewers commented upon the lyrics on both *Tiempos* and *Mundo*, discussing the emotional significance and "demanding" nature of the lyrics on *Tiempos* (Shuster, "Poetry"; John Swenson, "Ruben Blades") and noting the political and inspirational tone of *Mundo*'s lyrics (George Graham, "Ruben Blades: '*Mundo*,'" The World Wide Web Site of George D. Graham, 2002, http://georgegraham.com/reviews/blades.html; Judy Cantor, "Ruben Blades").

9. See my discussion in "Tropical Discourses."

10. Many critics were effusive in their praise of this album. For example, Ed Morales: "While its eclectic and original style may not conquer hard-core salseros or fans of Ricky Martin pop and Jennifer Lopez soul, Ruben Blades's *Tiempos* could be the best Latin record of the year. . . . [the album] is an impeccable, rich stew of flamenco, Afro-Cuban, Brazilian and obscure regional folk beats and melodies which propel lyrics that hauntingly describe Blades, disappointment with the end of his marriage, the economic desperation of Latin America and the corruption of its governments." Morales, "Review of *Tiempos*." Judy Cantor: "Emerging from the

singer's own soul-searching journeys into the barrio and the world beyond, Blades's latest CD, *Mundo*, is a daring production that speaks to this turbulent new global century." Cantor, "Ruben Blades." Critics online were similarly impressed: "*Mundo* is a complete album, without weaknesses, in which he [Blades] gives equal attention to the lyrics and the music." "*Mundo*" es un disco redondo, sin debilidades, en el que se le presta igual atención tanto a la letra como a la música." Tota, "Rubén Blades se burla con su 'mundo' del mercantilismo," *Tropicana Bogotá* (blog), September 30, 2002. Additionally, other sources argue that "*Tiempos* is definitely one of, or perhaps the best, high quality production of Rubén Blades" ("Definitivamente *Tiempos* es una producción, o quizás la mejor producción de alto calibre de Rubén Blades"). "Ruben Blades 'Tiempos' Un Grammy Para Todos," accessed November 11, 2019, http://portal.critica.com.pa/archivo/03032000/var1.html.

11. Aparicio, *Listening to Salsa*; Berrios-Miranda, "The Significance of Salsa Music"; Duany, "Popular Music in Puerto Rico"; Padilla, "Salsa Music"; Padilla, "Salsa"; Janson Pérez, "Political Facets of Salsa"; Román–Velázquez, "The Making of a Salsa Music Scene in London"; Rondón, *El Libro de La Salsa*; Santos-Febres, "Salsa as Translocation"; Leopoldo Tablante, *El dólar*; Waxer, "Situating Salsa"; Waxer, *The City of Musical Memory*.

12. Moreiras, *Exhaustion of Difference*, 32.

13. Heidegger, "The Thing."

14. See chapter 1 for debates concerning representation, including most notably Angel Rama's notion of representativity as an imperative for Latin American cultural production. *Writing Across Cultures: Narrative Transculturation in Latin America*. Translated by David Frye. Durham, NC: Duke University Press, 2012.

15. Mignolo, *The Idea of Latin America*; Rama, *La ciudad letrada*; Rama, *The Lettered City*.

16. Costa Rica's Programa Juvenil was created in 1972 to train musicians for the Orquesta Sinfónica Nacional ("Orquesta Sinfónica Nacional | Centro Nacional de la Música," accessed November 15, 2019, https://cnm.go.cr/orquesta-sinfonica -nacional/), and the Sistema Nacional de Educación Musical (SINEM) was founded in 2007 to broaden access to musical training beyond San José ("Sistema Nacional de Educación Musical," Ministerio de Cultura y Juventud, November 21, 2007, https://www.mcj.go.cr/espacios-culturales/instituciones-centros/sistema-nacional -de-educacion-musical). Costa Rica was also home to the Centro de Estudios Instrumentales, and Costa Rica's Ministry of Culture, Youth, and Sports was listed as the responsible institution. Created by the Organization of American States (OAS) in 1977 to train young orchestral musicians, the center was disbanded in 1996 (as confirmed in OAS budgets).

17. This locus is not merely the specific location from which something is enounced. For Mignolo, the locus of enunciation defines global designs such as "colonial difference" from which things are thought, said, and experienced in the specificities of that situation. This situatedness implicates the direction in which the production of knowledge moves: "Dependency theory was a political statement for the social transformation of and from Third World countries, while world-system analysis was a political statement for academic transformation from First World countries," offers Mignolo. Acknowledgment of these directions and the loci they outline (e.g., center and periphery) allows for identifying those excluded from

the discussion—for Mignolo, mostly indigenous peoples. Mignolo, "Geopolitics of Knowledge," 63.

18. The only precedent *Éditus* cites is the Argentine trio Vitale-Baraj-Gonzáles. Here's how the group described itself as of 2015:

> **ÉDITUS** is a Costa Rican musical group founded in **1990** that unifies modern and traditional jazz, **New Age** and classical music, authentic Latin American sounds, technical effects and academic research in a single artistic expression.
>
> **ÉDITUS** es un grupo musical costarricense fundado en **1990** que une el jazz moderno y tradicional, la música "**new age**" y clásica, sonidos auténticos latinoamericanos, efectos técnicos e investigación académica en una sola expresión artística.

"Editus," Editus, accessed November 15, 2019, https://edituscr.bandcamp.com.

19. Strauss, "Three Faces of Ruben Blades."

20. Andreas Villar, "Abrir Nuevos Horizontes," *Matices: Zeitschrift Zu Lateinamerika, Spanien, Und Portugal*, no. 25 (2000), https://www.matices-magazin.de/archiv/25-musik-ii/.

21. Blades, *Tiempos*, liner notes.

22. Blades, *Tiempos*, liner notes. For a different approach to the chacarera in a contemporary setting, see my discussion of the Argentine composer, arranger, and director Guillermo Klein. Moreno, "Past Identity."

23. Blades, *Tiempos*, liner notes.

24. George Rivera, "Q & A: A Conversation with Ruben Blades," http://salsaweb .com/blades.html [inactive link], Salsa Web, 2000.

25. Fairley, "The 'Local' and 'Global' in Popular Music," 273.

26. Morales, "Review of *Tiempos*."

27. Strauss, "Three Faces of Ruben Blades."

28. Deborah Pacini Hernández notes that salsa did not enjoy the benefits of being included in the world beat phenomenon during the 1980s and 1990s (Pacini Hernandez, "Amalgamating Musics"). While I do not take this exclusion from world beat to be a central feature of Blades's demands, it is worth noting that *Mundo* went on to receive the Grammy in the category World Music.

29. Blades, *Mundo*, liner notes.

30. This thesis was developed by tracing mitochondrial DNA analysis. Sykes, *The Seven Daughters of Eve*. The book was a popular science bestseller. In his lyrics, Blades refers to the clan Lara, argued to be the origin of human life.

31. Evan C. Gutierrez, "Rubén Blades, Rosa de Los Vientos, AllMusic Review," AllMusic, accessed November 6, 2019, https://www.allmusic.com/album/rosa-de -los-vientos-mw0000073114.

32. The party's name came from the Embera language, meaning "Madre Tierra."

33. Oscar Hernandez, Blades's longtime music director, served as music director for the show. Simon's score mixed doo wop, gospel, and Latin styles, but not rock or pop. Cowritten by Simon and Derek Walcott, the show dramatized the story of Salvador Agrón (1943–1986), a Puerto Rican migrant to New York City who was found guilty of a double murder in 1959 and later became an activist. The show opened up discussions about the representation of the "Latino experience," some arguing for its importance, no matter what the theme, others denouncing the possibility of pathologizing "Latino" criminality.

34. Blades, "Interview with Enrique Fernandez," 50.

35. In 1982, Miami Sound Machine, perhaps the standard for successful "Latin" crossover artists, was recording for CBS International. Only in 1984 did the influential ensemble move to the "American" Epic/Columbia label, their first hits in the US coming with "Conga," "Bad Boy," and "Words Get in the Way," from their 1985 *Primitive Love* album.

36. *Solar* can be translated as a lot (piece of land), usually an open area at the back of a house, but also as tenement, both translations evoking a form of familial sociability generally associated with the working class. There was a sort of intertextual reference. *Canciones del Solar de los Aburridos* (Songs from the Tenement of the Bored Ones) was the penultimate record Blades did for Fania, with Willie Colón, in 1981.

37. The film, directed and cowritten by Cuban-American Leon Ichaso, tells the story of Rudy Veloz, a fictional New York City salsa musician, as he tries to recalibrate his musical style to something closer to world music. *Dreams* figures a parable of rootedness, best expressed in the final musical number, a Blades's original entitled "Todos Vuelven" ("Everyone Returns") that proclaims how everyone returns to their birthplace.

38. Pacini Hernandez, *Oye Como Va!*, 145.

39. Pacini Hernandez, *Oye Como Va!*, 145.

40. Garofalo, "Black Popular Music," 229.

41. Brackett, "Musical Meaning"; Brackett, "Politics and Practice"; Garofalo, "Black Popular Music"; Garofalo, "Crossing Over"; Negus, *Music Genres and Corporate Culture*.

42. George, "Rhythm & The Blues." Nelson offers a sustained and scathing critique of crossover in his *The Death of Rhythm and Blues* (New York: Pantheon, 1988). For a discussion of George, whose position is described as "Going Under," in comparison with his critical opponent, Steve Perry, who interpreted 1980s crossovers as a force for racial integration and a response to changes in social relations, technology, and prevailing musical styles, see Garofalo, "Black Popular Music."

43. George, "Rhythm & The Blues."

44. George, "Rhythm & The Blues."

45. In the main, academic and critical debates around "crossover" in the US focus on questions of race. See, for example, Brackett, "Black or White?"; and Garofalo, "Black Popular Music."

46. Palmer, "The Pop Life."

47. The notion of a crossover dilemma appears in David Brackett's lucid analysis of the phenomenon in his book *Categorizing Sound*, 280–316.

48. Brackett, *Categorizing Sound*, 316.

49. Palmer, "The Pop Life."

50. Randel, "Crossing Over with Rubén Blades," 302.

51. Randel, "Crossing Over with Rubén Blades," 322.

52. Randel, "Crossing Over with Rubén Blades," 322.

53. I discuss "Buscando América" in depth in my article "Tropical Discourses."

54. Dávila, *Latinos, Inc.*

55. As discussed in chapter 1, these were the songs that noted Chicano scholar José David Saldívar heard as heralding a new constitution for America, given in the kind of literary hybridization of Blades's work. Saldívar, *Dialectics of Our America.*

56. Jürgen Schön, "Ein Rassistisches Etikett. Musiker Aus Der Dritten Welt Brauchen Keine Green Card, Um in Der Ersten Spielen Zu Dürfen. Sie Sind Talentiert, Keiner Muß Sie Entdecken," *RZ-Online*, July 8, 1999, http://archiv.rhein-zeitung.de/on/99/07/08/magazin/news/blades.html [inactive link].

57. Rockwell, "In Pop Music."

58. By "musical practices" I mean musicking, as explained in the introduction: an assemblage of actions (e.g., composing, arranging, executing) and conceptualizations (e.g., genre categorizations, Latin Americanisms themselves, etc.) through and in which music and the sonic are produced, experienced, known, and understood. My discussion does not include discussion of actual musical performances, a valuable analytic beyond this chapter's scope.

59. Moreiras, *Exhaustion of Difference*, 127.

60. Jenckes, "The 'New Latin Americanism'" (review-essay of Moreiras, *Exhaustion of Difference*; Levinson, *The Ends of Literature*; Williams, *The Other Side of the Popular*). These debates were a culmination of arguments that began earlier (late 1980s to early 1990s), when Mabel Moraña explained that "studies around notions of identity and nation, polarizations such as center/periphery, hegemony/subalternity, [and] 'high culture'/popular culture have given way to more fluid and, notably, less totalizing analyses, although in many cases no less risky in their labor of apprehending Latin American cultural specificity." Moraña, "Escribir en el aire," 279.

61. Cited in Jenckes, "The 'New Latin Americanism,'" 247.

62. Hartman, "Criticism and Restitution."

63. "Points of inscription" is Moreiras's expression, and "cognitive mappings" is Jameson's. See Moreiras, *Exhaustion of Difference*, 131; Jameson, *Postmodernism.*

64. Mignolo, "Colonial and Postcolonial Discourse," 123.

65. Levinson, *The Ends of Literature*, 119.

66. Moreiras, *Exhaustion of Difference*, 146.

67. Moreiras, *Exhaustion of Difference*, 127.

68. Moreiras, *Exhaustion of Difference*, 131. This analytic shows also that *Tiempos* and *Mundo* concern more than a desire to experiment with musical forms and to pursue projects of artistic renovation, which is how critics such as Fairley and Morales heard *Tiempos* and *Mundo*.

69. Zuñiga, "Éditus."

70. Zuñiga, "Éditus."

71. García Canclini, "State of War," 48. Hardt and Negri offer a more sinister analysis of connectivity through globalized communication networks: "communications industries integrate the imaginary and the symbolic within the biopolitical fabric, not merely putting them at the service of power but actually integrating them into its very functioning" (*Empire*, 33). There is no space here to elaborate this reading of connectivity. George Yúdice argued forcefully against confusing multiculturalism's politics of recognition for the more urgent task of access. Yúdice, "We Are Not the World."

72. Carvalho, "O olhar etnográfico," 136.

73. Martín-Barbero, *Al Sur de La Modernidad*, 13.

74. Camila Gallardo, "Entrevista Grupo Éditus." Full reference to Gallardo is not available anymore.

75. Martín-Barbero, *Al Sur de La Modernidad*, 16.

76. D'Addario, "El Trio Éditus."

77. Beck, "The Cosmopolitan Society and Its Enemies," 27. Speaking of Costa Rica, Blades said that it was by fortune that he first heard *Éditus* on a CD a friend gave him. "Costa Rica! I had no idea there were any musicians in Costa Rica—even though it borders on Panama [*sic*]. Then in 1998 I was there for an ecological conference—and they were playing at the reception!" Steward, "Tiempos fugit,"

78. Beck, "The Cosmopolitan Society and Its Enemies," 27.

79. Beck, "The Cosmopolitan Society and Its Enemies," 27.

80. Beck, "The Cosmopolitan Society and Its Enemies," 27.

81. Beck, "The Cosmopolitan Society and Its Enemies," 27.

82. Beck, "The Cosmopolitan Society and Its Enemies," 25–26.

83. Beck, "The Cosmopolitan Society and Its Enemies," 26.

84. Holston, "Razor Blades."

85. Hybridization has been used to describe processes of colonialization, globalization, border crossing and migration, and linguistic, communicational, and artistic mixtures. At this point in the argument, I focus on the latter, which might be termed broadly "cultural hybridity," but others appear in the analysis. This list of processes appears, slightly altered, in García Canclini, "Noticias Recientes Sobre Hibridación." Salient works on the concept of hybridity include Bhabha, *The Location of Culture*; García Canclini, *Culturas híbridas*; Hall, "Cultural Identity and Diaspora"; Hall, "The Local and the Global"; Hall, "Old and New Identities"; Kraniauskas, "Hybridity and Reterritorialization"; Kraniauskas, "Hybridity in a Transnational Frame"; Lowe, "Heterogeneity, Hybridity, Multiplicity"; Lowe, *Immigrant Acts*.

86. García Canclini, "Cultural Reconversion," 32.

87. García Canclini, "Cultural Reconversion," 39.

88. I use the more abstract sociological term "hybridization" instead of the anthropological term "hybrid" (e.g., "hybrid subjects") but recognize their inseparability. See Timothy Taylor, "Some Versions of Difference," for an overview of hybridity in Music Studies. My thanks to Professor Taylor for bringing his article to my attention.

89. According to García Canclini, "this term is used to explain the strategies through which . . . national bourgeoisies acquire the languages and necessary competences to reinvest their economic and symbolic capital in transnational circuits," after Bourdieu. "Se utiliza este término para explicar las estrategias mediante las . . . las burguesías nacionales adquieren los idiomas y otras competencias necesarias para reinvertir sus capitales económicos y simbólicos en circuitos transnacionales." García Canclini, "Noticias Recientes Sobre Hibridación." Here García Canclini draws on Bourdieu's *Distinction*, 155, 175, 354. Román de la Campa sees García Canclini's "cultural reconversion" "in light of transculturation theory as a new nexus between the subjectivity of popular culture produces and the hegemony of market economies" and his search as being "much more anchored in the material relations of the cultural market than in the processes of troping" that characterize border performativities (e.g., Guillermo Gómez-Peña). De la Campa, *Latin Americanism*, 69.

90. Cornejo Polar, "Mestizaje e hibridez." García Canclini offers a thoughtful response to Cornejo Polar in "Noticias Recientes."

91. García Canclini captures this intersection of temporalities, histories, and locations, as well as the intrinsic hybridizing character of Latin American modernity, when he casts modernization as "projects of renovation with which diverse sectors

take charge of the multi-temporal heterogeneity of each nation." García Canclini, *Culturas híbridas*, 15. Indeed, de la Campa remarks on "García Canclini's emphasis on the multitemporal aspect of multiculturalism, given Latin America's inherently transmodern history, an ongoing criss-crossing of disrupted modernities, with its lingering colonialism alongside its intermittent imperialisms." De la Campa, *Latin Americanism*, 70.

92. Latour, *We Have Never Been Modern*. Ana María Ochoa Gautier builds on this formulation, via the work of Richard Bauman and Charles Briggs, in her critique of the role purification has played in establishing folkloric music categories in Latin America. The argument goes to the heart of the many Latin Americanist operations of mixture, from mestizaje to transculturation. See Ochoa Gautier, "Sonic Transculturation."

93. Laclau, *Emancipation[s]*, 50.

94. The trajectory of Latin American cultural analysis, the reader is reminded, can be roughly sketched along three main models: transculturation (Fernando Ortiz, Ángel Rama), heterogeneity (A. Cornejo Polar), and hybridization (N. García Canclini), with mestizaje (Vasconcelos, Ricardo Rojas) being a key precedent. One may also include in this list Mary Louise Pratt's notion of "contact zone," from her influential *Imperial Eyes*.

95. Although not a case of neo-coloniality as such, this possibility calls to mind Homi Bhabha's notion of the constitutive ambivalence of colonial hybridity in which the disciplined perception of the other is accompanied by an unconscious desire for that other and by the possibility that the perceiver becomes unsettled and displaced by that desire. See Bhabha, *The Location of Culture*.

96. García Canclini, *Diferentes, Desiguales y Desconectados*.

97. I am aware of my critique of choice in relation to Blades's reinvention above. Here, I do not uphold a politics of choice, which may be a choice for some but not at all for others who must endlessly perform their traditions, ethnicities, or any other similar categories of identity. Choice, in short, does not operate in the same ways for all actors involved.

98. After Bhabha, Moreiras proposes "savage hybridity," an idea pivoting around a double consciousness that disavows its ontopological ground. Savage hybridity is "an expression of the radical finitude of all particularism," the "'other side' of the hegemonic relationship," "not so much a locus of enunciation as it is an atopic site, not a place for ontopologies but a place for the destabilization of all ontopologies, for a critique of totality." Blades's ontopological commitments mean that the "beyond" can only point toward this "atopic site." See Moreiras, *Exhaustion of Difference*, 294.

99. Derrida, *Specters of Marx*, 82.

100. Appadurai, *Modernity at Large*, 178.

101. Ochoa Gautier, *Músicas locales*.

102. Kun, *Audiotopia*, 185.

103. Kun, *Audiotopia*, 22–23.

104. Kun, *Audiotopia*, 23.

105. García Canclini, *Culturas híbridas*; García Canclini, "Cultural Reconversion"; García Canclini, "State of War"; Hardt and Negri, *Empire*; Kraniauskas, "Hybridity and Reterritorialization"; Kraniauskas, "Hybridity in a Transnational Frame"; Yúdice, *The Expediency of Culture*.

106. Kun, *Audiotopia*, 2. For discussion of the aporias of immobility and the dialectical openings of circulation among musicians, see Steingo, *Kwaito's Promise*. A classic study of circulation and the global imagination is Louise Meintjes's *Sound of Africa!*

107. Mignolo, *Local Histories/Global Designs*; Mignolo, *The Idea of Latin America*.

108. Spivak, *Death of a Discipline*.

109. Spivak, *Death of a Discipline*, 72.

110. Laclau, *Emancipation[s]*.

111. Laclau, *Emancipation[s]*, 38.

112. Hardt and Negri, *Empire*.

113. Adorno, *Negative Dialectics*, 5.

114. Richard, *Residuos y metáforas*, cited in Beasley-Murray, "'El Arte de La Fuga,'" 259.

115. Yúdice, "Postmodernity and Transnational Capitalism in Latin America," 21.

116. García Canclini, *Latinoamericanos buscando lugar en este siglo*.

117. Thanks to Andrew Niess for suggesting a connection here to syncopation and for the phrase "home in time, in this new century."

Chapter Three

1. Reydeltiempo, November 18, 2006, 10:34 p.m., comment on Casa Editorial El Tiempo, "Así fue el concierto de Shakira en el parque Simón Bolívar de Bogotá," *El Tiempo*, November 17, 2006, https://www.eltiempo.com/archivo/documento/CMS-3330559.

2. Duerden, "Sexiest Woman."

3. "Shakira estudia historia en UCLA."

4. Krohn, *Shakira*.

5. "Upon the release of her long awaited Spanish album *Fijación Oral, Vol. 1*, Shakira made musical and cultural history marking the biggest one-week sales and highest chart debut for a Spanish language release in the Soundscan era." "Shakira Follows Up." On April 5, 2006, *Business Wire* reported that "the album, which is the English counterpart to the triple platinum *Fijación Oral, Vol. 1*, was certified platinum this week with sales exceeding a million copies in the US. Both of Shakira's latest albums debuted in the top 5 of the Billboard Top 200 Album Chart, making Shakira the only artist ever to debut top 5 albums in English and Spanish in the same calendar year." "'Hits' Don't Lie."

6. Silverman, "Fans Unveil."

7. See González Henríquez, "Música Popular."

8. I do not discuss Shakira's "voice" in "musical" terms as such. Rather, my thinking corresponds to what Licia Fiol-Matta calls "the thinking voice" in her pathbreaking study of Puerto Rican women singers. Following Fiol-Matta, I regard Shakira as a "great woman singer" whose "thinking voice . . . [takes] residence, unleashing questions and providing answers—consciously or not—in response to the cultural moment of [her] times." As Fiol-Matta makes lucidly clear, in a "great woman singer" this happens no matter her political positioning and regardless of any overtly political content. Attending to the voice in its "conceptual dimension" and apart from facile notions of "natural or intuitive performance" means that the great woman

singer cannot be made to collapse under the corporate machine that sustains but is also transformed by her. Singing mobilizes listening and "reorder[s] a variety of injunctions, among them how enjoyment should proceed and where, how patriotic allegiances should be expressed . . . how politics should enter music lyrics, and how consumption should become the main activity of subjects in capitalism." Fiol-Matta, *Great Woman Singer*, 7, 8, 13.

9. In 1916, the port of Barranquilla received 6,362.7 kilograms of imported phonographs, gramophones, records, and replacement parts, far surpassing other ports' stocks. In 1919, the tonnage more than tripled. The country's total number of imported player pianos increased from 4 (1910) to 269 (1918). Velasquez Ospina, "(Re) Sounding Cities," 231, 228.

10. "The mechanical reproduction of music relocated the US as an aural referent of cosmopolitan modernization for Colombian cities. . . . Unlike Argentina, Mexico, and Brazil, in Colombia, American companies used the expertise and knowledge of local entrepreneurs to distribute products from American and Latin American centers of production." Velasquez Ospina, "(Re)Sounding Cities," 236.

11. Wade, *Music, Race and Nation*, 73.

12. Wade, *Music, Race and Nation*, 94. On bolero consumption in Colombia, see Santamaría-Delgado, *Vitrolas, rocolas y radioteatros*.

13. Turino, "Nationalism."

14. Law 198, 1995, article 6 stipulates that the National Institute of Radio and Television, Inravisión, must produce a fifteen-minute program on raising the national flag and must include the national anthem, an homage to the flag, and a commemoration of a Colombian hero or event in the history of national independence to be broadcast Sundays at 8:00 a.m. on channel 3 and national radio. Article 6 states that all twenty-four-hour radio television must broadcast the official version of the national anthem daily at 6:00 a.m. and 6:00 p.m. Stations with partial broadcast must broadcast the official version of the national anthem at the beginning and ending of their transmission. Colombian Congress, Ley 198 de 1995 (Julio 17), Artículo 6, Por la cual se ordena la izada de la Bandera Nacional y colocación de los símbolos patrios en los establecimientos públicos y educativos, instalaciones militares y de policía y representaciones de Colombia en el exterior, y se dictan otras disposiciones.

15. Turino, "Nationalism," 93–94. Turino's definition of cosmopolitanism refers solely to local and foreign contact, a division he maintains throughout his article.

16. The cosmopolitanism allowed in the anthem's state-sanctioned aesthetics contrasted sharply with Núñez's advocacy, in cohort with the Catholic Church, of a nearly virulent nationalistic politics. See Siskind, *Cosmopolitan Desires*, 169–70.

17. On the "deep roots" of a certain cosmopolitan tradition in the constitution of Latin America, see Fojas, *Cosmopolitanism in the Americas*, 1–2.

18. Siskind, *Cosmopolitan Desires*, 168. In 1894, Sanín Cano wrote that "[today] ideas and ideals spread with great haste. A people that wishes to make of their own [ideas and ideals] their exclusive patrimony is senseless, as if it expects that the foreign [ideas and ideals] do not mix with their own." Sanín Cano, "De lo exótico," cited in Siskind, *Cosmopolitan Desires*, 169, translation modified.

19. Abbas, "Cosmopolitan De-Scriptions," 210. This contradiction in modern cosmopolitanism is constitutive, and has been noted by critics such as Adorno, Arendt, Fanon, and Horkheimer.

20. Abbas, "Cosmopolitan De-Scriptions," 218.

21. Readers of García Márquez's 1985 novel *Love in the Time of Cholera* find Núñez there. The long trip at the novel's heart—upriver by steamboat from the Atlantic coast in the north to the country's capital in the interior—offers an idea of how distant most of the country was from the points of access of foreign goods at the time. During the first and second decades of the century, musical equipment was transported through a network of boats, railways, and mules. Velasquez Ospina, "(Re)Sounding Cities," 226–30.

22. On the interplay between phonographic reproduction and modernization in Colombia around the turn of the century, see Velasquez Ospina, "(Re)Sounding Cities."

23. Following Actor-Network-Theory, I consider actors to include humans and nonhumans alike. See Latour, *Reassembling the Social*.

24. Shakira has been the subject of a number of articles—particularly in the fields of media and communication and Latino studies (and, more recently, Latinx studies)—that focus on questions of gende , embodiment, sexuality, and identity. For a thorough analysis of issues I discuss here, such as Latinity/Latinidad, the recording industry, tensions around national and transnational citizenship, and migration, see Cepeda, *Musical ImagiNation*. The notion of cosmopolitanism I propose differs from and complements Cepeda's, which appeals to "imagined communities" and interstitial dwelling, and sees a tension between Latinity as "social identity" and "media/marketing tool."

25. Putnam, *Radical Moves*.

26. Garramuño, *Primitive Modernities*; Ortiz, *La africanía*, 105; Carpentier, *La música de Cuba*.

27. Cited in Brennan, *At Home*, 277. The relations nominated under cosmopolitanism cut across affective, formal, and material domains. Much depends then on the discursive form given to the networks connecting and separating those domains, following the idea that "a generalized rhetoric—which necessarily includes within itself a performative dimension—transcends all regional boundaries and becomes coterminous with the structuration of the social order." Laclau, "Universalism, Particularism," 229.

28. For excellent studies of rock music in Latin America, see Pacini Hernandez, Fernández L'Hoeste, and Zolov, *Rockin' Las Américas*.

29. "Eso no significa ocupar un cargo político sino la necesidad que tiene cada ciudadano de participar en el destino de su nación, del mundo, de la polis. Pero la polis se nos ha crecido y no es sólo Barranquilla ni Colombia: para todos es el mundo y debemos preocuparnos por el destino de la humanidad, de a dónde va la ecología, qué va a pasar con esos 75 millones de niños que no reciben educación en tantos lugares del mundo." "Shakira disfruta."

30. Yúdice, "La Industria."

31. Bender, "Will the Wolf Survive?"; Cepeda, "When Latina Hips"; Cepeda, *Musical ImagiNation*; Fiol-Matta, "Pop Latinidad"; Herrera, "Latin Explosion"; Tobey, "Latin Explosion."

32. "El espejo." "Like many Latin artists who have crossed into the English market, Christina Aguilera's foray into Spanish has yielded a mostly mainstream pop album with Latin inflections." "Latin: Christina Aguilera."

33. "El espejo."

34. In 2001, Andrés Pastrana, then the embattled president of Colombia, had declared the singer a "national goodwill ambassador." "Pastrana." Cepeda, in *Musical ImagiNation*, cautions against such official endorsements but confirms Shakira's role in destigmatizing Colombia abroad.

35. A representative sample: "Taking a cue from Canadian sister-in-song Alanis Morrissette . . . Shakira has injected her music with gritty rhythms (both acoustic and electronic), smart and sometimes sassy lyrics, and memorable melodies . . .Like Morrissette, emotion is at the center of Shakira's musical world." "Review of Shakira."

36. Marc Anthony's figures result from summing various individual country numbers and typically exclude Europe. There are no world sales numbers by themselves. Unfortunately, the Nielsen Soundscan, a good index, keeps its numbers mostly private. Still, the figures give a general picture of sales.

37. In polls conducted in Venezuela and Colombia to determine the most recognizable figures from each country, Venezuelans named Shakira first (at 28 percent), García Marquez second (15 percent), and Botero third (5 percent). Bisbal, "Medios y Cultura," 435.

38. Ochoa Gautier, "Sonic Transculturation."

39. "Shakira y Juanes."

40. Arias, "Y Shakira."

41. The Magdalena meets the Atlantic at Puerto Colombia, the largest Colombian port in that ocean, and very close to Barranquilla.

42. The congress took place in 2004. The hatchet buried, in 2016, Vives scored a major hit in a duet with Shakira, "La Bicicleta," sung entirely in Spanish.

43. Comments paraphrased and cited below all come from *El Tiempo*. See https://www.eltiempo.com/archivo/documento/CMS-3330559.

44. Anamatilde, November 18, 2006, 9:52 a.m., comment on Casa Editorial *El Tiempo*, "Así fue el concierto de Shakira en el parque Simón Bolívar de Bogotá," *El Tiempo*, November 17, 2006, https://www.eltiempo.com/archivo/documento/CMS -3330559. Comments are no longer live on this archived page; I documented comments in detail when they were still available online.

45. JotaT, November 18, 2006, 11:06 a.m., comment on Casa Editorial *El Tiempo*, "Así fue el concierto de Shakira en el parque Simón Bolívar de Bogotá," *El Tiempo*, November 17, 2006, https://www.eltiempo.com/archivo/documento/CMS-3330559.

46. Between 1996 and mid-2003, 1.6 million Colombians left the country and did not return; in 2003 there were an estimated 240,390 in Spain. Bérubé, "Colombia: In the Crossfire." Compare this number with the figure that "one in ten Colombians currently lives outside his or her homeland." Cepeda, *Musical ImagiNation*, 4.

47. ". . . y por si fuera poco Shakira se presentó en la final del Mundial de Fútbol en Alemania 2006 convirtiéndose en la primera cantante latina en hacerlo (Ricky Martin es hombre . . . hasta que no se demuestre lo contrario). Y sí, Shakira ha terminado convirtiéndose en una embajadora de Colombia para el mundo entero (ya todo el globo terraqueo sabe que 'en Barranquilla se baila así'); pero, Shakira no es Colombia, ni es lo que es por Colombia. Shakira es simplemente SHAKIRA, una artista colombiana que se ha impuesto en el mundo entero por su música. . . ." CINEFICO, November 18, 2006, 11:34 p.m., comment on Casa Editorial *El Tiempo*, "Así fue el concierto de Shakira en el parque Simón Bolívar de Bogotá," *El Tiempo*, November 17, 2006, https://www.eltiempo.com/archivo/documento/CMS-3330559.

48. On Shakira's stage representations of Colombian-ness, see Cepeda, "Shakira."

49. "SHAKIRA SHAKIRA!!!! tan COLOMBIANA como su acento ARGENTINO. . . . tan HUMILDE como su mansión en MIAMI. . . . . . . tan PATRIOTA como su baile ARABE. . . . haber DESPIERTEN . . . no es 'envidia' como achacan todos los que están furiosamente embelesados con ella, es REALISMO . . . no mágico, realismo a secas . . ."

50. Accent and dancing notwithstanding, the issue of living abroad had haunted other figures. The late García Márquez and Botero—both of whom resided abroad and rarely visited Colombia—were criticized for abdicating their responsibilities to their compatriots who shouldered the day-to-day weight of living *in situ* in a violent and insecure society. Residing abroad was considered a form of national refusal, despite Botero's heartfelt declarations that Colombia was his source of inspiration and his "greatest sorrow." Velásquez Urrego, "El arte contemporáneo."

51. "Shakira llena de satisfacción el deseo que tenemos los colombianos de ser observados desde una perspectiva diferente en el ámbito mundial." Interpretacion, November 18, 2006, 11:45 p.m., comment on Casa Editorial *El Tiempo*, "Así fue el concierto de Shakira en el parque Simón Bolívar de Bogotá," *El Tiempo*, November 17, 2006, https://www.eltiempo.com/archivo/documento/CMS-3330559.

52. "Felicitaciones a Shakira por su patriotismo y amor por su tierra. En el extranjero no hay regionalismos que causan fricciones . . . Todos somos COLOMBIANOS . . . y sin nos preguntan de donde somos respondemos 'COLOMBIANOS.' Lo más interesante de Colombia es la variedad de culturas y de gentes, esa identidad es la que nos hace ser diferentes." Juanc54321, November 18, 2006, 8:33 a.m., comment on Casa Editorial *El Tiempo*, "Así fue el concierto de Shakira en el parque Simón Bolívar de Bogotá," *El Tiempo*, November 17, 2006, https://www.eltiempo.com/archivo/documento/CMS-3330559..

53. Quoted in Gurza: "'No vimos la audiencia como si estuviera dividida,' dice Lee Stimmel, vicepresidente de mercadeo de Epic Records, que lanzó ambos álbumes el año pasado. 'Dijimos: esta música es demasiado importante y fantástica como para marginalizarla.'"

54. Cobo, "Shakira X2," 22–23.

55. Cobo, "Epic's Shakira," 5.

56. Cobo, "Epic's Shakira," 5. A Los Angeles–born Chilean, Lio Carvallo, taught Shakira English in Miami for eight months in 1998.

57. On Colombian-ness, see Cepeda, "Shakira."

58. The Telecommunications Act of 1996 "created a near-monopoly situation," with the biggest four media companies having 48 percent of all listeners and the top ten two-thirds. Seventy-six percent of all programming settled into fifteen formats, which helps explain the reticence about Shakira's then hard-to-define "style." See Taylor, *Music and Capitalism*, 50.

59. Cobo, "Latin Acts Expand Presence," 1.

60. Cobo, "Latin Acts Tread Carefully."

61. Cobo, "Shakira X2."

62. Cobo, "Epic's Shakira."

63. Mill, *Principles*.

64. Arendt, *Human Condition*, 24.

65. Arendt, *Human Condition*, 198.

66. This is reported by Diogenes Laertius in his biography and by the Alexandrian Jewish philosopher Philo. Pollock, "Cosmopolitanism and Vernacular," 50. The Cynics did not formulate the term "cosmopolitanism," but Diogenes's claim is regarded as the earliest expression of the notion's practice.

67. Anderson, *Powers of Distance.*

68. Plutarch, "On the Fortune"; Nussbaum, "Patriotism and Cosmopolitanism."

69. Appiah, *Cosmopolitanism.*

70. Brennan, *At Home,* 147.

71. On cosmopolitan "frames of intelligibility," see Siskind, *Cosmopolitan Desires.*

72. On exappropriation, see Derrida, *Specters of Marx.* On hospitality, see Derrida and Dufourmantelle, *Of Hospitality.*

73. On cosmopolitanism as it relates especially to modernity, colonialism, and Latin America, see Rabasa, *Inventing America*; Mignolo, "Many Faces of Cosmo-Polis"; Mignolo, *Local Histories/Global Designs*; and García Canclini, *Latinoamericanos buscando,* 23. For useful general critique, see Latour, "Difficulty of Being Glocal"; and Calhoun, "Class Consciousness."

74. García Canclini, *Latinoamericanos buscando,* 23. Here, "literary 'constitutions'" refers to "foundational fictions," texts through which readers came to desire their nations and to gain interest in other Latin American nations. Sommer, *Foundational Fictions.*

75. Pollock, "Cosmopolitanism and Vernacular," 16.

76. See Siskind, *Cosmopolitan Desires*; Darío, *Viajes*; Fojas, *Cosmopolitanism in the Americas.* The period 1870–1910 marks the "literary modernization of Latin America [which] saw a very broad and indiscriminate incorporation of modern literatures . . . the novelty rested in the breadth of literary incorporations, which began to encompass the whole of the West, guided by the saint signal of the most forward-looking metropolises: cosmopolitanism." Rama, *La crítica,* 85.

77. Siskind, *Cosmopolitan Desires,* 124.

78. Siskind, *Cosmopolitan Desires,* 3.

79. Siskind, *Cosmopolitan Desires,* 19.

80. Siskind, *Cosmopolitan Desires,* 4–5. Jorge Luis Borges offers one of the most cited registers of Latin Americanist cosmopolitan aspirations: "our [Latin American] tradition is the whole of Western culture . . . we must believe that our patrimony is the universe." Jorge Luis Borges, "Argentine Writer and Tradition."

81. Denning, *Noise Uprising.* On Colombia, see Velasquez Ospina, "(Re)Sounding Cities."

82. Wade, *Music, Race, and Nation,* 49–50.

83. Siskind, *Cosmopolitan Desires,* 19.

84. Denning, *Noise Uprising,* 2. On Colombia, see Wade, *Music, Race, and Nation.*

85. Denning, *Noise Uprising,* 4.

86. Denning, *Noise Uprising,* 6.

87. Erlmann, "Aesthetics of the Global Imagination"; Erlmann, *Music, Modernity*; Ochoa Gautier, *Músicas locales.*

88. Garramuño, *Primitive Modernities*; Moore, *Nationalizing Blackness*; Turino, *Nationalists, Cosmopolitans.*

89. Ochoa Gautier, *Músicas locales,* 29.

90. Ferguson, *Global Shadows.*

91. For a discussion of folklorists' stronghold on the study of Colombian music, see Miñana Blasco, "Entre el folklore."

92. Taylor, *Strange Sounds*, 3; Feld, "Sweet Lullaby," 145.

93. Stokes, "Musical Cosmopolitanism."

94. Erlmann, "Aesthetics of the Global Imagination"; Ochoa, *Músicas locales*; Stokes, "Musical Cosmopolitanism," 3.

95. Stokes, "Musical Cosmopolitanism," 3, 5.

96. Sloterdijk, *Im selbem Boot*, cited in Erlmann, "Aesthetics of Global Imagination," 478.

97. Sloterdijk, *Im selbem Boot*. The German philosopher is critical of this politics, advocating instead to return to the micropolitical and to restore the human to the human, not to an abstract and generalized humanity. See also Erlmann, "Communities of Style."

98. One aspect of these global times is precisely how it constitutes the "world" in "World Music." World music marked "a key moment in the transformation of the global recording industries as they struggle[d] to orient themselves to, and exploit, the rapidly changing soundscapes of first world cities." Stokes, "Musical Cosmopolitanism," 7. At the same time, a number of genres weren't included in "World Music" circuits, including those originating in Puerto Rico, New York City, Colombia, and Venezuela, along with merengue from the Dominican Republic. See Pacini Hernandez, *Oye Como Va!*, 142–62. On the cosmopolitan pathways through which cumbia comes to travel and on the expression "cosmopolatina," see Pacini Hernandez, *Oye Como Va!*, 106–41.

99. On colonial and imperial difference, see Mignolo, "Geopolitics of Knowledge." On Latin America as a literary subsystem within the worldwide long-distance aesthetic and intellectual community of letters, see Casanova, *World Republic of Letters*.

100. Stokes, "Musical Cosmopolitanism," 6. Stokes recalls Hannah Arendt's notion of the world as the space that human beings create through how they relate to one another. This world is at once something shared and something that separates us. See Arendt, *Human Condition*.

101. Feld, *Jazz Cosmopolitanism*, 49.

102. Stokes, "Musical Cosmopolitanism," 6, 7.

103. This perspective adheres to a view of interdependency in which cosmopolitanism is disavowed neither for its association with "hyperpolitics" (Sloterdijk) nor for how the local may offer a place for "resistance" to the global. Rather, each relation is observed according to which actors are involved and which alliances deployed: the possible is not a priori determined to be a political lie. Against the problematic "arts of the possible" of imperial cosmopolitanisms (according to Sloterdijk), Erlmann proposes an art of the impossible, like the interdependent model of cosmopolitanism I advocate. See Erlmann, "Communities of Style."

104. García Canclini, *Latinoamericanos buscando*, 19.

105. According to the Organization of American States, Colombia's migration reached its apex in the 1990s. "Colombia—Trends and Characteristics of Colombian Migration Policy since the Late Twentieth Century to the Present," accessed May 18, 2019, http://www.migracionoea.org/index.php/en/sicremi-en/266 -colombia-3-tendencias-y-caracteristicas-de-la-politica-migratoria-desde-fines-del -siglo-xx-a-la-actualidad-2.html [inactive link].

106. According to figures given by the World Bank, there occurred a spike in unemployment during the 1995–2005 period:

1995: 8.72%
1996: 11.81%
1997: 12.14%
1998: 15%
1999: 20.06%
2000: 20.52%
2001: 15.04%
2002: 15.6%
2003: 14.18%
2004: 13.7%
2005: 11.87%

"Desempleo, Total (% de La Población Activa Total) (Estimación Modelado OIT)," Banco Mundial, accessed May 18, 2019, https://datos.bancomundial.org/indicador/ SL.UEM.TOTL.ZS?locations = CO%2F-CO.

Index Mundi offers a similar breakdown for 1999–2005:

1999: 20%
2000: 20%
2001: 17%
2002: 17.39%
2003: 14.19%
2004: 13.6%
2005: 11.8%

"Unemployment Rate," Index Mundi, accessed May 18, 2019, https://www.index-mundi.com/g/g.aspx?c = co&v = 74&1 = es/ 8/.

Monthly figures by the Banco de la República (Colombia's national bank) from 2001 confirm these numbers. Tasas de Empleo y Desempleo," Banco de la República, accessed May 18, 2019, http://www.banrep.gov.co/es/tasas-empleo-y-desempleo.

107. Throughout the 1990s, Colombia had 971,607 migrants. Between 2000 and 2005, a total of 661,151 Colombians migrated, for a total of 1,632,758. These numbers are from the following sources at DANE's (Colombia's National Administrative Department of Statistics): *Estimación de la migración 1973–2005* (Bogotá, Colombia: Departamento Administrativo Nacional de Estadística [Colombia], 2008), https:// www.dane.gov.co/files/investigaciones/poblacion/migraciones/doc_est_mig_1973 _2005.pdf, 32; "Anuario Estadístico de Movimientos Internacionales-2006" (Departamento Administrativo Nacional de Estadística [Colombia], 2006), https://www .dane.gov.co/files/investigaciones/poblacion/migraciones/Anuario_2006.pdf (data for 1996–1999); "Demografía y Población-Movilidad y Migración," accessed May 28, 2019, https://www.dane.gov.co/index.php/estadisticas-por-tema/demografia-y -poblacion/movilidad-y-migracion, (data for 1990–1995).

108. Spain enjoyed a period of growth between 1995 and 2000, given here according to the GDP:

1995: 2.76%
1996: 2.68%

1997: 4.31%
1998: 3.7%
1999: 4.49%
2000: 5.29%

"GDP Growth (Annual %) | Data," World Bank, accessed May 28, 2019, https://data
.worldbank.org/indicator/NY.GDP.MKTP.KD.ZG?locations = ES.

109. In 1995, there were 6,992 Colombians residing in Spain, a 5.72 percent increase over the previous year. By 2000, the number had increased by 81.27 percent
over the previous year (13,627), to 24,702. These numbers were gathered from the
following sources at Spain's INE (National Institute of Statistics): "Fondo Documental.
Historia," Instituto Nacional de Estadística, accessed May 28, 2019, http://www.ine
.es/inebaseweb/25687.do, (1990–1995); "Anuarios Estadísticos de Inmigración,"
Portal de Inmigración, accessed May 28, 2019, http://extranjeros.mitramiss.gob.es/
es/ObservatorioPermanenteInmigracion/Anuarios/index.html [link inactive].

110. In 2000, students comprised the largest portion of Colombian immigrants to
Spain (2,421). The second largest was domestic service workers (2,023), while the
third was labeled as nonclassified (1,983). "Anuarios Estadísticos de Inmigración."

111. The split among Colombian residents in Spain in 2000 was 7,409 men and
17,114 women. "Anuarios Estadísticos de Inmigración."

112. Among the best known of these Los Angeles–based producers are Jorge Ca-
landrelli and Gustavo Santaolalla, both Argentine multi-Grammy winners.

113. Party, "Miamization"; Yúdice, *Expediency of Culture*, 192–213. See also
Cepeda, *Musical ImagiNation*; Grosfoguel, "Global Logics."

114. Yúdice, *Expediency of Culture*, 193, 192, 203.

115. Yúdice, *Expediency of Culture*, 205.

116. Yúdice, *Expediency of Culture*, 199; Firmat, "Salsa for All Seasons," 118–25.

117. Yúdice, *Expediency of Culture*, 199–200. By 1999, Crescent Moon was earn-
ing a gross of US$200 million yearly. Cepeda, *Musical ImagiNation*, 45.

118. Party, "*Miamization*," 66.

119. Ochoa Gautier, *Músicas locales*, 53.

120. Estefan had first recorded a Spanish album in 1993, *Mi Tierra* (Epic Records).
A tribute to Cuban music, the album was a commercial and critical success. She is
only credited as writer on the last track, "Tradición," but throughout the album as
arranger, composer, coro, primary artist, vocals. See https://www.allmusic.com/al-
bum/m%C3%AD-tierra-mw0000098094/credits.

121. Valdes-Rodriguez, "Shakira."

122. Fiol-Matta, *Great Woman Singer*, 194.

123. Maira, "Belly Dancing"; Dox, "Dancing Around Orientalism."

124. "All the credit apparently goes to the video of Shakira's hit single 'Whenever,
Wherever,' where she is seen belly dancing to jungle beats. According to choreogra-
pher and dance instructor Ritambhara Sahni, who runs The Belly Dance Institute in
Mumbai, the perception of the dance form got a much-needed boost due to the pop
star. 'It suddenly got accepted in India. Earlier, people looked down upon it. That
image has changed now,' says Sahni." Priyanka Jain, "Shakira Gets Credit for Popula-
rising Belly Dancing," *Hindustani Times*, January 26, 2012, https://www.hindustan-
times.com/art-and-culture/shakira-gets-credit-for-popularising-belly-dancing/story
-QNokhQxgeUTL0QXM8IR8MI.html. On September 3, 2015, BBC News reported

that "Dalia Kamal Youssef—known as the Egyptian Shakira . . . [was] arrested over their scantily-clad performances in videos." "Egypt Jails Belly Dancers for Videos," September 3, 2015, sec. Middle East, https://www.bbc.com/news/world-middle-east-34140406.

125. Powers, "Shakira's Dance."

126. Party, "Miamization," 66–67.

127. Party's exemplar is Gloria Estefan's "Don't Wanna Lose You," which appeared in Spanish with an identical backing track as "Si voy a perderte." Party, "Miamization," 69.

128. Party, "Miamization," 68, 66.

129. Party, "Miamization," 69.

130. Yúdice, *Expediency of Culture*, 198, 206–7.

131. Cepeda, *Musical ImagiNation*, 63.

132. Ochoa Gautier, *Músicas locales*, 54. In this new regime, national cultural industries are compelled to cater to distant audiences and to fuse with global enterprises: "in its last stage, the twentieth century delivered on its promise to unify us, as *transnational markets*." García Canclini, *Latinoamericanos buscando*, 31.

133. Party, "Miamization," 76.

134. Ochoa Gautier, "Sonic Transculturation."

135. Discussing the success of the hit TV show *Ugly Betty* (the US version of the Colombian show *Yo soy Betty, la fea*), Yeidy Rivero remarks that "this was not simply a Colombian show that became an international magnet. Rather, Betty was a transnational show from the beginning, in that the scriptwriter and 'showrunner' behind the show's success, Fernando Gaitán, understood his project as combining elements drawn from both US and Latin American television genres." Rivero, "New Export Product," 583. The reality show *The Moment of Truth*, which ran for two seasons (2008–2009), originally aired in Colombia in 2007 as *Nada más que la verdad*. Created by US producer Howard Schultz, it used Colombia as its first market and went on to be produced in forty-six countries.

136. Cepeda, *Musical ImagiNation*, 10.

137. José F. Promis, "Pies Descalzos—Shakira | Songs, Reviews, Credits," *AllMusic*, accessed May 18, 2019, https://www.allmusic.com/album/pies-descalzos-mw0000185569.

138. "Shakira Bio," *Rolling Stone*, accessed June 19, 2019, https://www.rollingstone.com/music/artists/shakira/biography/.

139. Harvey, *Brief History of Neoliberalism*, 42.

140. Taylor, *Music and Capitalism*, 46.

141. Pallotta, "Logo."

142. Klein, *No Logo*, 4.

143. Arvidsson, *Brands*, 13; Lury, *Brands*, 1, 2.

144. Hess, "What Happens."

145. Taylor, *Music and Capitalism*, 54.

146. Hess, "What Happens"; Klein, *No Logo*.

147. Pepsi spots featuring Shakira show considerable transformation between 1999 and 2003. Although sung in English, the first one ends with a Spanish voiceover by the singer saying *"pide más"* ("ask for more"). See Pablo Barron, *Shakira Pepsi Commercial (English) [1999]*, accessed June 7, 2019, https://www.youtube.com/

watch?v = v3VdqH554eY (1999); Shakira World, *Shakira—Pepsi Commercial (Objection Theme)*, accessed June 7, 2019, https://www.youtube.com/watch?v = N1hG5I-J9nCM (2003).

148. "With $2.2 billion in ad spending last year, Pepsi was the No. 4 advertiser in the US. Sony, with a total of $1.4 billion, came in 16th place." Spain, "Pepsi."

149. Spain, "Pepsi."

150. Spain, "Pepsi." "Thomas D. Mottola, the chairman and chief executive of Sony Music Entertainment, said he had been approached by several of Pepsi's competitors about forming a partnership with his company. But, Mr. Mottola said he began talks with Pepsi about a possible alliance in July largely because the companies had worked together to promote Shakira, the Colombian-born pop star. . . . Some of the product promotions that are likely to appear in the US are already selling well in Europe, Mr. Mottola said. As part of a separate endorsement deal between Shakira and Pepsi, cups of Pepsi fountain drinks at restaurants like Pizza Hut and Taco Bell are currently swathed with images of Shakira. Underneath the plastic caps on the drinks is a CD-ROM that includes interviews with Shakira, trivia questions and music videos." See Day, "Pepsi and Sony."

151. "Sony Music, Pepsi Forge Multifaceted Global Marketing Campaign," *CelebrityAccess* (blog), November 16, 2002, https://celebrityaccess.com/caarchive/sony-music-pepsi-forge-multifaceted-global-marketing-campaign/.

152. Charski, "Pepsi."

153. Wentz, "Pepsi Puts Interest."

154. Pier Dominguez, "Was There Ever."

155. Grogan, "Don't Be Fooled."

156. Critiques of the shift away from a rock aesthetic reflect the pervasiveness of "rock ideology." Rock music and musicians, despite being shaped by the culture industry and integrated in commercial enterprises, retain an unparalleled degree of autonomy and unburnished authenticity. Frith, *Sound Effects*.

157. Lash and Lury, *Global Culture Industry*, 6. See Taylor, *Music and Capitalism*, 55.

158. "Society of control" is Deleuze's name for the regime of social governmentality that replaces Foucault's "disciplinary society." In the society of control, institutional enclosures no longer hold individuals; instead, those activities are given over to the "dividual," the social unit replacing the old "individual" and defined by the internalization of the older imperatives of discipline and for its infinite capacity for self-division. See Foucault, *Discipline and Punish*; Deleuze, "Postscript on the Societies of Control."

159. Nealon, *I'm Not Like Everybody Else*, 11–12, 19.

160. Deleuze, *Difference and Repetition*, 100.

161. The rock bona fides of the track are established in the instrumental introduction, openly redolent of Pink Floyd's eerie guitar part in "Wish You Were Here." This part, written by Shakira's co-producer and musical director Tim Mitchell, cleverly moves from C-sharp minor (Dorian) to G-sharp minor, playing with the ambiguity of tonal center that modal minor "keys" afford. It rhythmically shifts from a freer unaccompanied time feel to a square, on the beat group of two notes that bring in the rhythm section with the full force of what producers call a "drop." The rhythm section drops right before the singer comes in, leaving only the *dumbek* to play what

will be the track's main rhythm feel. The mood and musical shifts are remarkable and reflect the care with which the track pushes all the right buttons.

162. Alex Henderson, "Laundry Service—Shakira," *AllMusic*, accessed May 15, 2019, https://www.allmusic.com/album/laundry-service-mw0000016418.

163. McCracken, *Transformations*, 293, 306, cited in Taylor, *Music and Capitalism*, 67, 68.

164. According to the World Bank, 15.34 percent of Colombians had internet access in 2006, compared to 62.2 percent in 2017. "Personas Que Usan Internet (% de La Población) | Data," Banco Mundial, accessed May 29, 2018, https://datos .bancomundial.org/indicador/IT.NET.USER.ZS?locations = CO.

165. Personal interview, Bogotá, May 2008. Monsalve and Sarmiento were co-founders of *Curupira*, an influential ensemble dedicated to experimental exploration of Colombian traditional popular music. Sarmiento has become one of the most important promoters of music from the Colombian countryside with his project Sonidos Enraizados and has been a member of the critically acclaimed band Los Aterciopelados.

166. Wheeler, *Designing Brand Identity*, 4, quoted in Taylor, *Music and Capitalism*, 56.

167. "Emotional branding" comes from Marc Gobé and refers to a "dynamic cocktail of anthropology, sensory experiences, and visionary approach to change." "Brand personality," coined by Jennifer Aaker, constitutes "the set of human characteristics associated with a brand." Aaker, "Dimensions of Brand Personality," cited in Taylor, *Music and Capitalism*, 57.

168. Lazzarato, "Immaterial Labor," 132.

169. Hardt and Negri, *Empire*, 30. The expression "immaterial labor" has since been disavowed, leaving "affective labor" as the operative term.

170. Wheeler, *Designing Brand Identity*, 48.

171. Delanty, "Cosmopolitan Imagination."

172. "Latunes," with a Latin beat and English lyrics and in vogue from the 1930s throughout the 1960s, used English as a "cognitive language" controlling the song's intellectual and affective content, as well as to domesticate Latin rhythms' "foreignness." Firmat, "Latunes." Thanks to Daniel Party for bringing this text to my attention.

173. Tenorio-Trillo, "On Monolingual Fears." In 1985, the pro-monolingualism group U.S. English had proposed to the Federal Communications Commission (FCC) to limit the growth of Spanish-language radio stations. "Cutting off American citizens from sources of information in the language of their country, fostering language segregation via the airwaves, these are major problems that warrant the steps we propose," wrote U.S. English's executive director. Quoted in Flores and Yúdice, "Living Borders/Buscando America," 71, 83. For a sustained treatment of radio in Spanish in the US, see Casillas, *Sounds of Belonging*.

174. Flores and Yúdice, "Living Borders/Buscando America."

175. Flores and Yúdice, "Living Borders/Buscando America," 63, 59, 68, 70, 69.

176. Flores and Yúdice, "Living Borders/Buscando America," 59.

177. Inter-lingualism, originally proposed to address linguistic practices in Chicano literature, sees Spanish and English not as separate systems but as a "space" of their constant interaction. See Bruce-Novoa, *RetroSpace*.

178. Anzaldúa, *Borderlands/La Frontera*.

179. Anzaldúa, *Borderlands/La Frontera*, 80.

180. Sommer, *Bilingual Aesthetics*, xi–xii, xii.

181. Pareles, "All About the Amor."

182. Compare with Pareles's assessment of another pop record released at the same time, *Sex and Love*, by Enrique Iglesias, the Spanish-born heartthrob: "The English songs are a virtual checklist of clichés, verbal and musical." Pareles, "All About the Amor."

183. Morales, "Mea Culpa."

184. Connor, "Edison's Teeth," 161.

185. The line is ascribed to George, *né* Jorge de, Santayana and cited in Tenorio-Trillo, "On Monolingual Fears," 431. This is different from Frances R. Aparicio's notion of "tropicalization," by means of which Latino and Latina writers (e.g., Sandra Cisneros, Gary Soto, Helena María Viramontes) publishing in English actively use literal (but unmarked) translations from Spanish or introduce phonetic representations of Spanish accent in their work. See Aparicio, "On Sub-Versive Signifiers."

186. Tenorio-Trillo, "On Monolingual Fears," 431.

187. Deleuze and Guattari, *Kafka*. To be clear, by "minor" the authors of the concept do not mean that which is produced by a minority (although this is a possibility, provided it is not an expression of their cultural essence), but rather that which happens within that major language as its signifying regimes are disrupted, what Deleuze and Guattari call deterritorialization.

188. Deleuze and Guattari, *Kafka*, 16. Cf. Sloterdijk's critique of a problematic "art of the possible" above, for which cosmopolitanism is an easy way out.

189. Although raised in the US since the age of three, "the decades of unrest and repression that left thousands 'disappeared' in Latin America inspired his first two books." Lidia Hernández-Tapia, "AQ Top 5 Storytellers: Daniel Alarcón," accessed May 17, 2019, https://www.americasquarterly.org/content/aq-top-5-storytellers-daniel-alarcon.

190. Vulliamy, "She Loves You."

191. Valdes-Rodriguez, "Shakira." In the same article, Emilio Estefan is cited as saying that Shakira's lyrics are "cerebral."

192. Rancière, *Emancipated Spectator*, 72.

193. Rancière, *Aesthetics and Its Discontents*, 23.

194. "Fito Páez se lanzó en picada contra Joaquín Sabina y Shakira," Cooperativa .cl, November 22, 2006, https://www.cooperativa.cl/noticias/entretencion/musica/fito-paez/fito-paez-se-lanzo-en-picada-contra-joaquin-sabina-y-shakira/2006-11-22/063238.html.

195. Steingo, *Kwaito's Promise*, 161–62.

Chapter Four

1. Fernández Moya and Leahy, "Irish Presence."

2. Interview with Vincent Cherico in New York City, interview by Jairo Moreno, July 14, 2015. For an account of this trip to Cuba, see also Blumenfeld, "NYC Pianist Arturo O'Farrill."

3. As Cherico recounted, the drum set, which was barely held together by wires and tape, was brought by bicycle, piece by piece, by its owner, who was delighted to lend it to the musicians.

4. "Como devolverlo a Cuba, de algún modo, a través de su música, tocarla aquí y con mi madre como espectadora de este evento. Sería un modo de cerrar el círculo espiritual, artístico, familiar, del reencuentro." Cuban Art News, "Arturo O'Farrill en Cuba: una leyenda del jazz regresa a casa," *Cuban Art News* (blog), accessed July 15, 2015, https://cubanartnews.org/es/2011/01/25/arturo-ofarrill-en-cuba -una-leyenda-del-jazz-regresa-a-casa/ [inactive link].

5. "El murió con el corazón roto, reconocía que nunca regresaría a su amada isla. Era en realidad la única emoción que provocaba sus lágrimas, su dolor emocional. Desde niño y luego de joven, sentí el dolor de mi padre." *Cuban Art News*.

6. "También implicaba pagar una deuda cultural. Porque si oyes la música de Chico O'Farrill, descubres que mucho de lo que ha evolucionado el mundo del jazz es música cubana. Algunos aspectos de esta música sólo pueden venir de ritmos, texturas y esquemas compositivos de influencia afrocubana. Yo buceé en esas aguas, y nunca tuve la oportunidad de devolverlas, de traerlas a casa. Para mí, la oportunidad de interpretar esta música es el modo de decir: gracias al pueblo cubano, a su cultura en general, por su fecunda influencia. Por supuesto, la otra parte es reconocer que la música cubana es aún incomprendida como fuente del jazz, como debiera ser." *Cuban Art News*.

7. O'Farrill was different from other notable Cuban composers and arrangers like Mario Bauzá, who built his career in the US, or Armando Romeu, who developed his style in Cuba. According to Leonardo Acosta, O'Farrill was "the only Cuban arranger who had great influence in Cuban and US jazz's orchestration [style], given that until the 1950s he travelled between the two countries. . . . He became the only Cuban arranger who entered directly in the history of jazz without having to go through 'Latin Jazz' when he wrote 'Undercurrent Blues' for Benny Goodman's band." Acosta, *Raíces del jazz latino*. Acosta is critical of what he considers the provincialism of US critics and historians who claim that Afro-Cuban jazz, mambo, or salsa were created or invented in New York City (Acosta, *Raíces del jazz latino*, 160). For an early appraisal of O'Farrill's work, see Dance, "Chico O'Farrill."

8. The Bush administration had stopped all musical interchange between the US and Cuba from 2003 until 2008, but the Obama administration relaxed traveling restrictions.

9. I adapt the phrase from Paul Carter's study of the acoustemological politics of cross-cultural communication: "Applying the term 'echoic mimicry' to situations of cross-cultural colonial encounter, to verbal habits of migrants whose host community's language is not their own . . . my interest has been similar: to indicate an environmental orientation. . . . As the orientation occurs through a process of doubling, in which the concept of origin ceases to have value, being replaced by a notion of beginnings repeatedly begun, any inward collapse towards semiosis of the spatio-temporal envelope it performs signifies a radical disorientation. It entails the collapse of an entire auditory topography." Earlier, Carter writes, "The much fetishised [sic] moment of initial cross-cultural encounter now forms part of a continuum of such events. The multi-channel communication affected by the migrant (mimetic, gestural, macaronic) recapitulates the beginnings of all communication. Instead of representing histories, actors turn out subconsciously to participate in an exact analogue of these places of attempted dialogue." Carter, "Ambiguous Traces."

10. Here takes place an interaction between an imperial transnationalism ani-

mated by broad geopolitical hegemonic continental relations and a minor transnationalism emerging from lateral transactions between migrant minorities (i.e., Cuban) and the US's minorities (i.e., African Americans). This minor transnationalism retains indelible traces of the asymmetries and verticality of imperial transnationalism manifest as the foreign-immigrant and citizen distinction in the US. See Moreno, "Imperial Aurality"; and Lionnet and Shih, *Minor Transnationalism*.

11. Arendt, *The Human Condition*, 199 passim.

12. The lexical constellation around "Cuba," "Latin," and "Jazz" is notoriously contentious. Armando Romeu, a co-founder of Cuban supergroup Irakere: "what they do [Chucho Valdés, Arturo Sandoval, Emiliano Salvador, Juan Pablo Torres, among others] is evolved contemporary Cuban music, and not jazz." Gonzalo Rubalcaba, the Cuban piano virtuoso: "What I do is not jazz . . . [it is] Cuban music with a new sense of improvisation; with a new way of using percussion and with a different structural conception." Rubalcaba regards "Latin Jazz" as "a commercial construct." Cited in Borge, *Tropical Riffs*, 157. Christopher Washburne offers a detailed discussion in his "Latin Jazz." See also Corti, *Jazz Argentino*.

13. Moreno, "Sonorous Specters."

14. See Taussig, *The Nervous System*, 6.

15. Benjamin, "Theses on the Philosophy of History," 254.

16. Benjamin, "Theses on the Philosophy of History," 254.

17. Oyarzún, *Walter Benjamin*, 22.

18. Video (2012) from the Afro Latin Jazz Alliance (ALJA), since 2007 the umbrella organization for O'Farrill's Orchestra, accessed July 10, 2019, https://web.archive .org/web/20171223152216/http://www.kennedy-center.org/Artist/A17184.

19. DeVeaux, "Constructing the Jazz Tradition," 551.

20. "Afro Latin Jazz Orchestra," Kennedy Center, July 2013, accessed July 10, 2019, https://web.archive.org/web/20171223152216/http://www.kennedy-center .org/Artist/A17184.

21. This and other quotes in this paragraph appear in "ALJO 10 Year Anniversary Interviews," accessed July 20, 2018, https://www.youtube.com/watch?v= vgl3yZwqb5g.

22. Only Walsh and McIntyre appeared in the ALJO's original lineup.

23. From the ALJA mission statement: "The Afro Latin Jazz Alliance (ALJA) is dedicated to preserving the music and heritage of big band Latin jazz." "Preservation— Afro Latin Jazz Alliance," Afro Latin Jazz Alliance, accessed July 10, 2019, https:// www.afrolatinjazz.org/preservation/.

24. Interview with Vincent Cherico, New York City, July 14, 2015.

25. I will use the expression "Black Americans" to refer to ethnically Black people from the US. For other authors, I use their preferred expression, either African-American or African American. My choice reflects the idea that nation shapes race, particularly in hemispheric contexts.

26. Ethan Iverson offers an insightful and comprehensive musical analysis of the contributions of the "Young Lions" and of the polemics surrounding their emergence. See "Young Lions of the 1980s," accessed July 27, 2015, http://dothemath.typepad .com/dtm/1-young-lion-jazz-of-the-1980s.html [inactive link].

27. On Marsalis's debt to Murray and Crouch, see Marsalis and Stewart, *Sweet Swing Blues*.

28. See Murray, *The Omni-Americans.*

29. See Kaplan, "When Ambassadors Had Rhythm." The article describes the "not well known" musicians, one of whom was Miguel Zenón (chapter 5), who toured West Africa as part of Rhythm Road. According to Maura Pally, acting assistant secretary of state for educational and cultural affairs, Rhythm Road's 2010 funding from the State Department was $1.5 million, nearly double the inaugural season's figure. See da Fonseca-Wollheim, "America's Musical Ambassadors." The program's musicians toured South Korea, China, Russia, the Philippines, Colombia, Uruguay, Saudi Arabia, Turkmenistan, and many others.

30. In 1991, Lincoln Center began a department dedicated to jazz, with seed money from the Lila Wallace–*Reader's Digest* Fund ($3.4 million) to support a national performing network for jazz. By 1996, Jazz at Lincoln Center became a full-fledged institution dedicated to the archiving, dissemination, education, and performance of jazz. In 2004, the doors opened at its multi-hall center at the Time Warner Center at Columbus Circle, in New York City (cost: $131 million). As of 2016, its annual budget was over $50 million.

31. Marsalis served as the series' co-producer and artistic director. Large corporations contributed to the series, and the series' branding of books, DVDs, and related merchandise made hundreds of millions of dollars. The jingoistic and American exceptionalist ethos were the target of much critique. See Pond, "Jamming the Reception"; Gabbard, "Ken Burns's 'Jazz'"; and Lipsitz, "Songs of the Unsung."

32. "May we say—without the blare of jingoism," asked Robert G. O'Meally, the founding organizer of the Jazz Study Group at Columbia University, an influential project in the academic study of jazz, "that jazz offers a vital model for free democratic operation and cooperation at the highest levels?" O'Meally, *The Jazz Cadence of American Culture,* xii. On jazz as the most and truest American of the nation-state's art forms, which embodies both the soft power of culture and the hard power of the US's global reach, see Brown, "Americanization at Its Best?"

33. Lipsitz, "Songs of the Unsung," 12.

34. Lipsitz, "Songs of the Unsung," 13.

35. Marsalis was signed with Columbia Records throughout the 1980s; in 1988, Columbia became part of Sony. Lewis, *A Power Stronger Than Itself,* 444, 594n20. See also Krin Gabbard, "Ken Burns's 'Jazz': Beautiful Music, but Missing a Beat," *Chronicle of Higher Education,* December 15, 2000, https://www.chronicle.com/article/Ken-Burnss-Jazz-Beautiful/2632. These debates failed to note the near-total omission of Latin American and Caribbean musicians in the series. On the neoliberal dimension of the project, see Laver, "Freedom of Choice."

36. Marsalis's role and relationship to Jazz at Lincoln Center is discussed in various scholarly publications. See, for example, Robert G. O'Meally et al., *Uptown Conversation*; Lee B. Brown, "Marsalis and Baraka"; and Laver, "Freedom of Choice."

37. Marsalis, "What Is Jazz." See also Russonello, "At 30, What Does Jazz at Lincoln Center Mean?"

38. Marsalis, "What Jazz Is—and Isn't." With "early jazz writers" with prejudices, I understand Marsalis to refer to white jazz critics. He doesn't name anyone. Throughout the chapter, I use "white critics" in this anonymous fashion. For a related critique of jazz criticism, see Jones, "Jazz and the White Critic." Jones, however, links the white establishment's critical outlook to questions of race that Marsalis will

refuse. On the impact of criticism in the constitution of jazz in the public sphere, see Gennari, *Blowin' Hot and Cool*. We are reminded how, "as a cultural expression, [Black music] is cast within and against the formations of racial ideology—as a sound form expressive simultaneously of both the difference of blackness and the relation of black to white." Radano, *Lying Up a Nation*, 279.

39. Hobsbawm and Ranger, *The Invention of Tradition*. On the centrality of the concept of "tradition" for social disciplines and, within these, of the problematic tradition/modernity, see Bauman, "Tradition, Anthropology Of."

40. Raymond Williams, *Marxism and Literature*. These three terms are not equivalent. Invention signifies a greater degree of intentionality than construction. Construction tends to be more heterogeneous in its processes than invention. Both processes solicit an idea of progressive occurrence often called "emergence" by their advocates, although perhaps construction comes to pass over longer periods of time. For a useful discussion of the problematic conflation of invention and construction, see Mato, "On the Theory."

41. Bauman and Briggs, *Voices of Modernity*, 11.

42. Wagner, *The Invention of Culture*. See also Holbraad, "The Relative Native." Note that in Wagner's groundbreaking critique—directed at the culturalist character of anthropology, particularly in the US—"invention" does not signify construction as such, but rather the sense that what culture does is, first and foremost, to invent. As Holbraad puts it, "Wagner recasts the idea of culture as the manner in which the world invents itself (culture does as nature is, one might say)." This is not a question of how things "might be 'represented,' 'known' . . . or for that matter 'constructed.'" "The Relative Native," 470.

43. Appadurai, "The Past as a Scarce Resource," 201.

44. Quasi-transcendental refers to those notions that while being posited as an origin are themselves of the time of the world, not of some otherworldly or metaphysically transcendent temporality. They are conceived to be manifest in the particular events of the society that claims it as its origin or foundation. Like a transcendental, a quasi-transcendental can never be presented as such, being a condition of possibility, but unlike the transcendent, it can be known.

45. Appadurai, "The Past as a Scarce Resource," 202.

46. Appadurai, "The Past as a Scarce Resource," 203. These forms recall Bauman and Briggs's notion of the discursive and mediational performatives of the concept of tradition.

47. Taking ownership of a narrative is key to the administration of one's archive. Marsalis's discourse constitutes both beginning (*arche*) and custodial power (*archon*) of something all too long denied to African American musicians. On the archive, see Derrida, *Archive Fever*.

48. The authors correspond to a proper name and person but also to a set of values underlying that person's individuality, an "author function." Foucault, "What Is an Author?" These values gain empirical density in the form of the capacious modern humanist individual Lawrence Grossberg describes thus: "(1) the subject as a position defining the possibility and the source of experience and, by extension, of knowledge; (2) the agent as a position of activity; and (3) the self as a mark of a social identity." Grossberg, "Identity and Cultural Studies," 97–98.

49. Gitelman, *Scripts, Grooves, and Writing Machines*, 15; Kittler, *Gramophone, Film, Typewriter*.

50. Taussig, *The Nervous System*, 3.

51. On the risks of records for a writing of jazz history, see Rasula, "The Media of Memory." On phonography and racial violence, see Stadler, "Never Heard Such a Thing." On Blackness and sound ownership, see Radano, "Black Music Labor." On the relationship between a genre-driven notion such as "jazz" and listening, see Shatz, "Kamasi Washington's Giant Step." "Washington often skips in conversation from Kendrick Lamar to Coltrane, and from Charlie Parker to Stravinsky. The reason that we don't see these connections, he says, is that we're captives of 'preconceived notions,' the most confining being the very idea of 'jazz.'" For Washington the issue is one of listening: "the problem is not merely that categories ghettoize forms of music, but that they prevent us from fully listening. All music, he believes, deserves a fair hearing." On Blackness, phonography, and modernity, see Weheliye, *Phonographies*.

52. For the notion of performance as "restored behavior," see Schechner, *Between Theater and Anthropology*, 36–37. Other definitions of performance are applicable: Victor Turner's sense of performance as a manner of completion and furnishing forth; Richard Bauman's sense of actual execution; Joseph Roach's understanding of it as "substitution" and "surrogacy." Turner, *From Ritual to Theatre*; Bauman, "Performance"; Roach, *Cities of the Dead*, 3.

53. Marsalis, "What Is Jazz," passim. Compare with George Lewis, who calls for exercising caution in stereotyping Black American musical creativity with characteristic features such as "fixed pulse" and "swing" but also in lumping Black American musical experimentalism with the total absence of phenomena such as regular pulse or recurrent harmonic, motivic, or melodic forms. See Lewis, "Gittin' to Know Y'all," 21–22.

54. Jackson, "Culture, Commodity, Palimpsest"; Moreno, "Imperial Aurality."

55. Moreno, "Imperial Aurality"; Brennan, *Secular Devotion*.

56. Important texts focusing on jazz in the Americas include Acosta, *Otra vision* (2004), *Descarga cubana* (2000), and *Descarga número dos* (2002); Balliache, *La historia del jazz en Venezuela* (1995); Borge, *Tropical Riffs* (2018); Corti, *Jazz argentino* (2015); Delannoy, *Carambola* (2005), *Convergencias* (2012), and *Caliente!* (2001); Derbez, *El jazz en México* (2001); Foster Steward, *Las expresiones musicales en Panamá* (1997); Karush, *Musicians in Transit* (2017); Malacara Palacios, *Catálogo casi razonado* (2005); Michelone, *El jazz habla español* (2014); Muñoz Vélez, *Jazz en Colombia* (2008); Jorge Olazo, *Jazz con sabor peruano* (2003); Sergio Pujol, *Jazz al sur* (1992); and Ruesga Bono, *Jazz en español* (2013).

57. Ancestry congregates jazz's musical, aural, and sonic network, along with the affective, communicative, and cognitive capacities held therein, as the work of "Afro-Americans" (Marsalis's expression). Thus, social-affective suffuses his figurations. Blues—not *the* blues—is non-naïve optimism, "down home sophistication." It has a "religious connotation" of "joy and lift"; swing is "constant coordination" on the face of an outright hostile environment; collective improvisation is "people getting together"; syncopation means "you're always prepared to do the unexpected, always ready to find your equilibrium"; call and response "is spontaneous. You invent it"; vocal effects are the transduction of vocality to musical instruments, coming, "for the most part, from the Negro tradition." Marsalis, "What Is Jazz," passim.

58. Marsalis's Messianic power—as legitimate historiographer (expert analyst, interpreter, and archival authority)—marshals a quintessential figure of modernity, the modern subject acting as agent in the production of knowledge, implement of

factual proof, and point of application of affective and cognitive experience. See Starobinski, *Montaigne in Motion*, 223.

59. Marsalis, "What Is Jazz," passim. He also refuses an account of the tradition that maps it according to a history of social contexts or that draws homologies between the social and the musical. Marsalis draws from Murray's rejection of Jones's ideas about the inextricable imbrication of jazz in racial and class politics and contexts. See Jones, *Blues People*; Murray, *Stomping the Blues*; Murray, *The Omni-Americans*; and Murray, "The Function of the Heroic Image." For Crouch's own disavowal of race as a determinant, see Crouch, *The All-American Skin Game*.

60. Porter, *What Is This Thing Called Jazz?*

61. Porter, *What Is This Thing Called Jazz?*, 292.

62. Gray, *Cultural Moves*, 37.

63. Miles, *Racism*, 75.

64. These bodies were male bodies, a skewed gender politics for which JALC was often critiqued.

65. Marsalis's positions and JALC's hiring practices drew accusations of "Crow Jim" or reverse racism, as well as charges of cronyism from Black journalists, cultural elitism and musical conservatism from musicians, and racism from whites, as well as ageism, nepotism, and sexism. In 1993, JALC executive director Ron Gibson "raised a furor by firing members of the jazz orchestra who were over 30. He later rescinded the action upon being told it was illegal." Blumenthal, "Director Leaves Jazz at Lincoln Center." For discussions of the JALC's polemics, see Porter, *What Is This Thing Called Jazz?*, 314; Sandke, *Where the Dark and the Light Folks Meet*, 128–29; Eric Nisenson, *Blue*; Gray, "Prefiguring a Black Cultural Formation"; and Pellegrinelli, "Dig Boy Dig,".

66. Hall, "What Is This 'Black' in Black Popular Culture?," 468.

67. Hall, "What Is This 'Black' in Black Popular Culture?," 468.

68. Gilroy, *Darker Than Blue*, 125.

69. Gilroy, *Darker Than Blue*, 128.

70. Shelby, "Cosmopolitanism, Blackness, and Utopia."

71. Fields and Fields, *Racecraft*. Many thanks to Guthrie Ramsey for bringing this text to my attention.

72. Fields and Fields, *Racecraft*, 16, 17, 18.

73. The authors draw from E. E. Evans-Pritchard's idea that belief is operative in spheres of rationality, as well as from related work by K. Anthony Appiah, Emile Durkheim, and W. E. B. Du Bois.

74. Fields and Fields, *Racecraft*, 198.

75. Fields and Fields, *Racecraft*, 205.

76. Fields and Fields, *Racecraft*, 203.

77. For a spirited example of this, see Floyd and Radano, "Interpreting the African-American Musical Past."

78. Fields and Fields, *Racecraft*, 201.

79. Rosaldo, *Culture and Truth*.

80. Latour, *Petite réflexion*, 15, cited in Viveiros de Castro, "The Relative Native," 490.

81. Wagner, *The Invention of Culture*, 39.

82. Viveiros de Castro, "The Relative Native," 491.

83. Wagner, *The Invention of Culture*, 30.

84. Raymond Williams, *Marxism and Literature*, 119.

85. For "cultural reconversion," see García Canclini, *Hybrid Cultures*.

86. Yúdice, *The Expediency of Culture*.

87. Miller and Yúdice, *Cultural Policy*, 1.

88. Alvarez, Dagnino, and Escobar, *Cultures of Politics*.

89. Miller, *Cultural Citizenship*, 35.

90. Miller, "Introducing . . . ," 3.

91. Miller, "Introducing . . . ," 35.

92. The critical tradition associated with the Birmingham school remarks of the transference of biological racism to a form of "cultural racism" (see Gilroy, *"There Ain't No Black in the Union Jack"*) and to a "cultural definitions of race" that permits race to play a significant role in projects of nation and national identity (Hall, "The Multi-Cultural Question").

93. Erlmann, *Music, Modernity, and the Global Imagination*, 6.

94. Erlmann, *Music, Modernity, and the Global Imagination*, 6.

95. Luker, *The Tango Machine*, 29.

96. Miller, *Cultural Citizenship*, 68. JALC's cultural policy was selective in its antagonisms. JALC blurred political horizons by, on the one hand, progressively declaring cultural affirmation of a historically aggrieved group while, on the other hand, asserting an arguably regressive aesthetic traditionalism. This selectivity is in accord with a classically modern politics of "fulfillment," in Gilroy's expression, in which the cultural politics of race mobilize music to demand that "bourgeois civil society live up to the promises of its own rhetoric," most crucially that it enact democratic inclusion. Gilroy, *The Black Atlantic*. For Gilroy, however, the best Black musical expression and creativity accomplishes what he calls a "politics of transfiguration" which "strives in pursuit of the sublime . . . to present the unpresentable" (38). See also Shelby, "Cosmopolitanism, Blackness, and Utopia."

97. Miller and Yúdice use reproduction and transformation in a different sense. Miller and Yúdice, *Cultural Policy*, 3.

98. Miller, *Cultural Citizenship*, 73.

99. This was especially the case for musicians like Bauzá who, in the 1940s, cofounded Machito and His Afro-Cubans. Moreno, "Bauzá-Gillespie-Latin/Jazz."

100. Nora, *Realms of Memory*, 1. Composition is meant in the broader sense of putting or placing together (com-posing). Unlike Nora's notion of *lieux de memoire*, my invocation here does not render such *lieux* as symbolic substitutes cataloguing, collecting, exhibiting, and organizing once-lived experiences of everyday *millieux*. For Nora, the symbolic substitution renders *lieux de memoire* as having "no referents in reality . . . pure signs" (19), in part because "the trace negates the sacred but retains its aura" (9) and because the present has "banished ritual" (6). The performance of music militates against this austere purified semiotics and anti-ritualistic understanding.

101. González Echevarría, *La Ruta de Severo Sarduy*, 102.

102. O'Farrill released two other recordings with his Afro-Cuban Orchestra: *Heart of a Legend* (1999), featuring distinguished guests such as Paquito D'Rivera, Arturo Sandoval, Israel "Cachao" Lopez, and Gato Barbieri and featuring "Trumpet Fantasy," a piece composed for Wynton Marsalis, and *Carambola* (2000). Prior to this

turning point, O'Farrill subsisted mostly as a composer of jingles. For information on O'Farrill's work with jingles, see Reich, "Arturo 'Chico' O'Farrill, 79"; Reich, "Back in the Swing"; "About Chico O'Farrill," *Arturo O'Farrill* (blog), accessed April 23, 2020, http://www.arturoofarrill.com/about-arturo/about-chico.

103. *Cuban Art News*, "Arturo O'Farrill en Cuba."

104. *Cuban Art News*, "Arturo O'Farrill en Cuba."

105. Christopher Washburne, "Latin Jazz," 96.

106. Asked about the emphasis on dance music of this record, O'Farrill commented, "If you listen to the Tito Rodriguez records, some of that stuff is really jazz. It's really unabashedly big band jazz. Even though it's set to a danceable rhythm, it exemplifies the very best of what we call harmony, big band writing, and brass writing." Chip Boaz, "Jazz News: Latin Jazz Conversations: Arturo O'Farrill (Part 3)," *All About Jazz* News, February 5, 2011, https://news.allaboutjazz.com/latin-jazz -conversations-arturo-ofarrill-part-3.php.

107. As Sherry Ortner remarks, it is particularly difficult to have access to these institutions. Sherry Ortner, "Access."

108. Washburne, "Latin Jazz," 96.

109. Thirteen out of fifteen musicians in the foundational Afro-Cuban ensemble, Machito and His Afro-Cubans, for example, were in fact Puerto Ricans. Flores, *The Diaspora Strikes Back*, 63.

110. Washburne, "Latin Jazz," 99.

111. "Introducing the Afro Latin Jazz Orchestra," interview with Arturo O'Farrill.

112. Washburne, "Latin Jazz," 98.

113. Acosta, *Raices del jazz latino*.

114. Interview with Juan Flores in Brooklyn, NY, interview by Jairo Moreno, May 8, 2008.

115. Jiménez Román and Flores, *The Afro-Latin@ Reader*, 2.

116. Jiménez Román and Flores, *The Afro-Latin@ Reader*, 2.

117. Jiménez Román and Flores, *The Afro-Latin@ Reader*, 1.

118. I affirm with Elizabeth Grosz that, rather than existing in a causal relation for "which present and future are given effects," the past constitutes "the ground from which divergence and difference erupt." Grosz, *In the Nick of Time*, 8.

119. "Most jazz musicians look upon Cuban music with great interest. They put on their lab coats and remark on how exotic those crazy rhythms are. Latin musicians put jazz on a marble pedestal and venerate the mighty gringos and their spang-a-lang. Neither side is fully accepting of the other; neither side understands that we are coinheritors of a mighty river that flows from the richness of Africa." O'Farrill, "We Speak African." On Marsalis and "ancestors," see Wynton Marsalis, "Convergence of Swing," accessed June 20, 2019, http://wyntonmarsalis.org/discogra phy/title/ congo-square.

For an account of links between Havana and Harlem and of jazz lovers in contemporary Havana, see Guridy, *Forging Diaspora*, 200–204. Guridy mentions a documentary premiered in Havana in 2004 but not yet shown in the US: *Nosotros y el jazz*, directed by Gloria Rolando. The film documents "the ways Afro-Cubans in the 1940s and 1950s encountered African American popular culture. . . . Dancing is portrayed as a way to enact memories of a diasporic experience, as opposed to an expression of an exoticized innate Africanness." Guridy, *Forging Diaspora*, 203.

120. Du Bois, *The Souls of Black Folk*; Radano, *Lying Up a Nation.*

121. Strathern, *The Gender of the Gift*; Busby, "Permeable and Partible Persons," 261–78.

122. Busby, "Permeable and Partible Persons."

123. Strathern, *The Gender of the Gift*, 13.

124. See Radano, "Black Music Labor."

125. The Orchestra's concert in Havana (Oct. 2010) was released as a double album, *Live in Cuba: Lincoln Center Jazz Orchestra with Wynton Marsalis* (Blue Engine Records, 2015). The concert was part of an official visit that included educational opportunities for Cuban musicians. Since then, the Center has presented programs dedicated to "Latin" and "Afro-Latin" music, including concerts curated by the Orchestra's bassist, Bronx-born virtuoso Carlos Hernandez ("The Music of Puente, Machito & Henriquez," June 12 and 13, 2015), features by Rubén Blades ("Una Noche con Rubén Blades," Nov. 2014, released as an album on Blue Engine Records, October 2018), and ongoing collaborations with other leading musicians such as Paquito D'Rivera.

126. Peebles, "The Anthropology of Credit and Debt." I adopt Peebles's formulation of the immanent relationality of credit and debt.

127. Scott DeVeaux, "Constructing the Jazz Tradition," 551.

128. Peebles, "The Anthropology of Credit and Debt," 230.

129. "Con Alma," *Jazz from Lincoln Center*, November 14, 1998, line 1.

130. "Con Alma," line 3.

131. "Arturo O'Farrill & the Afro Latin Jazz Orchestra," All About Jazz, September 28, 2004, https://www.allaboutjazz.com/arturo-ofarrill-and-the-afro-latin-jazz -orchestra-arturo-ofarrill-by-aaj-staff.php?width = 1440.

132. Marsalis, "Convergence of Swing."

133. Morrison, "Rootedness," 343, cited in Griffin, *"Who Set You Flowin'?,"* 5.

134. For African American creative responses to the encounter and confrontation with a modernity given in urbanization, labor in cities, and new demands on familial social organization, see Ramsey, *Race Music.* Afro-Modernism, in Ramsey's analysis, encompasses the social energies by which African Americans transacted passages to new locations during their migration North. Vernacular forms of the 1940s and 1950s were investigated and analyzed as being themselves modernist. As Ramsey holds, the pluralization of African American musical genres of that time decisively marked a form of Afro-Modernism different from that of the earlier Harlem Renaissance's lettered, cosmopolitan modernity. Such vernacular forms elaborated and extended earlier forms. Across this vast spectrum of music making, communities and traditions may intermingle and interrupt one another. It is only with the increasing social agitation of the late 1950s that new forms of collective association organized around music emerge. (I am thankful to my colleague, Professor Ramsey, for speaking at length with me about these matters.) See also Kelley, *Race Rebels*; and Denning, *The Cultural Front.*

135. Ingrid Monson points out that white jazz musicians also invoke the notion of ancestors, but do so to legitimate their own place within the jazz tradition. For Monson, this is undercut by the fact that any such ancestry is grounded in some kind of appropriation of African American musicking (swing and the blues). Monson identifies this appropriation as part of a "recursive cultural exchange" in which

African American musicking appropriates from white musicking notions of harmony. Such processes are recursive and not reciprocal, in Monson's analysis, because of the unequal power relations that inform these exchanges: "white localization of the blues and swing was not as frequently borrowed back into African American musical practice at a later point in time." Monson, *Freedom Sounds*. Deborah Kapchan discusses Moroccan Gnawa musicians who regard African American jazz musicians such as Randy Weston, Dexter Gordon, and others as ancestors. Kapchan, *Traveling Spirit Masters*, 218–19.

136. As Derrida notes, use-value is not mysterious for Marx: "If one keeps to use-value, the *properties* (*Eigenschaften*) of the thing (and it is going to be a question of property) are always very human, at bottom, reassuring for this very reason. They always relate to what is proper to man, to the properties of man: either they respond to men's needs, and that is precisely their use-value, or else they are the product of a human activity that seems to intend them for those needs." Derrida, *Specters of Marx*, 166.

137. *A Morte Como Quase Acontecimento.*

138. Music, particularly jazz—which demands for its reproduction on a constant restaging of its conditions of possibility (real-time, live improvisation)—seems eminently suited for this process.

139. Daphne A. Brooks speaks of spirit-rapping sessions in the pre–Civil War US as "radical act[s] of 'desegregating the dead,'" suggesting that, although these sessions were practiced mainly by whites, "spiritualism's philosophical basis on metamorphoses posed an ideological resistance to the cultural politics of segregation." Brooks, *Bodies in Dissent*, 15.

140. Chip Boaz, "Jazz News: Latin Jazz Conversations: Arturo O'Farrill (Part 4)," *All About Jazz* News, accessed June 21, 2019, https://news.allaboutjazz.com/latin -jazz-conversations-arturo-ofarrill-part-4.php.

141. *Arturo O'Farrill Brings His Afro-Cuban Jazz to Havana.*

142. Honig, *Democracy and the Foreigner.*

143. In some cases, the geopolitical outcomes of the Cuban Revolution and in all cases the imperial dissemination of US cultural forms plays a key role. Much of O'Farrill's thinking about conversations begun by Pozo and Gillespie in the 1940s and his father's contributions in the 1950s have to do with the radical breach caused by the 1959 Cuban Revolution. Here the idea that bodies with credit are less bound in their spatial displacement is complicated by the debt acquired precisely in the movement across nations and political systems. On spatial displacement and credit, see Munn, *The Fame of Gawa.*

144. Honig, *Democracy and the Foreigner.*

145. For the giver, this also takes the form of the unalienable possession that is at once given and kept. Such possessions enable hierarchies and create lasting social significance for the possessors. Weiner, *Inalienable Possessions*. Carol Muller deploys the notion in a musical context in *Rituals of Fertility.*

146. I am aware that both moments imply the possibility that JALC could only give and take away in its capacity as a hegemonic power in relation to "jazz." This would, however, only prove the burden associated with lending as part of the maintenance of hegemonic arrangements.

147. Esposito, *Communitas.*

148. Campbell, "Translator's Introduction."

149. Esposito, *Communitas*, 121.

150. Interview with Arturo O'Farrill, interview by Jairo Moreno, July 2015.

151. Ratliff, "Conclusion: 2017," 208–9.

152. Ochoa Gautier, "Sonic Transculturation."

153. Rancière, *Disagreement.*

154. Rancière, *Disagreement.*

155. Rancière, *Disagreement.*

156. The expression "part with no part," which I adopt here, is central to Rancière's political thought.

157. Rancière, *Disagreement*, 6.

158. Marsalis's jazz tradition confronts the paradox of having to *expropriate* the common in order to *appropriate* it as tradition, all while requiring that the common remain common to others to ensure its future reproducibility. Although I do not wish to dwell in the aporia this expropriation and appropriation creates, I should note the appearance here of what Derrida calls "exappropriation": the constitutive dependence of anything that claims a foundational relation to itself as its proper on an exteriority that will persist as exteriority no matter how insistent claims on it may be. This constitutes an existential condition that compels efforts toward auto-immunization, or the constant incorporation of exteriorities that help preserve the integrity of a formation's interior. In Derrida's words, "Un mouvement quasi-machinique d'exappropriation attache et arrache, selon une logique d'auto-immunité, à la religion, la famille, l'identité, l'ethos, le lieu, l'idiome." Jacques Derrida, *Foir et Savoir, Suive de Le Siècle et Le Pardon* (Paris: Seuil, 2000), 64.

159. Benjamin, "Theses on the Philosophy of History," 256.

160. Chakrabarty, *Provincializing Europe*, 107.

161. Chakrabarty, *Provincializing Europe*, 6.

162. On History 2, see Chakrabarty, *Provincializing Europe*; on local and global designs, see Mignolo, *Local Histories/Global Designs.*

Chapter Five

1. "Miguel Zenón—MacArthur Foundation," January 27, 2008, https://www.macfound.org/fellows/815/.

2. On the State's claims on jazz, see "A Concurrent Resolution Expressing the Sense of Congress Respecting the Designation of Jazz as a Rare and Valuable National American Treasure," Pub. L. No. H.Con.Res. 57 (1987). On modernization and liberal ideology and jazz, see Gebhardt, *Going for Jazz*; Brennan, *Secular Devotion*; O'Meally, *The Jazz Cadence of American Culture*; DeVeaux, *The Birth of Bebop*; Monson, *Freedom Sounds*; Porter, *What Is This Thing Called Jazz?*; Early and Monson, "Why Jazz Still Matters." On Afro-Modernity, see Gilroy, *The Black Atlantic*; Hanchard, "Afro-Modernity." On the aesthetics of Afro-Modernism, I follow Ramsey, *Race Music*. For discussion of bebop's Afro-Modernism as "abstraction and creative mobility" and the centrality of migration to its development, including the role of Cuban music, see Jesse Stewart, "No Boundary Line to Art."

3. Unless otherwise noted, comments by Zenón are from a personal interview conducted with the author in New York City, summer 2008. I address Zenón in two other articles, Moreno, "Imperial Aurality"; and Moreno, "Past Identity."

4. Ben Ratliff, "Inspired by the Complexities." The record was released on Marsalis, saxophonist Branford Marsalis's label. Research and fieldwork for *Jíbaro* was
carried out with help from a grant from the New York State Council of the Arts.

5. Hull, "*Jíbaro.*"

6. Holston, "Miguel Zenón: *Jíbaro.*"

7. Kelman, "Miguel Zenón, *Jíbaro.*"

8. Virtually every single exploration of Puerto Rican vernaculars by musicians
from other traditions has focused on Afro-diasporic forms of the *bomba* and *plena*,
forms perceived as being traditional but also urban. Zenón did go on to work on plena
in his *Esta Plena* (2009). Like *Jíbaro*, the later album was the result of research and
extensive fieldwork carried out on the Island, in this case a Guggenheim Fellowship.

9. These designs have been analyzed in, among countless others: Dussel, "Euro-
centrism and Modernity"; Dussel, *The Invention of the Americas*; Fabian, *Time and the
Other*; Ferguson, *Expectations of Modernity Myths and Meanings*; Grossberg, *Cultural
Studies*; Koselleck, *Futures Past*; Lander, *La colonialidad del saber*; and Mignolo, *Local
Histories/Global Designs*.

10. For a related discussion of an associated formation that I call "Black Caribbean" and of its effects on Afro-Cuban and US Black relations, see Moreno,
"Bauzà-Gillespie-Latin/Jazz."

11. Mintz, *Sweetness and Power*; Mintz, *Caribbean Transformations*.

12. Thanks in part to governmental intervention, *música jíbara* would survive the
unprecedented modernization projects in Puerto Rico after World War II, as the Island shifted from an agrarian base to a fully industrialized one. In the 1960s, the conservative, pro-statehood Partido Nuevo Progresista foregrounded music and other art
forms in proposals to emphasize "estadidad jíbara." See Méndez, *Posesión del ayer*,
122. The Instituto de Cultura Puertorriqueña (founded in 1955) played a key role in
determining what is being framed as "Puerto Rican," including establishing criteria
for making judgments of the authenticity of folk music, separating, for instance,
"peasant" and "African" genres. See Dávila, *Sponsored Identities*.

13. On modern nationalism, see Anderson, *Imagined Communities*; Sanders, "The
Vanguard of the Atlantic World." On Haiti, see Buck-Morss, *Hegel, Haiti, and Universal History*; and Fischer, *Modernity Disavowed*. Trouillot, "The Otherwise Modern";
and Scott, *Conscripts of Modernity*. On the Middle Passage, see Gilroy, *The Black
Atlantic*. See also Guerra, *Modernidad e independencias*; and Tenorio-Trillo, *Mexico at
the World's Fairs*.

14. The idea that modernity is a "project" and "projection" appears in Trouillot,
"The Otherwise Modern," 220–21. Inda discusses the Foucauldian scheme of this definition in "Analytics of the Modern." See Foucault, *The Government of Self and Others*.

15. Herlinghaus, *Renarración y descentramiento*. See Paz, *Los hijos del limo*. As for
so many Latin American intellectuals from the first part of the twentieth century,
modernity, for Paz, is a purely Occidental phenomenon that coheres around the Enlightenment, critical reason, liberalism, Marxism, and positivism, for which poetry
(rhythm, for him, more than reason) offers a most powerful response. Paz's views
have illustrious antecedents in Hegel, who in his *Lectures on the Philosophy of History*
deemed America a "non-place," "immature," and "incoherent," while at once proclaiming it the "land of the future, where, in the ages that lie before us, the burden of
the World's History shall reveal itself—perhaps in a contest between North and South

America" (Hegel, *Philosophy of History*, 86–87). Hegel's own ambivalence leads him to place "America" as geography without Spirit; that is, as a land prior to History. See the section "Geographical Basis of History" in the *Lectures*.

16. For Paz, see Habermas and Ben-Habib, "Modernity"; for Borges, see Foucault, *The Order of Things*; and Berman, *All That Is Solid Melts into Air*.

17. Herlinghaus, *Renarración y descentramiento*, 28.

18. Beatriz Sarlo discusses the case of Victoria Ocampo (1890–1979), an Argentine author, intellectual, and cultural agent who wagered on the powers of translation as a means to neutralize differences (Ocampo published translations of Camus, Malraux, and Sartre, partook in conversations with Cocteau and Lacan, and hosted Stravinsky and Tagore). Sarlo, *La máquina cultural*.

19. Sarlo, *Una modernidad periferica*.

20. Moreiras, *Exhaustion of Difference*.

21. Escobar, *Territories of Difference*, 14.

22. Pratt, "Modernity and Periphery," 32–35.

23. See Beverley, Aronna, and Oviedo, *The Postmodernism Debate in Latin America*; Herlinghaus and Walter, *Posmodernidad en la periferia*; de Toro, *Postmodernidad y Postcolonialidad*.

24. Incidentally, the Residencial Llorens Torres is where Rubén Blades is called out as a "jerk," in Edgardo Rodríguez Juliá's chronicle from *Cortijo's Wake*, the epigraph in chapter 1.

25. The general contour of this narrative of musical literacy is typical of much musical life there since the late nineteenth century, when, caught between the last vestiges of Spanish colonial rule and the imperial ambitions of the US, military music was abundant, as were armies of musicians able to read music. The influence of military band music in Puerto Rican musicians' literacy is discussed in Glasser, *My Music Is My Flag*. See also Brennan, *Secular Devotion*.

26. "Desarrollar y encauzar la innata sensibilidad artística de nuestro pueblo, mediante un plan sistemático de enseñanza, aprendizaje, experimentación, divulgación y formación del arte musical." Puerto Rico, House of Representatives, Ley Núm. 365 de 20 de abril de 1946 (Law 365, April 20, 1946).

27. Licia Fiol-Matta points out how the state "relied on music as a stand-in for culture, as evidence of progress, and as a placeholder of the aspirational model of class interpellating most Puerto Ricans in the E.L.A. [in the 1940s]." Although the project never passed into law, it helped launch key musical institutions such as the Conservatory and the Escuela Libre. Fiol-Matta, *The Great Woman Singer*, 102, 103.

28. "Se procura impartir al esfuerzo económico y a la libertad política unos objetivos armónicos con el espíritu del hombre, en su función de regidor más bien que de servidor de los procesos económicos . . . el pueblo de Puerto Rico espera ansiosamente mantenerse bondadoso y tranquilo en su entendimiento, en sus actitudes, mientras utiliza plena y vigorosamente todos los complejos recursos de la civilización moderna." "Fundación Luis Muñoz Marín | Biografía | Operación Serenidad," Proyecto Salón Hogar, accessed September 5, 2012, http://www.proyectosalonhogar .com/BiografiasPr/Munoz/op_serenidad.html.

29. "Admiraba a David Sánchez, Danilo Pérez y utilizando su música como norte con un toque latinoamericano más balanceado y moderno me fui encontrando." Ana Teresa Toro, "Hijo de La Fusión," Archivo Digital *El Nuevo Día*, Au-

gust 29, 2010, http://www.herencialatina.com/Miguel_Zenon/Hijo_de_la_Fusion
_agosto_Septiembre_2010.htm.

30. Harris, "Jazz on the Global Stage."

31. Gaonkar and Povinelli, "Technologies of Public Forms," 387.

32. Lee and LiPuma, "Cultures of Circulation," 192.

33. In 2009–2010, the percentage of the "domestic African-American student body" was 11 percent and that of the "domestic Hispanic student body" was 10 percent. "Facts and Statistics | Berklee College of Music." https://www.berklee.edu/about/facts-and-statistics.

34. Connolly, *Identity/Difference*. A robust argument in favor of "difference" in democratic politics appears in Young, *Justice and the Politics of Difference*.

35. García Canclini, *Hybrid Cultures*.

36. Chambers, "Signs of Silence, Lines of Listening," 47–62, 50. Later in this essay, under the subtitle of "Disrupting Modernity," Chambers presents music as a critical force in this enterprise.

37. Trouillot, "The Otherwise Modern," 226.

38. Readers will note the influence of Chantal Mouffe and Ernesto Laclau on this section. See Laclau and Mouffe, *Hegemony and Socialist Strategy*; Laclau, "Universalism, Particularism and the Question of Identity."

39. Trouillot, "The Otherwise Modern," 233.

40. Foucault, "What Is Enlightenment?," 42.

41. Foucault, "What Is Enlightenment?," 39.

42. Foucault, "What Is Enlightenment?," 45.

43. Foucault was famously unconcerned with issues of modernity outside Europe. For critiques of Foucault on this account, see Stoler, *Race and the Education of Desire*; and Chatterjee, *Our Modernity*.

44. Trouillot, "The Otherwise Modern," 231; emphasis original.

45. Butler, Laclau, and Žižek, "Questions," 8.

46. Spivak, *Outside in the Teaching Machine*, 165.

47. Grossberg, *Cultural Studies*, 289.

48. Grossberg, *Cultural Studies*, 268.

49. An earlier version of this idea, with "otherness" (a form of non-relational difference) in place of what he here calls "multiplicity," appears in his "Identity and Cultural Studies."

50. The series received support from the Banco Popular Foundation and the Luis A. Ferré Foundation, although Zenón paid for all musicians. The series was in conjunction with Revive la Música (Revive Music), a project to promote music education among youth by collecting and refurbishing old instruments, music textbooks, and scores. This initial plan was extended, and concerts continued until 2017. "Caravana Cultural—Miguel Zenón," accessed September 3, 2017, https://miguelzenon.com/caravana-cultural/. It's not clear that there won't be future dates, but the last date listed anywhere online is September 3, 2017. Zenón and Fundación Popular are both involved in the Berklee in Puerto Rico exchange. "Prestigious Berklee Educational Program Returns to Puerto Rico," *Fundación Banco Popular* (blog), April 21, 2015, https://www.fundacionbancopopular.org/en/art-and-culture/prestigious-berklee-educational-program-returns-puerto-rico/ [inactive link].

51. Of the six towns the Caravan visited until 2013, the largest one, Yauco, has a population around 42,000, and the smallest, Maunabo, 14,500.

52. "Hay ciertas áreas del País que no han tenido la exposición que se ha tenido en la zona metropolitana, quizás porque lo ven como música de un alto sector. Pero eso no es así. Queremos llegar a la gente que no tiene la oportunidad de ir a festivales para que aprendan y puedan apreciarla sin tener que pensar en dinero o viajar." Guzmán, "Regala dos años de jazz" (site discontinued).

53. "Conversation with Miguel Zenon Webcast | Library of Congress," accessed April 15, 2018, http://www.loc.gov/today/cyberlc/feature_wdesc.php?rec=7830.

54. "Conversation with Miguel Zenon Webcast."

55. "Nos fuimos a la pizzería de la esquina. . . . Una señora que andaba con los nenes le dijo a otra que a las tres de la tarde iba 'para lo de jazz' que tenían en el Anexo. El evento era en un salón adjunto a la Casa Alcaldía, en la misma plaza de Maunabo. Parecería que todo el pueblo estaba enterado." ("Caravana," *80grados*, March 9, 2012, http://www.80grados.net/caravana/, accessed Sept. 9, 2018.)

56. "Cuando dieron las tres no cabía la gente en el Anexo. En el espacio caben unas 300 personas. Miguel tomó el micrófono y empezó la primera parte del evento, una charla de una hora. La conferencia está dividida en tres partes: la improvisación, el jazz y su historia, y la vida y obra del homenajeado, en este caso Coltrane. La gente escuchó en silencio. Había viejitos, niños y jóvenes." "Caravana," *80grados*.

57. Since 2015, the project has offered small grants to students to help purchase instruments and pay lessons. "Conversation with Miguel Zenon Webcast."

58. "'Válgame Dios, por fin.' El público se rió y aplaudió. 'Los pueblos pequeños no tenemos un gran presupuesto para actividades culturales y que alguien se nos acerque y nos traiga un proyecto de la calidad de este para nuestro pueblo es una bendición.' Entonces la gente aplaudió vigorosamente." "Caravana," *80grados*.

59. "Simplemente música. Al enfocarnos específicamente en la música de jazz, tenemos también como objetivo eliminar cualquier estigma social o cultural con que el que se pueda relacionar este estilo." Doris Angleró, "Miguel Zenón en Maunabo," *80grados*, February 17, 2012, http://www.80grados.net/miguel-zenon-en-maunabo/.

60. Rancière, "The Ethical Turn of Aesthetics and Politics," 109–10.

61. For more on the critique of "distinction," see Moreno and Steingo, "Rancière's Equal Music."

62. As a critic of the insertion of virtuous action in the networks of corporate philanthropy, Puerto Rican sociologist Arturo Torrecilla might disavow the Caravana, which was supported in part by the Fundación Banco Popular and the Fundación Luis A. Ferré. But as an advocate of virtuosic acts, Torrecilla might interpret Zenón's in terms of how "virtuosity corresponds to everyone whose ethics do not rest in a calculus of algorithmic consequences, that is, necessarily predictable" ("El virtuosismo corresponde a todo aquel cuya ética no descansa en un calculo deconsecuencias algorítmico, es decir, necesariamente predecible"); virtuosic work is ephemeral, "consumes itself in the act," and "gathers in one go separated spheres of existence," all of which breaches "modernity's moral culture and political economy." Torrecilla, *La ansiedad de ser puertorriqueño*, 133, 136. Torrecilla's "virtuoso" comes from Paolo Virno. See Virno, *A Grammar of the Multitude*.

63. Hallward, "The Universal and the Transcendental." Hallward does not ignore the performative contradiction of his claims, or that of those he opposes: these dynamic processes "are transcendental to any particular human experience because no

such experience would be conceivable without them (including the effort to deny them their transcendental status)" (182).

64. Hallward, "The Universal and the Transcendental," 179; emphasis original.

65. Hallward, "The Universal and the Transcendental," 179, 183.

66. Hallward, "The Universal and the Transcendental," 183; emphasis original.

67. "Quisiera tener el peritaje para hablar críticamente de la música que ocurrió allí el domingo, pero no lo tengo. Sé que me gustó, me conmovió la generosidad de Miguel. Me quedé pensando que así se construye un país." "Caravana," *80grados*.

68. "Fui parte de ese evento maravilloso, la profecionalidad [*sic*] del Sr. Zenón, sus conocimientos del jazz , mas la forma sencilla de transmitir estos, hicieron de esa tarde una clase magistral de JAZZ [*sic*]." "Caravana," *80grados*.

69. Badiou, *Ethics*, 25-26.

70. Hallward, "Consequences of Abstraction," 3. On this, see also Agamben's "whatever singularity."

71. Badiou, *Ethics*, 27.

72. Hallward, "Translator's Introduction," in Badiou, *Ethics*, xiv.

73. The following summary does not attempt to discuss in any depth the extensive and heterogeneous work of Badiou. Key references are Badiou's *Being and Event*, as well as the simpler and useful *Ethics*. There is less here of his follow-up to *Being and Event*, *Logics of Worlds: Being and Event II*. Thorough introductions appear in Hallward, *Badiou*; and Bosteels, *Badiou and Politics*.

74. Badiou, *Ethics*, 42-43.

75. Badiou, "Eight Theses on the Universal."

76. Badiou, "Eight Theses."

77. Badiou, *Ethics*, x.

78. Badiou, *Ethics*, xiii.

79. "Ésa es la idea. . . . Intentar romper esa desconexión que hay de la masa popular con este tipo de música específicamente." Acuña, "El Jazz de Miguel Zenón."

80. Bosteels, *Badiou and Politics*, xi.

81. Hallward, *Absolutely Postcolonial*, x`x.

82. Bhabha, *The Location of Culture*, 242.

83. Bhabha, *The Location of Culture*, 243.

84. The Commission is a twenty-three-member group "tasked by Congress to provide a report on the creation of a potential Museum of the American Latino, which would focus on American Latino life, art, history and culture." Selected by the president and bipartisan congressional leaders, its members include media, education, entertainment, and business figures. They have conducted open forums across the country to solicit local input. As the Commission's site announces, "one primary theme resonated clearly throughout the forums—Latinos are part of the fabric of this nation, and there is an urgency, desire, and need for a museum to highlight and preserve this great heritage for the benefit of all Americans." "American Latino Museum: About," American Latino Museum, accessed September 21, 2012, http:// americanlatinomuseum.org/welcome/about/.

85. "Cuando me llamaron para mí era obvio que la situación de Puerto Rico era distinta a la de cualquier otro lugar en Estados Unidos. Y así fue, con opiniones a favor y en contra pero sentí que mi responsabilidad tenía que ver con que se pensara sobre la cultura y la música puertorriqueña fuera de los parámetros de lo que significa ser o no puertorriqueño." Toro, "Hijo de La Fusión."

86. "Dejó claro que en asuntos de cultura—o en cualquier otro plano—no tiene problemas de identidad." Toro, "Hijo de La Fusión."

87. "Hablar de los de aquí y los de allá; ese debate siempre existe pero en el caso de la música hay que decir que es de todos, viene de la misma raíz y en ese sentido no hay mucho que debatir. No tengo ninguna duda sobre mi identidad. Soy puertorriqueño, me fui a Estados Unidos porque lo que quería hacer no podía hacerlo en Puerto Rico. No estaba y me fui a buscarlo allá." Toro, "Hijo de La Fusión."

88. Flores, *The Diaspora Strikes Back*.

89. Carlos Romero Barceló, cited in Negrón-Muntaner, *None of the Above*, 3.

90. Negrón-Muntaner, *None of the Above*, 5.

91. Negrón-Muntaner, *None of the Above*.

92. *Downes v. Bidwell*, 182 U.S. 244 (1901); "Puerto Rico belongs to but is not part of the United States" (Foraker Act, 1900).

93. Hallward, *Badiou*, 285.

94. Here, Olivia Bloechl summarizes my analysis of Zenón. Bloechl, Lowe, and Kallberg, "Introduction," 40.

95. Billy Pierce, personal interview, Boston, February 17, 2010.

96. Moreno, "Imperial Aurality."

97. Benjamin, "Theses on the Philosophy of History, XIII," 260–61.

98. Benjamin, "Awakening," 462.

99. Benjamin, *The Arcades Project*, 255.

100. Benjamin, "Awakening," 262.

101. Benjamin, "Awakening," 262–63.

102. Benjamin, "Awakening," 255.

103. Benjamin, "Awakening," 255.

104. The formulation of a time living inside another appears in Karen Barad, "Troubling Time/s and Ecologies of Nothingness," lecture. See European Graduate School Video Lectures, *Karen Barad. Troubling Time/s and Ecologies of Nothingness* (2017), https://www.youtube.com/watch?v=RZHurGcoRmQ.

105. Didi-Huberman, *Images in Spite of All*.

106. Draper, *Afterlives of Confinement*, 102.

107. Didi-Huberman, *Images in Spite of All*, 170.

Conclusion

1. Wallis and Malm, *Big Sounds from Small Peoples*, 88.

2. Schouten, Theory Talk #13: Immanuel Wallerstein.

3. Franco, *The Decline and Fall of the Lettered City*, 261.

4. Franco, *The Decline and Fall of the Lettered City*, 4, 5.

5. See Ochoa Gautier's carefully attuned account of aurality in nineteenth-century Colombia in *Aurality*.

6. In the aftermath of this general attenuation, however, many phenomena attest to salsa's vitality. For example, the award-winning Spanish Harlem Orchestra (launched in 2002), the ongoing Salsa Day in San Juan, Puerto Rico, international salsa congresses and meetings held annually, and Colombian salsa schools, dance troupes with elaborate and highly popular shows. Salsa dancing concentrates the most active field, being a global phenomenon today. See García, *Salsa Crossings*;

Hutchinson, *Salsa World*; McMains, *Spinning Mambo into Salsa*. On the death of salsa musicians and its effects on a disappearing living archive, see Moreno, "La salsa y sus muertes."

7. Morris, "Lil Nas X."

8. Garsd, "Calle 13."

9. Milian, *Latining America*.

BIBLIOGRAPHY

Aaker, Jennifer. "Dimensions of Brand Personality." *Journal of Marketing Research* 34 (1997): 347–56.

Abbas, Ackbar. "Cosmopolitan De-Scriptions: Shanghai and Hong Kong." In *Cosmopolitan De-Scriptions: Shanghai and Hong Kong*, edited by Dipesh Chakrabarty, Homi K. Bhabha, Sheldon Pollock, and Carol A. Breckenridge, 209–28. Durham, NC: Duke University Press, 2002.

Achugar, Hugo. "Local/Global Latin Americanisms: 'Theoretical Babbling,' apropos Roberto Fernández Retamar." *Interventions* 5, no. 1 (2003): 125–41.

Acosta, Leonardo. *Descarga cubana: El jazz en Cuba 1900–1950*. Havana: Ediciones Unión, 2002.

———. *Descarga número dos: El jazz en Cuba 1950–2000*. Havana: Ediciones Unión, 2002.

———. *Otra vision de la música popular cubana*. Havana: Editorial Letras Cubanas, 2004.

———. "Perspectives on 'Salsa.'" *Centro Journal* 16, no. 2 (Fall 2004): 6–13.

———. *Raices del jazz latino: Un siglo de jazz en Cuba*. Barranquilla: Editorial La Iguana Ciega, 2001.

Acuña, Xiomara. "El jazz de Miguel Zenón." *Claridad*, January 25, 2011.

Adorno, Theodor W. *Negative Dialectics*. Translated by E. B. Ashton. New York: Continuum, 1983.

Alberdi, Juan Bautista. *Bases y puntos de partida para la organización política de la República Argentina*. Buenos Aires, 1852.

Alvarez, Sonia E., Evelyn Dagnino, and Arturo Escobar. *Cultures of Politics, Politics of Cultures: Re-Visioning Latin American Social Movements*. Boulder, CO: Westview Press, 1998.

Anderson, Amanda. *The Powers of Distance: Cosmopolitanism and the Cultivation of Detachment*. Princeton, NJ: Princeton University Press, 2001.

Anderson, Benedict. *Imagined Communities: Reflections on the Origin and Spread of Nationalism*. 2nd ed. London: Verso, 1991.

Andrade, Mário de. *Ensaio sobre a Música Brasileira*. São Paulo: Martins, 1962.

Antelo, Raúl. *Crítica acéfala*. Buenos Aires: Grumo, 2008.

Anzaldúa, Gloria. *Borderlands/La Frontera: The New Mestiza*. San Francisco: Spinsters/Aunt Lute, 1987.

Aparicio, Frances. *Listening to Salsa: Gender, Latin Popular Music and Puerto Rican Cultures*. Middletown, CT: Wesleyan University Press, 1998.

————. "On Sub-Versive Signifiers: Tropicalizing Language in the United States." In *Tropicalizations: Transcultural Representations of Latinidad*, edited by Frances Aparicio and Susana Chávez-Silverman, 194–212. Dartmouth, NH: University Press of New England, 1997.

Appadurai, Arjun. "Disjuncture and Difference in the Global Cultural Economy." *Theory Culture Society* (7) (1990): 295–310.

————. *Modernity at Large: Cultural Dimensions of Globalization.* Minneapolis: University of Minnesota Press, 1996.

————. "The Past as a Scarce Resource." *Man* 16, no. 2 (1981): 201–19.

Appiah, Kwame Anthony. *Cosmopolitanism: Ethics in a World of Strangers.* New York: W. W. Norton & Company, 2006.

Ardao, Arturo. *Génesis de la idea y el nombre de América Latina.* Caracas: Centro de Estudios Latinoamericanos, 1980.

Arendt, Hannah. *The Human Condition.* Chicago: University of Chicago Press, 1998.

Arias, Eduardo. "Y Shakira, ahí . . ." *Semana*, August 31, 2006. https://www.semana.com/on-line/articulo/shakira-ahi/80712-3.

Arvidsson, Adam. *Brands: Meaning and Value in Media Culture.* London: Routledge, 2006.

Asad, Talal. *Formations of the Secular: Christianity, Islam, Modernity.* Palo Alto, CA: Stanford University Press, 2003.

Avelar, Idelber. "Ritmos do popular no erudito: Política e música em Machado de Assis." In *A Obra de Machado de Assis.* Ensaios Premiados No 10 Concurso Internacional Machado de Assis. Brasília: Ministério das Relações Exteriores, 2006. https://docplayer.com.br/50255438-Ritmos-do-popular-no-erudito-politica-e-musica-em-machado-de-assis-1-idelber-avelar.html.

————. "Transculturation and Nationhood." In *Literary Cultures of Latin America: A Comparative History: Institutional Modes and Cultural Modalities*, edited by Mario J. Valdés and Djelal Kadir, 251–57. Oxford: Oxford University Press, 2004.

Badiou, Alain. *Being and Event.* Translated by Oliver Feltham. London: Continuum, 2005.

————. "Eight Theses on the Universal." Lacan.com, November 19, 2004. http://www.lacan.com/badeight.htm.

————. *Ethics: An Essay on the Understanding of Evil.* New York: Verso, 2001.

————. *Logics of Worlds: Being and Event II.* Translated by Alberto Toscano. 1st ed. New York: Continuum, 2009.

Badiou, Alain, Pierre Bourdieu, Judith Butler, Georges Didi-Huberman, Sadri Khiari, and Jacques Rancière, eds. *What Is a People?* New York: Columbia University Press, 2016.

Baker, Houston A. Jr. *Blues, Ideology, and Afro-American Literature: A Vernacular Theory.* Chicago: University of Chicago Press, 1984.

Balliache, Simón. *La historia del jazz en Venezuela.* Caracas: Editorial Ballagrub, 1995.

Banerjee, Prathama. *Politics of Time: "Primitives" and History-Writing in a Colonial Society.* New York: Oxford University Press, 2006.

Baraka, Amiri. "Apple Cores #6." In *Black Music.* New York: William Morrow, 1967.

Barthes, Roland. *Writing Degree Zero.* New York: Hill and Wang, 1953.

Bauman, Richard. "Performance." In *International Encyclopedia of Communications*, 262–66. New York: Oxford University Press, 1989.

———. "The Remediation of Storytelling: Narrative Performance on Early Commercial Sound Recordings." In *Telling Stories: Building Bridges Among Language, Narrative, Identity, Interaction, Society and Culture*, 23–43. Washington, DC: Georgetown University Press, 2010.

———. "Tradition, Anthropology Of." In *International Encyclopedia of the Social and Behavioral Sciences*, edited by Neil J. Smelser and Paul B. Baltes, 15819–24. London: Elsevier, 2001.

Bauman, Richard, and Charles Briggs. *Voices of Modernity: Language Ideologies and the Politics of Inequality*. Cambridge: Cambridge University Press, 2003.

Bauman, Zygmunt. *Liquid Modernity*. New York: John Wiley & Sons, 2000.

Beasley-Murray, Jon. "'El Arte de La Fuga': Cultural Critique, Metaphor and History." *Journal of Latin American Studies* 9, no. 3 (2000): 259–72.

———. "Introduction: Towards a New Latin Americanism." *Journal of Latin American Studies* 11, no. 3 (2002): 261–64.

———. *Posthegemony: Political Theory and Latin America*. Minneapolis: University of Minnesota Press, 2010.

Beck, Ulrich. "The Cosmopolitan Society and Its Enemies." *Theory, Culture & Society* 19, no. 1–2 (April 1, 2002): 17–44.

Belknap, Jeffrey, and Raúl Fernández. "Introduction." In *José Martí's "Our America": From National to Hemispheric Cultural Studies*, edited by Jeffrey Belknap and Raúl Fernández. Durham, NC: Duke University Press, 1998.

Bender, Steven W. "Will the Wolf Survive? Latino/a Pop Music in the Cultural Mainstream." *Denver University Law Review* 78 (2001): 719–51.

Benítez-Rojo, Antonio. *The Repeating Island: The Caribbean and the Postmodern Perspective*. 2nd ed. Translated by James E. Maraniss. Durham, NC: Duke University Press, 1996.

Benjamin, Walter. "Awakening." In *The Arcades Project*. Cambridge, MA: Belknap Press, 1999.

———. *The Arcades Project*. Cambridge, MA: Belknap Press, 1999.

———. "The Author as Producer." In *Reflections: Essays, Aphorisms, Autobiographical Writing*, edited by Peter Demetz, translated by Edmund Jephcott, 220–38. New York: Schocken Books, 1986.

———. "The Storyteller." In *Illuminations*, edited by Hannah Arendt, translated by Harry Zohn. New York: Schocken Books, 1968.

———. "Theses on the Philosophy of History." In *Illuminations: Essays and Reflections*, edited by Hannah Arendt, translated by Harry Zohn, 253–64. New York: Schocken Books, 1968.

Berman, Marshall. *All That Is Solid Melts into Air: The Experience of Modernity*. New York: Simon and Schuster, 1982.

Berrios-Miranda, Marisol. "The Significance of Salsa Music to National and Pan-Latino Identity." PhD dissertation, University of California, Berkeley, 1999.

Bérubé, Myriam. "Colombia: In the Crossfire." *Migration Policy Institute* (blog), November 1, 2005. https://www.migrationpolicy.org/article/colombia-crossfire.

Beverley, John. *Latinamericanism after 9/11*. Durham, NC: Duke University Press, 2011.

————. *Subalternity and Representation: Arguments in Cultural Theory.* Durham, NC: Duke University Press, 1999.

Beverley, John, Michael Aronna, and José Oviedo, eds. *The Postmodernism Debate in Latin America.* Durham, NC: Duke University Press, 1995.

Bhabha, Homi K. *The Location of Culture.* London: Routledge, 1994.

Bisbal, Marcelino. "Medios y cultura en la integración Colombo-Venezolana." *Cuaderno Venezolano de Sociología* 14, no. 3 (2005): 429–37.

Blades, Rubén. "Interview with Enrique Fernandez." *Musician*, 1986.

Bloechl, Olivia Ashley, Melanie Diane Lowe, and Jeffrey Kallberg, eds. "Introduction." In *Rethinking Difference in Music Scholarship.* New York: Cambridge University Press, 2015.

Blumenfeld, Larry. "NYC Pianist Arturo O'Farrill Finds Himself in Cuba, and Brings His Father Home." *The Village Voice*, February 23, 2011. http://www.villagevoice.com/music/nyc-pianist-arturo-ofarrill-finds-himself-in-cuba-and-brings-his-father-home-6430123.

Blumenthal, Ralph. "Director Leaves Jazz at Lincoln Center." *New York Times.* December 16, 2000. http://www.nytimes.com/2000/12/16/arts/director-leaves-jazz-at-lincoln-center.html.

Boal, Augusto. *Teatro del oprimido y otras poéticas políticas.* Buenos Aires: Ediciones de la Flor, 1974.

Bohlman, Philip. *Jewish Music and Modernity.* Oxford: Oxford University Press, 2008.

Bolívar, Simón. "Bolívar, Jamaica Letter." In *El Libertador: Writings of Simón Bolívar*, edited by David Bushnell. New York: Oxford University Press, 1998.

Borge, Jason. *Tropical Riffs: Latin America and the Politics of Jazz.* Durham, NC: Duke University Press, 2018.

Borges, Edgar. *Vínculos: Apuntes con Rubén Blades.* Pamplona: Leer-e, 2014.

Borges, Jorge Luis. "The Argentine Writer and Tradition (1956)." In *Selected Non-Fictions*, edited by Eliot Weinberger, translated by Esther Allen. London: Penguin Books, 1999.

Bosteels, Bruno. *Badiou and Politics.* Durham, NC: Duke University Press, 2011.

Bourdieu, Pierre. *Distinction: A Social Critique of the Judgement of Taste.* Cambridge, MA: Harvard University Press, 1979.

————. "Outline of a Sociological Theory of Art Perception." *International Social Science Journal* 20, no. 4 (1968): 589–612.

Brackett, David. "Black or White? Michael Jackson and the Idea of Crossover." *Popular Music and Society* 35, no. 2 (2012): 169–85.

————. *Categorizing Sound: Genre and Twentieth-Century Popular Music.* Berkeley: University of California Press, 2016.

————. "Musical Meaning: Genres, Categories and Crossover." In *Popular Music Studies*, edited by David Hesmondhalgh and Keith Negus, 65–83. London: Arnold, 2002.

————. "The Politics and Practice of 'Crossover' in American Popular Music, 1963–65." *The Musical Quarterly* 78, no. 4 (1994): 774–97.

Brecht, Bertolt. "Against Georg Lukács." In *Aesthetics and Politics*, edited by Ronald Taylor, translated by Stuart Hood. London: Verso, 2007.

————. *On Theatre: The Development of an Aesthetic.* Translated by John Willett. New York: Hill and Wang, 1964.

————. *Werke: Grosse kommentierte Berliner und Frankfurter Ausgabe.* Edited by Werner Hecht. Vol. 21. Berlin: Suhrkamp, 1992.

Brennan, Timothy. *At Home in the World: Cosmopolitanism Now.* Cambridge, MA: Harvard University Press, 1997.

————. *Secular Devotion: Afro-Latin Music and Imperial Jazz.* London: Verso, 2008.

Brooks, Daphne A. *Bodies in Dissent: Spectacular Performances of Race and Freedom, 1850–1910.* Durham, NC: Duke University Press, 2006.

Brossard, Sébastien de. *Dictionnaire de musique,* s.v. "Syncope." Paris: Christophe Ballard, 1702.

Brown, Lee B. "Marsalis and Baraka: An Essay in Comparative Cultural Discourse." *Popular Music* 23, no. 3 (2004): 241–55.

Brown, Robin. "Americanization at Its Best? The Globalization of Jazz." In *Resounding International Relations: On Music, Culture, and Politics,* 89–109. New York: Palgrave Macmillan, 2005.

Bruce, La Marr Jurelle. "Interludes in Madtime: Black Music, Madness, and Metaphysical Syncopation." *Social Text* 35, no. 4 (2017): 1–31.

Bruce-Novoa, Juan. *RetroSpace: Collected Essays on Chicano Literature.* Houston: Arte Público, 1990.

Bruckner, D. J. R. "Stage: 'Pedro Navaja.'" *New York Times,* August 8, 1986, sec. Theater. https://www.nytimes.com/1986/08/08/theater/stage-pedro-navaja.html.

Brunner, José Joaquín. "América Latina en la encrucijada de la modernidad." *FLACSO* 22 (April 1992): 1–36.

————. "Notes on Modernity and Postmodernity in Latin American Culture." *Boundary 2* 20, no. 3 (Autumn 1993): 34–51.

Buck-Morss, Susan. *Hegel, Haiti, and Universal History.* Pittsburgh: University of Pittsburgh Press, 2009.

Buenaventura, Enrique. "De Stanislavski a Brecht." *Mito* 4, no. 21 (1958).

Busby, Cecilia. "Permeable and Partible Persons: A Comparative Analysis of Gender and Body in India and Melanesia." *Journal of the Royal Anthropological Institute* 3, no. 2 (1997): 261–78.

Bushnell, David, and Neill Macauly. *The Emergence of Latin America in the Nineteenth Century.* 2nd ed. New York: Oxford University Press, 1994.

Butler, Judith, Ernesto Laclau, and Slavoj Žižek. "Questions." In *Contingency, Hegemony, Universality: Contemporary Dialogues on the Left.* London: Verso, 2000.

Calderón, Fernando, Martín Hopenhayn, and Ernesto Ottone. *Esa esquiva modernidad: Desarrollo, ciudadanía y cultura en América Latina y el Caribe.* Caracas: Editorial Nueva Sociedad, 1996.

Calhoun, Craig. "The Class Consciousness of Frequent Travelers: Toward a Critique of Actually Existing Cosmopolitanism." *South Atlantic Quarterly* 101, no. 4 (October 1, 2002): 869–97.

Călinescu, Matei. *Five Faces of Modernity: Modernism, Avant-Garde, Decadence, Kitsch, Postmodernism.* Durham, NC: Duke University Press, 1987.

Campa, Román de la. *Latin Americanism.* Minneapolis: University of Minnesota Press, 1999.

Campbell, Timothy. "Translator's Introduction: Bíos, Immunity, Life: The Thought of Roberto Esposito." In *Bíos: Biopolitics and Philosophy*, translated by Timothy Campbell. Minneapolis: University of Minnesota Press, 2008.

Cantor, Judy. "Ruben Blades: *Mundo* 'Sony International.'" *Miami New Times*. October 10, 2002.

Carpentier, Alejo. *La música de Cuba*. Mexico City: Fondo de Cultura Económica, 1946.

Carter, Paul. "Ambiguous Traces: Mishearing and Auditory Space." Australian Sound Design Project. Accessed June 8, 2019. http://www.sounddesign.unimelb.edu.au/site/papers/mishearing.html [inactive link].

Carvalho, José Jorge de. "O olhar etnográfico e a voz subalterna." *Horizontes Antropológicos* 7, no. 15 (July 2001): 107–47.

Casanova, Pascale. *The World Republic of Letters*. Cambridge, MA: Harvard University Press, 2004.

Casillas, Dolores Ines. *Sounds of Belonging: U.S. Spanish-Language Radio and Public Advocacy*. New York: New York University Press, 2014.

Celis Albán, Francisco. "Blades: 'No me pidan que apoye a este lado o al otro.'" *El Tiempo*, January 20, 2011. http://www.eltiempo.com/archivo/documento/CMS-8792014.

Cepeda, María Elena. *Musical ImagiNation: U.S.-Colombian Identity and the Latin Music Boom*. New York: New York University Press, 2010.

———. "Shakira as the Idealized, Transnational Citizen: A Case Study of Colombianidad in Transition." *Latino Studies* 1, no. 2 (2003): 210–32.

———. "When Latina Hips Make/Mark History: Music Video in the 'New' American Studies." *Women & Performance* 18, no. 3 (November 2008): 235–52.

Chakrabarty, Dipesh. *Provincializing Europe: Postcolonial Thought and Historical Difference*. Princeton, NJ: Princeton University Press, 2000.

Chambers, Iain. "Signs of Silence, Lines of Listening." In *The Post-Colonial Question: Common Skies, Divided Horizons*, edited by Iain Chambers and Lidia Curti. New York: Routledge, 1996.

Charski, Mindy. "Pepsi Gets a Latino 'Movement.'" *Adweek*, July 29, 2002. https://www.adweek.com/brand-marketing/pepsi-gets-latino-movement-57891/.

Chatterjee, Partha. *Our Modernity*. Rotterdam and Dakar: SEPHIS-CODESRIA, 1997.

Chino, Jorge. "Rubén Blades: La vanguardia musical de fin de siglo." *El Andar*, 1999.

Clément, Catherine. *Syncope: The Philosophy of Rapture*. Translated by Sally O'Driscoll and Deirdre M. Mahoney. Minneapolis: University of Minnesota Press, 1994.

Cobo, Leila. "Epic's Shakira 'Serves' a Bilingual Album. (Cover Story)." *Billboard*, November 10, 2001.

———. "Latin Acts Expand Presence at Arenas. (Cover Story)." *Billboard*, October 19, 2002.

———. "Latin Acts Tread Carefully With Crossover Bids." *Billboard*, January 24, 2004.

———. "Shakira X2." *Billboard*, May 28, 2005.

Connolly, William E. *Identity/Difference: Democratic Negotiations of Political Paradox*. Ithaca, NY: Cornell University Press, 1991.

Connor, Steven. "Edison's Teeth: Touching Hearing." In *Hearing Cultures: Essays on Sound, Listening and Modernity*, edited by Veit Erlmann, 153–72. New York: Berg, 2004.

Cornejo Polar, Antonio. "Mestizaje e hibridez: Los riesgos de las metáforas." *Revista de Crítica Literaria Latinoamericana* 24, no. 47 (1998): 7–11.

Corti, Berenice. *Jazz Argentino: La música "negra" del país "blanco."* Buenos Aires: Gourmet Musical, 2015.

Cowell, Henry. "Music." *The Americana Annual* [1929]: 501.

Crouch, Stanley. *The All-American Skin Game, or The Decoy of Race.* New York: Pantheon Books, 1994.

Cruz, Bárbara. *Rubén Blades: Salsa Singer and Social Activist.* Berkeley Heights, NJ: Enslow Publishers, 1997.

Curet Alonso, Catalino. "Memoirs of a Life in Salsa." In *Situating Salsa: Global Markets and Local Meaning in Latin Popular Music*, translated by Lise Waxer, 187–200. New York: Routledge, 2002.

D'Addario, Fernando. "El trio Éditus, de Costa Rica: Raíces universales." *Pagina 12.* Accessed November 12, 2019. https://www.pagina12.com.ar/2001/01-10/01 -10-07/PAG35.HTM.

Dance, Helen. "Chico O'Farrill: The Well-Rounded Writer." *DownBeat*, February 23, 1967.

Darío, Rubén. *Viajes de un cosmopolita extremo.* Edited by Graciela Montaldo. Mexico City: Fondo de Cultura Económica, 2013.

Dávila, Arlene M. *Culture Works: Space, Value, and Mobility across the Neoliberal Americas.* New York: New York University Press, 2012.

———. *El Mall: The Spatial and Class Politics of Shopping Malls in Latin America.* Berkeley: University of California Press, 2016.

———. *Latinos, Inc.: The Marketing and Making of a People.* Berkeley: University of California Press, 2001.

———. *Sponsored Identities: Cultural Politics in Puerto Rico.* Philadelphia: Temple University Press, 1997.

Day, Sherri. "Pepsi and Sony Are Partners in a Cross-Promotional Campaign for Soft Drinks and Music." *New York Times*, November 12, 2002, sec. Business Day. https://www.nytimes.com/2002/11/12/business/media-business-advertising -pepsi-sony-are-partners-cross-promotional-campaign.html.

De Toro, Fernando. *Brecht en el teatro Hispanoamericano.* Ottawa: Girol Books, 1984.

Degiovanni, Fernando. *Vernacular Latin Americanisms: War, the Market, and the Making of a Discipline.* Pittsburgh: University of Pittsburgh Press, 2018.

DeLanda, Manuel. *Assemblage Theory.* Edinburgh: Edinburgh University Press, 2016.

———. *A New Philosophy of Society: Assemblage Theory and Social Complexity.* London: Continuum, 2006.

Delannoy, Luc. *Caliente! Una historia del jazz latino.* Mexico City: Fondo de Cultura Económica, 2001.

———. *Carambola. Vidas en el jazz latino.* Mexico City: Fondo de Cultura Económica, 2005.

———. *Convergencias.* Mexico City: Fondo de Cultura Económica, 2012.

Delanty, Gerard. "The Cosmopolitan Imagination: Critical Cosmopolitanism and Social Theory." *British Journal of Sociology* 57, no. 1 (2006): 25–47.

Deleuze, Gilles. *Difference and Repetition*. Translated by Paul Patton. New York: Columbia University Press, 1995.

———. "Postscript on the Societies of Control." *October* 59 (1992): 3–7.

Deleuze, Gilles, and Félix Guattari. *Kafka: Toward a Minor Literature*. Minneapolis: University of Minnesota Press, 2003.

Denning, Michael. *The Cultural Front: The Laboring of American Culture in the Twentieth Century*. New York: Verso, 1998.

———. *Noise Uprising: The Audiopolitics of a World Musical Revolution*. New York: Verso, 2015.

Derbez, Alain. *El jazz en México*. Mexico City: Fondo de Cultura Económica, 2001.

Derrida, Jacques. *Archive Fever: A Freudian Impression*. Chicago: University of Chicago Press, 1996.

———. *Specters of Marx: The State of the Debt, the Work of Mourning, and the New International*. Translated by Peggy Kamuf. New York: Routledge, 1994.

Derrida, Jacques, and Anne Dufourmantelle. *Of Hospitality: Anne Dufourmantelle Invites Jacques Derrida to Respond*. Translated by Rachel Bowlby. Palo Alto, CA: Stanford University Press, 2000.

DeVeaux, Scott. *The Birth of Bebop: A Social and Musical History*. Berkeley: University of California Press, 1997.

———. "Constructing the Jazz Tradition." *Black American Literature Forum* 25, no. 3 (1991): 525–60.

Díaz-Quiñones, Arcadio. *La memoria rota: Ensayos sobre cultura y política*. 1st ed. San Juan: Ediciones Huracán, 1993.

———. "Puerto Rico y las lenguas de su soledad." In *Ciudadano insano: y otros ensayos bestiales sobre cultura y literatura*, edited by Juan Duchesne Winter, 1st ed., 39–48. San Juan: Ediciones Callejón, 2001.

Didi-Huberman, Georges. *Confronting Images: Questioning the Ends of a Certain History of Art*. University Park: Pennsylvania State University Press, 2005.

———. *Images in Spite of All: Four Photographs from Auschwitz*. Chicago: University of Chicago Press, 2008.

Dominguez, Daniel. "Las mujeres que formaron a Rubén Blades." *La Prensa*, November 11, 2016. https://impresa.prensa.com/vivir/mujeres-formaron-Blades _0_4618038235.html.

Dominguez, Pier. "Was There Ever an Authentic Shakira? A Look at Her Controversial Crossover." *Remezcla*, October 12, 2016. https://remezcla.com/features/music/shakira-crossover/.

Dox, Donnalee. "Dancing Around Orientalism." *TDR: The Drama Review* 50, no. 4 (December 5, 2006): 52–71.

Draper, Susana. *Afterlives of Confinement: Spatial Transitions in Postdictatorship Latin America*. Pittsburgh: University of Pittsburgh Press, 2012.

Du Bois, W. E. B. *The Souls of Black Folk*. New York: Dover, 1994.

Duany, Jorge. *Blurred Borders: Transnational Migration between the Hispanic Caribbean and the United States*. Chapel Hill: University of North Carolina Press, 2011.

———. *La nación en vaivén: Identidad, migración y cultura popular en Puerto Rico*. San Juan: Ediciones Callejón, 2010.

———. "Popular Music in Puerto Rico: Toward an Anthropology of Salsa." *Latin American Music Review* 5, no. 2 (1984): 186–216.

Duerden, Nick. "The Sexiest Woman in Music Today: Shakira." *Blender*, March 2003.

Dussel, Enrique. "Eurocentrism and Modernity." *Boundary* 2, no. 20 (1993): 64–74.

———. *The Invention of the Americas: Eclipse of "the Other" and the Myth of Modernity*. New York: Continuum, 1995.

Early, Gerald, and Ingrid Monson. "Why Jazz Still Matters." *Daedalus* 148, no. 2 (March 21, 2019): 5–12.

Egan, Linda. *Carlos Monsiváis: Cultura and Chronicle in Contemporary México*. Tucson: University of Arizona Press, 2004.

"El espejo de los otros: ¿Qué piensan algunos famosos de la colombiana?" *Semana*, March 9, 2001. https://www.semana.com/el-espejo-otros-que-piensan-algunos-famosos-colombiana/48533-3/.

Erlmann, Veit. "The Aesthetics of the Global Imagination: Reflections on World Music in the 1990s." *Public Culture* 8, no. 3 (1996): 467–89.

———. "Communities of Style: Musical Figures of Black Diasporic Identity." In *The African Diaspora: A Musical Perspective*, edited by Ingrid Monson, 83–100. New York: Routledge, 2000.

———. *Hearing Cultures: Essays on Sound, Listening, and Modernity*. Oxford: Berg, 2004.

———. *Music, Modernity, and the Global Imagination: South Africa and the West*. New York: Oxford University Press, 1999.

Escobar, Arturo. *Territories of Difference: Place, Movements, Life, Redes*. Durham, NC: Duke University Press, 2008.

Espinoza Agurto, Andres. "Una Sola Casa: Salsa Consciente and the Poetics of the Meta-Barrio." PhD dissertation, Boston University, 2014. http://undefined/docview/1556761003/abstract/E36F4270BD5B4BD3PQ/1.

Esposito, Roberto. *Communitas: The Origin and Destiny of Community*. Translated by Timothy Campbell. Palo Alto, CA: Stanford University Press, 2010.

Fabian, Johannes. *Time and the Other: How Anthropology Makes Its Object*. New York: Columbia University Press, 1983.

Fairley, Jan. "The 'Local' and 'Global' in Popular Music." In *The Cambridge Companion to Pop and Rock*, edited by Simon Frith, Will Straw, and John Street, 272–89. New York: Cambridge University Press, 2001.

Feld, Steven. *Jazz Cosmopolitanism in Accra: Five Musical Years in Ghana*. Durham, NC: Duke University Press, 2012.

———. "A Sweet Lullaby for World Music." *Public Culture* 12, no. 1 (2000): 145–71.

Feres Júnior, João. *Histoire du concept d'Amérique latine aux Etats-Unis*. Translated by Yves Gounot. Paris: L'Harmattan, 2010.

Ferguson, James. *Expectations of Modernity Myths and Meanings of Urban Life on the Zambian Copperbelt*. Berkeley: University of California Press, 1999.

———. *Global Shadows: Africa in the Neoliberal World Order*. Durham, NC: Duke University Press, 2006.

Fernández Moya, Rafael, and Annette Leahy. "The Irish Presence in the History and Place Names of Cuba." *Irish Migration Studies in Latin America* 5, no. 3 (2007): 189–97.

Fernández Retamar, Roberto. "Caliban: Notes towards a Discussion of Culture in Our America." *The Massachusetts Review* 15, no. 1–2 (Winter–Spring 1974): 7–72.

———. "Modernismo, noventiocho, subdesarrollo." In *Para el perfil definitivo del hombre*, 207–18. Havana: Editorial Letras Cubanas, 1981.

Fields, Karen E., and Barbara J. Fields. *Racecraft: The Soul of Inequality in American Life*. New York: Verso Books, 2012.

Fiol-Matta, Licia. *The Great Woman Singer: Gender and Voice in Puerto Rican Music*. Durham, NC: Duke University Press, 2017.

———. "Pop Latinidad: Puerto Ricans in the Latin Explosion, 1999." *Centro Journal* 14, no. 1 (2002): 26.

Firmat, Gustavo Pérez. "Latunes: An Introduction." *Latin American Research Review* 43, no. 2 (2008): 180–203.

———. "Salsa for All Seasons." In *Life on the Hyphen: The Cuban-American Way*, 95–125. Austin: University of Texas Press, 2012.

Fischer, Sibylle. *Modernity Disavowed: Haiti and the Cultures of Slavery in the Age of Revolution*. Durham, NC: Duke University Press, 2004.

Flores, Juan. *The Diaspora Strikes Back: Caribeño Tales of Learning and Turning*. New York: Routledge, 2009.

———. *Divided Borders: Essays on Puerto Rican Identity*. Houston: Arte Público Press, 1993.

———. *From Bomba to Hip-Hop: Puerto Rican Culture and Latino Identity*. New York: Columbia University Press, 2000.

Flores, Juan, and George Yúdice. "Living Borders/Buscando America: Languages of Latino Self-Formation." *Social Text*, no. 24 (1990): 57–84.

Floyd, Samuel A., and Ronald Radano. "Interpreting the African-American Musical Past: A Dialogue." *Black Music Research Journal* 29, no. 1 (2009): 1–10.

Fojas, Camilla. *Cosmopolitanism in the Americas*. West Lafayette, IN: Purdue University Press, 2005.

Fonseca-Wollheim, Corinna da. "America's Musical Ambassadors." *Wall Street Journal*, June 17, 2010, sec. Life and Style. https://www.wsj.com/articles/SB1 0001424052748704324304575306603221333096.

Foster Steward, Noel. *Las expresiones musicales en Panamá. Una aproximación*. Panama City: Editorial Universitaria, 1997.

Foucault, Michel. *Discipline and Punish: The Birth of the Prison*. Translated by Alan Sheridan. New York: Vintage, 1979.

———. *The Government of Self and Others: Lectures at the Collège de France 1982–1983*. Edited by Frédéric Gros, Francois Ewald, and Alessandro Fontana. Translated by Graham Burchell. London: Palgrave Macmillan UK, 2010.

———. *The Order of Things: An Archaeology of the Human Sciences*. New York: Pantheon Books, 1971.

———. "What Is an Author?" In *Language, Counter-Memory, Practice*, edited by Donald F. Bouchard, translated by Donald F. Bouchard and Sherry Simon, 124–27. Ithaca, NY: Cornell University Press, 1977.

———. "What Is Enlightenment?" In *The Foucault Reader*, edited by Paul Rabinow. New York: Pantheon Books, 1984.

Franco, Jean. *The Decline and Fall of the Lettered City: Latin America in the Cold War*. Cambridge, MA: Harvard University Press, 2002.

———. "Latin American Intellectuals and Collective Identity." *Social Identities* 3, no. 2 (1997): 265–74.

———. *The Modern Culture of Latin America: Society and the Artist.* New York: F. A. Praeger, 1967.

Frith, Simon. *Sound Effects: Youth, Leisure, and the Politics of Rock.* London: Constable, 1983.

Frye, Northrop. *Anatomy of Criticism: Four Essays.* Princeton, NJ: Princeton University Press, 1957.

Gabbard, Krin. "Ken Burns's 'Jazz': Beautiful Music, but Missing a Beat." *Chronicle of Higher Education,* December 15, 2000. https://www.chronicle.com/article/Ken-Burnss-Jazz-Beautiful/2632.

Gallardo, Camila. "Entrevista Grupo Éditus." n.d.

Gaonkar, Dilip Parameshwar. "On Alternative Modernities." In *Alternative Modernities,* edited by Dilip Parameshwar Gaonkar, 1–23. Durham, NC: Duke University Press, 2001.

Gaonkar, Dilip Parameshwar, and Elizabeth A. Povinelli. "Technologies of Public Forms: Circulation, Transfiguration, Recognition." *Public Culture* 15, no. 3 (2003): 385–98.

García Canclini, Néstor. "Anthropology: Eight Approaches to Latin Americanism," *Journal of Latin American Studies* 11, no. 3 (2002): 265–78.

———. "Cultural Reconversion." In *On Edge: The Crisis of Contemporary Latin American Culture,* edited by George Yúdice, Juan Flores, and Jean Franco, 29–44. Minneapolis: University of Minnesota Press, 1992.

———. *Culturas híbridas: Estrategias para entrar y salir de la modernidad.* Mexico: Grijalbo, 1990.

———. *Diferentes, desiguales y desconectados: Mapas de la interculturalidad.* Barcelona: Gedisa, 2004.

———. *Hybrid Cultures: Strategies for Entering and Leaving Modernity.* Translated by Christopher L. Chiappari and Silvia L. Lopez. Minneapolis: University of Minnesota Press, 1995.

———. *Latinoamericanos buscando lugar en este siglo.* Buenos Aires: Editorial Paidos, 2002.

———. "Noticias Recientes Sobre Hibridación." *TRANS-Revista Transcultural de Música* 7 (2003). https://www.sibetrans.com/trans/articulo/209/noticias-recientes-sobre-la-hibridacion.

———. "The State of War and the State of Hybridization." In *Without Guarantees: In Honour of Stuart Hall,* edited by Paul Gilroy, Lawrence Grossberg, and Angela McRobbie, 38–52. London: Verso, 2000.

García, Cindy. *Salsa Crossings: Dancing Latinidad in Los Angeles.* Durham, NC: Duke University Press, 2013.

Garcia, David. *Liner Notes for Siembra, by Rubén Blades.* New York: Fania Records, 1978.

García, David F. *Arsenio Rodríguez and the Transnational Flows of Latin Popular Music.* Philadelphia: Temple University Press, 2006.

García, Luis Ignacio. "Brecht y América Latina: Modelos de refuncionalización." *A Contracorriente: A Journal on Social History and Literature in Latin America,* 2012.

García Liendo, Javier. *El intelectual y la cultura de masas: Argumentos latinoameri-*

canos en torno a Ángel Rama y José María Arguedas. West Lafayette, IN: Purdue University Press, 2016.

Garofalo, Reebee. "Black Popular Music: Crossing Over or Going Under." In *Rock and Popular Music: Politics, Policies, Institutions*, edited by Tony Bennett, Simon Frith, Lawrence Grossberg, John Shepherd, and Graeme Turner, 229–48. New York: Routledge, 1993.

———. "Crossing Over: 1939–1989." In *Split Images: African Americans in the Mass Media*, edited by Jannette L. Dates and William Barlow, 57–121. Washington, DC: Howard University Press, 1990.

Garramuño, Florencia. *Primitive Modernities: Tango, Samba, and Nation*. Translated by Anna Kazumi Stahl. Palo Alto, CA: Stanford University Press, 2011.

Garrett, Charles Hiroshi. *Struggling to Define a Nation: American Music and the Twentieth Century*. Berkeley: University of California Press, 2008.

Garsd, Jasmine. "Calle 13, on Being Loved and Hated in Latin America." NPR, March 9, 2020. https://www.npr.org/2014/04/05/299180900/calle-13-on -being-loved-and-hated-in-latin-america.

Gebhardt, Nicholas. *Going for Jazz: Musical Practices and American Ideologies*. Chicago: University of Chicago Press, 2001.

Gennari, John. *Blowin' Hot and Cool: Jazz and Its Critics*. Chicago: University of Chicago Press, 2006.

George, Nelson. "The Rhythm & The Blues." *Billboard*, August 31, 1985.

Giddens, Anthony. *Modernity and Self-Identity: Self and Society in the Late Modern Age*. Cambridge: Polity Press, 1991.

Gilroy, Paul. *The Black Atlantic: Modernity and Double Consciousness*. Cambridge, MA: Harvard University Press, 1993.

———. *Darker Than Blue: On the Moral Economies of Black Atlantic Culture*. Cambridge, MA: The Belknap Press of Harvard University Press, 2010.

———. *"There Ain't No Black in the Union Jack": The Cultural Politics of Race and Nation*. Chicago: University of Chicago Press, 1991.

Gitelman, Lisa. *Scripts, Grooves, and Writing Machines: Representing Technology in the Edison Era*. Palo Alto, CA: Stanford University Press, 1999.

Glasser, Ruth. *My Music Is My Flag: Puerto Rican Musicians and Their New York Communities, 1917–1940*. Berkeley: University of California Press, 1995.

Glissant, Edouard. *Caribbean Discourse: Selected Essays*. Translated by Michael Dash. Charlottesville: University Press of Virginia, 1989.

Gomart, Emilie, and Antoine Hennion. "A Sociology of Attachment: Music, Amateurs, Drug Users." In *Actor Network Theory and After*, edited by John Law and John Hassard, 220–47. Malden, MA: Blackwell Publishing, 1999.

González, Aníbal. *A Companion to Spanish American Modernismo*. Woodbridge, UK: Tamesis, 2007.

———. *La Crónica modernista hispanoamericana*. Madrid: José Porrúa Turanzas, 1983.

González Echevarría, Roberto. *La ruta de Severo Sarduy*. Hanover, NH: Ediciones del Norte, 1987.

González Henríquez, Adolfo. "Música popular e identidad en Barranquilla, 1940–2000. De la cultura tropical a la identidad global." In *Música popular e identidad en Barranquilla, 1940–2000*, 114–31. Bogotá: Editorial Universidad del Rosario, 2009.

Gray, Herman. *Cultural Moves: African Americans and the Politics of Representation.* Berkeley: University of California Press, 2005.

———. "Prefiguring a Black Cultural Formation: The New Conditions of Black Cultural Production." In *Between Law and Culture: Relocating Legal Studies,* edited by Lisa C. Bower, David Theo Goldberg, and Michael C. Musheno, 74–94. Minneapolis: University of Minnesota Press, 2001.

Griffin, Farah Jasmine. *"Who Set You Flowin'?": The African-American Migration Narrative.* Oxford: Oxford University Press, 1995.

Grogan, Siobhan. "Don't Be Fooled by the Pictures." *The Guardian,* December 2, 2002, sec. Music. https://www.theguardian.com/music/2002/dec/02/artsfeatures.popandrock.

Grosfoguel, Ramón. "Global Logics in the Caribbean City System: The Case of Miami." In *World Cities in a World-System,* edited by Paul L. Knox and Peter J. Taylor, 156–70. Cambridge: Cambridge University Press, 1995.

Grossberg, Lawrence. *Cultural Studies in the Future Tense.* Durham, NC: Duke University Press, 2011.

———. "Identity and Cultural Studies: Is That All There Is?" In *Questions of Cultural Identity,* edited by Stuart Hall and Paul du Gay, 87–107. London: Sage, 1996.

Grosz, Elizabeth. *In the Nick of Time: Politics, Evolution, and the Untimely.* Durham, NC: Duke University Press, 2004.

Guerra, François-Xavier. *Modernidad e independencias: Ensayos sobre las revoluciones hispánicas.* Madrid: Editorial MAPFRE, 1992.

Guerra Vilaboy, Sergio, and Alejo Maldonado Gallardo. *Los laberintos de la integración latinoamericana: Historia, mito y realidad de una utopía.* Morelia, México: Facultad de Historia de la Universidad Michoacana de San Nicolás de Hidalgo, 2002.

Guridy, Frank Andre. *Forging Diaspora: Afro-Cubans and African Americans in a World of Empire and Jim Crow.* Chapel Hill: University of North Carolina Press, 2010.

Gutkin, David. "The Modernities of H. Lawrence Freeman." *Journal of the American Musicological Society* 72, no. 3 (December 1, 2019): 719–79.

Guzmán, Marcos Billy. "Regala dos años de jazz." Archivo Digital *El Nuevo Día,* January 5, 2011. http://www.adendi.com/archivo.asp?Xnum=856460&year=2011&mon=1&keyword=caravana%20cultural [inactive link].

Habermas, Jürgen, and Seyla Ben-Habib. "Modernity—An Incomplete Project." In *Postmodern Culture,* edited by Hal Foster, 3–15. London: Pluto Press, 1985.

Hall, Stuart. "Conclusion: The Multi-Cultural Question." In *Un/Settled Multiculturalism: Diasporas, Entanglements, "Transruptions,"* edited by Barnor Hesse, 209–41. London: Zed Books, 2000.

———. "Cultural Identity and Diaspora." In *Identity: Community, Culture, Difference,* edited by Jonathan Rutherford, 222–37. London: Lawrence and Wishart, 1990.

———. "The Local and the Global: Globalization and Ethnicity." In *Culture, Globalization and the World-System: Contemporary Conditions for the Representation of Identity,* edited by Anthony D. King, 19–39. Minneapolis: University of Minnesota Press, 1997.

———. "Old and New Identities, Old and New Ethnicities." In *Culture, Global-ization and the World-System: Contemporary Conditions for the Representation of Identity*, edited by Anthony D. King, 41–68. Minneapolis: University of Minnesota Press, 1997.

———. "What Is This 'Black' in Black Popular Culture?" In *Stuart Hall: Critical Dialogues in Cultural Studies*, 465–75. London: Routledge, 1996.

Hallward, Peter. *Absolutely Postcolonial: Writing Between the Singular and the Specific*. Manchester, UK: Manchester University Press, 2001.

———. *Badiou: A Subject to Truth*. Minneapolis: University of Minnesota Press, 2003.

———. "The Universal and the Transcendental." In *Absolutely Postcolonial: Writing between the Singular and the Specific*, 179–82. Manchester, UK: Manchester University Press, 2001.

Hallward, Peter, ed. "Introduction: Consequences of Abstraction." In *Think Again: Alain Badiou and the Future of Philosophy*. New York: Continuum, 2004.

Hamill, Peter. "Hey, It's Rubén Blades: A Latin Star Makes His Move." *New York*, August 19, 1985.

Hanchard, Michael. "Afro-Modernity: Temporality, Politics, and the African Diaspora." In *Alternative Modernities*, edited by Dilip Parameshwar Gaonkar, 272–98. Durham, NC: Duke University Press, 1999.

Hardt, Michael, and Antonio Negri. *Empire*. Cambridge, MA: Harvard University Press, 2000.

Harootunian, Harry. *History's Disquiet: Modernity, Cultural Practice, and the Question of Everyday Life*. New York: Columbia University Press, 2000.

———. "Some Thoughts on Comparability and the Space-Time Problem." *Boundary 2* 32, no. 2 (2005): 23–52.

Harris, Jerome. "Jazz on the Global Stage." In *The African Diaspora: A Musical Perspective*, edited by Ingrid Monson, 103–34. London: Routledge, 2003.

Hartman, Geoffrey. "Criticism and Restitution." *Tikkun* 4, no. 1 (1989).

Harvey, David. *A Brief History of Neoliberalism*. New York: Oxford University Press, 2005.

Hegel, Georg Wilhelm Friedrich. *Philosophy of History*. Translated by J. Sibree. Buffalo, NY: Prometheus Books, 1991.

Heidegger, Martin. "The Thing." In *Poetry, Language, Thought*, translated by Albert Hofstader. New York: Harper & Row, 1971.

Helmreich, Stefan. *Sounding the Limits of Life: Essays in the Anthropology of Biology and Beyond*. Princeton, NJ: Princeton University Press, 2016.

Hennion, Antoine. "Loving Music: From a Sociology of Mediation to a Pragmatics of Taste." *Comunicar* 17, no. 34 (2010): 25–33.

Herlinghaus, Hermann. *Renarración y descentramiento: Mapas alternativos de la imaginación en América Latina*. Madrid: Iberoamericana, 2004.

Herlinghaus, Hermann, and Mabel Moraña. *Fronteras de la modernidad en América Latina*. Instituto Internacional de Literatura Latinoamericana. Pittsburgh: University of Pittsburgh Press, 2003.

Herlinghaus, Hermann, and Monika Walter, eds. *Posmodernidad en la periferia: Enfoques latinoamericanos de la nueva teoría cultural*. Berlin: Langer Verlag, 1994.

Herrera, Brian Eugenio. "Latin Explosion: Latinos, Racial Formation and Twentieth Century U.S. Popular Performance." PhD dissertation, Yale University, 2008.

Hess, Amanda. "What Happens When People and Brands Are Just Brands?" *The New York Times Magazine*, May 1, 2018. https://www.nytimes.com/2018/05/01/magazine/what-happens-when-people -and-companies-are-both-just-brands.html.

Hess, Carol A. *Representing the Good Neighbor: Music, Difference, and the Pan American Dream*. New York: Oxford University Press, 2013.

"'Hits' Don't Lie; Shakira's *Oral Fixation Vol. 2* Storms Back into the Top Ten as Album Goes Platinum." *Business Wire*, April 5, 2006.

Hobsbawm, Eric, and Terence Ranger, eds. *The Invention of Tradition*. Cambridge: Cambridge University Press, 1983.

Hoggart, Richard. *The Uses of Literacy*. London: Penguin, 1972.

Holbraad, Martin. "Turning a Corner: Preamble for 'The Relative Native' by Eduardo Viveiros de Castro." *HAU: Journal of Ethnographic Theory* 3, no. 3 (2013): 469–71.

Holmberg, Arthur, and Carlos Solorzano. *World Encyclopedia of Contemporary Theatre: Volume 2: The Americas*. New York: Routledge, 2014.

Holston, Mark. "Miguel Zenón: *Jíbaro*." *Jazziz*, August 2005. 194446261. Music Periodicals Database.

———. "Razor Blades." *Hispanic*, February 2000.

Honig, Bonnie. *Democracy and the Foreigner*. Princeton, NJ: Princeton University Press, 2001.

Hopenhayn, Martin. *No Apocalypse, No Integration: Modernism and Postmodernism in Latin America*. Translated by Cynthia M. Hopkins and Elizabeth Rosa Horan. Durham, NC: Duke University Press, 2002.

Hull, Tom. "*Jíbaro*." *The Village Voice*, 2006.

Hutchinson, Sydney, ed. *Salsa World: A Global Dance in Local Contexts*. Philadelphia: Temple University Press, 2014.

Inda, Jonathan Xavier. "Analytics of the Modern: An Introduction." In *Anthropologies of Modernity: Foucault, Governmentality, and Life Politics*. New York: John Wiley & Sons, 2008.

Iverson, Ethan. "Young Lions of the 1980s." *Do the Math*. Accessed July 27, 2015. http://dothemath.typepad.com/dtm/1-young-lion-jazz-of-the-1980s.html [inactive link].

Jackson, Travis A. "Culture, Commodity, Palimpsest: Locating Jazz in the World." In *Jazz Worlds/World Jazz*, edited by Philip V. Bohlman and Goffredo Plastino, 381–401. Chicago: University of Chicago Press, 2016.

Jameson, Fredric. "The End of Temporality." *Critical Inquiry* 29, no. 4 (2003): 695–718.

———. *Postmodernism, or, The Cultural Logic of Late Capitalism*. Durham, NC: Duke University Press, 1991.

———. *A Singular Modernity: Essay on the Ontology of the Present*. New York: Verso, 2002.

Janson Pérez, Brittmarie. "Political Facets of Salsa." *Popular Music* 6, no. 2 (May 1987): 149–59.

Jenckes, Kate. "The 'New Latin Americanism,' or the End of Regionalist Thinking?" *CR: The New Centennial Review* 4, no. 3 (2004): 247–70.

Jiménez Román, Miriam, and Juan Flores, eds. *The Afro-Latin@ Reader: History and Culture in the United States*. Durham, NC: Duke University Press, 2010.

Johnson, Julian. *Out of Time: Music and the Making of Modernity*. New York: Oxford University Press, 2015.

Jones, LeRoi. *Blues People: Negro Music in White America*. New York: HarperCollins, 1963.

———. "Jazz and the White Critic." *DownBeat*, August 15, 1963.

Kane, Brian. "*L'Objet sonore maintenant*: Pierre Schaeffer, Sound Objects and the Phenomenological Reduction." *Organised Sound* 12, no. 1 (2007): 15–24.

Kapchan, Deborah A. *Traveling Spirit Masters: Moroccan Gnawa Trance and Music in the Global Marketplace*. Middletown, CT: Wesleyan University Press, 2007.

Kaplan, Fred. "When Ambassadors Had Rhythm: Photo Exhibition Revisits State Department Program That Sent Jazz Greats Abroad." *New York Times*, June 29, 2008, sec. Music. https://www.nytimes.com/2008/06/29/arts/music/29kapl.html.

Karush, Matthew B. *Musicians in Transit: Argentina and the Globalization of Music*. Durham, NC: Duke University Press, 2017.

Kelley, Robin D. G. *Race Rebels: Culture, Politics, and the Black Working Class*. New York: The Free Press, 1994.

Kelman, John. "Miguel Zenón, *Jíbaro*." *All About Jazz*, June 17, 2006.

Kember, Sarah, and Joana Zylinska. *Life After New Media: Mediation as a Vital Process*. Cambridge, MA: MIT Press, 2021.

Kheshti, Roshanak. *Modernity's Ear: Listening to Race and Gender in World Music*. New York: New York University Press, 2015.

Kittler, Friedrich A. *Gramophone, Film, Typewriter*. Palo Alto, CA: Stanford University Press, 1999.

Klein, Naomi. *No Logo: Taking Aim at the Brand Bullies*. New York: Picador, 1999.

Koselleck, Reinhart. *Futures Past: On the Semantics of Historical Time*. Translated by Keith Tribe. New York: Columbia University Press, 2004.

Kraniauskas, John. "Hybridity and Reterritorialization." *Travesía* 1, no. 2 (1992): 143–51.

———. "Hybridity in a Transnational Frame: Latin-Americanist and Postcolonial Perspectives on Cultural Studies." *Nepantla: Views from the South* 1, no. 1 (2000): 111–37.

Krohn, Katherine. *Shakira*. Minneapolis: Twenty-First Century Books, 2007.

Kun, Josh. *Audiotopia: Music, Race, and America*. Berkeley: University of California Press, 2005.

Kusch, Rodolfo. *Indigenous and Popular Thinking in América*. Translated by Joshua M. Price and María Lugones. Durham, NC: Duke University Press, 2010.

"La verdadera historia de Pedro Navaja @ Miami. | HispanicAd.Com." Accessed September 13, 2018. http://hispanicad.com/blog/news-article/had/art-literature/la-verdadera-historia-de-pedro-navaja-miami.

Laclau, Ernesto. *Emancipation(s)*. New York: Verso, 1996.

———. "Universalism, Particularism and the Question of Identity." In *Emancipation(s)*. New York: Verso, 1996.

———. "Why Do Empty Signifiers Matter in Politics?" In *Emancipation(s)*, 36–46. London: Verso, 1996.

Laclau, Ernesto, and Chantal Mouffe. *Hegemony and Socialist Strategy: Towards a Radical Democratic Politics*. New York: Verso, 1985.

Lander, Edgardo. *La colonialidad del saber: Eurocentrismo y ciencias sociales*. Buenos Aires: CLASCO, 2005.

Landes, Donald A. "Le Toucher and the Corpus of Tact: Exploring Touch and Technicity with Jacques Derrida and Jean-Luc Nancy." *L'Esprit Créateur* 47, no. 3 (2007): 80–92.

Larraín Ibañez, Jorge. *Modernidad, razón e identidad en américa latina*. Santiago: Editorial Andres Bellow, 1996.

Larsen, Neil. "Latin Americanism without Latin America: 'Theory' as Surrogate Periphery in the Metropolitan University." *A Contracorriente: Una Revista de Historia Social y Literaria de América Latina/A Journal on Social History and Literature in Latin America* 3, no. 3 (2006): 37–46.

———. *Reading North by South*. Minneapolis: University of Minnesota Press, 1996.

Lash, Scott, and Celia Lury. *Global Culture Industry: The Mediation of Things*. Cambridge: Polity Press, 2007.

"Latin: Christina Aguilera." *Billboard*, September 16, 2000.

Latour, Bruno. "On the Difficulty of Being Glocal." Art-e-Fact: Strategies for Resistance. Accessed May 19, 2019. http://artefact.mi2.hr/_a04/lang_en/index_en.htm.

———. *Petite réflexion sur le culte moderne des dieux faîtiches*. Le Plessis/Robinson: Institut Synthélabo, 1996.

———. *Reassembling the Social: An Introduction to Actor-Network-Theory*. New York: Oxford University Press, 2005.

———. *We Have Never Been Modern*. Translated by Catherine Porter. Cambridge, MA: Harvard University Press, 1993.

Laver, Mark. "Freedom of Choice: Jazz, Neoliberalism, and the Lincoln Center." *Popular Music and Society* 37, no. 5 (October 20, 2014): 538–56.

Lazzarato, Maurizio. "Immaterial Labor." In *Radical Thought in Italy: A Potential Politics*, edited by Paolo Virno and Michael Hardt, 132–46. Minneapolis: University of Minnesota Press, 1996.

Lee, Benjamin, and Edward LiPuma. "Cultures of Circulation: The Imaginations of Modernity." *Public Culture* 14, no. 1 (January 1, 2002): 191–213.

Lefebvre, Henri. *Introduction to Modernity: Twelve Preludes, September 1959–May 1961*. Translated by John Moore. London: Verso, 1995.

Levinson, Brett. *The Ends of Literature: The Latin American "Boom" and the Neoliberal Marketplace*. Palo Alto, CA: Stanford University Press, 2001.

Lewis, George E. "Gittin' to Know Y'all: Improvised Music, Interculturalism, and the Racial Imagination." *Critical Studies in Improvisation/Études Critiques en Improvisation* 1, no. 1 (2004): 1–33.

———. *A Power Stronger Than Itself: The AACM and American Experimental Music*. Chicago: University of Chicago Press, 2008.

Lionnet, Françoise, and Shu-mei Shih. *Minor Transnationalism*. Durham, NC: Duke University Press, 2005.

Lipsitz, George. "Songs of the Unsung: The Darby Hicks History of Jazz." In *Uptown Conversation: The New Jazz Studies*, edited by Robert G. O'Meally, Brent Hayes Edwards, and Farah Jasmine Griffin, 9–26. New York: Columbia University Press, 2004.

―――. *Time Passages: Collective Memory and American Popular Culture.* Minneapolis: University of Minnesota Press, 1990.

Lomas, Laura. *Translating Empire: José Martí, Migrant Latino Subjects, and American Modernities.* Durham, NC: Duke University Press, 2008.

López de Jesús, Lara Ivette. *Encuentros sincopados: El Caribe contemporáneo a través de sus prácticas musicales.* Ciudad de México: Siglo XXI Editores, 2003.

Losilla, Javier. "Ruben Blades: De Panamá para el Mundo." *Esquina Latina,* 2000.

Lowe, Lisa. "Heterogeneity, Hybridity, Multiplicity: Marking Asian American Differences." *Diaspora: A Journal of Transnational Studies* 1, no. 1 (1991): 24–44.

―――. *Immigrant Acts: On Asian American Cultural Politics.* Durham, NC: Duke University Press, 1996.

Ludmer, Josefina. *Aquí América Latina: Una especulación.* Buenos Aires: Eterna Cadencia Editora, 2010.

Luker, Morgan James. *The Tango Machine: Musical Culture in the Age of Expediency.* Chicago: University of Chicago Press, 2016.

Lury, Celia. *Brands: The Logos of the Global Economy.* London: Routledge, 2004.

Lyotard, Jean-Francois. *The Postmodern Condition: A Report on Knowledge.* Edited by Geoffrey Bennington and Brian Massumi. Minneapolis: University of Minnesota Press, 1979.

―――. *Postmodern Fables.* Minneapolis: University of Minnesota Press, 1997.

Madrid, Alejandro L. *Nor-tec Rifa! Electronic Music from Tijuana to the World.* New York: Oxford University Press, 2008.

―――. *Sounds of the Modern Nation: Music, Culture, and Ideas in Post-Revolutionary Mexico.* Philadelphia: Temple University Press, 2008.

Maira, Sunaina. "Belly Dancing: Arab-Face, Orientalist Feminism, and U.S. Empire." *American Quarterly* 60, no. 2 (June 13, 2008): 317–45.

Malacara Palacios, Antonio. *Catálogo casi razonado del jazz en México.* Mexico City: Fondo Nacional para la Cultura y las Artes, 2005.

Man, Paul de. "Literary History and Literary Modernity." *Daedalus* 99, no. 2: *Theory in Humanistic Studies* (1970): 384–404.

Manuel, Peter. "Musical Representations of New York City in Latin Music." In *Island Sounds in the Global City: Caribbean Popular Music and Identity in New York,* edited by Ray Allen and Lois Wilcken, 23–43. Brooklyn: Institute for Studies in American Music, 1998.

―――. "Puerto Rican Music and Cultural Identity: Creative Appropriation of Cuban Sources from Danza to Salsa." *Ethnomusicology* 38, no. 2 (Spring–Summer 1994): 249–80.

Marchart, Oliver. "In the Name of the People: Populist Reason and the Subject of the Political." *Diacritics* 35, no. 3 (2005): 3–19.

Mariategui, José Carlos. *Seven Interpretative Essays on Peruvian Reality.* Translated by Jorge Basadre. Austin: University of Texas Press, 1971.

Marsalis, Wynton. "What Is Jazz, an Interview with Toni Scherman." *American Heritage Magazine,* 1995. http://www.americanheritage.com/articles/magazine/ ah/1995/6/1995_6_66_print.shtml [inactive link].

―――. "What Jazz Is—and Isn't." *New York Times,* July 3, 1988, sec. Editorial.

Marsalis, Wynton, and Frank Stewart. *Sweet Swing Blues on the Road.* New York: W. W. Norton, 1994.

Martí, José. "Nuestra América." *La Revista Ilustrada*, January 10, 1891.

Martín-Barbero, Jesús. *Al sur de la modernidad: Comunicación, globalización y multiculturalidad*. Pittsburgh: Instituto Internacional de Literatura Iberoamericana, University of Pittsburgh, 2001.

———. "Between Technology and Culture: Communication and Modernity in Latin America." In *Cultural Agency in the Americas*, edited by Doris Sommer, 37–51. Durham, NC: Duke University Press, 2006.

———. *Communication, Culture and Hegemony*. London: Sage, 1992.

———. *De los medios a las mediaciones*. Bogotá: Convenio Andrés Bello, 2003.

Mato, Daniel. "On the Theory, Epistemology, and Politics of the 'Social Construction' of Cultural Identities in the Age of Globalization: Introductory Remarks to Ongoing Debates." *Identities* 3, no. 1–2 (1996): 61–72.

McCracken, Grant David. *Transformations: Identity Construction in Contemporary Culture*. Bloomington: Indiana University Press, 2008.

McGuinness, Aims. "Searching for Latin America: Race and Sovereignty in the Americas in the 1850s." In *Race and Nation in Modern Latin America*, edited by Nancy P. Appelbaum, Anne S. Macpherson, and Karin Alejandra Rosemblatt, 87–107. Chapel Hill: University of North Carolina Press, 2003.

McHale, Brian. *Postmodernist Fiction*. New York: Methuen, 1987.

McMains, Juliet. *Spinning Mambo into Salsa: Caribbean Dance in Global Commerce*. New York: Oxford University Press, 2015.

Meintjes, Louise. *Sound of Africa!* Durham, NC: Duke University Press, 2003.

Méndez, Mario Ramos. *Posesión del ayer: La nacionalidad cultural en la estadidad*. San Juan: Isla Negra Editores, 2007.

Michelone, Guido. *El jazz habla español*. Milan: EDUCatt, 2014.

Mignolo, Walter D. "Colonial and Postcolonial Discourse: Cultural Critique or Academic Colonialism?" *Latin American Research Review* 28, no. 3 (1993): 120–34.

———. "The Geopolitics of Knowledge and the Colonial Difference." *South Atlantic Quarterly* 101, no. 1 (January 1, 2002): 57–96.

———. *The Idea of Latin America*. Malden, MA: Blackwell Publishing, 2005.

———. *Local Histories/Global Designs: Coloniality, Subaltern Knowledges, and Border Thinking*. Princeton, NJ: Princeton University Press, 2000.

———. "The Many Faces of Cosmo-Polis: Border Thinking and Critical Cosmopolitanism." In *Cosmopolitanism*, edited by Dipesh Chakrabarty, Homi K. Bhabha, Sheldon Pollock, and Carol A. Breckenridge, 15–53. Durham, NC: Duke University Press, 2002.

Miles, Robert. *Racism*. London: Routledge, 1989.

Milian, Claudia. *Latining America: Black-Brown Passages and the Coloring of Latino/a Studies*. Athens: University of Georgia Press, 2013.

Mill, John Stuart. *Principles of Political Economy: With Some of Their Applications to Social Philosophy*. London: Longmans, Green, and Company, 1909.

Miller, Nicola, and Stephen Hart, eds. *When Was Latin America Modern?* New York: Palgrave Macmillan, 2007.

Miller, Toby. *Cultural Citizenship: Cosmopolitanism, Consumerism, and Television in a Neoliberal Age*. Philadelphia: Temple University Press, 2007.

———. "Introducing . . . Cultural Citizenship." *Social Text* 19, no. 4 (2001): 1–5.

Miller, Toby, and George Yúdice. *Cultural Policy*. London: Sage, 2002.

Miñana Blasco, Carlos. "Entre el folclor y la etnomusicología: 60 años de estudios sobre la música popular tradicional en Colombia." *A Contratiempo: Revista de Música En La Cultura* 11 (2000): 36–49.

Mintz, Sidney. *Caribbean Transformations*. Chicago: Aldine Publishing Co., 1974.

———. *Sweetness and Power: The Place of Sugar in Modern History*. New York: Viking Press, 1985.

Monsiváis, Carlos. *A ustedes les consta: Antología de la crónica en México*. 2nd ed. Ciudad de México: Era, 1981.

———. "Ídolos populares y literatura en américa latina." *Boletín Cultural y Bibliográfico* 21, no. 1 (1984): 47–57.

———. "Penetración cultural y nacionalismo." In *No intervención, autodeterminación y democracia en América Latina*. Ciudad de México: Siglo XXI Editores, 1983.

Monson, Ingrid T. *Freedom Sounds: Civil Rights Call Out to Jazz and Africa*. New York: Oxford University Press, 2007.

Montaldo, Graciela. "Latin Americanism: The Disciplining of Culture, Globalization, and Regional Agendas." In *Tinker Board Forum*, 2000.

Moore, Robin. *Nationalizing Blackness: Afrocubanismo and Artistic Revolution in Havana, 1920–1940*. Pittsburgh: University of Pittsburgh Press, 1997.

Mora, G. Cristina. *Making Hispanics: How Activists, Bureaucrats, and Media Constructed a New American*. Chicago: University of Chicago Press, 2014.

Morales, Ed. "Mea Culpa." *The Village Voice*. January 5, 1999.

———. "Review of *Tiempos*." *Rolling Stone*, 1999.

Moraña, Mabel. "Boom of the Subaltern." In *The Latin American Cultural Studies Reader*, edited by Ana del Sarto, Alicia Ríos, and Abril Trigo. Durham, NC: Duke University Press, 2004.

———. "Escribir en el aire: 'Heterogeneidad' y 'Estudios Culturales.'" *Revista Iberoamericana* 61, no. 170 (1995): 279–86.

Moreiras, Alberto. *The Exhaustion of Difference: The Politics of Latin American Cultural Studies*. Post-Contemporary Inventions. Durham, NC: Duke University Press, 2001.

———. "Introduction: The Conflict in Transculturation." In *Literary Cultures of Latin America: A Comparative History*, edited by Mario J. Valdés and Djelal Kadir. New York: Oxford University Press, 2004.

———. "On Latin Americanism. A Comment to Tenorio-Trillo." Infrapolitical Deconstruction (and Other Issues Related and Unrelated.), August 18, 2017. https://infrapolitica.com/2017/08/18/on-latin-americanism-a-comment-to-tenorio-trillo/.

Moreno, Jairo. "Bauzá-Gillespie-Latin/Jazz: Difference, Modernity, and the Black Caribbean." *The South Atlantic Quarterly* 103, no. 1 (January 30, 2004): 81–99.

———. "Corpus Delicti: 'Pedro Navaja' como palabra y escucha." In *Relaciones caribeñas. Entrelazamientos de dos siglos. Relations caribéennes. Enchevêtrements de deux siècles*, edited by Liliana Gómez and Gesine Müller, 195–212. Frankfurt: Peter Lang Verlang, 2011.

———. "Imperial Aurality: Jazz, the Archive, and U.S. Empire." In *Audible Empire: Music, Global Politics, Critique*, edited by Ronald Michael Radano and Tejumola

Olaniyan, 135–60. Refiguring American Music. Durham, NC: Duke University Press, 2016.

———. "La salsa y sus muertes." In *El son y la salsa en la identidad del Caribe,* edited by Darío Tejeda and Rafael Emilio Yunén, 473–80. Santo Domingo: Centro León, 2008. Reprinted in *Cocinando suave: Ensayos de salsa en Puerto Rico,* edited by César Colón-Montijo, 29–38. San Juan: Ediciones Callejón, 2015.

———. "Past Identity: Guillermo Klein, Miguel Zenón and the Future Jazz." In *Music and Youth Culture in Latin America: Identity Construction Processes from New York to Buenos Aires,* edited by Pablo Vila, 81–105. New York: Oxford University Press, 2014.

———. "Sonorous Specters: On Some Recent Histories and Economies of Afro-Latin Jazz." *Journal of Latin American Cultural Studies* 25, no. 3 (July 2, 2016): 397–417.

———. "Tropical Discourses: Community, History, and Sentiment in Rubén Blades's Latin Music(s)." *Journal of Popular Music Studies* 13, no. 2 (2001): 133–63.

Moreno, Jairo, and Gavin Steingo. "Rancière's Equal Music." *Contemporary Music Review* 31, no. 5–6 (2012): 487–505.

Morris, Wesley. "Lil Nas X Is the King of the Crossover." *New York Times,* March 11, 2020, sec. Magazine. https://www.nytimes.com/interactive/2020/03/11/magazine/lil-nas-x-old-town-road.html.

Morrison, Toni. "Rootedness: The Ancestor in Afro-American Fiction." In *Black Women Writers at Work: A Critical Evaluation,* edited by Mari Evans, 339–45. Garden City, NY: Anchor Press, 1984.

Moten, Fred. *In the Break: The Aesthetics of the Black Radical Tradition.* Minneapolis: University of Minnesota Press, 2003.

Mouffe, Chantal. *The Democratic Paradox.* New York: Verso, 2000.

Muller, Carol Ann. *Rituals of Fertility and the Sacrifice of Desire: Nazarite Women's Performance in South Africa.* Chicago: University of Chicago Press, 1999.

Munn, Nancy D. *The Fame of Gawa: A Symbolic Study of Value Transformation in a Massim (Papua New Guinea) Society.* Cambridge: Cambridge University Press, 1986.

Muñoz Vélez, Enrique. *Jazz en Colombia.* Barranquilla: La Iguana Ciega, 2008.

Murray, Albert. "The Function of the Heroic Image." In *The Jazz Cadence of American Culture,* edited by Robert G. O'Meally, 569–79. New York: Columbia University Press, 1998.

———. *The Omni-Americans: Black Experience and American Culture.* New York: Da Capo Press, 1990.

———. *Stomping the Blues.* New York: McGraw-Hill, 1976.

Nancy, Jean-Luc. "Communism, the Word." In *The Idea of Communism,* edited by Costas Douzinas and Slavoj Žižek. London: Verso, 2010.

———. *Le discours de la syncope: I. Logodaedalus.* Paris: Flammarion, 1976.

———. *The Discourse of the Syncope: Logodaedalus.* Translated by Saul Anton. Palo Alto, CA: Stanford University Press, 2008.

Nancy, Jean-Luc, and Philippe Lacoue-Labarthe. *The Literary Absolute: The Theory of Literature in German Romanticism.* Albany: State University of New York Press, 1988.

Nealon, Jeffrey T. *I'm Not Like Everybody Else: Biopolitics, Neoliberalism, and American Popular Music*. Lincoln: University of Nebraska Press, 2018.

Negrón-Muntaner, Frances, ed. *None of the Above: Puerto Ricans in the Global Era*. New Directions in Latino American Cultures. New York: Palgrave Macmillan, 2007.

Negus, Keith. *Music Genres and Corporate Culture*. New York: Routledge, 1999.

Newsweek Staff. "Way, Way Off Broadway." *Newsweek*, August 29, 2004. http://www.newsweek.com/way-way-broadway-126649.

Nisenson, Eric. *Blue: The Murder of Jazz*. Cambridge, MA: Da Capo Press, 1997.

Nora, Pierre. *Realms of Memory: Rethinking the French Past (Vol. I: Conflicts and Divisions)*. Edited by Lawrence D. Kritzman. Translated by Arthur Goldhammer. New York: Columbia University Press, 1996.

Novak, David. *Japanoise: Music at the Edge of Circulation*. Durham, NC: Duke University Press, 2013.

Nuez, Iván de la. "Mis diez personajes latinoamericanos: 1810–2010." Blog. *Iván de la Nuez*, November 29, 2009. http://www.tumiamiblog.com/2009/11/mis-diez-personajes-latinoamericanos.html.

Nussbaum, Martha. "Patriotism and Cosmopolitanism." *The Boston Review*, October 1, 1994. https://bostonreview.net/articles/martha-nussbaum-patriotism-and-cosmopolitanism/.

Ochoa Gautier, Ana María. *Aurality: Listening and Knowledge in Nineteenth-Century Colombia*. Durham, NC: Duke University Press, 2014.

———. "García Márquez, Macondismo, and the Soundscapes of Vallenato." *Popular Music* 24, no. 2 (May 2005): 207–22.

———. *Músicas locales en tiempos de globalización*. Bogotá: Editorial Norma, 2003.

———. "Silence." In *Keywords in Sound*, edited by David Novak and Matt Sakakeeny, 183–92. Durham, NC: Duke University Press, 2015.

———. "Sonic Transculturation, Epistemologies of Purification and the Aural Public Sphere in Latin America." *Social Identities* 12, no. 6 (2006): 803–25.

O'Farrill, Arturo. "We Speak African: Arturo O'Farrill on U.S./Cuba Exchange." *JazzTimes* (blog). Last modified April 25, 2019. Accessed July 10, 2019. https://jazztimes.com/features/columns/we-speak-african-arturo-ofarrill-on-u-s-cuba-exchange/.

O'Gorman, Edmundo. *The Invention of America: An Inquiry into the Historical Nature of the New World and the Meaning of Its History*. Bloomington: Indiana University Press, 1961.

Olazo, Jorge. *Jazz con sabor peruano*. Lima: El Cocodrilo Verde Ediciones, 2003.

O'Meally, Robert G., ed. *The Jazz Cadence of American Culture*. New York: Columbia University Press, 1998.

O'Meally, Robert G., Brent Hayes Edwards, and Farah Jasmine Griffin, eds. *Uptown Conversation: The New Jazz Studies*. New York: Columbia University Press, 2004.

Ong, Walter J. *Orality and Literacy: The Technologizing of the Word*. London: Methuen, 1982.

Ortiz, Fernando. *Contrapunteo cubano del tabaco y el azúcar*. Caracas: Biblioteca Ayacucho, 1978.

———. *Cuban Counterpoint: Tobacco and Sugar*. Translated by Harriet de Onís. Durham, NC: Duke University Press, 1995.

————. *La africanía de la música folklórica de Cuba*. Havana: Editora Universitaria, 1965.

Ortner, Sherry. "Access: Reflections on Studying Up in Hollywood." *Ethnography* 11, no. 2 (2010): 211–33.

Otero Garabís, Juan. "Esquinas y/o encrucijadas: Una mirada al caribe urbano en música y literatura." *Revista Iberoamericana* 75, no. 229 (October 2009): 963–81.

————. *Nación y ritmo: "Descargas" desde el Caribe*. 1st ed. San Juan: Ediciones Callejón, 2000.

"Otro edificio que se nos va: El Teatro Musical de La Habana." *CiberCuba*, July 31, 2018. https://www.cibercuba.com/noticias/2018-07-31-u73624 -e73624-s27061-otro-edificio-nos-teatro-musical-habana-fotos.

Oyarzún, Pablo. *La desazón de lo moderno: Problemas de la modernidad*. Santiago: Cuarto Propio/Arcis, 2001.

Oyarzún, Pablo, trans. *Walter Benjamin: La dialéctica en suspenso (Fragmentos sobre historia)*. Santiago: Ediciones LOM, 2014.

Pacini Hernandez, Deborah. "Amalgamating Musics: Popular Music and Cultural Hybridity in the Americas." In *Musical Migrations: Transnationalism and Cultural Hybridity in Latin/o America, Volume I*, edited by Frances R. Aparicio and Cándida F. Jácquez, 13–32. New York: Palgrave Macmillan, 2003.

————. *Oye Como Va! Hybridity and Identity in Latino Popular Music*. Philadelphia: Temple University Press, 2010.

Pacini Hernandez, Deborah, Héctor D. Fernández L'Hoeste, and Eric Zolov, eds. *Rockin' Las Américas: The Global Politics of Rock in Latin/o America*. Pittsburgh: University of Pittsburgh Press, 2004.

Padilla, Felix M. "Salsa Music as a Cultural Expression of Latino Consciousness and Unity." *Hispanic Journal of Behavioral Sciences* 11, no. 1 (1989): 28–45.

————. "Salsa: Puerto Rican and Latino Music." *Journal of Popular Culture* 24, no. 1 (1990): 87–104.

Padura Fuentes, Leonardo. "Salsa y conciencia." *Guaraguao* (2002): 119–23.

Palamides, Costa. "Compañía Nacional de Teatro: El trienio inicial." *Latin American Theatre Review* (1998): 69–72.

Palmer, Robert. "The Pop Life: Ruben Blades' Salsa." *New York Times*, April 4, 1984.

Palomino, Pablo. *The Invention of Latin American Music: A Transnational History*. New York; Oxford University Press, 2020.

Pallotta, Dan. "A Logo Is Not a Brand." *Harvard Business Review*, June 15, 2011. https://hbr.org/2011/06/a-logo-is-not-a-brand.

Pareles, Jon. "It's All About the Amor." *New York Times*, March 27, 2017. https:// www.nytimes.com/2014/03/28/arts/music/new-music-by-shakira-juanes -enrique-iglesias-and-wisin.html.

Parry, Benita. "Aspects of Peripheral Modernisms." *Ariel* 40 (2009): 27–55.

Party, Daniel. "The Miamization of Latin-American Pop Music." In *Postnational Musical Identities: Cultural Production, Distribution, and Consumption in a Globalized Scenario*, edited by Ignacio Corona and Alejandro L. Madrid, 65–80. Lanham, MD: Lexington Books, 2007.

"Pastrana: 'Shakira, nuestra embajadora internacional.'" *El Tiempo*, February 23, 2001. https://www.eltiempo.com/archivo/documento/MAM-607268.

Paz, Octavio. *Los hijos del limo: Del romanticismo a la vanguardia*. 1st ed. Barcelona: Seix Barral, 1974.

Peebles, Gustav. "The Anthropology of Credit and Debt." *Annual Review of Anthropology* 39 (2010): 225–40.

Peixoto, Fernando. "Brecht, nuestro compañero." *Conjunto: Revista de Teatro Latinoamericano*, no. 69 (1986).

Pellegrinelli, Lara. "Dig Boy Dig." *The Village Voice*, November 7, 2000.

Pellettieri, Oswaldo. "Brecht y el teatro porteño." In *De Bertolt Brecht a Ricardo Monto. Teatro en lengua alemana y teatro argentino (1900–1994)*. Buenos Aires: Galerna, 1994.

Peñalosa, David. *The Clave Matrix: Afro-Cuban Rhythm: Its Principles and African Origins*. Edited by Peter Greenwood. Redway, CA: Bembe Books, 2009.

Pérez Villalón, Fernando. "Modernidad sincopada: Música, rítmo y nación en la obra de Mário de Andrade." *Revista Chilena de Literatura* 90 (2015): 223–44.

Perkinson, Jim. "Constructing the Break: 'Syncopated Tricksterism' as Afro-Diaspora Kairos Inside Anglo-Capitalist Chronos." *Social Identities* 8, no. 4 (2002): 545–69.

Phelan, John Leddy. "Pan-Latinism, French Intervention in Mexico (1861–1867) and the Genesis of the Idea of Latin America." In *Conciencia y autenticidad históricas. Escritos en homenaje a Edmundo O'Gorman*, 279–98. Mexico City: Universidad Nacional Autónoma de México, 1968.

Pianca, Marina. "De Brecht a Nueva York: Caminos del teatro latinoamericano." *Conjunto*, 1986.

Pier, John. "Metalepsis." In *The Living Handbook of Narratology*. Hamburg: Hamburg University Press, 2013. https://www.lhn.uni-hamburg.de/node/51.html.

Pietrobruno, Sheenagh. *Salsa and Its Transnational Moves*. Lanham, MD: Lexington Books, 2006.

Pimentel-Otero, Juan. "Latin Americanism in the Music of Rubén Blades." *Sociology and Anthropology* 4, no. 4 (2016): 241–48.

Plutarch. "On the Fortune or the Virtue of Alexander." In Plutarch, *Moralia, Volume IV*, translated by Frank Cole Babbitt, 380–489. Cambridge, MA: Harvard University Press, 1936.

Polin, Bruce. "A Visit with Ruben Blades." *The Descarga Newsletter*, 1996.

Pollock, Sheldon. "The Cosmopolitan Vernacular." *Journal of Asian Studies* 57, no. 1 (February 1998): 6–37.

———. "Cosmopolitanism and Vernacular in History." In *Cosmopolitanism*, edited by Dipesh Chakrabarty, Homi K. Bhabha, Sheldon Pollock, and Carol A. Breckenridge, 15–53. Durham, NC: Duke University Press, 2002.

———. "India in the Vernacular Millennium: Literary Culture and Polity, 1000–1500." *Daedalus*, Early Modernities, 127, no. 3 (Summer 1998): 41–74.

———. *The Language of the Gods in the World of Men: Sanskrit, Culture, and Power in Premodern India*. Berkeley: University of California Press, 2006.

Pond, Steven F. "Jamming the Reception: Ken Burns, 'Jazz,' and the Problem of 'America's Music.'" *Notes*, 2nd series, 60, no. 1 (2003): 11–45.

Porter, Eric. *What Is This Thing Called Jazz? African American Musicians as Artists, Critics, and Activists*. Berkeley: University of California Press, 2002.

Posada, Francisco. *Lukács, Brecht y la situación actual del realismo socialista*. Buenos Aires: Galerna, 1969.

Povinelli, Elizabeth A. *Empire of Love: Toward a Theory of Intimacy, Genealogy, and Carnality*. Durham, NC: Duke University Press, 2006.

Powers, Ann. "Shakira's Dance of Dynamism." *LA Times*, August 17, 2006. https://www.latimes.com/archives/la-xpm-2006-aug-17-wk-shakira17-story.html.

Pratt, Mary Louise. *Imperial Eyes: Travel Writing and Transculturation*. London: Routledge, 1992.

———. "It Takes Two to Tangle." *Social Text* 28, no. 3 (2010): 151–57.

———. "Modernity and Periphery: Toward a Global and Relational Analysis." In *Beyond Dichotomies: Histories, Identities, Cultures, and the Challenge of Globalization*, edited by Elisabeth Mudimbe-Boyi, 21–47. Albany: State University of New York Press, 2002.

Prieto, Adolfo. *El discurso criollista en la formación de la Argentina moderna*. Buenos Aires: Editorial Sudamericana, 1988.

Pujol, Sergio. *Jazz al sur*. Buenos Aires: EMC, 1992.

Putnam, Laura. *Radical Moves: Caribbean Migrants and the Politics of Race in the Jazz Age*. Chapel Hill: University of North Carolina Press, 2013.

Quijada, Mónica. "Sobre el origen y difusión del nombre 'América Latina' (o una variación heterodoxa en torno al tema de la construcción social de la verdad)." *Revista de Indias* 57, no. 214 (1998): 595–619.

Quijano, Aníbal. "Coloniality and Modernity/Rationality." *Cultural Studies* 21, no. 2–3 (2007): 168–78.

———. "Coloniality of Power, Eurocentrism and Social Classification." In *Coloniality at Large: Latin America and the Postcolonial Debate*, edited by Mabel Moraña and Enrique Dussel. Durham, NC: Duke University Press, 2008.

Quintero-Herencia, Juan Carlos. *La máquina de la salsa: Tránsitos del sabor*. San Juan: Ediciones Vértigo, 2005.

Quintero Rivera, Ángel. *Cuerpo y cultura: Las músicas "mulatas" y la subversión del baile*. Madrid/Frankfurt: Iberoamericana, Vervuert, 2009.

———. "Salsa, entre la globalización y la utopía." *Cuadernos de Literatura* 4, no. 7–8 (1998): 91–106.

———. *¡Salsa, sabor y control! Sociología de la música "tropical."* 2nd ed. Mexico City: Siglo XXI Editores, 1998.

———. "Sensibilidades y comunicación en las músicas populares afro latinoamericanas." Accessed November 3, 2019. http://facultad.pucp.edu.pe/comunicaciones/ciudadycomunicacion/wp-content/uploads/2014/11/Quintero-Sensibilidades-y-comunicacion.pdf.

Rabasa, José. *De la invención de América. la historiografía española y la formación del eurocentrismo*. Mexico City: Universidad Iberoamericana, 2009.

———. *Inventing America: Spanish Historiography and the Formation of Eurocentrism*. Norman: University of Oklahoma Press, 1994.

Radano, Ronald. "Black Music Labor and the Animated Properties of Slave Sound." Edited by Gavin Steingo and Jairo Moreno. *Boundary 2*, Econophonia: Music, Value, and Forms of Life, 43, no. 1 (2016): 173–208.

———. *Lying Up a Nation: Race and Black Music*. Chicago: University of Chicago Press, 2003.

Rama, Ángel. *La ciudad letrada*. Hanover, NH: Ediciones del Norte, 1984.

———. *La ciudad letrada*. Santiago: Ediciones Tajamar, 2004.

————. *La crítica de la cultura en américa latina*. Edited by Sonowski Saúl and Tomás Eloy Martínez. Caracas: Biblioteca Ayacucho, 1985.

————. *The Lettered City*. Translated by John Charles Chasteen. Latin America in Translation. Durham, NC: Duke University Press, 1996.

————. *Writing Across Cultures: Narrative Transculturation in Latin America*. Translated by David Frye. Durham, NC: Duke University Press, 2012.

Ramos, Julio. *Divergent Modernities: Culture and Politics in Nineteenth-Century Latin America*. Translated by John D. Blanco. Durham, NC: Duke University Press, 2001.

————. "Los tiempos caribeños de Amadeo Roldán y Luis Palés Matos." Columbia University, New York, 2013.

Ramsey, Guthrie P. *Race Music: Black Cultures from Bebop to Hip-Hop*. Berkeley: University of California Press, 2003.

Rancière, Jacques. *Aesthetics and Its Discontents*. Translated by Steven Corcoran. Cambridge: Polity, 2009.

————. *Disagreement: Politics and Philosophy*. Minneapolis: University of Minnesota Press, 1999.

————. *The Emancipated Spectator*. Translated by Gregory Elliot. New York: Verso, 2008.

————. "The Ethical Turn of Aesthetics and Politics." In *Aesthetics and Its Discontents*, translated by Steven Corcoran. Cambridge: Polity, 2009.

————. *The Philosopher and His Poor*. Durham, NC: Duke University Press, 2004.

————. *The Politics of Aesthetics: The Distribution of the Sensible*. Translated by Gabriel Rockhill. London: Continuum, 2004.

————. *The Politics of Literature*. Translated by Julie Rose. Cambridge: Polity, 2011.

————. "Ten Theses on Politics." In *Dissensus: On Politics and Aesthetics*, translated by Steven Corcoran, 27–44. New York: Continuum, 2010.

————. "What Intellectual Might Mean." In *Moments Politiques*. New York: Seven Stories Press, 2014.

Randel, Don Michael. "Crossing Over with Rubén Blades." *Journal of the American Musicological Society* 44, no. 2 (Summer 1991): 301–23.

Rappaport, Joanne, and Tom Cummins. *Beyond the Lettered City: Indigenous Literacies in the Andes*. Durham, NC: Duke University Press, 2012.

Rasula, Jed. "The Media of Memory: The Seductive Menace of Records in Jazz History." In *Jazz Among the Discourses*, 134–64. Durham, NC: Duke University Press, 1995.

Ratliff, Ben. "Conclusion: 2017." In *Future of Jazz*, edited by Yuval Taylor and Will Friedwald, 208–9. Chicago: A Cappella Books, 2002.

————. "Inspired by the Complexities of Back-Country Troubadours." *New York Times*, June 5, 2004.

Reich, Howard. "Arturo 'Chico' O'Farrill, 79." *Chicago Tribune*, June 29, 2001. https://www.chicagotribune.com/news/ct-xpm-2001-06-29-0106290259-story.html.

————. "Back in the Swing." *Chicago Tribune*, August 20, 2000. https://www.chicagotribune.com/news/ct-xpm-2000–08–20–0008200041-story.html.

"Review of Shakira: MTV Unplugged." *Billboard*, March 4, 2000.

Reynolds, Andrew. *The Spanish American Crónica Modernista, Temporality and Material Culture: Modernismo's Unstoppable Presses.* Lanham, MD: Bucknell University Press, 2012.

Ribeiro de Oliveira, Solange. *De mendigos e malandros: Chico Buarque, Bertolt Brecht, John Gay—uma leitura transcultural.* Ouro Preto, Brazil: Editora da UFOP, 2011.

———. "Musical Comedy and Cultural Memory in Brazil: Chico Buarque's Transcultural Reading of John Gay's *The Beggar's Opera* and Bertolt Brecht's *Threepenny Opera.*" In *Methods for the Study of Literature as Cultural Memory,* edited by Raymond Vervliet. Leiden: Brill, 2000.

Richard, Nelly. "Intersecting Latin America with Latin Americanism: Academic Knowledge, Theoretical Practice, and Cultural Criticism." In *The Latin American Cultural Studies Reader,* edited by Ana del Sarto, Alicia Ríos, and Abril Trigo, 686–705. Durham, NC: Duke University Press, 2004.

———. *Residuos y metáforas: Ensayos de crítica cultural sobre el Chile de la transición.* Santiago: Editorial Cuarto Propio, 1998.

Rimmon-Kenan, Shlomith. *Narrative Fiction: Contemporary Poetics.* New Accents. London: Routledge, 2002.

Rivero, Yeidy. "A New Export Product: Yo Soy Betty, La Fea Goes Global." In *The Colombia Reader: History, Culture, Politics,* edited by Ann Farnsworth-Alvear, Marco Palacios, and Ana María Gómez López. Durham, NC: Duke University Press, 2017.

Roach, Joseph R. *Cities of the Dead: Circum-Atlantic Performance.* New York: Columbia University Press, 1996.

Robbins, Dylon. "Polyrhythm and the Valorization of Time in Three Movements." *Brasiliana: Journal of Brazilian Studies* 4, no. 1 (2015): 82–109.

Rockhill, Gabriel. "The Politics of Aesthetics: Political History and the Hermeneutics of Art." In *Jacques Rancière: History, Politics, Aesthetics,* edited by Gabriel Rockhill and Philip Watts, 195–215. Durham, NC: Duke University Press, 2009.

Rockwell, John. "In Pop Music, the Races Remain Far Apart." *New York Times,* March 18, 1984.

Rodó, José Enrique. *Ariel.* Translated by Margaret Sayers Peden. Austin: University of Texas Press, 1988.

Román-Velázquez, Patria. "The Making of a Salsa Music Scene in London." In *Situating Salsa: Global Markets and Local Meanings in Latin Popular Music,* edited by Lise Waxer, 259–87. New York: Routledge, 2002.

Rondón, César Miguel. *El libro de la salsa. crónica de la música del caribe urbano.* Caracas: Ediciones B, 2007.

Rosaldo, Renato. *Culture and Truth: The Remaking of Social Analysis.* Boston: Beacon, 1993.

Rotker, Susana. *The American Chronicles of José Martí: Journalism and Modernity in Spanish America.* Translated by Jennifer French and Katherine Semler. Hanover, NH: University Press of New England, 2000.

———. *La invención de la crónica.* Mexico City: Fondo de Cultura Económica, 2005.

Ruesga Bono, Julián, ed. *Jazz en español: Derivas hispanoamericanas.* Xalapa, México: Biblioteca Universidad Veracruzana, 2013.

Russonello, Giovanni. "At 30, What Does Jazz at Lincoln Center Mean?" *New York*

Times, September 13, 2017, sec. Arts. https://www.nytimes.com/2017/09/13/arts/music/jazz-at-lincoln-center-30th-anniversary.html.

Safa, Helen. "The Social Cost of Dependency: The Transformation of the Puerto Rican Working Class from 1960 to 1990." In *The Anthropology of Lower Income Urban Enclaves: The Case of East Harlem*, edited by Judith Freidenberg, 75–96. New York: Academy of the Sciences, 1995.

Sagramoso, Uberto. "Rubén Blades: Música e identidad latinoamericana." *El Espectador*. July 3, 1983, Magazin Dominical No. 16 edition.

Said, Edward. *Culture and Imperialism*. New York: Knopf, 1993.

Salazar, Max. "The Pioneers of Salsa." *Latin Beat Magazine*, 2001.

———. "Salsa Music Rivalries and Battles." *Latin Beat Magazine*, 2003.

Saldívar, José David. *Dialectics of Our America: Genealogy, Cultural Critique, and Literary History*. Durham, NC: Duke University Press, 1991.

Salomon, Noël. "José Martí y la toma de conciencia latinoamericana." In *Lectura crítica de la literatura americana: La formación de las culturas nacionales*, edited by Saúl Sosnowski, 223–38. Caracas: Biblioteca Ayacucho, 1972.

Sanabria, Izzy. "Ruben Blades. Singer, Poet, Philosopher." *Latin New York* 3, no. 11 (1980): 32–37, 58–60.

Sanders, James E. "The Vanguard of the Atlantic World: Contesting Modernity in Nineteenth-Century Latin America." *Latin American Research Review* 46, no. 2 (2011): 104–27.

Sandke, Randal. *Where the Dark and the Light Folks Meet: Race and the Mythology, Politics, and Business of Jazz*. Lanham, MD: Scarecrow Press, 2010.

Sanín Cano, Baldomero. "De lo exótico." *Revista Gris*, 1894.

Santamaría-Delgado, Carolina. *Vitrolas, rocolas y radioteatros: Hábitos de escucha de la música popular en Medellín, 1930–1950*. Bogotá: Universidad Javierana/Banco de la República, 2014.

Santana Archbold, Sergio, ed. *Yo, Rubén Blades: Confesiones de un relator de barrio*. Medellín: Ediciones Salsa y Cultura, 1997.

Santiago, Midaglia. "Ruben Blades: Lleva Maestra Vida al teatro." *El Mundo*, January 31, 1981.

Santos-Febres, Mayra. "Salsa as Translocation." In *Everynight Life*, edited by Celeste Fraser Delgado and José Esteban Muñoz, 175–88. Durham, NC: Duke University Press, 1997.

Saona, Margarita. "Orden y progreso: Modernización a la brasilera en Opera do Malandro de Chico Buarque." New York: Department of Spanish and Portuguese, Columbia University, 1994.

Sarlo, Beatriz. *La máquina cultural: Maestras, traductores y vanguardistas*. Buenos Aires: Ariel, 1998.

———. *Una modernidad periferica: Buenos Aires, 1920 y 1930*. Buenos Aires: Nueva Vision, 1988.

Sarmiento, Domingo Faustino. *Argirópolis*. Buenos Aires, 1916.

Sartinger, Kathrin. "Rewriting als produktive Differenz: Chico Buarque de Hollandas Ópera Do Malandro als brasilianische Wiederkehr von John Gay's *The Beggar's Opera*." In *John Gay's The Beggar's Opera, 1728–2004 Adaptations and Re-Writings*. Amsterdam: Rodopi, 2006.

Sartorius, David, and Micol Siegel. "Introduction: Dislocations across the Americas." *Social Text* 28, no. 3 (2020): 1–10.

Schechner, Richard. *Between Theater and Anthropology*. Philadelphia: University of Pennsylvania Press, 1985.

Schouten, Peter. Theory Talk #13: Immanuel Wallerstein. Accessed August 4, 2008. http://www.theory-talks.org/2008/08/theory-talk-13.html.

Schwarz, Roberto. "Altos e baixos da atualidade de Brecht." In *Sequências Brasileiras: Ensaios*, 113–48. São Paolo: Companhia das letras, 1999.

———. "The Relevance of Brecht: High Points and Low." Translated by Emilio Sauri. *Mediations* 23, no. 1 (Fall 2007): 27–61.

Scott, David. *Conscripts of Modernity: The Tragedy of Colonial Enlightenment*. Durham, NC: Duke University Press, 2004.

"Shakira disfruta de la tranquilidad de Bahamas." *El Universal*, July 2, 2009. http://archivo.eluniversal.com.mx/notas/609092.html/.

"Shakira estudia historia en UCLA." *Vanguardia*. Accessed April 10, 2020. https://vanguardia.com.mx/shakiraestudiahistoriaenucla-40707.html.

"Shakira Follows Up Spanish Smash with All New English Album *Oral Fixation, Vol. 2*." *Business Wire*, October 10, 2005.

"Shakira y Juanes tienen su carácter." *Semana*, December 8, 2006. https://www.semana.com/enfoque/enfoque-principal/articulo/shakira-juanes-tienen-su-caracter/82582-3.

Shatz, Adam. "Kamasi Washington's Giant Step." *New York Times Magazine*, January 21, 2016. https://www.nytimes.com/2016/01/24/magazine/kamasi-washingtons-giant-step.html.

Shelby, Tommie. "Cosmopolitanism, Blackness, and Utopia: A Conversation with Paul Gilroy." *Transition*, no. 98 (2008): 116–35.

Shellhorse, Adam Joseph. *Anti-Literature: The Politics and Limits of Representation in Modern Brazil and Argentina*. Pittsburgh: University of Pittsburgh Press, 2017.

Shepard, Richard F. "Stage: 'Navaja,' from Puerto Rico." *New York Times*, August 10, 1985, sec. Theater. https://www.nytimes.com/1985/08/10/theater/stage-navaja-from-puerto-rico.html.

Shuster, Fred. "Poetry in Music Latin Singer's New Album Combines Emotional Lyrics with Costa Rican Sounds." *The Fresno Bee*, 1999.

Silverman, Stephen M. "Fans Unveil 6-Ton Metal Statue of Shakira." *People*, November 16, 2006. https://people.com/celebrity/fans-unveil-6-ton-metal-statue-of-shakira/.

Singer, Roberta. "Puerto Rican Music in New York City." *New York Folklore* 14, no. 3 (1998): 139–50.

Siskind, Mariano. *Cosmopolitan Desires: Global Modernity and World Literature in Latin America*. Evanston, IL: Northwestern University Press, 2012.

Sloterdijk, Peter. *Im selbem Boot: Versuch über die Hyperpolitik*. Frankfurt: Suhrkamp, 1993.

Small, Christopher. *Musicking: The Meanings of Performing and Listening*. Middletown, CT: Wesleyan University Press, 1998.

Sommer, Doris. *Bilingual Aesthetics: A New Sentimental Education*. Durham, NC: Duke University Press, 2004.

———. *Foundational Fictions: The National Romances of Latin America*. Berkeley: University of California Press, 1991.

Spain, William. "Pepsi, Sony in Music Marketing Pact." *MarketWatch*, Novem-

ber 12, 2002. https://www.marketwatch.com/story/pepsi-digs-pop-music
-promos-in-pact-with-sony /.

Spitta, Silvia. *Más allá de la ciudad letrada: Crónicas y espacios urbanos*. Pittsburgh: Biblioteca de América, Instituto Internacional de Literatura Iberoamericana, University of Pittsburgh, 2003.

Spivak, Gayatri Chakravorty. *Death of a Discipline*. New York: Columbia University Press, 2003.

———. *Outside in the Teaching Machine*. New York: Routledge, 1993.

Stadler, Gustavus. "Never Heard Such a Thing: Lynching and Phonographic Modernity." *Social Text* 28, no. 1 (2010): 87–105.

Stallings, Stephanie N. "Collective Difference: The Pan-American Association of Composers and Pan-American Ideology in Music, 1925–1945." PhD dissertation, Florida State University, 2009.

Starobinski, Jean. *Montaigne in Motion*. Translated by Arthur Goldhammer. Chicago: University of Chicago Press, 1986.

Steingo, Gavin. *Kwaito's Promise: Music and the Aesthetics of Freedom in South Africa*. Chicago: University of Chicago Press, 2016.

Sterne, Jonathan. *The Audible Past: Cultural Origins of Sound Reproduction*. Durham, NC: Duke University Press, 2003.

Steward, Sue. "Tiempos fugit." *Time Out* (July 12–19, 2000), 23.

Stewart, Jesse. "No Boundary Line to Art: 'Bebop' as Afro-Modernist Discourse." *American Music* 29, no. 3 (Fall 2011): 332–52.

Stokes, Martin. "On Musical Cosmopolitanism." In *The Macalester International Roundtable 2007*. Macalester College, 2007. http://digitalcommons.macalester .edu/intlrdtable/3/.

Stoler, Ann Laura. *Race and the Education of Desire: Foucault's History of Sexuality and the Colonial Order of Things*. Durham, NC: Duke University Press, 1995.

Strathern, Marilyn. *The Gender of the Gift: Problems with Women and Problems with Society in Melanesia*. Berkeley: University of California Press, 1988.

Strauss, Neil. "The Three Faces of Ruben Blades." *New York Times*, August 29, 1999. http://www.nytimes.com/1999/08/26/arts/the-pop-life-the-three -faces-of-ruben-blades.html.

Swenson, John. "Ruben Blades Looks for the Source." United Press International, 1999.

Sykes, Bryan. *The Seven Daughters of Eve: The Science That Reveals Our Genetic Ancestry*. New York: W. W. Norton, 2001.

Tablante, Leopoldo. *El dólar de la salsa: Del barrio latino a la industria global de fonogramas, 1971–1999*. Madrid, Frankfurt: Iberoamericana, Vervuert, 2014.

Taussig, Michael. *The Nervous System*. New York: Routledge, 1992.

Taylor, Charles. *Modern Social Imaginaries*. Durham, NC: Duke University Press, 2003.

Taylor, Diana. "Brecht and Latin America's 'Theatre of Revolution.'" In *Brecht Sourcebook*, edited by Henry Bial and Carol Martin, 173–84. New York: Taylor & Francis, 2014.

Taylor, Timothy. *Music and Capitalism: A History of the Present*. Chicago: University of Chicago Press, 2015.

———. "Some Versions of Difference: Discourses of Hybridity in Transnational Musics." In *Global Currents: Media and Technology Now*, edited by Patrice Petro and Tasha G. Oren, 219–44. New Brunswick, NJ: Rutgers University Press, 2004.

———. *Strange Sounds: Music, Technology & Culture*. New York: Routledge, 2001.

Tenorio-Trillo, Mauricio. *Latin America: The Allure and Power of an Idea*. Chicago: University of Chicago Press, 2017.

———. *Mexico at the World's Fairs: Crafting a Modern Nation*. Berkeley: University of California Press, 1996.

———. "On Monolingual Fears." *Public Culture* 19, no. 3 (2007): 425–32.

Thomaz, Anderson Luis, Maurini de Souza, and Marcelo Fernando de Lima. "Categorias sociais da Ópera Do Malandro." *Aletria: Revista de Estudos de Literatura* 26, no. 2 (October 1, 2016): 47–64.

Thompson, Donald, and Francis Schwartz. *Concert Life in Puerto Rico, 1957–1992: Views and Reviews*. San Juan: Editorial de la Universidad de Puerto Rico, 1998.

Thompson, Emily. *The Soundscape of Modernity: Architectural Acoustics and the Culture of Listening in America, 1900–1933*. Cambridge, MA: MIT Press, 2002.

Tobey, Cheryl. "The Latin Explosion: Spanish and Latin-Inspired Dance, Theatre, and Art in Chicago." *PAJ: A Journal of Performance and Art* 26, no. 3 (2004): 72–77.

Toro, Alfonso de, ed. *Postmodernidad y postcolonialidad: Breves reflexiones sobre latinoamérica*. Teoría y Crítica de La Cultura y Literatura; Theorie und Kritik der Kultur und Literatur, vol. 11. Frankfurt am Main: Vervuert, 1997.

Torrecilla, Arturo. *La ansiedad de ser puertorriqueño: Etnoespectáculo e hiperviolencia en la modernidad líquida*. San Juan: Ediciones Vértigo, 2004.

Trigo, Abril. "General Introduction." In *The Latin American Cultural Studies Reader*, edited by Ana del Sarto, Alicia Ríos, and Abril Trigo, 1–14. Durham, NC: Duke University Press, 2004.

Trouillot, Michel-Rolph. "The Otherwise Modern: Caribbean Lessons from the Savage Lot." In *Critically Modern: Alternatives, Alterities, Anthropologies*, edited by Bruce Knauft, 220–37. Bloomington: Indiana University Press, 2002.

Tsing, Anna Lowenhaupt. *Friction: An Ethnography of Global Connection*. Princeton, NJ: Princeton University Press, 2005.

Turino, Thomas. "Nationalism and Latin American Music: Selected Case Studies and Theoretical Considerations." *Latin American Music Review* 24, no. 2 (Fall–Winter 2003): 169–209.

———. *Nationalists, Cosmopolitans, and Popular Music in Zimbabwe*. Chicago: University of Chicago Press, 2000.

Turner, Victor. *From Ritual to Theatre: The Human Seriousness of Play*. New York: Performing Arts Journal Publications, 1982.

Ugarte, Manuel. *El destino de un continente*. Alicante: Biblioteca Virtual Miguel de Cervantes, 2016.

———. *El porvenir de la américa latina: La raza, la integridad terriorial y moral, la organización interior*. Alicante: Biblioteca Virtual Miguel de Cervantes, 2017.

Ulloa, Alejandro. "La salsa: Una memoria histórico musical." *Nexus* (July 2008).

Valdes-Rodriguez, Alisa. "Shakira, a Pop-Rock Success in Latin America, Seems to Have What It Takes to Be a Smash with the English-Speaking U.S. Will She Be the . . . : Queen of Crossover?" *LA Times*, April 18, 1999. https://www.latimes.com/archives/la-xpm-1999-apr-18-ca-28407-story.html.

Vasconcelos, José. *The Cosmic Race/La Raza Cósmica*. Baltimore: Johns Hopkins University Press, 1997.

Vega, Carlos. "Mesomúsica: Un ensayo sobre la música de todos." *Revista del Instituto de Investigación Musicológica "Carlos Vega,"* Año 3, no. 3 (1974): 4–16.

Velasquez Ospina, Juan Fernando. "(Re)Sounding Cities: Urban Modernization, Listening, and Sound Cultures in Colombia, 1896–1930." PhD dissertation, University of Pittsburgh, 2018.

Velásquez Urrego, Liliana. "El arte contemporáneo es terrible." *El País*, July 8, 2007.

Versényi, Adam. "1985 Festival Latino." *Latin American Theatre Review* 19, no. 2 (Spring 1986): 111–20.

———. "Brecht, Latin America and Beyond." *Theatre* 17, no. 2 (1986): 42–46.

Villoro, Juan. *Tiempo transcurrido: Crónicas imaginarias*. 4th ed. Mexico City: Fondo de Cultura Económica, 2015.

Virno, Paolo. *A Grammar of the Multitude: For an Analysis of Contemporary Forms of Life*. Los Angeles: Semiotext(e), 2004.

Viselli, Antonio. "In Possession of a Stolen Weapon: From John Gay's Macheath to Rubén Blades' Pedro Navaja." *Imaginations: Journal of Cross-Cultural Image Studies* 3, no. 1 (2012): 45–60.

Viveiros de Castro, Eduardo. "The Relative Native." *HAU: Journal of Ethnographic Theory* 3, no. 3 (2013): 473–502.

Volpi Escalante, Jorge. *El insomnio de Bolívar: Cuatro consideraciones intempestivas sobre américa latina en el siglo XXI*. 1st ed. Mexico City: Debate, 2009.

"Vuelve a Editarse 'Siembra,' El Disco Que Dividió En Dos La Historia de La Salsa." *El Tiempo*, March 9, 2009. https://www.eltiempo.com/archivo/documento/CMS-4867436.

Vulliamy, Ed. "She Loves You . . . Sí, Oui, Ja: How Pop Went Multilingual." *The Observer*, April 6, 2019. https://www.theguardian.com/music/2019/apr/06/latin-spanish-pop-takes-over-from-english-language.

Wade, Peter. *Music, Race and Nation: Música Tropical in Colombia*. Chicago: University of Chicago Press, 2000.

Wagner, Roy. *The Invention of Culture*. Rev. and expanded ed. Chicago: University of Chicago Press, 1981.

Wallis, Roger, and Krister Malm. *Big Sounds from Small Peoples: The Music Industry in Small Countries*. New York: Pendragon Press, 1984.

Warner, Michael. *Publics and Counterpublics*. New York: Zone Books, 2002.

Washburne, Christopher. "Latin Jazz, Afro-Latin Jazz, Afro-Cuban Jazz, Cubop, Caribbean Jazz, Jazz Latin, or Just . . . Jazz: The Politics of Locating an Intercultural Music." In *Jazz/Not Jazz: The Music and Its Boundaries,* edited by David Ake, Charles Garrett, and Daniel Goldmark, 89–107. Berkeley: University of California Press, 2012.

———. *Sounding Salsa: Performing Latin Music in New York City*. Philadelphia: Temple University Press, 2008.

Waxer, Lise. *The City of Musical Memory: Salsa, Record Grooves, and Popular Culture in Cali, Colombia*. Middletown, CT: Wesleyan University Press, 2002.

Waxer, Lise, ed. *Situating Salsa: Global Markets and Local Meanings in Latin Popular Music*. New York: Routledge, 2002.

———. "Situating Salsa: Latin Music at the Crossroads." In *Situating Salsa: Global Markets and Local Meanings in Latin Popular Music*, 3–22. New York: Routledge, 2002.

Webb, Simon. "Masculinities at the Margins: Representations of the Malandro and the Pachuco." In *Imagination Beyond Nation: Latin American Popular Culture*, edited by Eva Paulino Bueno and Terry Caesar. Pittsburgh: University of Pittsburgh Press, 1998.

Weheliye, Alexander G. *Phonographies: Grooves in Sonic Afro-Modernity*. Durham, NC: Duke University Press, 2005.

Weiner, Annette. *Inalienable Possessions: The Practice of Keeping While Giving*. Berkeley: University of California Press, 1992.

Wentz, Laurel. "Pepsi Puts Interest before Ethnicity: Aided by Range of Shops, Marketer Proves That Passion Comes First." *Advertising Age*, July 7, 2003.

Wheeler, Alina. *Designing Brand Identity: An Essential Guide for the Whole Branding Team*. 4th ed. Hoboken, NJ: John Wiley and Sons, 2009.

White, Hayden. "The Fictions of Factual Representation." In *Tropics of Discourse: Essays in Cultural Criticism*, 121–34. Baltimore: Johns Hopkins University Press, 1978.

Williams, Gareth. *The Other Side of the Popular: Neoliberalism and Subalternity in Latin America*. Durham, NC: Duke University Press, 2002.

Williams, Raymond. *Marxism and Literature*. New York: Oxford University Press, 1977.

Young, Iris Marion. *Justice and the Politics of Difference*. Princeton, NJ: Princeton University Press, 1990.

Yúdice, George. "Estudios culturales y sociedad civil." *Revista de Crítica Cultural* 8 (1994): 44–45.

———. *The Expediency of Culture: Uses of Culture in the Global Era*. Durham, NC: Duke University Press, 2003.

———. "La industria de la música en la integración América Latina–Estados Unidos." In *Las Industrias Culturales En La Integración Latinoamericana*, edited by Néstor García Canclini and Carlos Moneta, 115–61. Buenos Aires: EUDEBA, 1999.

———. "Postmodernity and Transnational Capitalism in Latin America." In *On Edge: The Crisis of Contemporary Latin American Culture*, edited by George Yúdice, Jean Franco, and Juan Flores, 1–28. Minneapolis: University of Minnesota Press, 1992.

———. "We Are Not the World." *Social Text* 31–32 (1992): 202–16.

Zea, Leopoldo. *América latina en sus ideas*. Mexico City: Siglo XXI Editores, 1986.

———. *Dialéctica de la conciencia americana*. Mexico City: Alianza Editorial Mexicana, 1976.

Zuñiga, Alberto. "Éditus: Un Filtro de Texturas (Entrevista)." *La Nación*, February 28, 1999.

Discography

Afro Latin Jazz Orchestra with Arturo O'Farrill. *Una Noche Inolvidable*. Palmetto Records, 2005.

Blades, Rubén. *La Rosa de Los Vientos*. Sony Tropical, 1996.

———. *Tiempos*. Sony Music Latin, 1999.

———. *Mundo*. Sony Music International, 2002.

Iglesias, Enrique. *Sex and Love*. Republic Records, 2014.

Marsalis, Wynton, and Jazz at Lincoln Center. *Live in Cuba: Lincoln Center Jazz Orchestra with Wynton Marsalis*. Blue Engine Records, 2015.

O'Farrill, Arturo, and the Afro Latin Jazz Orchestra. *Cuba: The Conversation Continues*. Motéma Music, 2015.

O'Farrill, Chico, and His Afro-Cuban Orchestra. *Heart of a Legend*. Milestone Records, 1999.

———. *Pure Emotion*. Milestone Records, 1995.

———. *Carambola*. Milestone Records, 2000.

Shakira. *Pies Descalzo*. Epic Records, 1995.

———. *Laundry Service*. Epic Records, 2001.

———. *Fijación Oral, Vol. 1*. Epic Records, 2005.

———. *Oral Fixation, Vol. 2*. Epic Records, 2005.

———. *Shakira*. RCA Records, 2014.

Shakira, and Alejandro Sanz. *La Tortura*. Epic Records, 2005.

Shakira, and Carlos Vives. *La Bicicleta*. Sony Music Latin, 2016.

Zenón, Miguel. *Jíbaro*. Marsalis Music, 2005.

———. *Esta Plena*. Marsalis Music, 2009.

Filmography

Afro Latin Jazz Orchestra. 2012. https://www.youtube.com/watch?v=vg13yZw qb5g [inactive link].

Arturo O'Farrill Brings His Afro-Cuban Jazz to Havana. 2013. https://www.youtube .com/watch?v=sRGPMwq9kcM.

Arturo O'Farrill and the Afro-Latin Jazz Alliance Programs. 2015. https://vimeo .com/127726818.

A Morte Como Quase Acontecimento. 2009. https://www.youtube.com/watch?v= nz5ShgzmuW4.

Crossover Dreams. 1985. Directed by Leon Ichaso.

Jazz. 2000. Ken Burns, Lynn Novick, and Geoffrey C. Ward. Washington, DC: PBS. DVD.

INDEX

Page numbers in italics refer to illustrations.

13; Latin American Studies and, 15; Bruno Latour on, 109; legacies of, 212; "liquid," 158; musicking and, 16, 242; Music Studies and, 15, 17, 258n72; New York City and, 81; North Atlantic modernity, 212; "peripheral," 215; plurality of modernities, 221; progress and, 13, 20; Puerto Rico and, 226, 237; racial attitudes and, 12; Shakira and, 168; spatial dimensions, 14; storytelling and, 44; syncopation and, 13, 240; temporal dimensions, 14; temporality and, 13, 82, 212, 238–39; temporal lag, 212, 214, 237, 240; translation and, 168; Michel-Rolph Trouillot on, 221; the US and, 3

modernization, 217–18; literature and, 244

monolingualism, 99, 130, 167; Shakira's challenge to in the US, 24; Mauricio Tenorio-Trillo on, 289n173; in the US, 162, 289n173

Monsiváis, Carlos: hearing of, 52, 54; on 1980s Latin American culture, 50; on "Pedro Navaja," 49

Moreiras, Alberto: definition of Latin Americanism, 9; on "the exhaustion of difference," 215

Morrison, Toni, on ancestry, 198

multiculturalism, 102; branding and, 154; Miami and, 149; Shakira and, 149; in the US, 149

Muñoz Marín, Luis, Operación Serenidad (Operation Serenity), 217

music: affect and, 53–54; belonging and, 230, 234; biopolitics and, 156–57; Blackness and, 183; branding and, 153; circulation of, 125, 143; consumption and, 153; cosmopolitanism and, 144; as entertainment, 61, 67, 69, 70; equality and, 76–77, 79; event and, 230; as event, 5; experience and, 47; futurity and, 54; globalization and, 143–45; history and, 53; identity formation and, 153; incommensu-

rability and, 74; intelligibility of, 33; irony and, 37; language and, 78; literacy and, 216, 303n25; literature and, 78, 141; mediation and, 5, 189; neoliberalism and, 153; as object, 5; protest and, 60, 61; sociality and, 71, 72; "universal language" trope, 234; virtuality and, 159; world and, 243–44

musical instruments: accordion, 91, 92; alto saxophone, 218; bagpipes, 93; bass, 209; berimbau, 91, 92; *Bombo Legüero*, 91; bongos, 34; bouzouki, 94; *Caja Peruana*, 91; charango, 157; conga, 32, 33, 34, 91; didgeridoo, 93; drums, 209; *dumbek*, 157, 288n161; electric bass, 35, 87; guitar, 87, 91, 110, 157; Irish flute, 93; maracas, 91; piano, 35, 87, 91, 209; player piano, 279n9; *siku*, 157, 159; soprano saxophone, 91, 110; synecdoche and, 91; timbales, 34, 91; trombone, 31, 32, 37, 38; tuba, 33; vibraphone, 97; violin, 87, 91, 110

musical Latin Americanism: attunement and, 12; defined, 11; record industry and, 12

musical theater, 96, 273n33; in New York City, 67, 68; in Puerto Rico, 65; salsa and, 67

music education, in Panama, 247. *See also* pedagogy

musicking, 49, 203, 241; defined, ix, 4, 22; ecumenical, 107; the idea of Latin America and, 11; literarized, 49; as mode of production, 169

Music Studies, 17; modernism and, 258n72; modernity and, 15, 17, 258n72

myth, 51; jazz and, 178, 179

nationalism, 106, 140, 279n14; Colombia and, 123; hearing and, 123; national anthems and, 122, 123; in Puerto Rico, 233, 235; Shakira and, 129–30, 131, 132, 133

ness," 31; Latin Americanism and, 85; of Latinity, 57; mediation and, 85; migrant creativity and, 2; music and, 31; as politics, 117; politics of, 31, 241; representability, 85–86; representativeness, 42, 44, 57; salsa and, 43, 78, 86; Shakira and, 130, 131; sonic representation, 91; sonic representation of Latin America, 94; space and, 80; style and, 76; in theater, 67; truth and, 68; voice and, 78

resonance, 29, 242; co-constitution with modernity, 16; defined, 4; as event, 5; fathoming and, 4, 5; as method, 4

rhythm, 91; African musics and, 20; Afro-Brazilian, 88; Ayoub, 157; *chacarera*, 92; cross-rhythm, 37; *cumbia*, 92; groove, 92; historical, 19; huapango, 37; indexicality and, 91; jazz and, 176; polyrhythms, 20, 260n101; as produced by dislocation, 13; "ritmo," 92; *rumba*, 93; synecdoche and, 91; "Western" isorhythms, 20. *See also* clave

"ritmo." *See under* genre

rock, 126; circulation of, 150; Latin America and, 50; transculturation and, 56

salsa, 57, 172, 201, 243, 245; addressing Latin America, 61; aesthetics and, 79; arrangements, 32–33; attunement and, 81; audiences and, 63, 99, 100; aural equality and, 33, 73, 75, 76; behind-the-beat style, 77; bitonality in, 37–38; call-and-response in, 34, 35; the Caribbean and, 73; the chronicle and, 35; class and, 74, 82; class in, 39; Colombia and, 58; as commodity, 27; as the common, 69, 70, 75; crossover and, 98; dance and, 33, 36, 61, 62, 70, 74; defined variously, 42–43; democratization of, 69, 74, 75; diaspora and,

26–27; distribution of the sensible and, 74, 75; formal conventions of 1970s salsa, 34; form and, 31–32, 76; futurity and, 60; gender and, 74; Édouard Glissant on, 26–27; harmony and, 31; indexicality and, 49; intelligibility and, 73, 75, 76; language and, 73; Latin America and, 85; Latinity and, 27; Latino Latin Americanism and, 83, 102; Latinos and, 73; listening and, 70; literature and, 81; lyrics, 73; mimesis and, 43; musical theater and, 67; New York City and, 36, 61, 246; New York City–style dancing, 36; Nuyoricans and, 79; Panama and, 58; "Pedro Navaja" as greatest salsa hit, 60; percussion in, 32, 34–35; performativity and, 70; politics and, 14–15, 24, 44, 57, 60, 79, 84, 86; politics of, 27–28, 43; propriety and, 76; race and, 39, 74; representation and, 78, 86; "ruined salsa," 64; *salsa con consciencia* (salsa with consciousness), 43, 60, 72; songwriting and, 73; *son montuno*, 61; storytelling and, 60–61, 63, 70; syncopation and, 75; temporality and, 39; transculturation and, 56; transnationalism and, 43; urbanism and, 63; "urban *son*" ("*son urbano*"), 33, 263n34; Venezuela and, 58; voice and, 50

samba, 36, 125, 142

selfhood, 215; cosmopolitanism and, 158–61; language and, 163

sense, 70–71, 74, 227; branding and, 160; consensus and, 71; racecraft and, 184. *See also* distribution of the sensible

sexism, 296n65

sexuality, 227, 280n24; difference and, 220; listening and, 234

Shakira, 242, 243–44; accent of, 132, 167; Christina Aguilera on, 126; audibility of, 129; audiences and, 130–36; aural equality and, 129,